MANAGEMENT AND
THE WORLD OF
TOMORROW

MANAGEMENT AND THE WORLD OF TOMORROW

*Key issues for management in
economic growth, technological change
and human welfare*

*The proceedings of
the 18th CIOS World Management Congress*

Gower

Published in the United Kingdom by Gower Publishing Company Limited, Westmead, Farnborough, Hampshire, England by arrangement with Oxford & IBH Publishing Co., 66 Janpath, New Delhi, India

ISBN 0 566 02239 7

Printed in India at Oxonian Press Pvt. Ltd., Faridabad

Preface

Established in 1926, CIOS—World Council of Management (originally Conseil International pour l'organisation Scientifique) or Conseil Mondial de Management is a non-political, non-government and non-profit organisation of representative management organisations throughout the world. It promotes scientific and professional management, furthering, through its member organisations, research, education, training, development and practice, as well as exchange of information, knowledge and experience among its member organisations. A partner in other international organisations, CIOS has a consultative status with UNESCO and UNIDO as well as an observer status with the ILO.

In December 1978, the 18th CIOS World Management Congress was held at New Delhi. It was hosted by the All India Management Association. The theme of the Congress was 'Management Perspectives for Economic Growth and Human Welfare'. It was the first time that a CIOS Congress was held outside the developed world and in the Third World and therefore the emphasis on human welfare and quality of life during the deliberations was particularly appropriate. A 1200-strong community of professional managers and management experts from the developing as well as the developed world participated and made discussions very meaningful with their deliberations on critical management issues.

The then Prime Minister of India Mr. Morarji Desai, who inaugurated the Congress set the tone by exhorting the managers to observe highest standards of ethics in performance of their jobs, and not to forget the importance of human welfare in working for other people. "The real art of management", said Mr. Desai, "is taking the best from every person with whom the manager has to work. But that can only happen when he himself gives his best."

Dr. Bharat Ram, one of the leading industrialists of India and President of the CIOS, in his Presidential address emphasised the significance of 'economic growth' and 'human welfare'. "Talking of 'economic growth', 'human welfare' or even 'perspectives' does not appear as easy today as it did even a few decades back....Concepts like economic growth, human welfare and management can be understood only in the context of the fundamental requirements of human life.....It is my belief that by setting up a variety of largish projects, a developing country does not necessarily make a dent in the poverty problem. A more diffused entrepreneurial and managerial effort might be the answer. This should require the identification and training of a new kind of manager/entrepreneur." Whilst not touching upon specific issues that were to be considered by the delegates, Dr. Bharat Ram emphasised that "growth without welfare is no more acceptable than welfare which is unsustained by growth."

The purpose of this book is to bring to readers the very profound and expert opinions expressed by professional managers of the world at the Congress. Prof. Peter Drucker, the doyen of world management, delivered the keynote address. Dr. S.S. Ramphal, Secretary-General of the Commonwealth Secretariat, presented the valedictory address. Both these papers have been given as the first and second articles, in the book. Thereafter the papers have been put under the common headings, the sub-themes and topics, under which they were delivered at the Congress. A brief profile of the speaker, and the position held by him at the time of the Congress, have been included to introduce him to the reader.

I would be failing in my duty if at this point I did not acknowledge the active participation of eminent personalities who 'Chaired' the various sessions: Air Chief Marshall P.C. Lal (Retd.), Chairman, Air India and Indian Airlines; Mr. Richard K.M. Eu, President, Singapore Institute of Management; Sir J.A. Thomson, High Commissioner for Britain in India; Mr. Ronald K. Miller, National President, Australian Institute of Management; Mr. Mohd. Fazal, Chairman and Managing Director, Engineering Projects India Ltd.; Prof. M.G.K. Menon, Secretary, Department of Science and Technology, India; Dr. S.C. Bhattacharjee, Chairman, State Trading Corporation of India; Mr. M.K. Raju, Chairman, M.K. Raju Consultants Pvt. Ltd., India; Mr. A. Ray, Chairman, James Warren & Co. India Ltd.; Mr. Kan D. Mariwalla, Chairman and Managing Director, National Industrial Development Corporation Ltd., India; Dr. Charat Ram, Chairman, The Jay Engineering Works Ltd., India; Mr. G.V.K. Rao, Secretary, Ministry of Agriculture, India; Mr. R.K. Swamy, Chairman and Managing Director, R.K. Swamy Advertising Associates, India; Mr. S.C. Budhiraja, Overseas Director, Al Futtaim & Co., UAE; Mr. J.O. Haworth, President, The New Zealand Institute of Management Inc.; Mr. David L. Pank, President, AAMO, Australia; Dr. I.G. Patel, Governor, Reserve Bank of India; Mr. Naval H. Tata, Deputy Chairman, Tata Group of Companies, India; Dr. U. Ruhle, Rationalisierungs— Kuratorium der Deutschen Wirtschafte. V, West Germany; Dr. S.S. Marathe, Secretary, Ministry of Industry, India; Dr. Eric M. Scheid, Honorary CIOS President, West Germany; Mr. Keshub Mahindra, Chairman, Mahindra & Mahindra Ltd., India and Dr. Ram S. Tarneja, General Manager, Bennett Coleman & Co. Ltd., India. Mr. Prem Pandhi and Dr. Minoo D. Daver deserve special mention as they played a leading role in organising the Congress as the then President and Vice-President respectively of AIMA.

It is hoped that this unique and memorable experience, in terms of sheer breadth of the horizons of international communication and interaction that this Congress afforded, will prove to be invaluable to all readers.

New Delhi

August 19, 1980

MR. A.R. SARAOGI

President

All India Management Association

Contents

1. The Issues Facing Management Today and Tomorrow

Peter F. Drucker

Prof. Peter F. Drucker is the most well-known Management thinker and writer of our times.
Born in Vienna in 1909, Prof. Drucker was educated there and in England, and lives in Claremont, California, practising as a management consultant specialising in business and economic policy and in top management organisation. His contribution to modern management thought ranges over 16 books—translated into more than 20 languages—editorial columns in the Wall Street Journal, articles in various periodicals and three well-known series of management films. As keynote speaker at the 18th CIOS World Management Congress, Prof. Drucker made his first visit to India.

Management is a child of this century. The first CIOS World Management Congress took place less than sixty years ago. And at the first CIOS World Management Congress which I attended—the Congress in Paris in 1957—most of the participants, especially the Europeans and the participants from the Third World, were still very skeptical about management. It was something that fitted others, but had very little relevance to them, their own companies and institutions and their own countries. And in those years, the communist countries were quite certain that management was a capitalist invention which had absolutely no meaning for them—and was indeed totally incompatible with anything that could be called "socialist" or "Marxist". As social institutions go, management is thus a mere infant still.

But the child has been growing up very, very fast. Few people today would doubt that management is essential. When some of us, in Paris, dared suggest that management and managers were the essential key resource for economic and social development, we were practically booed. Today, this is commonplace. And the Soviet Union which, only fifteen yerrs or so ago, still considered management a "capitalist heresy" that would disappear with the dawn of communism or socialism, now has institutes of advanced manage-

1

nesses irrelevant. A genius at production, all by himself, is incapable of producing results. He does not know how to sell and he cannot read the simplest financial statement. But you do not have to have a very large organisation before you can give this person a salesman who can sell the stuff he can turn out, and a book-keeper who can at least keep the books straight. And then it does not matter that the production man does not know how to sell and does not know how to add and to subtract—what then matters is that he knows how to produce. This is what "organisation" means. And so we in management will increasingly have to face up to our responsibility for putting people where their strength will be productive and where their weaknesses do not really matter very much. This, let me emphasise, is particularly important in developing countries where the human resource is in such short supply. There you have to work twice as hard at putting people where they can really produce results. There you have to go through your organisation at least once a year—I like to do it twice a year—and ask: "Are the people in the organisation who are capable of performance where they can really perform?" And there you have to make sure that you ask everyone of the people in your managerial, your professional, your technical organisation, at least once a year: "What do we, in this organisation and especially what do I as your boss, do that helps you do the work you are being paid for?" and "What does this organisation, and I do that hampers you?" And then do more of what helps and get rid of what hampers. It is the responsibility of the manager to enable people to perform. It is the responsibility of the manager to make resources productive.

This also applies to the other resources—especially to the resource that is capital. It is the manager's responsibility to put capital where it can produce results, and to withdraw capital where it cannot produce results. One feeds opportunities and one starves problems. One does not use money as a substitute for thinking—something that is all too common in organisations, and especially in large ones. Accept the fact that, of all the resources we have, money likes to be exploited. Money does not get tired. Money does not charge overtime. Money does not join unions. Money does not need vacations. Money likes to work seven days a week, twenty-four hours a day. And the harder you work money, the better money likes it. So go to work on making resources productive—and especially on managing capital; capital is going to remain scarce for the rest of this century.

I am always being asked what objectives I would set for businesses. Now clearly, every single individual organisation needs to think through its own objectives. There is no general prescription. But there is one prescription for all organisations—and not just for businesses, but for hospitals and universities and government agencies as well. Five to ten years from now, you should be able to do twice the amount of work you are doing, without adding a single person to the payroll. Ten years from now, you should be able to have double the productivity of the human resource. And you do this mainly by working on the development of people and by working on their assignments. And ten years from now, you should be able to do at least twice the amount of work you are doing now without putting in one additional penny of capital.

It will be felt that this is "impossible". No, it is not "impossible". It is only difficult. For the fact of the matter is that in every single country and in every single industry, the leaders already operate at twice the productivity of both the human resource and the capital resource at which the average operates. And what one man has done, another man can always do again. And if the leaders in your country, as well as in mine—and in all other countries—already operate at twice the productivity of the key resources at which even organisations that consider themselves "well-managed" operate today, then doubling productivity is not innovation; it is not genius; it is not creativity. It is simply hard work. For what one man has done, another man can always do again by working hard.

There is one additional task, and it lies well within the definition of the function of management as that organ of society responsible for resources and their productivity. That is the productivity of management in the public sector—in hospitals and universities and schools and government agencies.

Twenty years ago, when you talked about management in the public sector, you were considered somewhat of a lunatic, or at least very eccentric. Public service institutions, it was believed, produced because of their good intentions. Today, we know better. At the same time, in every country the public sector increasingly employs resources; increasingly absorbs highly trained people and scarce capital; and increasingly has to satisfy fundamental expectations of our society. Increasingly, therefore, management in the public sector is becoming a priority task of management.

We know a good deal about managing in the public sector—but we do not do much about it. In part, this is because we are not willing or able to abandon anything in the public sector. In the private, the business sector of the economy, we are forced to abandon, especially there are even rudiments of a market system still in place. But in the public sector it is exceedingly difficult to abandon anything. Yet it is true that whatever is being done in the public sector is forever. We, in the United States for instance, will very soon realise that the proud achievement of the nineteenth century, the Postal Service, is obsolete. It simply makes no sense to transport half a pound of paper for the sake of one gramme of ink that is put on it. Electronic transmission is both infinitely faster and infinitely cheaper, and infinitely more reliable. And in a developed country, such as the United States, everybody has the tool to transmit and to receive graphic communications at practically no cost—everybody has either a television set or a telephone or both, and both are basically printing equipment. And so the postal system of which the nineteenth century was understandably so very proud, is rapidly becoming obsolete. But the same goes for a great many other things which the public sector performs.

today's methods by new and better equipment and methods; and above all, there is the capital needed both to create the job needed tomorrow both to maintain the market position of the business and to enable society to grow and to develop. I am quite sure that any business represented here today, if it were to think through and work out its future capital needs, would discover that it does not operate at a "profit". It operates at a deficit. It probably even fails to cover the genuine cost of capital. And by now we know that there are no resources that do not cost something. There is a genuine cost of capital—and it is high. It is the minimum a business has to earn to discharge its social responsibility. But over and above the cost of capital, there is the need to create enough new capital stock to provide for the capital needs of society and economy of tomorrow—and especially to provide the capital needed to create the jobs of tomorrow. A management that does not operate with high enough profitability in its business to provide for the capital needs of its society tomorrow is clearly remiss in its social responsibility and clearly guilty of depleting and destroying the resources committed to its keeping.

Then comes the second responsibility in the management of resources: the responsibility to employ them for results, to employ them for productivity. This is the entrepreneurial function of management. We all know that it is the function of the entrepreneur to move resources from less productive to more productive employment. This, of course, implies the need to think through what our business is, what it is not, what it should not be. But it then also increasingly implies the responsibility to organise abandonment of businesses, activities, markets and products which no longer produce, and which no longer serve. The abandonment function is not popular today—it never has been popular. Every human being, and certainly every adult human being, likes to cling to the known, familiar, and traditional. Yet it is the function of management to put every market, every activity on trial for its life ever so often—maybe every three years—and to ask: "Knowing what we now know, would we still go into this product, this market, this activity today?" And if the answer is "no", don't say "Let's make another study." Say instead, "How fast can we get out?" It is your responsibility to put resources, and especially the scarce resources of competent people and of capital where the results are.

But increasingly, the responsibility to employ resources where the results are will mean that management, both in developing and in developed countries, will have to learn to manage "production sharing". In all developed countries, including the developed countries of the communist world, that is European Russia and her European satellites, we face a major shortage of people to do the traditional jobs—especially traditional labour-intensive manufacturing jobs. It is not a matter of wage cost primarily. It is a matter of the availability of people, both because birth-rates in the developed countries are so very low, and because so many of the young people in the developed countries go in for higher education and thus become basically disqualified for traditional work.

In all developing countries, on the other hand, we face fifteen to twenty years during which there will be an incredibly large supply of young people qualified for little but the traditional labour-intensive jobs in manufacturing. And in most of the developing countries, the only way these young people can possibly find employment is in manufacturing for export. There are only a very few countries—India may be one of them—in which there is a potential domestic market large enough to absorb the output of masses of new young workers, workers who need jobs and who are easily trainable for the traditional manufacturing work. In the rest of the world manufacturing jobs and jobs in export industries, will mean increasingly that the world will see a new pattern of economic integration—a pattern that I have called "production sharing". You already see it all around you. Here is the large European textile manufacturer, a German/Dutch company, who spins, weaves and dyes in the Common Market and then airfreights the cloth to such countries as Morocco or Algeria or Thailand, where the cloth is converted into suits and shirts and rugs and bedding, to be airfreighted back and sold in the Common Market. There is the American shoe retailer—the largest shoe retailer in the world, perhaps. The hides to make the leather tend to be American, if only because America has the largest livestock population. They are being shipped to Brazil to be tanned and made into leather there, to be shipped to such places as Haiti and the British Virgin Islands where they are being made into shoes, to be assembled into finished shoes in Puerto Rico, for sale in the American market and for export to Europe. And so it goes—with the electronic industry perhaps the foremost practitioner of "production sharing".

Increasingly, we will have to learn to manage a system under which the developing countries will find employment for their abundant resources of young trainable people in production for export in those stages of production that are labour-intensive; while the developed countries will furnish management, technology and capital and, above all, the markets.

Increasingly, the multinational company of tomorrow will be a marketing company rather than a manufacturing company. It will sell where the markets are, and this means primarily in the developed countries. But it will have the goods made where the work force is—that is in the developing countries. And thus, production sharing will increasingly become a major managerial task—both in the developed and in the developing countries—and one that requires close cooperation between the two.

Finally, there is the task of making resources productive. Insofar as we are talking of human resources, we face the challenge of placing people, assigning people, of putting them where their strengths can be productive. The one advantage modern organisation has is that it is the one design known to us that is capable of making human strengths productive and human weak-

ment, publishes books on management, and regularly complains about the backwardness of management in its industries or in the industries of the European satellite countries. Indeed, even in China, where under Mao management was clearly taboo, there is now a sharp shift. If the new communist line in mainland China means anything, it means an assertion of the central importance of managers and management in the development of Chinese society and Chinese economy.

But with this acceptance of management as a key function in society have come ever-increasing demands on the manager. He will increasingly have to satisfy very great expectations. Indeed the greatest expectation in respect to manager and management is that managers discharge the *function of management* in today's society. What then is the basic function of management?

It can be stated simply: Management is responsible for the development, the allocation and the productivity of resources. In nineteenth century liberal capitalism, it was believed that resources developed themselves and are allocated by the "invisible hand". In nineteenth century socialism and twentieth century communism, it is believed that the development of resources is a function of the "system"—which is another form of the "invisible hand". We know better today. Resources are developed by managers, are allocated by managers, and managers are responsible for their productivity. It is, above all, productivity which is the first mission of management and its first responsibility. And the management task today, and increasingly the management task of tomorrow, will centre on the productivity of resources.

Yet very few of us in management take this responsibility seriously enough. And few of us are willing to make sure that our societies understand that this is the function of management. It is a new function, and one that needs being explained, being understood and, above all, one that needs to be practised effectively.

Resources are not made by nature. They are made by man. And this is particularly true of two key resources—the human being and capital. Indeed, the human being as such is not a "resource". He becomes a resource only if trained, developed and allocated to productive work. This is a central task of management. It is particularly important in developing countries. There are many people in developing countries, in some of them, perhaps more than can be productively employed. But there are far too few productive human beings in developing countries. It is the essence of being a developing country that effective, productive, competent people are in very short supply. One of the central management tasks in a developing country is development of people into human resource—a task of training, of developing, of managing. It requires that managers seriously work on managing work. We know how to do this. In fact, it was with the discovery that work can be managed and needs to be managed that the history of management begins. Far too few of us take seriously our responsibility for managing work; for analysing it; for thinking through its constituent parts—whether the work is manual work or knowledge work; for synthesising the work into a job; for providing the tools and the information and the feedback to the worker from the results back to his activities. But we also need to practice managing the worker—and this is something totally different, and something that requires increasingly that we demand responsible participation from the individual worker, whether he be skilled or unskilled, manual worker or knowledge worker.

We are not doing enough to make the human resource productive. We are guilty of far too many sins of omission.

When it comes to creating the other resource—capital—we are again guilty of far too many sins of omission. In many ways, capital is perhaps even more crucial, especially in developing countries, than the human resource. And capital can only be obtained by providing a surplus from today's production over today's costs—otherwise, capital formation cannot take place. Capital formation may be the crucial factor in the development of developing countries. It is also the crucial factor in the continuing prosperity of the developed countries. Yet we in management have made it almost impossible for our fellow-citizens in our nations to understand the importance of capital.

We have been guilty of grossly misleading our societies—and then we complain that they do not understand what we are doing. As long as we in management keep on talking nonsense about "profits" we will make it almost impossible to have capital formation adequate to the needs of our societies. There is no such thing as "profit"; the very word is a misunderstanding. There are only costs of the past and cost of the future. And the greatest cost of the future is not even the risk of economic activity with its inherent uncertainties. The greatest cost of the future is the capital needed to provide the *jobs* for tomorrow.

Everyone of us knows that there are no jobs unless we can invest a substantial amount of capital. Even in developing countries, in which a good deal of activity is, and should be, labour-intensive, the capital cost of a new job is very high and is going up rapidly. In fact, you may well say that the greatest drawback, the greatest weakness of developing countries in their desperate search for employment opportunities, is the lack of enough capital to create jobs. The consumer demand is there—what is lacking is the capital to create the jobs which in turn would create the goods to satisfy consumer demand. As long as we talk about "profits", we obscure understanding. What we need to talk and talk increasingly, is the need of our society for adequate capital formation for the jobs of tomorrow.

The place to begin is one's own company, one's business. Is one actually forming enough capital for the needs of tomorrow? One can, with considerable probability, figure out the minimum profitability of a business needed to satisfy society's demands for capital formation. There is risk premium needed to defray the insurance costs for the uncertainty of economic activity and the uncertainty of committing today's scarce resources to an unknown and unknowable future; there is the capital needed to replace today's equipment and

In fact, the rate of obsolescence in the public sector may be faster than in the private sector. For in the public sector population changes have much faster and much more immediate impact—and this is the century in which demographics change very fast indeed. Thus, in the developed countries we face the rapid obsolescence of the retirement system which we so proudly put in the last hundred years—simply because the age 65 which, one hundred years ago, was senility, is now highly performing and healthy middle age for most of our people.

Therefore, the public sector needs to think through what it allocates resources to. It needs to organise for abandonment. And above all, it needs to organise for performance. This, as all of us in management know, means first that one has to think through what performance is expected and then has to judge, if not to measure, performance by feedback from results. Increasingly in the public sector, we will have to become result-focussed.

Additionally, in the public sector we have focussed on effort rather than on result. We have considered the amount of money spent a fair measure of what is important and effective, rather than looking at the results obtained for society. The public sector, the public service institutions—that is the institutions that do not, by definition, produce and distribute economic good and services—are going to be the frontier of management. Our societies are becoming critical of the public sectors, to the point where some of our societies in the developed countries are openly cynical of the public sector—and this is quite clearly just as true in the communist developed countries as it is in Western Europe, the United States and even in Japan. They are critical because they do not see results. They are critical because they no longer believe that greater efforts necessarily mean greater performance—all they mean is greater costs. Increasingly, we demand management in the public sector. And management in the public sector will thus become, with certainty, the area in which the rest of this century will see the greatest activity, the greatest controversies, the greatest demand for effective management.

I have covered very specific things. But I have also covered a major shift in the orientation and the values of management. Almost three hundred years ago, in the early years of the eighteenth century, a British pamphleteer, De Mandeville, wrote a rhymed pamphlet, *The Fable of the Bees*, in which he anticipated classical economics and the values and principles of the nineteenth century altogether by declaring that in a good society "private vices" become "public benefits"—and especially the private vice of greed. That this system produced the economic goods, we all know. But it also produced a moral revulsion. In everyone of the great political philosophies it is taken for granted that the good society must rest on private virtues. And so the declaration that public benefits are produced by private vices violated everything political philosophers and moralists had been teaching us. And so we found ourselves caught in a dilemma between a moral basis of society which could not produce the desired results for the masses, and the need for the results obtainable only by accepting what we felt was immoral or at least amoral.

The emergence of management means, in effect, that we are transcending the *Fable of the Bees*. It is the essence of management that it believes that private *virtues* produce benefits. It is management's task to make resources productive. It is management's task to enable human beings to perform through putting their strengths to work. It is management's task to obtain results for society by allocating resources to where the results are which society needs, wants and is willing to work and to pay for. This is "virtue", in the most elementary, most primitive, most fundamental sense of the word.

The emergence of management is therefore more than an emergence of techniques, of processes, or even of new knowledge. It is basically the dialectic transcendence of the dilemma between an amoral society producing results and a moral society producing only poverty, stagnation and suffering. The emergence of management means that we can now assert—indeed we have to assert—that it is the task of the manager and management and the specific function of both to make private virtues rebound to public benefits.

And this is the fundamental issue facing management today and tomorrow—the issue of making productive for society, the individual, and our world altogether, the strength of people and the inherent performance potential of resources altogether.

is generally believed. Forty-eight jobs, for example, were lost in the period 1962–1975 in Germany as a result of technological change for every one lost to developing country imports. The world's managers know better than most that the short-term gains of protectionist policies are being bought at quite unacceptably high cost in terms of the health of the world economy.

Perhaps an even greater danger is that protectionism is being given a 'management' image. "Orderly marketing arrangements", "voluntary export restraints", non-tariff "regulatory measures" suggest, and are calculated to suggest, better management of the world economy. But management for whom? Management for what? Protectionism is, in fact, the antithesis of management, certainly it is the negation of management for economic growth and human welfare. It is resistance to change, repudiation of global interdependence, masquerading as 'management' of the world economy. What all this tragically ignores is the enlarging empirical evidence that global change responsive to the imperatives of interdependence is in the interest of rich and poor alike; that the 'management' the world needs is the management of interdependence.

Moments of crisis represent the best opportunity for imaginative change, for courageous action. Significant change, structural reform, certainly does not flow from 'better' times. When the last war ended, and Europe lay exhausted, the United States was only half as rich as it is today. But it took the bold step of committing a very much larger proportion of its GNP than it now gives to all the developing nations to underpin the economic reconstruction of Western Europe. The Marshall Plan's contribution to the restoration of world economic activity—without doubt the most creative chapter in the history of international economic cooperation—did not impoverish the United States. Recovery in Europe in fact lent fresh stimulus to the American economy, in a healthy transatlantic symbiosis which in turn triggered a remarkable surge of worldwide growth.

The chronic dislocations of today call for similarly bold initiatives. And there can be little doubt of the capacity of the Third World to inject a new dynamism into the world economy, once given the chance. That the logic of this call is being deeply pondered by Northern leaders is beyond doubt; witness the declaration of interdependence issued by the Bonn Summit earlier this year. But must it forever be the case that "between the conception and the creation, between the emotion and the response, falls the shadow"?

While the major responsibility for responding to these imperatives for change rests with the political leadership of the North, other influential elements within Northern societies have a share in that responsibility. It is, after all, the nature of the democratic process that political leaders must be sensitive to the moods of their constituencies.

The press is one institution in the 'North' that can exert a major influence on that mood. It can be an agent of enlightenment by applying its educative potential towards widening awareness of the realities of interdependence and of the need for change. But it can also be a bulwark of the status quo, fortifying resistance to change by capitalising on fear. In pursuit of wider circulation and greater profit, the press can—and, sadly, often does—fall prey to the temptation to magnify local and transient discomforts while ignoring their wider implications in the context of interdependence. Giving the readers what they want becomes an alibi for failure to live up to the highest tradition of journalism. When it fails to serve the cause of change, the press by default, if not purpose, serves the cause of reaction.

The press is, however, only one, if a major one, of the sources of influence on the public mood. Various institutions, various groups within society, have the capacity to influence both public opinion and decision making. Among these, the management community has a singularly important contribution to offer in the creation of an environment hospitable to enlightened and courageous policy decisions in the economic field. But it has, also, an autonomous responsibility, because of its pervasive role in contemporary economic life, to respond through its own actions to the challenges raised by an inequitable and unstable world. The management community has a responsibility, I suggest, to take a hand in the management of global change.

This is not purely a moral compulsion, a professional variant of noblesse oblige, but an obligation which derives from a hardheaded assessment of the self-interest of managers and the institutions they serve. In industrialised societies, prompted by the pressures and signals from an alert public, managers have come to recognise the prudence of sensitivity to community needs and objectives. In a world which technology has woven together as never before, that sensitivity must now reach out beyond community and nation to answer the call for social justice at the global level.

The management community in industrialised countries has the duty to widen public awareness of the self-defeating character of protectionism and the long-term benefits of Third World development, to press for effective adjustment policies to restructure domestic industries which have lost their competitive edge. Among the decision makers of Northern society few are better placed than management to appreciate the ultimate wisdom of adherence to the proven paths of comparative advantage.

Northern managers have also the capacity to help redress the several imbalances which both reflect and perpetuate global economic disparities; imbalances in investment, in technology, in research and development, in expertise. It is within their power too to seek to minimise the concentration of Northern resources on activities of minimal value to human welfare—on the production of ever more lethal weaponry, ever more plentiful gadgetry and ever more numerous products designed for rapid obsolescence.

Over the years, developing countries have become sensitive to the impact on their domestic circumstances of economic decisions taken elsewhere. As this sensitivity has increased, so have the tensions between governments and foreign companies operating on their soil. Today, the transnational corpora-

more strongly the opposite way. And those who would postpone action for 'better days' fail to discern or, while discerning, fail to acknowledge that better days may never come if the necessary structural changes in the world's economic system are not made now to ensure that these better days do come for all mankind.

It is now a long time since Mahatma Gandhi warned that "the earth provides enough to satisfy every man's need but not every man's greed." Yet, it has taken the economic cataclysms of the last few years to bring us to the awareness of the finiteness of many of the world's vital resources. Amid the profligacy with which a small minority of the world's people continue to consume those resources, we have begun to acknowledge the need for prudence in their use, as well as for more intensified efforts to develop alternatives to them if mankind is to develop a strategy of survival worthy of his claim to both wisdom and sentience.

Just as OPEC jolted the world into recognition of its interdependence in the field of energy, so the global food crisis of 1973 has brought us to realise the precarious balance between population and food supply. An unequal world which ordains that many must go hungry is an unsafe world. Islands of affluence within seas of want are more than an affront to morality or a challenge to piety. They are provocations to anger and invitations to conflict. A world of such disparities in the human condition contains within it the tinder that could endanger the survival of all its inhabitants.

Perhaps it was considerations such as these that prompted Zbigniew Brzezinski to comment recently:

"Previously dormant people have become active, demanding, assertive. Under the impact of literacy and modern communications, hundreds of millions of people are becoming aware, both of new ideas and of global inequity....If we try to create artificial obstacles to change for the sake of the status quo, we will only isolate ourselves—and, eventually, threaten and undermine our own national security."

There is no lack of perception at the highest levels of global leadership of the dangers facing humanity. What is not yet manifest is the will to act to avert the dangers so clearly before us. The case for better global management and for the effective management of global change is unanswerable; yet the action it calls for remains largely deferred. One tragic result is the ever widening disparity in the human condition.

In Victorian Britain at a time of industrial explosion and social turmoil, Disraeli alerted his countrymen to the dangers of allowing two nations to emerge within one polity; a nation of the rich and a nation of the poor. In later times, developed countries have heeded that message in the ordering of their domestic affairs, in making the welfare of their poor a responsibility of the community as a whole, in regulating the free play of market forces in favour of the underprivileged, in effecting domestic structural change to promote social justice and equality of opportunity. Now, nearly a century later, we face a global version of Disraeli's divided nation.

As in 19th century Britain, voices are raised—in compassion, in protest, in warning. Poverty is described, analysed, debated. Reams of statistics document the maldistribution of the world's wealth. But poverty and maldistribution remain unaffected. In the developed world, newspapers bring accounts of the deprivation of poverty to breakfast tables; television brings images of suffering to the comfort of the living room. Conscience is prodded and compassion summoned. Some urge charity, and many respond. But, as Dickens expounded in his day, poverty will not be banished by a 'little daily gruel or a roll of bread on Sunday'. Charity may ease the troubled mind of the giver; it may assuage the hunger of some and dull the anguish of some others. But it is only a pain-killer, not a cure—or even curative treatment. Yet, poverty is not inevitable and need not be terminal.

In its World Development Report published earlier this year, the World Bank laid a graphic message at our door. On the basis of 'business as usual' projections for the developed world and almost inexplicably optimistic assumptions of growth in the developing countries, the result by 1985 would be virtually no impact on absolute poverty; and, by the end of the century, a world in which there would remain more than 600 million people still living at the very margin of existence. Its clear lesson is that real improvement in the human condition worldwide simply cannot be secured with a mix of more of the same inadequate responses that have characterised the development efforts of the post-war era.

As with charity within nations, so with aid on the global scale. It will never be a sufficient answer to the problems of poverty. The poor must be enabled to earn their own livelihood and meet their basic needs through their own purchasing power. They must be assisted to secure employment and increase production; there must be markets for what they produce, and fair prices for what they market. I was glad to see the prominence given in the Congress' Keynote address to these needs—and to their being met in a more managed, and more efficiently and equitably integrated, world economy. But let us have no illusions about the gap between perception and performance, or about the inertial force of the status quo in leaving that gap unbridged.

Already the developing countries, as they reach out for a fairer share in world production, as they expand their trade horizons and export capability, see one barrier after another thrown up against them. Despite the voices of caution and the ritual bows to liberalism the Northern view has become increasingly myopic. Protectionism becomes the last refuge of senile and uncompetitive domestic industries, and the cost of this protection, in terms, for example, of inflationary prices to consumers is suppressed or ignored—as are the implications of the contraction in demand for Northern exports resulting from the forced reduction in the export earnings of developing countries. Protectionist measures do save some jobs, to be sure—though far fewer than

2. Management of Global Change

Shridath S. Ramphal

Dr. Ramphal is Secretary-General of the Commonwealth Secretariat, London. A citizen of Guyana, Dr. Ramphal had a distinguished legal career before he became Minister of State for External Affairs, Guyana. He is the recipient of several international honours and has written prolifically on legal, political and international affairs.

The focus at this meeting is on "Management Perspectives for Economic Growth and Human Welfare". That one should identify human welfare as a managerial goal in its own right and elevate it to at least equal status with economic growth is wholly gratifying. Too often there has been a tendency to worship at the shrine of economic growth on the complacent assumption that human welfare follows as an automatic benediction—that as the economic cup overflows for a few its bounty will trickle down to enlarge the welfare of the many. Within few societies does that faith any longer hold sway. Western societies, in particular, have led the way in economic and social transformation at home directed to the enhancement of human welfare in its own right.

But the response to the need for social and economic justice within nations has not carried over to the call for equity between nations—even though the challenge of human welfare is universal in its summons. Such double standards could not for long withstand enquiry. The result today is that the effort to reconcile these twin but separate goals of modern society— economic growth and human welfare—can no longer be safely confined within national borders. It is a global pursuit deeply relevant to relations between States. Indeed it is becoming increasingly clear that the search for a less unequal world will be the major global concern of the last quarter of this century.

In my Commonwealth vocation I see much of global disparities; for the Commonwealth mirrors the world's division between rich and poor, or, in the euphemistic usage of our time, between "North" and "South". The search for a more equitable international order has become a central Commonwealth preoccupation, and its perspectives will inform my effort to respond to the challenge underlying the theme of this Congress.

As the era of decolonisation, born with the historic emergence into freedom of India in 1947, draws to a close, there is accumulating evidence that political independence must be the first phase of a more profound democratisation of the international community and that the norms of freedom and justice which, together, infused the right of self-determination with its own special morality must now equally provide the ethical basis for economic relations between nations. As that era of decolonisation closes, another has begun—characterised by a movement from status to contract and by new insights of our world as a single community. For both reasons, it is an era of negotiation of what Harlan Cleveland has called "a planetary bargain".

To all save those who would not see, the last few years have shown that we are at a moment of transition in history—transition from a world of political power and economic dominance to a world more mindful of the limits of power and the dangers of economic disparities. It is a transition induced and made inevitable by the reality of interdependence. The obvious interdependencies in such areas as food, energy, raw materials, population and the environment, and the inter-relationship of these and such other issues as disarmament, science and technology, the exploration of the sea bed and outer space, have made us at once each other's guardian and each other's ward. We are both trustee and beneficiary in a world of mutual interests. But it is a world not yet won.

It will only be won through global change; and it is with the management of that change—from a world rooted in an adversary system of winners and losers to an interdependent world committed to the harmonising of human interests—that our generation must be essentially concerned. The management of interdependence is, I believe, the true message of this theme; and it is to that message that I express my opinion.

Amid the economic confusions and discontinuities of the last few years one truth has emerged above all else. It is that tinkering with the existing world economic system, fine-tuning the machine, will no longer suffice. The machinery, quite simply, is obsolete. And from the point of view of the developing countries whose future depends so much on a fresh approach to a global development strategy, every day brings aggravation. Each year the problems they face become more daunting, more intractable and more entrenched.

The palpable disintegration of the world's economic system, the increasing uncertainty and instability wnich has long been the way of life for poor countries but which rich countries are beginning to feel as well, the heightening of tensions between nations as economic anxieties induce protectionist policies: all these argue for acknowledgement of global interdependence; but they derive in fact from our denial of its imperatives. They are the manifestations of the old economic order struggling to reassert itself in tidewaters running ever

tion is exposed to the full glare of public scrutiny in its foreign operations. Beneath the alarm so manifest in the Third World over the role of TNCs lies the very real perception that such companies, by virtue of their immense bargaining power, can exert an influence, for good or ill, far disproportionate to their proper status as economic or commercial units. While circumstances vary considerably from country to country, from continent to continent, the role and responsibilities of transnational management are gradually taking a new shape.

Third World countries, for example, will no longer tolerate as the price of TNC contribution to their development, the excesses of transfer pricing or the unfairness of industrial patterns that deny to the countries that produce commodities the benefits of added value to be obtained through processing, blending and packaging them. And it is a particular source of disquiet in developing countries that enterprises which accommodate themselves to regulatory provisions dictated by the public interest within the "North" are less ready to allow their behaviour to be informed by the same respect for public interest in the "South". Examples in the food products, tobacco and pharmaceutical fields illustrate well how the unalloyed pursuit of profit all too readily assumes ascendancy over concern with human welfare—once allowed to. The current demand for a new economic order receives its impulse from the need of developing countries to free themselves from these and other inequities of the old.

But external constraints are not the only ones on Third World development: and their removal will not guarantee development—only facilitate it. The primary and the ultimate responsibility rests with developing countries themselves. In responding to such better opportunities for development as movement towards a new international order will offer, the Third World needs to acknowledge to a much greater degree than it now does that management will be a determinant of success. In large measure, development is management; certainly, without sound management, development will be forever elusive—however propitious the international climate or the structures of the global economic system.

This means that there is a role for the management community not merely in the process of effecting global change but in bringing management on acceptable terms to the process of development that such change facilitates. And, of course, it requires not merely an awareness of the need for such a role by developing countries themselves but a readiness on the part of the political leadership to facilitate and indeed to ensure efficient management of the development process. Each country must decide for itself what dependence it needs to place on foreign management expertise; but if management is to come wholly from within, the challenge to, and the burden upon, indigenous management cadres is made that much more onerous.

Development demands management; development with a socialist orientation—which is the path many developing countries wish to pursue—requires as much, certainly not less, management than development more reliant on private enterprise. Management is not a sinister instrument of capitalism but a necessary tool for all development. These are realities with which developing countries must come to terms.

But there are corresponding realities which the management community must accommodate. Among these is the likelihood that in the developing world the public sector will bear a somewhat higher profile than in the already industrialised countries—irrespective of ideological persuasions. Ideology will influence the composition of the public/private sectoral mix; in some countries the private sector will be more prominent than in others; but in very few developing countries will the public sector not occupy a significant place in the development process.

Peter Drucker has said:

"....the public sector will thus become with certainty, the area in which the rest of this century will see the greatest activity, the greatest controversies, the greatest demand for effective management."

Mr. Drucker may have been speaking of a public sector narrowly defined:

"....the public service institutions—that is the institutions that do not, by definition, produce and distribute economic goods and services...."
"....hospitals and universities and schools and government agencies".

I am speaking of the public sector in wider terms—of a public sector which embraces enterprises that do produce and distribute economic goods and services. But I would agree with his judgement, even in this wider context—that for the rest of this century the greatest demand (and, I would add, the greatest need) would be for effective management in this public sector.

If the management community is to assist Third World development it must do so in this context, adjusting its attitudes and its techniques to a milieu different from that of the industrialised world from which it springs. Almost by definition, it should be ready to respond to the need for that adjustment. To decline to do so would be to concede limits to management which are not warranted by its potential or by its record of innovation and creativity. The facilitation of management could be a critical factor in determining the course of world development over the remainder of this century. There is a management role of massive proportions in shaping the kind of world that will greet the 21st century.

If a responsibility for the management of global change rests on the international management community, a rather special responsibility devolves on the managers of the South. I have said that development is management; but it is of real development that I speak and, therefore, of management qualitatively attuned to its needs. Not only is there no morality, there is no efficiency either, in global change which facilitates less inequality between nations if it is not matched by change at the national level which generates greater equality within States—and within the States of the developing world in particular.

The management community of the South is among its most privileged people. It can be as defensive of an unequal status quo at home as the North has tended to be of an unequal world; but the message of interdependence is as pertinent nationally as it is internationally. The rich cannot prosper without progress by the poor. There is no future for a society in which the few are more than the many. For the South, elimination of international poverty must begin at home. Real development demands change within developing countries directed to dismantling those structures of elitism and privilege that help to sustain poverty.

Neither psychological shackles to Northern models nor elitist isolation within corporate sanctuaries must lead the managers of the South to stand aloof from these processes of domestic reform—still less to obstruct them. The management ethic of efficiency and enlightened self-interest alone should encourage them to play a constructive role in facilitating such reform. They must not be left guarding the fortress of economic growth long after the international management community has reached the higher ground of human welfare.

Let me end, by recalling Gandhiji's teaching that all wealth and talent belongs to "Daridra Narayan", the Lord of the Poor, and that those fortunate to be endowed with them hold them in trust for all mankind. The world's management community is so endowed; it needs to understand and respond to this universal truth. It needs to contribute to the management of that global change in relations between States and between peoples that a union of economic growth and human welfare implies and that our era of interdependence demands.

Management Culture

3. An Appropriate Management Technology

Sixto K. Roxas

Dr. Roxas is currently Vice-Chairman of American Express International Banking Corporation, New York. A specialist on the Asian management scene, Dr. Roxas was born in the Philippines in 1927 and educated there and in the U.S.A. He is closely associated with a number of business and professional bodies in Asia and in the West and is the recipient of several professional honours. He has occupied senior positions in the Philippines Government as Chairman, National Economic Council; Chairman, National Land Authority; Presidential Adviser on Economic Affairs, etc. Dr. Roxas is also the Co-Chairman of Asian Institute of Management, Manila.

Economic growth is not necessarily identical with improvement in human welfare. It is interesting that the typically modern disease is cancer which is a growth that kills. Growth by itself can be malignant as well as benign.

A management perspective applied to the development process views it as a matter of organisation rather than ideology, as a job to be done rather than a subject for intellectual speculation. It really does not serve a functional purpose to array free enterprise against socialism, free market against planning, Russian communist against Maoist. The critical problems of the world's poor demand action. Action means organisation: the clear definition of goals, the establishment of well-defined key result areas, the definition of responsibilities and their effective distribution, the establishment of rigorous standards of performance and precise measures, incentives, rewards and sanctions, cheques and balances. The Latin principle is critical here "Primum Vivere diende philosophari"—life comes first, philosophy later.

In the sub-continent of Asia, including India, Pakistan and Bangladesh the management profession is brought face to face with the realities of the human condition. According to the World Bank, on this sub-continent are found the majority of the 800 million of the world's population that dwell in absolute poverty. Here as well, lest the illusions of the capital cities of the world deceive us into a fool's euphoria over the successes of our modern science and technology, we view our most humbling failures. Here professional management faces its greatest challenge.

To view the development process from a management perspective, however, does not assure that it will be viewed objectively, on its own terms. Management perspectives carry with them the peculiar biases of the diverse cultures out of which managers emerge. This leads us to the sub-theme that has been assigned to me: management culture.

Every profession develops an implicit set of accepted principles, beliefs, standards for testing the validity of cognition, criteria for judging good and the bad, all of which, put together, set the framework by which practitioners reach conclusions and make decisions. For this reason, the professionals are said to have a common point of view, a standard set of approaches. The term paradigm is applied to these principles and standards.

The profession of management as it has developed through the years shares such a set of paradigms. These derive from a whole complex of antecedents: history, ideology, philosophy particularly of the societies in which the leaders of the art have emerged and in which their greatest successes have been demonstrated.

In this sense, every system of management naturally carries with it the cultural equipment it derives from the peculiar history and circumstances of the society from which it evolved.

In its historic origins modern management is American. It is in America that the art and science became an art separate from business as such or from administration or statecraft (which is European). It is rooted, therefore in the American free and private enterprise system.

Under the system the vital functions of community are distributed between two sectors: the government and the private sector.

The government maintains order, public health, public safety, education and investment in infrastructure.

The private sector does almost everything else, but it is free to choose what it will do within broad constraints established by the government. The constraints are embodied in laws and regulations governing such things as land zoning, building codes, sanitary and health codes, commercial laws and so forth. The private sector provides most of the jobs, makes most of the investments, owns most of the facilities, performs trade, provides most of the improvement and undertakes the greater portion of land development, housing and building construction.

The theory is that between the direct activity of the government and the regulatory framework it imposes on the one hand and the profit-seeking activities of the private sector on the other, all the vital tasks in the community will get done—efficiently and adequately.

In this system, management is typically associated with the business enterprise. The business firm is the exemplar of all sectoral organisation. Why so? Because business is a well-defined organisation. It is a discrete manageable unit; it has a specific objective, say, to produce and sell textiles; a defined purpose, say, to provide a profit for both investors and manager; a measured complement of resources: land, plant and machinery, inventory, cash, workforce; a specific technology of operations, production, market, finance, organisation and controls, etc.; and a rigorous set of performance standards, sales, profit margins, returns on investments, embodied in a consistent set of accounts.

Over the years business has developed a professional corps of managers imbued with the enterprise philosophy and perspective, educated in the science and technology of profit-seeking, and trained in the arts required to control organisations, mobilise resources and wage the warfare of market competition.

Economic progress has come to be identical precisely with the growth and development of this sector that accounts for some 75 to 90 per cent of economic activity in various countries.

The experience with the system of developing countries with large rural populations, has not been entirely satisfactory. Private enterprise is naturally biased towards picking out only those activities that offer the most attractive returns. In theory, markets and the price mechanism are supposed to ensure that the profitable activities are also the essential tasks to be performed in the community by and large. If, in the instance, this is not the case, government policy and intervention can correct the situation.

In fact, markets direct resources towards demands that are backed by purchasing power. Because less essential goods tend to be demanded by consumers of higher incomes, the pattern of purchases rapidly becomes biased towards less and less essential goods. There is circular causation here. The more talented, privileged or the most powerful manage to accumulate wealth. The demands of the wealthy begin to dictate where resources go so that eventually private enterprise creates an enclave where those who are relatively well-off get wealthier catering to one anothers' demands. The majority of the population becomes more and more marginal to the so-called progressive enclaves.

Land gets appropriated for low density, high income housing while the marginal majority becomes increasingly congested in the poor areas. These areas become classified as blight zones. Housing gets more and more luxurious for the minority and more and more squalid for the majority. Health services become more and more elaborate and sophisticated for the minority and become less and less accessible to the majority. Education, transport, recreation facilities, right down the line follow the same path.

This mode of distributing responsibilities breeds a tendency to view human settlements in physical rather than in human terms. The whole art for managing communities is biased towards building buildings and buying hardware instead of towards organising communities that are communal in the sense of mobilising human participation in common life and organic in the sense of possessing vital, functioning organs that sustain life, health, growth, fulfillment.

The whole bias, in favour of physical structures, grows to a point where these and not people become the centre of attention. People no longer become the principal beneficiaries of urban development. They are the problems, the principal obstacles. They build slums and pollute the landscape. They have to be got out of the way to make room for the buildings, roads, factories, warehouses, dams and all manner of engineering structures.

The distribution of functions between the government and private sector then leaves a large number of vital community functions untended.

The Search for Alternatives

Countries therefore have been trying to find the proper balance between State and the private sector through various modalities for modifying the enterprise system.

Two main currents have been established. One consists of substituting *State* for *private* enterprise. The second has consisted mainly of substituting *planned* for *free* enterprise.

In the first case the balance is sought by transferring the ownership and control of enterprise to the State through nationalisation. In a system where private profit is the ruling motive, community welfare seems to take a junior position in the order of priorities. It is argued that since the State does not seek profits, the community's welfare will come first in the operations of State-owned enterprise. The trouble is that in private enterprise, profit is not merely a reward that accrues to ownership; it is also the measure of efficiency and performance. When once this test of efficiency is removed, then the organisation deteriorates very rapidly. In the end, public welfare suffers because the quality of the performance of State enterprises drops to substandard levels.

In the second case, the bulk of economic activity remains in the private sector but its freedom is curtailed by the dictates of State planning. These are translated into production and capacity quotas, marketing allotments, price controls and subsidy programmes and so forth. The experience has been, however, that economic planners, no matter how rigorous and sophisticated in method, are never able to balance the multitudes of considerations required to meet effectively and efficiently the diverse requirements of society. Furthermore, State programmes have been found more effective in curtailing business than in pushing business to do the essential functions that are unattractive.

The search for an ideal balance between private efficiency and State concern for human welfare has caused different regimes to swing over a spectrum, now towards the private and free enterprise now towards State and centralised control. In the world today various regimes exist with varying degrees of one or the other, none really fully satisfactory.

In the Third World, the most objectionable character of the enterprise approach is that it induces a "high-grading" of opportunities in a country in exactly the same sense that a fly-by-night mining company picks only the most attractive ore in a body, leaving the lower grade ores beyond hope of economic recovery.

In the Third World, countries are precisely underdeveloped because the chores of development have to be done in significant, interrelated clusters. They must be planned and executed in a critical mass in order for any single project in the cluster to be viable at all. Any approach that merely picks the most immediately feasible and profitable projects to do singly is necessarily disintegrative. It is like a bus company that merely serves the routes with the attractive traffic. This renders it impossible for anyone to serve the routes that do not yet have the traffic.

But, is there really another alternative? As we have seen, the alternatives that have been tried apply various qualifications to the enterprise system— State over private enterprise; planning and controls over free enterprise. Only a third alternative remains unexplored and untried. Should we try a suitable alternative to the enterprise system altogether?

It might be argued that the enterprise technique which has produced the wealthiest and most powerful nation on earth, the United States, must be of proven soundness. No one can dare challenge its record.

In fact, the conditions of North American development, that of some Latin American countries, involve a process radically different from that which the Third World countries in Asia must achieve. For those continents the starting point involved no large indigenous rural population crowding on scarce land. There were only clusters of indigenous and aboriginal tribes to whom the early Spanish conquistador gave the name Indios or Indians.

For the immigrant populations in North America, the object of development was not to uplift the lives of these Indians but to displace them so as to settle immigrant Europeans. The disastrous effects of this mode of development on the indigenous peoples was not considered a failure of the process. The new colonial settlements were the focus of the policy and the strategy.

It must be obvious that the application of the same approach to countries in our part of the world is fraught with danger. In Asia, the indigenous rural populations are the principals of the development drama. The disintegration of their original communities is no minor matter to be remedied ultimately in the same manner as the European immigrant "remedied" the Indian problem, by putting them in reservations.

From this perspective the American model must be totally inapplicable. What is relevant for Asia in it is not its success in producing wealthy settlements but its failure in integrating the indigenous population into society. The experience we must seek, the technology that is relevant for our purpose is one that has demonstrated success in developing countries with large indigenous rural populations. For this only three examples loom large in the history of the last century: China and Japan and more recently South Korea.

The Chinese hierarchy of organisations: the commune, the brigade and the production team—is an interesting system that, at least since the Cultural Revolution (1968) makes the traditional communal settlements the units of organisation, of management and of accounting. The divisions now coincide by and large with the corresponding centuries-old hierarchy of Chinese settlements: the town, the village and neighbourhood.

The commune encompasses a system of villages with their market town and may have a population of about 25,000 to 30,000 people. Each village corresponds to a brigade with about 200 families. The brigade in turn would have about eight to ten production teams with about 20 to 25 families each belonging to a common neighbourhood, working roughly contiguous farms.

The brigade is really the basic unit of accounting and it is at this level, I believe, that the production and income accounts are consolidated. But the team is the ultimate unit of production, as it were, and a unit of management as well since it makes resource allocation decisions, production plans, capital formation budgets, savings-investment trade-offs and determines income distribution patterns.

The brigade itself is a community with its natural resource endowment, e.g., agricultural land, water, its physical plant, infrastructure facilities, community service units, schools, hospitals and clinics, utilities.

The most interesting aspect of the Chinese system is precisely this identification of the unit of organisation, management and accounting with the natural human community. In a country where 80 per cent of the population is rural this makes eminent sense. It is, I believe, the key to the Chinese capacity for mobilising human resources in highly labour-intensive modes of capital formation: building of dikes, reclamation of land, etc.

Since the Cultural Revolution in 1968, the management of these units have had a lot of leeway in formulating their own planes. They are urged to emulate successful effort:

"In agriculture learn from Tachai.
In industry learn from Taching."

These are references to a successful rural commune and a progressive industrial commune in the oil district. But they have a surprising degree of autonomy.

This mode of organisation develops managers who are perforce community-oriented and whose economising decisions are focussed on maximising productivity and incomes at community levels. The community's welfare is their business.

The Japanese orientation towards community rather than individual goals is equally strong but has its own modes.

Japanese society has always exercised a rigorous control over the import of foreign culture patterns. The Japanese systematically brought in western science and technology by importing the literature and launching a programme of translation and distribution. They also sent regulated numbers of scholars to the universities on the European continent. The dissemination was phased such that the adoption of new ideas could be integrated into the traditional structure and ideology of the society. There was no question here of permitting free entry and circulation of Westerners to proselytise and disorganise the indigenous society.

At the end of World War II then, Japanese society had values that were still rooted in its own history and traditions. The main characteristics of these were:

1) A strong collective rather than individualistic and atomistic character. In fact, in the civil code of 1898 the collective family was the basic legal entity rather than the individual.

2) The firmly established idea was that individualism and individual independence were contrary to fundamental Japanese virtues and traditions.

3) Village solidarity and communality remained the most powerful cohesive force in the nation. Politically, the village power structure had been integrated into the national polity.

4) In the economy, a well-knit structure existed between the large capital-intensive, higher-technology industrial operation on the one hand and the traditional small- and medium-scale, largely craft- and guild-oriented operations on the other. Competition was not totally free-wheeling and unbridled, and therefore was not permitted to destroy the close links between large-scale and small-scale industry. The keynote was to have the modern forms of production integrate with the older, traditional forms.

The occupation-sponsored reforms at the end of World War II attempted to change the structure and introduce American ideas of free enterprise competition and anti-trust action. In practice the measures were tempered since it became desirable to restore Japanese economic strength as an added resource for the Allies in the cold war with the U.S.S.R.

In fact, the reforms accomplished several critical changes.

The purge of Zaibatsu family members from industry and of the top executives involved in the war effort catapulted the younger professional managers into the positions of control.

The break-up of ownership concentration muted the voice of shareholders in the running of Japanese industry and firmly established the viewpoints of professional managers.

At the same time, the fundamental ideology and character of Japanese business were preserved: the strong collective orientation, the commitment to community at least on the same level as the commitment to shareholders, the familial and paternalistic system flowing over to labour and employee relations.

Notwithstanding the introduction of U.S. anti-trust jurisprudence into the Japanese legal system, the oligopolistic structure of large-scale industry remained, and far more important, for our theme here, the strong organic links between large-scale and small- and medium-scale, more traditional industry.

These features remained a basic character of the economy all through the spectacular growth of the 1960's and the 1970's.

There is very little written on South Korea that describes the Korean synthesis of the traditional culture and a successful modernisation.

We only get occasional glimpses that are however most illuminating, such as the paper given by Dr. Kim Kyung Won at the recent Williamsburg Conference in Thailand.

Belying the impression that Korean success owed anything to an American-type individualistic enterprise approach, Dr. Kim said:

"The values once considered 'pre-modern', such as the Confucian discipline and sense of hierarchy, are now found to have played an enormously important role in the modernisation of South Korea as experienced and valued by Koreans themselves.

"Put a little more dramatically, it seems that the 'individualism' once so reverentially regarded as the essence of modernity can be actually counterproductive, if allowed to function unmodified in a nation historically accustomed to more socially oriented values and mores."

One of the manifestations of the collective-orientation of Korean business in the industrial structure are the linkages maintained by the large capital-intensive businesses with medium-, small-scale and cottage industries which are kept viable and integral with the modernised firms. A structure, if my Korean friends will forgive me for saying so, closely resembling the Japanese system.

A Community as a Unit of Management

I am proposing that for purposes of macroeconomic management, the human settlement should be the primary unit of management, of organisation and of accounting. The community unit should be defined to include a resource base and a size that gives it the capacity to provide livelihood sources from within its own boundaries and from trade with other units. This makes it a viable ecological system although not necessarily a totally self-sufficient one.

There must be a scientific model of human settlement that provides the analytical basis for the technology of its operation, just as the economic theory of the business firm provides the scientific basis for the technology of the enterprise. We require a theory of the human settlement that encompasses its many facets: its geographical and resource base, its socio-cultural configuration, its economic systems, its political or power system, its physical system and organisational structure, etc.

The operative word is of course human. And if the theory is to be operational, i.e., provide the scientific basis for an art of management, then the theory must bring out the laws of its behaviour as a human organisation. This behaviour is governed by immanent factors such as anthropological patterns, value systems, culture forms and conditioned by the opportunities and constraints of geography and environment (including other human settlements).

The art of medicine is possible because "nature" in the concrete provides fairly unambiguous norms of health. The healthy or normal human being provides the model for defining health and, by deviations from the model, sickness as well. Nature in the concrete does not provide as unambiguous a set of norms for the healthy human settlement.

The norms on the one hand, and the modalities of human settlement behaviour with its systems of causality, its processes of adjustment, the occurrence of predictable and chance phenomena—provide the materials for a technology of "control" in the management sense. On this, much of the controversy hinges, not so much around the question of *management* of the human community as around the modalities of control systems. In the debate between free enterprise and "planned systems", between democracy and dictatorship, no one really poses extreme choices between total central control and total *laissez faire*. The debate has to do with the degrees of participation given to the population in the selection of their managers, the formulation of decisions, and the areas of freedom that will remain. All these elements become part of an appropriate "control system".

Finally, the human settlement should have a suitable legal personality and a system of accounting. There are many modes to choose from—the chartered municipality, the development authority, the new town corporation with the appropriate accounts, etc.

Development Franchise Areas

Development projects in this scheme would encompass whole areas and be typically multi-purpose. It is possible then to structure them as development franchises.

Countries would be divided into development franchise areas. Each area would be defined to encompass certain natural resources, a given population, such that a viable development plan could be designed for it. Part of the test of viability would be that the process of development would generate sufficient incomes to compensate a prime total development contractor.

Through some politico-legal process, duly institutionalised, the community would define the general elements of development it desires and then seek to get a prime contractor that will translate the development goals into a suitable practical strategy and into the corresponding business elements. The prime contractor then would mobilise the consortium of enterprises that would be required to execute the individual elements of the development and business strategy.

It would have a franchise over the territory under a contract with the community. The contract would spell out the minimum specifications of the resulting developments in the area and in the community at each phase, and the manner in which the prime contractor and the consortium members would get compensated for their performance under the principal contract and sub-contracts.

There would be provisions for audit and inspection to avoid exploitation and ensure the proper balance between profit-seeking and community welfare.

The essential point here is that the totality of the undertaking by a prime contractor should build into the design of the strategy the optimum balance between projects that enhance the income and welfare of the community and the projects that provide revenues to the contractors. The practicability of this whole procedure hinges on the assumption that the optimum development strategy for a defined community will generate enough incomes that can accrue to and motivate a private business group if the contracts are designed properly.

What are the implications of such an approach for private investors?

This really forces investors to form themselves into consortia in order to build up the capability for multiple lines of enterprise. If the basic resource is a mineral deposit, the logical prime contractor is a mining company. However, the mining leases will specify responsibilities for undertaking settlement or resettlement projects with all the elements of land development, infrastructure construction, housing, building of commercial centres, health and education facilities, plus the establishment of firms to operate transport, communications, waterworks, agro-business enterprises, small-scale manufacturing, etc.

The design will sort out the projects that government will have to undertake directly and which it will finance out of budget funds and borrowing. In general, the activities allotted to governments will be those in which the benefits accruing from the investments cannot be appropriated through a market price and must be recaptured through taxation. All the projects that produce a marketable commodity or service will be sub-contracted to private parties.

At first blush, the responsibility for undertaking all these other lines of business seems an awfully onerous burden for the private industry to assume, but firms that operate company towns usually do most of the functions set forth here. They provide housing, schools, health facilities, recreation, power and utilities, transport, etc. They generally do not feel, however, that they have the responsibility down the years to provide the diversified sources of livelihood for the growing community. The expansion and logical extensions of their own business are the paramount consideration. If these plans provide additional employment for the community, well and good; if they are inadequate, too bad. The government is really responsible for overall growth in employment opportunities.

Nor am I suggesting that private enterprises subsidise the community. Not at all. In undertaking the responsibility for supplying, say, suitable transport, private enterprise is expected to structure the transport operations as a viable business in itself. The "prime contractor" is asked simply to assist in promoting the venture, raising the capital and initially overseeing the operations.

The same would be so of the diversified small-scale industries. It is up to the prime contractor to set up the marketing and distribution network, get the design and production supervisory personnel who will then get the local craftsmen trained and organised to fabricate the goods according to vigorous specifications and time schedule. Again, with proper management, it should be possible to structure the operation so it more than pays for itself.

Development Contracts

The development of these franchise areas could be covered by specific legal contracts. To accomplish this for integrated area development projects, they must be translated into appropriate development contracts with specific parties assuming obligations to perform specific functions according to a coordinated time-table. The contract structure will involve a prime contractor that serves as a *chef de file* for the entire project. Among the parties to the contract will be government and private sector spanning the whole range of public sector agencies from public works departments to water resource development entities, private engineering consulting firms, surveyors, construction firms as well as commercial and industrial entities.

The mother contract is a total area development agreement. The principal party to it would have to be the community incorporated through a legal entity of some form similar to a city or municipal charter but encompassing a geographical area that is meaningful as a unit for integrated development; e.g., a whole river valley.

The basic accounting framework which will be used to define *desiderata* and measure results from the viewpoint of the people will be a system of community resource, production and income statements. This set of accounts will be used to define a development path for the community—specific objectives, translated into targets, resource utilisation patterns and budgets.

Within this framework, particular investment, production, trade and service functions will be subcontracted to private business. This approach makes the terms of reference of private business fit naturally into the community's development goals.

The New Managers

New systems breed new managers. The kind of manager this would breed is an interesting one. His commitment as a first instance is to a community rather than a product line. He is no tractor salesman viewing communities purely as a market for tractors or a rice trader viewing his territory as a source of the commodity.

His commitment is to the community and he must determine the totality of the community's needs and determine what lines of business will fill those needs in what orders of priority and in what sequence of time.

As a manager he is just as concerned with the optimum use of resources, achieving cost-effectiveness in supply of goods to the community, with markets. His concern, however, goes beyond merely selling or sourcing single products. The maintenance and growth of income streams for the community is in fact his principal business and the measure of his performance, as the community's business manager.

The accounts for which he is responsible are the community's product and income accounts. That is his equivalent profit and loss statement.

The science and art of managing a community "business" is sadly under-developed. This in itself is a dramatic symptom of the cavalier attention this all-important task has received the past many years. Although economics up to perhaps the time Steuart before Adam Smith was part of the art of state-craft and was a chapter in manuals for "The Prince".

But no matter. The analytical tools exist to fashion a science of economic management for communities; the economics of social overhead costs, the determination of how best to balance the public utility principle with the free competitive principle. In what spheres it is best to establish regulated mono-polies; in what spheres to induce free competitive activities; what activities to charge against overall social overhead and what to leave to competitive market pricing.

I cite these because when one divests the whole matter of ideological colour, when they are couched in purely economic management terms, the problems are no different in character or scale from those that businesses which are sectorially specialised deal with from day to day.

The concept can be made quite practical and operational.

Let me conclude with an anecdote from the life of my favourite Middle East character: Mulla Nasruddin.

Mulla had lost his donkey and he had everyone in his village madly searching everywhere. In the midst of all this frantic activity, one villager observed Mulla sitting nonchalantly in his house. "Mulla, your donkey is missing. Why are you not out looking with everybody else?" Mulla looked up at him and said, "You see that far distant hill on the horizon. When you have looked there and have not found my donkey, then I shall worry."

In our search for the ideal model, this may not be the last hill yet. But, perhaps, it is best to start worrying.

4. Management Culture

James L. Hayes

Mr. James L. Hayes is President and Chief Executive Officer of American Management Associations (AMA) since 1971. Management development has long been Mr. Hayes' speciality. He has conducted management training activities for key executives in many parts of the world. Prior to joining AMA, Mr. Hayes was Dean of the School of Business Administration, Duquesne University, Pittsburgh, for 11 years. He continues to be a faculty member of the renowned Stonier Graduate School of Banking, Rutgers University.

We have been asked to talk for about 20 minutes on the topic "Management Culture". I think I would have preferred giving the history of mankind in five minutes within this time. Indeed, the real impact that the two would make upon the public was described very well by the fact that the assemblers of this Congress passed out papers to all of you just a little while ago. I feel it is fortunate that each of us should take a slightly different point of view on the topic and I have tried to take mine from a bit of reading, reading from a few research papers during the great opportunity that I have had over the years to visit so many countries in the world. This is my second time standing on this platform and I have also been the host to many of you in the United States. I see couples before me that have been kind to me. I see men and women here, and I find that very often the best comments on the Culture of the Manager come from the wives. Somewhat like an aeroplane trip, their reactions range from frustration to relaxation, seldom touching satisfaction.

There are people who have taught me so much, many of you from many countries, that I think it is best to stay away from my own country because sometimes the accusations that are made about us are generalisations and a bit unfair.

I think *all* countries are developing countries, developing in different aspects. All countries have developed to some point more than all other countries. So, to characterise countries only by economic achievements may be incorrect. When I stand away from my own country a little bit, what do I see round the world when managers come together? What are the things that mark management culture as being different from all other cultures? Differing quickly from the cultures within a country are the national cultures which indeed are unique to that country and, probably, not fully understood from outside. I recall Matthew Arnold, one of the social critics of England. He said that the immediate aim of a culture is setting ourselves to train our sights on what perfection is and to make it prevail. A culture, therefore, is an assembly of traditions, of history, of practices, and even of some prejudices and biases.

Now if you look at managers, what is it that you want to change? It is often more things in general than the things that "separate" us. Let me tell you what I see around the world for purposes of discussion, because the real purpose here is discussion. Managers, if they could always get the knowledge would fill every opening that we have for managers in this world. But knowledge alone would not do. Somehow we still have the feeling that if we can send people to courses, if we can give them more books to read, eventually they will come out as managers. But it does not work this way.

Management is *attitude*. Management is *skill*. Management is *health*. At a very early age we catch something in the management spirit and we see it in young men and women throughout the world. I have never understood the statement that managers were born and not made. I have been puzzled as to how managers are born into a certain family. We have reason to believe that management can be transmitted but what would happen to our culture, to young entrepreneurial spirit where a small organisation has grown to be a very compact organisation?

We have lost our way just a little bit because we forget that managers are pragmatic in any country, in any job, and a sense of pragmatism marks a manager. The result may be profit. It may be governing more efficiently. This may involve better hospital care or even better productivity for the university. These require management indeed. This *ad hoc* aspect of practicality, however, is very implicit because it does not give many managers an opportunity to get a vision of the job. Most of them are driven by the complexity of organisation to get something done *today*. So we find that universities have led the way down the management path. I do not think that is correct. Universities have simplified management practices and made it possible for managers to see their jobs in a broader perspective because it is the manager with vision at the top and the practitioner at the bottom that must come together in any well-organised grouping. So there is this urgency in patience, respect for high productivity, profit maximisation, real achievement and often social orientation that have strong local and *ad hoc* overtones. These are the things throughout the world that managers are adjusting themselves to in their particular cultures. I do not find many managers who really have a great drive for social welfare, for leisure, for a long-term social change or even for undemonstrated theory throughout the world. That the people of the universities really understand this is doubtful. Have they ever played some role outside the university? On the contrary, the people of the universities wonder when they will get a vision of the things that I have just mentioned. At some places they must come together. Yet at the same time the manager has to know that from the university he will get an accountant. He wants experts, engineers, sociologists. But where do we put them together? Where have we changed from the breakdown of the subject "management" to see what the practical manager does in making decisions to come together?

You cannot produce managers without effective organisation. You cannot have organisation without *doing* something. Without communication you cannot talk. Without any of these things you cannot control your pattern. In many cases the manager senses this. He or she does not prescribe that work but that is what they do. And it seems to be true throughout the world. Some say there is long-range planning and short-range planning. Impossible! If you have both short-range and long-range planning you will implement the former and *file* the latter. Bringing them together is not correct. Some people say plans are for three years, five years or ten years. This varies by local culture. But there is no variation in the fact that the most practical long-range plan is the one on which you are going to make a decision today. That is true in every country. The general culture shows that they want recognition. Recognition does not have to be in the eyes of many but only in the manager's organisation. Isn't it that part of our objective and the reason why we do planning? This is implemented in many ways. We usually do not see planning as a preventive part of management. But management culture is one of problem prevention rather than problem solution—although we do have to solve problems as long as there is management.

Taking a cue from the outline which was given to us, I would like to be a little critical of the way we develop some of our management organisations, in the U.S. and throughout the world. When did we get ever so deeply ingrained in management that we put top personnel away from where the action is? Why do we think that we should keep them apart and not have them mingle with the workers? When did we ever say that there should be this separation? It is *separation* which causes many problems within our cultures. I have talked often about the practice of decision-making, something most managers can easily understand. But the supervisory tree and the communication tree are quite different. I believe strongly that people in top management position can have the most successful enterprises in the world if they have a strong concern for getting down to the bottom and finding out what is going on as a regular way of work. They should not believe just what a report says or what the computer prints out. What happens to the organisation with regard to a room like this one, for example? The President may come in with his Vice-President and say "What a beautiful room. I like this yellow colour on the wall. Did you think of *green* when you were doing this?" The Vice-President says, "We did consider it and thought that this would be the right colour." Later, the Vice-President says to an assistant, "Hayes said green. This wall should be light green." The assistant goes down one more level and says, "Did you hear? Hayes wants the auditorium painted green." Finally, he says "put them on overtime and get this repainted *tonight.*" I see this kind of communication problem in India, I can also see it in Japan, in the Netherlands and in the Soviet Union—the same kind of reaction. "Hayes wanted it green. Why didn't you make that decision in the first place?" We re-do things and spend money wastefully. And, if this is not enough, my wife will come to me and and say "many people in your organisation admire your taste." This culture is uniform throughout the world—it is world-wide. Supervision means getting out of our offices but still being leaders within our cultures. Let us get down and listen to the people at the bottom.

Where did unions come from? Unions came because people wanted someone to *listen* to them. Sometimes we forget that it is good to listen. How many cultures do we find in which managers believe they are different from the culture of the people? And how many times do we find that religious sects are treating managers as though they were not people? We should get away from this. All managers know that they have powers, but they are frequently less conscious of it than their wives. Managers know they have power and wish they could somehow share it.

Most of us know that the management theory is based on production theory. The building trade is a first manifestation. The world today is getting very much subservient; much more so in the countries that call themselves underdeveloped. We have lost our sense of service. We have forgotten our customers. Governments have lost the voters. Hospitals have forgotten their patients and we have forgotten that jobs bring satisfaction to other people. There is economic exchange in almost any system, and in an exchange the parties must think that more is gained than what is sacrificed. But why do we forget that an exchange takes place only when there is *satisfaction* first.

I have a feeling that in most organisations there are classes of society and classes, of course, isolate people rather than help people. In my country, (I know it varies in very many ways throughout the world), we find that getting the world work down to all kinds of people is very important. You know our problem—we have some disadvantaged people; but they are not really. If you put them into a job, they can be helpful, can be self-satisfying. Some of my friends here might have heard my story of what happens when someone says you can put disadvantaged people to work. It is said that eventually they would compete, would want better education, would have a skill and—sometime beyond all our time—we would have solved that kind of social problem. Very important today, so far as management is concerned, is providing volunteers to work with disadvantaged people. I have often told the story of a President of a company in my country who might attend a luncheon where he is impressed by talk of the need to help the disadvantaged or minorities.

He agrees to hire several and returns from lunch to tell his subordinate. He offers an explanation which is rather flattering, but when the message comes down one more level it translates into "see what he has brought back?" It goes down one more level—to the floor level—and they will say, you know that job you have open, well you have one of *them* to fill it. What I am saying is that in very many societies, as we go down through management the level of bias tends to increase because the history of mankind has been one of people trying to block other people out on false promises in order to gain the advantage for themselves—a very selfish thing. But, now, what happens on that job? The person starts working at the machine he has been assigned to and the foreman says, let me show you how we do it. You put your foot on the machine like this, press down on the foot lever and pull back on the hand lever. Try it. No. Try it again. No. That is a reject. Try it again. No. He now goes up to his superior and says, that man cannot learn. His disadvantage has deprived him of skills. His boss says, but we need someone on that job. Any suggestions? Then the first line supervisor says, well, I have a brother. The boss says, bring him in and teach your brother the job. So, he does. He says, come in brother, let me show you how you do this. You put your foot on the machine like this. Clap the side of the handle on this particular machine and then quickly step down on the foot lever. Try it brother. Beautiful ! See what happens? I am going to use a word that I think we as managers, in all our management cultures, have tended to be ashamed of. When I *love* you, I teach you the *art* of the job. When I *tolerate* you, I teach you the *technology*. Much of management culture throughout the world has been guilty of technological transfer without a shred of love. Some day, we who are in management, assuming leadership, *must* get back to the philosophers we have known within our national cultures, or our religious cultures, and see if we can put back, some of these qualities that I think management needs so badly. You all know about planning. You all know about controlling mechanisms and the way we use computers and these kinds of things. But, we should never forget what our philosophers taught us, namely, that we need humility to listen and to delegate, otherwise it is a simple posture of "tolerance" and less than a practice. But it takes a little patience to do some planning and hope that you will get to a point where you can take care immediately; a little modesty to get down with people and listen to those that don't have the same opportunity that you do. We are all brothers and worthy of transmitting a part of the art. In our country, we come up on one of our seasons now, one of our big occasions, called Christmas. As you know, at Christmas time we give gifts and it is commonplace to get these gifts from our stores. Often, these gifts come with "easy to follow directions". Parents get together on Christmas eve and with great frustration try to put these pieces together following those instructions. I used to go through this as a parent. I would take a red wire in my left hand and a green wire in my right hand, put them together and still not get the light that was supposed to go on. I would go to my neighbour and say, please help me. Certainly, he would say just take the red wire in your left hand, the green wire in your right hand, put them together, then just apply a little bit of saliva, and—there was the light! I read the instructions in which the word 'saliva' did not appear even once! These were very expensive toys and I did not say this to my neighbour, but where did he learn this? It was a touch of the common man; one that could be transmitted. Or, as another example of this, have you ever driven down a very busy highway in the various countries of the world and come to the conclusion that the brilliant engineer who puts up the directional signs *already* knew where he was going? It takes many engineers at all levels to transmit the art and no matter what we may do with education throughout the world, no matter what we may do with developing the art, in country after country, unless we find great groups of managers who care enough to be leaders of little groups, breaking things down to understandable small units and transmit the art of the job, on the job, we will not have successful enterprises or successful Governments, and we will not have successful social services. I feel that some place we have lost touch in all organisations for the fact that we have so much that is similar in our cultural managements—things which we can exchange. I want to know how you do it in your country. I am not sure it is adaptable to ours, but if I do not know it there is nothing I can do about it.

This is why we are here, to exchange management culture in highly technical points and in the way of understanding each other. And, at a meeting of this sort, my association with you is coming in the way of that transfer, if my position or yours gets in the way of that transfer, if your Government or mine gets in the way of that transfer, our professional stance should be to disown all of them, because the one thing about the business manager is that he or she wants to know how to do it better in order to be successful. I have never seen a professional manager who did not have a deep interest in people. *We* are those who provide the climate for the satisfaction of millions of people, and our culture has a transfer element. But we must first be managers before we try to transfer the technology.

5. Regional Characteristics of Management

John Marsh

Dr. Marsh is Chairman of W.D. Scott & Co (UK) Ltd and Consolidated Safeguards Ltd. He was Director General of the British Institute of Management during 1961–73 and subsequently its Assistant Chairman until 1976. He was also Director of the Institute of Personnel Management from 1947–49, and Director of the Industrial Welfare Society from 1950–61. He specialises in management and social problems of industrialisation in developed and developing countries.

If this paper is unorthodox in its content and presentation, I do not apologise, for we are, I believe, in an age when orthodoxy leads too often to dullness and inaction: giving undue importance to the *status quo* of managers and their organisations; too much time is spent on *its* preservation while excessively talking about change; change, it would seem, when technologically based and driven, has its own momentum; and it is above all precipitated by market forces; we and our fellow employees are also in the market forces—modern economic life is somewhat incestuous.

A New Era is Here

It has been my privilege to visit some fifty countries in all continents and of political systems and cultures; further, one has seen and has been part of managements and managers 'tasks in the good sellers' marked years of 1945–70. That era in domestic and international markets produced its own rather easier management attitudes and performances. The turbulent, disturbing 1970's, the buyers' market years, brought overnight differences, urgencies and struggles for economic viability and survival often both nationally and internationally; corporate managements have had the biggest shake-up in their thinking and behaviour yet recorded. It is still with us......'cash flow' is a new form of measuring economic haemorrhages.

The years 1970–80 are, in my view, the climacteric years of the century, heralding a prolonged period of uneasiness and adaptation which may last through to the 21st century. Who indeed can foresee a period with calmness and confidence for more than a year or two? The factors of inflation, recession, incipient unemployment or underemployment in most economies, energy problems, and the changing significance, even 'pecking order', of nations able to supply raw materials, oil, bauxite, copper, surplus food, etc. More nations, as they industrialise with relative success, will cope domestically with finished primary, secondary and tertiary products and then wish to trade competitively in that final determinant, 'the international market'.

Common and Divergent Characteristics

Against this background let me enunciate eight of my beliefs, which have effect on all regional characteristics of nations, organisations and those who work in industry.

First: economic and quality of life expectations of a greatly increased world population will demand greater performance by corporate managements and managers; both are part (not apart) of the workforce.

Second: the organics of managing (basic rules, organisation, systems) are broadly the same in all regions, countries and cultures; government controls or otherwise, local market factors, attitudes of people *to* work, speeds, and standards, the processes of management control, may differ.

Third: in talking of management we invariably think of yesterday and today, yet the emphasis needs to be on survival, development and growth tomorrow and the day after; we must learn to 'think things through' more effectively *with* our employees.

Fourth: management above all, means getting things done through people; there are racial, geographical, cultural, religious, family and individual/ group differences in attitude and emphasis by habit and tradition. Races and creeds are at best part of the human glory and variety.

Fifth: those who wish to be well-informed on the Regional Characteristics of Management can best find out the plus and minus points by consulting transnational corporations: they know by the realites of doing (often the same kind of business) in, say, a hundred differing countries with all their languages, regional and local habits and customs. Their information and advice has the 'cutting edge' of hard won, not always temporary, success out of early failures.

Sixth: the 'newness' of industrial management and managers in a newly industrialising country may mean learning much by what is rightly called 'the hard way'. However, there is no need to invent the wheel; management fundamentals are best learnt by action based pilot schemes with experienced help from outside.

Seventh: we must ask ourselves what is the yardstick by which 'successful management' is to be judged? Is it only profitability, if so profit for whom? More production of goods and services? Productivity? Their national and international marketability? Or a combination of 'economic' progress, provision of effective work and the quality of life? Not to mention the ephemeral and dogmatic pronouncements of politics!

Eighth: economic groupings in the *long term* will affect management styles. In the European Economic Community, Eastern Europe, Middle East, ANDEAN, ASEAN Groups, etc., we have seen the emergence of economic groupings in which common characteristics of management cultures and policies and practices continue to show themselves. Notable examples are the COMECON Group of countries with totally planned economies for the past 35-50 years. Their centralised characteristics are very differently viewed by employees, customers and competitors alike.

More recently the emergence of the European Economic Community whereby "harmonisation policies" are leading to many political, economic and social changes, including a strong emphasis on the emergence of more accountable, participative styles of management in the social democracies of Western Europe. Various forms of standardisation in technical and managerial policies and practices are evolving.

It could perhaps be argued that free-for-all trading atmosphere of Middle Eastern countries during the recent oil bonanza years has shown a dramatic return to the *laissez faire* systems of the 19th century. This has had a marked catalytic effect on other 'exporting' economies in expectations, competitiveness and results—the latter increasingly edging towards disillusionment to both parties.

Managers are Human in all Cultures

Without being impertinent, but in an effort to stress that managers are human beings, let us all admit that in *all* countries and cultures, managers as people, both men and women, young and old, of whatever colour or culture, language or career-origin, are to be found in many types; a few are described, in no order of precedence or frequency:

The Pragmatic: those who believe in the law of the situation and will tackle problems with their brand of commonsense. They are robust, not given to much dialogue but rather to command.

The Cautious: usually accurate with facts; those who keep things 'close to the chest'; are not easy in communication, and who are seemingly mistrustful unless speaking from a common basis of established fact: accountants are much given to this! And lawyers; who are further prone to seek second opinions from other lawyers!

The Risk-takers: clearly the entrepreneur, but I refer more to 'change agents', those who keep themselves up-to-date; who are investigative and thoughtful and who declare for one or two options to the solution of problems, (to be backed up by the second in a fall-back position). Are 5 per cent of managers genuine innovators? Do we need more as catalysts of change? Can they be respected leaders too?

The Bureaucratic: those who seem to be more interested in procedures than results. These are people who have never been accustomed to personal accountability, i.e., civil servants and local government bureaucrats who can hide their errors in the labyrinth of committees or in an early assimilation of the skill of 'buck-passing'. To be held responsible for results early on in life is a valuable foundation for a decision-making management career in all cultures; on this latter point I am utterly dogmatic and unrepentant.

The Technocratic: those who have studied management theory too literally and have an undue confidence in the results of academic teaching of management subjects; they wish for people and events to conform to theory and are somewhat inflexible. To them people do not seem to count so much as techniques and systems; in free societies (and one suspects in the not so free) ordinary people will outwit and frustrate systems. Technocrats are not necessarily inherent democrats. "Democracy is the worst possible system, except for all the others!" (Churchill).

The Elitist: those who have by inheritance, influence of education been led to believe that it confers on them a 'divine right' to manage or control others. Nevertheless, in all cultures, some 'tribal' and family groups often have a better managerial application than others by decisiveness, single mindedness, shrewdness and other qualities acquired at an early age. There are longstanding managerial Mafias!

The Stylistic: many managers, by the nature of their professions, industries or trades, develop special characteristics which, towards the end of this managerial century are becoming marked in many regions and cultures.

Proximity to the customer, satisfied or irate, brings an urgency to managerial manners and decision-making, i.e.,

a) The manager of a shop, service industry—garage, household equipment, supply and maintenance.

b) Building and associated trades—a special category these, victims of the professional niceties of architects and surveyors, the weather, casual labour, emergency interruptions.

c) Agricultural industries and the vagaries of climate, crop cycles, markets.

d) Hospitals—managing in a vastly complex organisation with great medical expertise, professional and vocational dedication, ancillary services, costs—and above all the survival of the patient. Here managerial responsibilities and skills need to be shared, in close partnership with others.

e) Education and other social services—this 'software' area of life, for the knowledge-based society, demands continuous education throughout life to cope with change and its application. In this area, management as an old art and a new science will escalate in importance (and difficulty)—who is to judge what results, how and when? There are, alas, too many managerial fads, fashions, gimmicks, techniques and Gurus.

f) Managing in commerce has in many countries meant the management of white collar employees. With competition for administrative employees and trade union growth in this area, the gaps between blue and white collar workers are disappearing rapidly. Even managers are resorting to union protection—in my view a short-sighted, retrograde step which will ultimately destroy professional credibility.

The Expert and Specialist: as in medicine, managerial proliferation into permanent as well as, hopefully, temporary specialisms, has been a feature of its growth during the past three decades. Organisations have been built to accommodate specialisms—*but* they must not be exempt from frequent audit—"Is this specialism helping to increase productivity?"—"What is its own productivity, what indeed is that of management and managers?" "Expert knowledge is limited knowledge."

The Professional: the professional manager has been a strong emergence in the 1970's. Professional managers, whether general or specialist, usually have no financial stake in the business, except their careers, on the basis of being hired in the market place. Many are mobile and move several times in a lifetime; indeed, it could be argued that mobility in attitude, experience and location is desirable for at least 20 per cent of a nation's managerial force, if they are to play a dynamic, wealth-creating, change agent role giving vitality and leadership to organisations and employees.

Ownership is Significant to Managerial Cultures

It is increasingly evident in mixed economies that managers working for private enterprise have more insecurity, though sometimes bigger immediate rewards (before tax). Those working in State enterprises have greater security, less personal accountability and their rewards are rising through strong trade union action at lower levels. Cooperative societies and enterprises are bound more by an ideology which could, with enlightened management, prosper greatly in an age of 'industrial democracy'.

Multinationals tend uniformly to pay higher wages and give better conditions in many countries than local employers. They are often pace-setters.

The family-owned industry is increasingly giving way to employing more professionals at the higher levels; taxation and inheritance legislation in many countries is leading to the disappearance of all but the very small family business. And yet, at all employee levels, some industries and organisations have attracted several generations of families to work in them—the 'family' round the industrial work situation has its positive, but taken for granted, role.

State and International Infrastructures for Survival ?

In the Western advanced industrial countries, the impact of greater unemployment is having a surprising effect on attitudes towards work. In the late 70's there is less fear than that which existed during similar world slumps, pre-1939. People, employed or not, believe that the international, interdependent, capitalistic, technology-based economic systems can and will provide the basic needs for living even in times of recessions, when many millions of people are unemployed or underemployed. The 'welfare state' provisions, though stretched, have assisted greatly but only insofar as taxes have been paid to keep going a national 'cash flow' often with the aid of the IMF and other funds. Let us not forget that many industrialising countries have scarcely laid the foundations for these provisions.

These trends give no answer to the serious poverty and chronic unemployment in so many developing countries. It is not the task of this paper to deal with this vital 'humane need', to which the attention of politicians in all countries needs to be increasingly focussed; the intensification and redirection of the wealth creating services of international agencies—UNO, UNIDO, ILO, UNDP, FAO, WHO, OECD, UNCTAD, and Regional Organisations, etc.—will still prove inadequate.

All these organisations need to audit, review, reset their priorities at ten -year intervals.

All managements and managers of local, national, and international resources will need to redouble or treble their commitment and effort in the dimensions of the new economic world order for progress to be made.

Who gives the clarion call to such Agencies; surely the inequalities, inadequate economic and social standards of the world's *so far unclamant* deprived millions should be the spur to our individual and collective consciences? The media has at least placed many of us in a position not to deny knowledge of this aspect of human agony?

The Media and its Contribution to Expanding Hopes/Horizons

Therefore, the all-pervasive influence of the media especially television, radio and the press, has brought about a greater public awareness of economic and social problems, but almost to the point of saturation and boredom. Human expectations become greater as more modern communications succeed—but the motivation for greater productive effort does not follow. In all cultures and regions people understandably have local horizons as a prime interest. We seem to think that for our politicians to talk about issues, the North-South dialogue, means that things happen; political motion does not also mean action though the battle of words is an essential part of democratic options—for options there surely must be.

Organic Rights of Association?

I believe that the post-1945 growth of trade unionism in advanced industrial societies has passed its peak in many ways. The new industrial overlords are the trade union leaders who can, by their influence and decisions, bring industries and even countries to a halt. Through media participation more and more citizens in their common sense are challenging the credibility of the power of trade union leaders.

Trade Union leaders, with businessmen, are becoming public scapegoats; both groups are influencing power and are influenced by it. It must never be forgotten that trade unions and employers band together their members—

To preserve the rights of association,

To prevent exploitation by third parties,

To bargain with each other and third parties (customers, government, regional agencies, ILO, etc.)

There are plusses and minusses for all institutions, but in my view both kinds of institutions and professional bodies are part of the total wealth creating process of our time in free (all) societies.

Imperial and Colonial Legacies

Those nations that have emerged from the British Empire have developed systems and even industrial and social cultural habits. Similarly, those nations that have emerged from French influence and that of Holland, Portugal and Spain. It is significant that the present-day imperialism of Soviet Russia and the seemingly colonial dependencies of the Eastern Block countries may indicate that the Eastern Block itself is 50 years behind at least in achieving some basics of emancipation that can come from the application of modern industrial and managerial ideals.

Summary

The Development of management and managers, individually or in the round, is part of the organic development of organisations; this process will gradually narrow some of the productively inhibiting differences in management culture and regional characteristics. It is, of course, a matter for each nation to determine its policies, programmes, pace and performance.

The world is, at one and the same time, a very complex amalgam of industrial and social systems, yet with the rationalisation brought about by science and technology, we are nearer to understanding each other's processes in adding to the wealth, health and happiness of people.

In conclusion, I would say, that in all regional cultures let us:

—Concentrate on the basics of organising work simply;

—Monitor our managerial systems and techniques, (many are really short-lived) so that the lay worker can be helped towards fulfilment;

—Avoid-jargon and eliminate the mystiques of this new art and science; like religions the essential message is for the individual to understand, embrace and practice; but let us not make management a new religious cult with its hierarchial priesthood and acolytes;

—Have a sense of humour about ourselves.

How do *we* fit into the perspective of our time? and in the eyes of others?

Finally, in all cultures, work systems, and organisations, let us remember Lao Tse's advice (A.D. 600):

"Fail to honour people
And they will fail to honour you".

But the challenge remains........

Life is not a cup to be drained: it is a measure to be filled.
Before a hungry man God may not appear except in the form of bread.

—Mahatma Gandhi

6. Regional Characteristics of Management

T. Shiina

Mr. T Shiina, whose management career spans half a century, joined Sumitomo Metal Industries Ltd, Japan, in 1929 and rose to become the Executive Vice-President of Sumitomo Corporation in 1965, and Vice-Chairman in 1977. Mr. Shiina is currently Senior Adviser of Sumitomo Petroleum Development Corporation.

To begin with, I would like to copy away the expression given by Dr. Drucker. Japan *was* a child till recently. The child has been growing very very fast. It was in 1868 that Japan set out on a course of modernisation when the Shogunate regime gave way to the Meiji Restoration putting an end to the centuries-old "closed-door policy". The new Government wanted to bring about modernisation by closely following in the footsteps of the western civilisation and most of the subsequent Governments continued to pursue this course.

Can then we regard the development of Japan in the same light as we see in Western countries? The answer is an emphatic 'no'. And I think with its respective systems of business management the difference between Japan and Western countries is most conspicuously evident.

The traditional employment system—the life-time employment system in Japan: Generally people in Japan will stay and work for the span of their working life at the business enterprise at which they found their first employment. This is a life-time employment system. In Japan, therefore, a big enterprise is not just where we go and work to get our pay cheques. An enterprise is often likened to a ship, and its employees to the complement manning the ship. This is very true. To the employees the enterprise is truly a ship that sails with them, carrying aboard their joys and sorrows. These mutual relations between the enterprise and the employees generate on the part of the employees a deep sense of loyalty to the enterprise and on the part of the enterprise a warm feeling of consideration towards the employees. Even an employee at the lowest level, when speaking of the enterprise he works for, will have no hesitation to call it "my company".

Trade unions: The rights of the working class are well established and fully protected in Japan under the most advanced system of labour laws enacted after the Second World War on the model of the labour laws of the United States of America. There is, however, a fundamental difference here which should not be lost sight of. Whereas modern labour-capital relations in the West are based on the premise that there exists an inevitable conflict of interests between labour and capital, the relations between the labour and the capital in Japan are predominantly influenced by the traditional thinking of labour and capital having a complementary role to play in each other's interests. In Japan, therefore, the unions are basically individual enterprise unions which combine into respective industrial associations of industrial enterprise unions. These industrial associations are then organised to form national federations of industrial associations such as the General Council of Japanese Trade Unions and the Liaison Council of Neutral Unions of Japan called 'Sohyo' and 'Churitsu Roren' respectively. Throughout this vertical organisation structuring of the trade unions in Japan, the independent will of individual enterprise unions is not forcibly subject to higher-level decisions.

The seniority system: Although with a life-employment system, we have in Japan the so-called seniority system of promotion and it is probably the most characteristic feature of the employment system in Japan. I will now explain how the seniority system operates. In Japanese enterprises where life-time employment is a well-established tradition, senior vacancies are usually filled by promotion from among the employees within the enterprises, and such promotions are most frequently made according to the seniority in age. This is the seniority system. In individual applications of the system, however, it would be far from the truth to say that ability is under-rated in favour of seniority. The system operates with due consideration both for ability and seniority. So it may perhaps be better termed the modulated competence system.

Selection of the executives and managers: In line with the seniority system stated above, it is customary in Japan that managerial staff and even senior executive officers are selected by promotion from within the enterprise. A majority of company presidents in Japan are such who have reached that position by promotion. Presidents in Japan could be compared to managing directors in other countries. The various positions in the enterprises in Japan are filled with a series in intra-organisational promotions and also with job experiences in various lines of business of their respective enterprises. Accordingly, Japanese executives at the top management have a thorough knowledge of personnel and material capabilities of the enterprises. On the other hand they tend to be rather indifferent to other unrelated enterprises and industries. This system of selecting executives and managers by intra-organisational promotions operates on the principle radically different from the Western concept of management skill.

Decision-making: The decision-making system in Japan is also very unique. First I would like to speak about the general meeting of the shareholders. The majority of Japanese enterprises are incorporated as joint-stock companies with limited liabilities. These joint-stock companies come under the ownership of the investors or the shareholders, to be exact. Under the code of laws the supreme decision-making power at the joint-stock companies is vested in the general shareholders' meeting. However, the fact of the matter is that bankers carry a considerably more weight over and above the shareholders, when it comes to making corporate decisions in Japanese enterprises. This is because enterprises in Japan depend overwhelmingly on banks and other financial institutions for a continued supply of working capital and operating funds rather than on the shareholders.

An analysis of the list of shareholders of big businesses in Japan would show that more than two-thirds of the issued shares are often held by enterprises having some close business relations with such other big businesses and also that the exclusive interest in holding these shares is thereby to ensure the continuation of their business relations. There are also many cases where shares are held on a reciprocal basis, that is, one enterprise holds shares of the other enterprise and vice versa.

Ownership and management associations: Whilst on the subject of general meeting of the shareholders, I should mention that executives and managers of big businesses in Japan own only a very negligible share in the equity of their business. For example, in one of the biggest motor car manufacturing companies, Toyota, only 2 per cent of the shares are held by the Toyota family. That is a good example.

The Board of Directors: This Board is vested with the supreme decision-making power in regard to management and administration. Big businesses in Japan tend to have more and more directors elected to the Board. These directors are usually nominated intra-organisationally and are for that reason habitually hesitant to express themselves freely at the board meetings before the president and senior members of the board who have themselves been selected under the seniority system, which we have already reviewed. Individual enterprises do have their own internal guidelines for the agenda of the board meetings which are, however, just minimal to satisfy the requirements under the code of law. In this manner the board which has necessarily an essential legal function to perform, has shrunk to its bare bones.

Executive Council: Parallel to the board of directors we have in Japan what we call the Jomu Kai or the Executive Council consisting of the president and a number of selected executive directors and thereby forming the core, top management of an enterprise, which in many instances performs the function of corporate management, administration, decision-making in place of the board meeting. Despite its real importance, however, the executive council has no foundation on the code of law and is no more than a voluntary institution within an enterprise.

Representing directors: For the management and administration of the business of an enterprise, representing director/directors is/are held finally responsible; the president holds an extraordinary power, principally because the board of directors, shrunk to its bare bones as I have previously mentioned, fails often to exercise a restraining influence over the president. Here perhaps I should also mention that quite a large number of Japanese big businesses have chairmen ranking above presidents in the organisational chart and leaving management and administration to their presidents. But in some rare cases we find chairmen in giant businesses vested with a strong power for executive decision-making.

The 'Ringi' system of decision-making: 'Ringi' is a Japanese word for which there seems to be no suitable English translation. It is a traditional system of decision-making, characteristic of Japanese enterprises and I would like to explain how this system works. Under the Ringi system matters for which decision is being sought, are first documented in writing at the level seeking a decision in the form of proposals which document is again referred to as the 'Ringi-sho' and is accompanied, whenever required, by all the available supporting data and information considered necessary for decision-making. The Ringi-sho is next submitted by the proposing level through respective organisational decision-making levels on the operating lines with their concurrence to the highest managerial level for decision and approval. Through this process the proposals documented in the Ringi-sho receive the stamp of management approval. Generally speaking, the Ringi system of decision-making is a very time-consuming process, but at the same time it has its own merits, one of which is that errors of judgement can be minimised because the system is exposed to views and opinions at different levels; it may also benefit from comments and judgements of the capable staff at different levels which help correct possible shortcomings of the seniority system.

The transfer of management abroad: Japanese overseas investment figures showed US $ 1.2 billion in 1966. In 1973 the figure was at the US $ 10 billion mark and went up to US $ 22.2 billion up to March 1978. Geographically Asia and North America take a major part of US $ 6.3 and US $ 5.4 billion respectively. In a type of business invested by Japan, it is noticeable that commercial enterprises take a major portion in the industrially advanced countries and manufacturing and mining industry in the developing countries. With the advance of overseas investment, Japan's management technology has been transferred abroad. Generally speaking, there may be fields which are comparatively easily transferable, such as production and sales management as well as those where some form of adjustment should be required in the industry invested, such as personnel and labour administration. There are such points worth taking into consideration such as the other side's adaptability to Japanese way of management, and the ways as to how full understanding and cooperation on the other side can be assured in order to make it possible to display Japanese technology as it is originally intended. Therefore, it is vitally important that the Japanese side should not press its way of management but should be prepared to give away whenever asked.

What I have described are, in my opinion, some of the characteristic features of business management in Japan today. In their respective practical areas these features have difficult problems of their own to solve and stand on the brink of changes of some magnitude coming on in the wake of our new age. At the same time, in Japan, the concept of business enterprises belonging to the community, is firmly taking hold with the incidence of environmental pollutions and the heightening of cosmology. It is therefore incumbent on the top management of enterprises today to concern itself seriously not only with the affairs of the enterprise but also with the affairs of the community.

Before concluding I am deviating from my main topic to mention something about Japanese businessmen and their activities in the world of business. Besides our own chambers of commerce and industry along with similar chambers of commerce in the countries of the world, we have in Japan a large number of economic/business institutions such as the Federation of Economic Organisations (Keidanren), the Japan Federation of Employers' Associations (Nikkeiren), the Japan Committee for Economic Development (Doyukai), the Kansai Economic Federation (Kankeiren). These institutions horizontally transcend and cross over the barriers of specific businesses and industries. There are other organisations for more specific groupings of business or industry such as Japan Chemical Industry Association, Japan Spinners Association and so on and so forth. Many Japanese businessmen are members concurrently of several of these institutions and organisations and play an active role in the pursuance of general and sub-committee economic programmes. At the same time the institutions and organisations themselves are active in making recommendations to the ministries of the Government on general or specific economic matters of national interest and concern and also arranging visits of economic missions to and from countries overseas for the purpose of promoting economic good will and intercourse.

7. Changing Public Policies and Management

Sir James Lindsay

Sir James Lindsay is currently Director of International Programmes at the Administrative Staff College, Henley-on-Thames, U.K. Actively interested in the management movement in India while he carried out top management assignments in this country, Sir James has served as President, All India Management Association; First Vice-President, Asian Association of Management Associations of CIOS; and President, Associated Chambers of Commerce and Industry, India.

We have been asked to examine the role and responsibility of managements in promoting economic growth and human welfare; how they should identify, respond to, or anticipate public policy in the contemporary climate of opinion and attitudes. Public policies can be seen to depend on a diverse range of forces at work in society; in particular, they are influenced ultimately by society's values and beliefs. We are concerned, with the consequences, the changing values become articulated with increasing stridency by different interest groups, and eventually find expression in the output of parliaments and public administrators; also with the fact that governments and other major interest groups such as the trade unions and the civic action bodies, all exert their own day-to-day influence on company affairs.

The Role of Management

I start from the standpoint that the role of business which management runs, is to service the present and future needs of the community, and to create wealth. This is its justification for the use it makes of capital, people and materials [1]. Its aims are achieved by satisfying the interests of its stakeholders; namely, the shareholders, customers, employees, the government, specific interest groups, and the community at large. Ongoing profitability measures its success or failure. Profit is paramount in the sense that without it, the enterprise would not have the means to achieve either its economic or its societal aims. The concept of "on-going" profit precludes the expediency of the "fast buck": the over-riding priority is corporate survival in the long term.

Governments' Limitations as Interpreters of the Public Interest

It might be convenient for managements to regard the government as the sole arbiter of the public interest; but it would be unwise, even in Third World countries where so much economic activity is subject to governmental intervention. This is because governments often have short terms of office, and are therefore tempted to proclaim as public policy what will bring in the votes at the next election, rather than what is in the longer-term public interest. This dilemma may even affect the way in which ministries are structured. In some countries, labour ministries, influential because they are presiding over labour's rewards, can by their policies gain public support for the government; while the ministries of industry, separately responsible for the productivity to which those rewards relate, are less influential with the voter than the national interest demands. In any case, governments are not omniscient. For example, in the early days of India's First Five Year Plan, companies who thought that the proclaimed planning targets enabled them to dispense with the need to do their own market research, found—only after they had installed manufacturing capacity—that the demand did not in practice exist. The conclusion is inescapable: the management must determine for themselves the balance of interests vis-a-vis their different stakeholders, and that doing so is an essential function of management. Among the stakeholders government is always important and has periodically to be negotiated with; so, in future, will an increasing number of stakeholders. If, over time, managements get their priorities wrong in balancing these interests, survival of their business will be at stake.

Monitoring the Environment

For guidance on what are the public policies, present and future, to which the enterprise must respond, it is necessary to scan the environment of influences in which business operates. Management does this anyway in the more general context of corporate strategy. It should, in its environmental analysis, be specifically concerned to identify societal influences, constraints and threats which call for a corporate response. Also to identify opportunities for societal involvement that will promote the interests both of the community and the firm. Figure 1 illustrates how a company and its customers share the same environment of interacting systems: ethical, socio-cultural, political, economic and technical. A study of this interaction reveals five themes that I would like to develop. They are:
— The interdependence of the world economy;
— The effect of instant communication;
— The fast-changing values and value-laden situations to which managements must respond;
— The growing role of influence group on company affairs;
— The complexity of the multiple environments a company encounters when it starts to operate transnationally.

An Independent World

More than ever before, the world can be seen as an economically interdependent and tightly-coupled system; a joggle in one area may affect the
whole system. The market for grain is worldwide: the USSR.'s recourse to the
granaries of the west puts up prices in western supermarkets as well as in
Third World bazaars. The OPEC shock has affected every country, including
China. "Shock" is the right word for the first successful contemporary challenge by the South to Northern economic dominance. The effect on employment of new micro-process technology is global. Previously autarkic
centrally-planned countries such as the U.S.S.R. and Eastern Europe have
been hit by the downturn in the West. In the North-South dialogue, the
governments of the rich OECD nations now accept, if only in principle, that in
their longer-term interest they should pay more attention to the economic
well-being of the developing countries. It is morally, economically, politically
and strategically necessary to eliminate the more grinding levels of poverty in
those countries and to build up their purchasing power as customers. This interdependence favours the operations of the transnational corporations (as
the United Nations have re-christened the multinationals) who have a significant role to play in contributing to the industrialisation of the South; provided they can come to terms with their home-based trade unions, who are
highly suspicious of all investment made aboard; as well as with the priorities
of host-country governments.

The Effect of Instant Communications

The advent of instant communication (the radio-telephone, telex, video-
phone, telstar, computer terminals, television printouts, jet travel, etc.) contributes to this interdependence, affects value systems round the world, and
has implications both for public policies and for managements. The effect
on the United States' foreign policy of gory scenes of Vietnam battles, communicated day after day into American homes on colour-TV, was conclusive:
it stopped a war. Another important effect—with social, political and economic consequences—is the worldwide growth of expectations. In the overcon-
suming West, the 'man-in-the-gilded-street' expects progressively to improve
his material living standards. Comrades in the centrally-planned economies
of Europe increasingly aware—after generations of austere five-year plans—
of the consumption standards in other societies, are demanding the diversion
to consumption of a larger share of national resources. The 20 per cent of
mankind—some 800,000,000 souls living in Third World countries "in absolute
poverty", to quote Robert McNamara—simply have to improve their lot.

Consumption standards communicate not only across, but within, national boundaries. In India, for example, it is not uncommon to find that the
peasant and the townsman both aspire to the ownership of a bushshirt made
of synthetic fibre. On the outskirts of some Latin American cities, in the
shape of shanty towns constructed from corrugated iron sheets and packing

wood—that can be seen on the way in from the airports—the "imitated" consumption patterns of the rich are evidenced by a forest of colour-TV antennas sprouting from the shacks.

The consequences for public policy are obvious. The situation in which almost the whole of mankind is articulating growing expectations must result in worldwide public policies aimed at improving the material condition and quality of life. This demand for betterment has to be considered in the light of some adverse trends in demography and the finiteness of certain material resources: the production of too many babies but insufficient food and energy. Nevertheless, no government in the First, Second, or Third Worlds will choose a national strategy which does not predicate growth. Thus, in declining order of justice, the workers in the opulent West, the less-opulent East, and the poverty-stricken South—the workers of the whole world—all have growing expectations.

Fast Changing Values

Not only expectations are changing. It was Peter Drucker, who first referred to the present as being "an age of discontinuity", meaning that the pace of change is so fast that the past-present-future continuum becomes almost unintelligible. Prediction no longer flows fluently and logically from an interpretation of the past and an understanding of present realities. With no claim to originality [2, 3] I list some of the very wide-ranging value changes and societal situations to which managements must respond:

Values
— The decline of the growth ethic (and in some industrial societies, the work ethic) and the reaction against technology;
— The escalation of social aspirations from quantitative to qualitative requirements of life (cf. Maslow's *Hierarchy of Human Needs*);
— A rise in the use of strong-arm tactics in industrial action, and the increasing dominance of unions in the political field;
— The use of terror to achieve political (or criminal) ends leading to a rise in crime rate;
— The emergence of equal rights demands for woman and people of different races;
— The heightened interest in civic rights generally;
— The demand for political devolution by ethnic minorities;
— The demand for workers' participation in decision-making and ownership;
— The growing interest in mysticism and the occult;
— The large-scale addictive drug and alcohol problem.

Situations
— The arrival of an age of affluence (which means the co-existence of over-consumption in the industrialised North and the under-consumption and

under-nourishment in the developing South);
— Enhanced expectations (already referred to) on a worldwide scale;
— An ecological collision-course as a consequence of affluence, and the pro-
fligate use of energy;
— An increasing appreciation of the finiteness of material resources and the
need for control of the physical environment;
— The growing gap between physical and social technology.

The above underlie, or are in themselves, matters of political and economic significance on which managements need not only to take a view, but
also to take action. Foreknowledge of them would have been invaluable to
public policy-makers and managements alike; yet few were forecast. Whereas there are well-established methodologies for attitude research, very little has
been done on human values which determine attitudes, and of which motivation is an aspect. To improve the predictive tools required to forecast the
changes to which enterprises must respond, better value analysis is necessary.
To assess present realities, some kind of cross-impact analysis is worth considering: the influence groups are listed against their likely impact on different
parts of the business or on a particular project. The same process may be
carried out to consider the effect of a legislative enactment. One large company which does this, constructs what it describes as a 'Social Response Assessment Matrix'.

The Growing Role of Influence Groups

In many parts of the world, management authority is limited by the practices of pressure groups in society. It has been successfully challenged by *government action* (nationalisation, direct investment, regulation of prices and
wages, company law provisions); by *trade unions* in alliance with political
parties (monopoly power closed shop, the vulnerability of modern technology,
worker participation, planning agreements); and by *social pressure groups*
(conservation, anti-pollution, consumer protection, equal opportunities).
Government intervention is on the increase. In Europe, the power of the
unions has increased to the extent that they can, and do, prevent the implementation of company plans, including investment projects in other countries. In Britain, union power has already affected the distribution of wealth.
Consumer protection groups are holding the marketeer to his marketing concept of satisfying consumer needs. The Consumer Association is demanding
that the government should make the consultative machinery quadruple
putting it on par with the two sides of industry, the Trade Union Congress
and the Confederation of British Industry who, in theory (and perhaps on
a day in practice!) might conspire together to exploit the consumer for the
benefit of wage—and dividend-earners. All over the industrial northern world,
the environmentalists are a force to be reckoned with. Suppliers' points of
view must be taken note of as more material resources are seen to be finite.

The problem is not so much to decide whether steps should be taken to involve the principal influence groups, but how should it be done. In Europe and North America the situation is approaching where planning and major decision-making, if it is not going to be thwarted, requires the prior agreement of these groups. Otherwise plans will abort if they involve sensitive issues such as laying-off personnel, reducing manning levels, introducing new technology, using atomic energy or locating new factories. In these conditions, management becomes a more political process as is illustrated in Table 1 describing two styles of planning [4]. It has been said [5] that instability (or uncertainty), not change, is the challenge of our time. The increasing power of the non-shareholding stakeholder adds to the uncertainty. To handle this and cope with lower growth in highly competitive world markets and in traditional industries, the manager must develop his capability to live with uncertainty, to manage strategically, in a proactive rather than a reactive way, and to be future- rather than past-orientated. He will have often to operate like a politician, maintaining formal and informal contracts with other interest groups; negotiating and bargaining with them, forming alliances with friendly groups, and trying to influence potential opponents. Indeed, corporate planning [4] "needs to be developed as an inter-organisational process so as to include relationships with other organisations and interest groups (inside and outside the business) whose decisions and actions are likely to have an important impact on them."

The Complex World Environment of the Traditional Corporation

As an enterprise moves its activities abroad, it has to take into account not only the domestic environments of each of the countries in which it operates, but also some specifically international variables (see fig. 1). Managerial issues thus become more complex and also more politicised. More stakeholders are involved, and we are brought to the key dilemma of the transnational corporation: reconciling the interest of the shareholders with those of the other stakeholders in the home and host countries. There is now a new variable, as companies operating in southern Africa have found, namely, the world community. There the TNC is not expected to behave as a good corporate citizen of its host country: local norms clash with those of the international community, so the latter apply. Furthermore, transnational business is now so large that many home *and* host country stakeholders (particularly the government and the employees' representatives) and the international community, are unhappy that the control of them is in non-governmental hands. Hence the setting up of the UN Center on Transnational Corporations and the demand for codes of conduct to which a number of agencies have readily responded; to wit, the UN, UNCTAD, ILO, OECD, EEC and some individual governments. Hence the proliferation of public policies, affecting the operation of TNCs, which have been translated into national legislation all round the world.

The Special Requirements of the Developing Countries

The economies of scale vis-a-vis monopoly and concentration

Turning to the developing nations, there is no dispute that monopolistic practices are undesirable; governments are quite right to be concerned about them, and about excessive concentration when used to the common detriment. Nevertheless, at a stage of economic growth when a developing country is entering into many new industrial fields for the first time, an initial and temporary monopoly may be unavoidable. Indeed, it would be beneficial where the volume of demand does not permit more than one economic unit. But government ensures that sooner, rather than later, competition emerges with the growth of demand, as is fully borne out by the Indian experience of the past thirty years, in developing purely Indian competition to the multinationals who were permitted to introduce new industries. I would like to urge that a premature preoccupation with the problem of monopoly should not be allowed to come in the way of the establishment of units of optimum size. The concentration of economic power needs to be seen in the perspective of the countries' prospective world markets for manufactured goods. Some of the largest units in developing countries are small by world standards. If a product is susceptible to substantial economies of scale, the experience curve and allied concepts of the Boston Consulting Groups show that, in certain industries, costs reduce by 20 per cent every time the volume of goods produced (over time, not annually) is doubled. To enter many export markets a substantial domestic market base is required to provide indispensable volume throughout. In these cases, the more advanced products that only the transnationals may be able to offer, make a joint venture (on equitable terms) an attractive proposition, even to the more highly industrialised developing countries.

Mutual Needs? The Transnationals vis-a-vis the Developing Countries

I believe I am on safe ground in saying that countries develop to the extent that they succeed in mobilising their own human and material resources. In support of this they need—and the TNCs are in a position to supply—technology, managerial skills, management and technical development, plant, equipment, and capital. Thus, the one's need is the other's opportunity, and vice versa (see fig. 2), so long as the commercial opportunities the TNCs seek are consistent with the host countries' needs as expressed in their planning priorities.

In such circumstances, why do the developing countries hesitate? They have firmly in their hands the means of attracting selectively, the right multinational into the product area in which it is needed, and of controlling it once it is there. India is an example of a country which is very good at this. With such powers of control available to them, why do the developing countries hold back? It is because they are restrained by distrust and fear.

They do not trust the corporation to keep its promises:
— Will they really export, develop import substitutes, and train locals as managers fast enough?
— Will they deal fairly? Or will they make too much profit and seek to evade the control on their remittances by under-invoicing their products, taking extra payment in other countries?
— Will they be good corporate citizens, paying proper regard to the host country's priorities, or will they, in emergency, bring in pressures to bear from their home governments?

They fear:
— The impact of the enterprise on the balance of payments;
— They may perhaps be giving up resources that may one day be needed (for example, after that hole-in-the-ground is exhausted);
— The impact on the country's culture (for example, the fear that the TNC will promote the growth of a "client class", in the shape of the intellectually expatriate elite whose consumption pattern is imported, so deepening the effects of the dual economy within the country);
— It will impede the development of local industry.

There is also the debilitating effect on decision-making of political ambivalence about big business, if not about the whole private sector, and certainly—never far below the surface—about foreigners.

On the other side of the coin is the standpoint of the transnational. For it, the host country's need represents opportunity to manufacture nearer to markets, raw materials or cost-effective labour; or to establish additional launching pads for the products of its R&D, more outlets for its goods and services that a saturated home market cannot absorb. Common needs and opportunities constitute the driving forces impelling the developing country and the TNC towards each other. But the hesitancy is two-sided: the TNC is also beset by the restraining forces of distrust, and fear (see fig. 2), including the fear, after pioneering the introduction of a new product in the market, of not being allowed by the host government to increase production capacity to meet the burgeoning demand. And there are daunting challenges to management. The TNC entering a developing country is, in effect, an agent of change. Going into the situation with its eyes wide open, the company knows it will be expected to reconcile its goals with the planning priorities of the host government, the differing objectives of the company's own local employees, customers and suppliers, local shareholders and those back home. The job of an international manager is to achieve a workable reconciliation of these interests in a new culture in which private enterprise is not necessarily taken for granted. Typically there is a dual economy and the gap between the haves and the have-nots is immense, and he will be identified with the haves. In crisis situations his "foreignness" will count against him: it may be exploited by the trade unions, by his competitors, even by his customers and perhaps by the government itself.

The two sides of the picture are clear. What is required is to decrease the restraining influences, reducing by deeds the mutual fear and distrust. The driving forces will be strengthened by enhancing the knowledge and improving communications about specific developing country needs on the one hand, and the matching TNC resources on the other. The UN Centre on Transnational Corporations could undertake a creative activity in this area in addition to data-gathering with codes of conduct in mind.

In these circumstances, the message for the transnational rings out loud and clear: their objectives in initial (and indeed in all) negotiations with a Third World government, should be for a fair share of the benefits of whatever the project may be. Let me say, as an aside, that it is beyond the skill of any foreign businessman I know to get the better of our host government of this very moment, the Government of India, though not all Third World country governments are so sophisticated.

Living with the Investment

Once the project is installed, the joint venture management has to "live with the investment". Being a good corporate citizen is, I believe, governed by principles which are generally applicable. Operating in someone else's country means that a more conscious effort has to be made to interpret and implement those principles. In a developing country, a company's stake-holders rapidly identify themselves; the high importance of coming to terms with the government is soon obvious, and is facilitated by government's readiness to be accessible. It is easy for a foreign company to acquaint itself with the host government's priorities; and, once established in the country, the company has ample opportunity to communicate how it proposes to contribute to development in areas defined by host national priorities.

Coming to general principles, Milton Friedman's argument that social responsibility, by diverting business from profit-seeking, may endanger a free society [6] is still quoted seriously. If the view is accepted that business loses legitimacy when it fails to match society's expectations [7], then the changing values we have already discussed make it clear that corporate conduct is under scrutiny, and that strategic responsiveness [9] (the ability to anticipate or react to environmental change) has a social dimension that cannot be ignored. To accommodate a concern for social issues into the operation of the firm is no minor challenge; especially when the company is beset by the more traditional economic, technological and competitive forces.

A useful analysis which illustrates contemporary thinking about how to tackle these problems is ably set out by S. Prakash Sethi in his *Three-State Scheme for Classifying Corporate Behaviour* [9, 10] (see Table 2). The broad classification are:

State 1: Social obligation

What a company must do to satisfy legal and economic criteria only;

equating profitable operations with fulfilling social expectations.

State 2: Social responsibility

A company accepts the reality that legal and economic criteria are of limited relevance, and is willing to consider broader, extra-legal and extra-market criteria for measuring its corporate performance and its social role.

State 3: Social responsiveness

The company accepts its role as defined by the social system and subject, therefore, to change. Ongoing profitability is an important criteria, but others are included.

In State 1, the company is concerned, in its search for profit, to do what it has to do within the law. In State 2 it recognises that there are things it ought to do in the interest of long-term survival, ongoing profitability, and reducing the likelihood of hostile legislation being enacted: its posture is reactive. In State 3, the company's outlook is proactive and it positively seeks activities in which, from its own resources (possibly in conjunction with other bodies, public or private) it makes a unique contribution to the solution of some social problem at a local, national, regional or international level, or puts society in a position to enjoy amenities which would not otherwise be available.

Companies which take social responsiveness seriously will, sooner or later, be confronted with the problem of developing (singly or in collaboration with others) criteria with which to measure how well they are discharging their social responsibilities. They will need to establish such criteria for three reasons:

— As a guide to such company's own corporate performance on social issues;
— To determine the firm's legitimate social responsibility, what response is appropriate, and how the response is to be managed;
— To be ready with tested criteria against the day when someone outside the firm, endeavours to impose externally generated (and possibly hostile) criteria upon it.

International Business in the Future

Transnational operations constitute only one of the ways of conducting international business. They involve [11]:

a) Equity-based control,
b) Ultimate control by a nationally-owned company, and
c) Integrated international production systems.

To change one of these variables is to alter the total situation. In the eyes of the developing countries, there is a significant identification of the transnational companies with ex-colonial powers. One view about their future is that they will not survive in their present form because, potentially, they are non-profitable: "ultimate control by a nationally-owned company", being not acceptable to important influence groups. I personally believe that the transnationals will survive because they are intelligent, resourceful, and have much useful potential. But they will have to be highly adaptive: already they are operating in a number of countries on a contractual basis; receiving fees for services rendered rather than profit in return for risk-taking. If that is not already a trend, it is likely to become one.

Summary

1) *The challenge of management:* Pursuing economic growth objectives, at the same time as responding to public attitudes and policies concerning human welfare.

2) *Management's use of resources* is justified when they are servicing the present and future needs of the community; albeit within the constraint of safeguarding corporate survival.

3) *Government cannot be the sole arbiters of the public interest* because of the day-to-day pressures on them to provide short- rather than long-term benefits.

4) *Management must identify the societal influences* to which it must respond. *Cross-impact analysis* is a worthwhile technique. To be considered are:
— The interdependence of the world economy;
— The effects of escalation of expectations brought about by the communication explosion;
— The fast-changing value systems: the need for better value analysis;
— The growing role of influence groups, prior agreement becoming a precondition of effective corporate planning; the growing political context of the management process;
— The complexity of the changing environment of international business.

5) *The special requirements of the developing countries:*
— The economies of scale are essential for successful competition in many world markets for standard goods: caveat about heavy-handed anti-trust activities which stunt growth of manufacturing units which are not large enough by world standards.
— Mutual needs/opportunities: Developing countries need the resources that transnational corporations can provide. The TNCs need the outlets for their products and processes: they must be prepared to accept governments' development priorities, negotiate only for a fair share of the benefits, and recognise that developing country governments are steadily enhancing their negotiating skills. Management has to develop its skills in living with its overseas investments.

6) *Living with the investment* successfully, and over time, means business taking seriously the concept of strategic responsiveness: this may mean progression from social obligation to social responsibility and social responsiveness. Companies in their own interest should take active steps to develop criteria for judging the effectiveness of their social response.

7) *Transnational operations* comprise only one of the ways of conducting international business. TNCs may find it necessary to operate more on a contractual, than an investment basis. In any case, they will have to be highly adaptive in their strategic response to hostile opinion on the part of some of their stakeholders both at home and abroad.

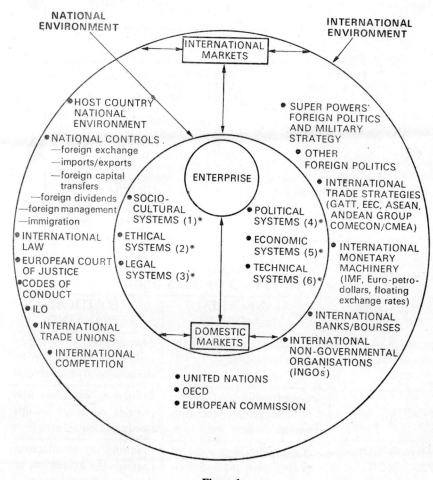

Figure 1

KEY*
1. Literacy, education, customs, classes, castes, media, employees, social mobility, relationships
2. Religions, personal values, assumptions, beliefs, professional codes
3. International, regional, national, state, municipal
4. Central and state governments, legislatures, municipalities, parties, trade unions
5. Finance, taxation, competition, tariffs, currency stability, exchange control, shareholders, suppliers, employers, consumers, media
6. Technology, products, processes, management, pollution control, R&D, universities, scientific institutions

Figure 2

THE TRANSNATIONAL COMPANY AS A RESOURCE FOR DEVELOPING COUNTRIES—DRIVING/RESTRAINING FORCES

Table 1
TWO STYLES OF PLANNING

	MANAGERIAL PLANNING	POLITICAL PLANNING
POWER	Management's authority is unquestioned	Management's authority is limited in practice by the actions of other groups
FOCUS	Coordination and control of management decisions within the firm	Influences decisions and policies of other groups inside and outside the firm
THEORY OF PLANNING	A "scientific" process of problem-solving and decision-making	Planning, to be effective, requires the agreement of the major power groups
PLANNING METHODS	Management formulates objectives, strategies and plans; other groups receive and implement them. Management makes the final decision	Management maintains information networks, forms alliances, uses persuasion and coercion, negotiates and bargains with other groups

Source: B. Taylor. *Corporate Planning—The Political Dimension,* World Planning Conference Paper, September 1978.

Table 2

A THREE-STATE SCHEME FOR CLASSIFYING CORPORATE BEHAVIOUR

Dimensions of Behaviour	State One: Social Obligation Prescriptive	State Two: Social Responsibility Prescriptive	State Three: Social Responsiveness Anticipatory and Preventive
1	2	3	4
Search for legitimacy	Confines legitimacy to legal and economic criteria only; does note violate laws; equates profitable operations with fulfilling social expectations.	Accepts the reality of limited relevance of legal and market criteria of legitimacy in actual practice. Willing to consider and accept broader —extralegal and extramarket —criteria for measuring corporate performance and social role.	Accepts its role as defined by the social system and therefore subject to change; recognises importance of profitable operations but includes other criteria.
Ethical norms	Considers business value neutral; managers expected to behave according to their own ethical standards.	Defines norms in community related terms, i.e., good corporate citizen. Avoids taking moral stand on issues which may harm its economic interests or go against prevailing social norms (majority views).	Takes definite stand on issues of public concern; advocates institutional ethical norms even though they may be detrimental to its immediate economic interest or prevailing social norms.
Social accountability for corporate actions	Construes narrowly as limited to stockholders; jealously guards its prerogatives	Construes narrowly for legal purposes, but broadened to include groups affected by	Willing to account for its actions to other groups, even those not directly affected by

1	2	3	4
	against outsiders.	its actions; management more outward looking.	its actions.
Operating strategy	Exploitative and defensive adaptation. Maximum externalisation of costs.	Reactive adaptation. Where identifiable, internalise previously external costs. Maintain current standards of physical and social environment. Compensate victims of pollution and other corporate related activities even in the absence of clearly established legal grounds. Develop industry-wide standards.	Proactive adaptation. Take lead in developing and adapting new technology for environmental protectors. Evaluates side effects of corporate actions and eliminates them prior to the actions being taken. Anticipates future social changes and develops internal structures to cope with them.
Response to social pressures	Maintains low public profile, but if attacked, uses PR methods to upgrade its public image; denies any deficiencies; blames public dissatisfaction on ignorance or failure to understand corporate functions; discloses information only where legally required.	Accepts responsibility for solving current problems; will admit deficiencies in former practices and attempt to persuade public that its current practices meet social norms; attitude toward critics conciliatory; freer information disclosures than State One.	Willingly discusses activities with outside groups; makes information freely available to public; accepts formal and informal inputs from outside groups in decision-making. Is willing to be publicly evaluated for its various activities.
Activities pertaining to governmental	Strongly resists any regulation of its activities except	Preserves management discretion in corporate deci-	Openly communicates with government; assists in en-

actions	when it needs help to protect its market position; avoids contact; resists any demands for information beyond that legally required.	sions, but cooperates with government in research to improve industry-wide standards; participates in political processes and encourages employees to do likewise.	forcing existing laws and developing evaluations of business practices; objects publicly to governmental activities that it feels are detrimental to the public good.
Legislative and political activities	Seeks to maintain status quo; actively opposes laws that would internalise any previously externalised costs; seeks to keep lobbying activities secret.	Willing to work with outside groups for good environmental laws; concedes need for change in some status quo laws; less secrecy in lobbying than State One.	Avoids meddling in politics and does not pursue special-interest laws; assists legislative bodies in developing better laws where relevant; promotes honesty and openness in government and in its own lobbying activities.
Philanthropy	Contributes only when direct benefit to it clearly shown; otherwise, views contributions as responsibility of individual employees.	Contributes to noncontroversial and established causes; matches employee contributions.	Activities of State Two, *plus* support and contributions to new, controversial groups whose needs it sees as unfulfilled and increasingly important.

REFERENCES

1. J. Hargreaves and J. Dauman. *Business Survival and Social Change*, Associated Business Programmes, London, 1975.
2. H.I. Ansoff, R.D. Declerk and R.L. Hayes. *From Strategic Planning to Strategic Management*, Wiley, 1976.
3. G. Rattray Taylor. *Prediction and Social Change*, Futures, Vol. 9 No. 5, October, 1977.
4. B. Taylor. *Corporate Planning—The Political Dimension*, World Planning Conference Paper, September, 1978.
5. G. Vickers. *Freedom in a Rocking Boat*, Penguin Books, 1972.
6. M. Friedman. *Capitalism and Freedom*, University of Chicago, 1962.
7. R.W. Ackerman. *Putting Social Concern into Practice*, European Business, Winter/Spring, 1974.
8. R.M. Jalland. *Proceedings of the 6th Annual Conference of the European Foundation for Management Development—External Affairs and the International Enterprise: Corporate Citizenship in Theory and Practice* (Paris), May, 1977.
9. S.P. Sethi. *Dimensions of Corporate Social Performance: An Analytical Framework*, California Management Review, Spring, 1975.
10. See reference 1 above which proposes a similar three-level model.
11. R.D. Robinson. *International Business Management*, Holt Rinehart & Winston, 1977.

Other reference material relevant to the text
D. Bell. *The Coming of Post-industrial Society*, Penguin Books, 1976.
British Institute of Management. *Changing Social Values*, Occasional Paper, New Series 014.
S. Cole, J. Gershuny and I. Miles. *Scenarios of World Development*, Futures, Vol. 10 No. 1, February, 1978.
R. Dahrendorf. *The New Liberty—1974 BBC Reith Lectures: Survival and Justice in a Changing World*, Routledge and Keagan Paul, London, 1975.
A. van Dam. *Joint Planning for an Interdependent World*, Long Range Planning, December, 1975.
P.F. Drucker. *Concept of the Corporation*, New American Library, 1972.
M.P. Fogarty. *The New European Enterprise*, New Europe, Spring, 1977.
J.K. Galbraith. *The Defense of the Multinational Company*, Harvard Business Review, March/April 1978.
G. Goyder. *Some Thoughts on Trusteeship*, C.C. Desai Memorial Lecture at the Administrative Staff College of India, February, 1978.
W.W. Harman. *An Incomplete Guide to the Future*, San Francisco Book Company, 1976.
P.R. Hayden and J.H. Burns. *Canada's Control of Multinationals*, Journal of Business Law (Canada), January, 1976.

B. Hedley. *A Fundamental Approach to Strategy Development*, Long Range Planning, December, 1976.

F. Hirsh. *Social Limits to Growth*, Routledge & Keagan Paul, 1977.

G.C. Hughes. *Antitrust Caveats for the Marketing Planner*, Harvard Business Review, March/April, 1978.

N.H. Jacoby. *Corporate Power and Social Responsibility*, Macmillan, 1973.

J.A. Lee. *Cultural Analysis in Overseas Operations*, Harvard Business Review, March/April 1966

R. & J.G. Likert. *New Ways of Managing Conflict*, McGraw-Hill, 1977.

H.V. Perlmutter, F.R. Root and L.V. Planet. *Responses of US-based MNCs to Alternative Public Policy Futures*, Columbia Journal of World Business, Fall 1973.

B. Taylor. *New Dimensions in Corporate Planning*, Long Range Planning, December, 1976.

G. Rattray Taylor. *How to Avoid the Future*, New English Library, 1977.

United Nations. *Activities of Transnational Corporations in Southern Africa and the Extent of the Collaboration with Illegal Regimes*, ECOSOC Secretarial Report, April 6, 1977.

R. Vancil and P. Lorange. *Strategic Planning in Diversified Companies*, Harvard Business Review, January/February, 1975.

T.D. Weinshall (ed). *Culture and Management*, Penguin, 1977.

M.H. Wolff. *Multinational Corporations: A Framework for the European Community*, Commercial Law Journal (USA), July, 1795.

8. Changing Public Policies and Management

P.J. Fernandes

Mr. Fernandes is currently UN Adviser at the Centre for Public Enter-prises in Developing Countries, Yugoslavia. A distinguished civil servant of the Indian Administrative Service, Mr. Fernandes was Secretary in the Ministry of Finance, Government of India, prior to taking up his current assignment.

Let me start off by questioning a popularly held myth. In recent years, there has been a great deal of talk about government and business. Political leaders have been demanding from business what they call "social reponsibi-lity". Owners and managers of enterprises have viewed with alarm and irritation what they consider to be unwarranted interference of the State in the affairs of business. Books are being written on the subject, Chambers of Industry and Commerce discuss it, management schools are conceptualising theories about it, and now we have a World Management Congress which is considering the subject. The underlying assumption seems to be a brief that something new is appearing on the scene and that only recently the shadow of State intervention has begun to fall on the sheltered corridors of business power. There is nothing to warrant this assumption. Indeed, throughout the course of world history, from times immemorial, there has been a confronta-tion between public authority and business interests. Kings, emperors, des-pots of a bygone age, in the exercise of sovereign rights, have considered it their prerogative to look into the affairs of business. Perhaps the only chance which has come about in recent years is that public authority is being backed by the voice of public opinion and that we are today beginning to conceptua-lise and rationalise the problem.

This being the case, it would be of considerable interest to scrutinise and analyse the nature of public intervention. What does the State seek to inter-vene in? For what purpose? And towards what objective? Whose interests is the State seeking to uphold? The State has always considered itself to be an arbiter and umpire of national affairs and even in the most extreme forms of free enterprise society, to be found largely only in textbooks, the State would at least be expected to ensure that the rules of the game are observed. But the State has gone a little further. Recognising that there are weaker elements in society, the State has progressively emerged as a protector of the weak against the strong. It is this Lord Protector role which we should first look at. Who are these weaker interests?

The Interests of the Working Classes

In its classical form, business enterprise involved Capital and Labour, entrepreneurs and owners on one side and paid employees on the other. Let it not be forgotten that the origin of western industrial society has been based on a ruthless exploitation of the working classes. The great prosperous societies of America, Britain and Western Europe emerged out of the 19th century industrial revolution on the frail backs of the exploited working man. One does not have to read economic history or governmental reports to understand this. The novels of Charles Dickens depict in a graphic manner the sordid and sad story—Underpaid workers, child labour, ruthless working hours, the total absence of any form of health or social insurance. It was the loud outcry of public opinion which brought about the intervention of public authority for the protection of the working classes. In due course, a body of labour legislation came into being—guarantee of minimum wages, the prevention of child labour, special facilities to women labour, health insurance, old-age pensions, and other welfare measures. What is more, State legislation recognised the rights of working men to organise themselves into trade unions so that they could fight their own battles, and created legislation for regulating industrial disputes. Today all this seems to be taken for granted and is part of normal business and economic life. But when the State first started intervening over a century ago in matters concerning the conditions of the working class, there was horror and indignation in the minds of owners of business enterprises who considered it an unwarranted intrusion into the laws of economics. No doubt if there was at that time a World Management Congress, it would have considered the new labour legislation as a part of changing public policies!

In connection with the attitudes of business towards workers, a new element has now arisen. With the increasing democratisation of societies all around the world, there is a cry for greater human involvement of all sections of society in the affairs of the nation. This reveals itself in a demand for political decentralisation and in terms of management it calls for a much higher degree of participation in decision-making at all levels. In many countries public authorities are directly intervening to ensure that this happens. Workers' participation in management is being prescribed by law in many countries. The recent Bullit Report has created a fairly strong controversy in Britain. I, for one, believe that it is not a viable proposition to prescribe participation by law. To my mind a participative process must be part of an environment of involvement. It would seem that the very concept of participation is opposed to the concept of compulsion. Here again the world management movement has a significant role to play to foster and encourage new styles of participative management, not because it is fashionable to do so, not because it is a kind of acceptance of socialist ideology, but essentially because it happens to be the most effective way of running organisations. The old despots of world industry are, thank God, or at least I hope they are, things of the past. Professional management and the concept of management by objectives, both demand a commitment and involvement of all levels of managers and workers.

The Interests of the Consumer

Businesses are set up to sell their products, goods and services to customers and the buying public. It is a native assumption that the competitive system would by itself provide adequate protection to consumer interests. But what did happen in practice? —peddling of low quality goods, adulteration, sometimes downright cheating in weights and measures, ganging together of enterprises to form trusts and cartels—all these steps at the ultimate expense of the paymaster, namely the consuming public. The State was forced to intervene once again and rules and regulations emerged for the standardisation of weights and measures, establishment of public institutions for quality control, and legislation to prevent unfair business practices, restrictive practices and the formation of cartels. The Kefauver Report on the American drug industry speaks for itself. The Sherman Antitrust Act was imposed because of the potential threat of the cartels to genuine competitiveness. Most countries today have adopted legislation for monopolies and restrictive practices.

The Interests of the Environment

Quite recently a new interest has grown. Citizens view with alarm the filth, dirt and pollution which modern industry is forcing on them. The beautiful landscapes of nature have been despoiled by man. Once again, we have a case for State intervention to protect the environment from the grosser forms of the abuse of pollution. Even now debates go on as to the economics of anti-pollution measures. Recently a most astonishing battle commenced in Britain where a company running Britain's biggest toxic waste dump was hauled up for having put more poisons into the dump than was permitted under its existing licence. The astonishing part of the story was that the company challenged the right of local authorities to place restraints. While admitting that they had in fact dumped more poisons than permissible under the licence, they claimed that they had been doing so for many years and therefore had gained the prescriptive right to continue! This would of course provide a magnificent defence for Jack the Ripper who, after having committed over 40 brutal murders, could claim the prescriptive right to continue his interesting profession! In the matter of environment it is not merely a question of pollution. Modern industry places enormous strains on local resources.

Housing has to be provided for the workers and an infrastructure of public health and sanitation as well as education has to be created. Transportation facilities have to be expanded. The question is what contributions do industries make for supporting the environment in meeting the problems created by themselves?

The Interest of the Owner

Now it may seem rather absurd that the State should intervene to protect the owners of the enterprises from themselves. But this arises out of the structure of current ownership patterns. The ownership of business enterprises is often widely diffused. What protection has the individual shareholder against the possible misdemeanours of controlling interests and management? And thus a new set of intervention begins, company law to ensure that balance sheets and profit and loss accounts are fairly prepared; independent audit and a whole set of rules to ensure the proper disclosures of relevant information to shareholders. One would therefore have to concede that the growing intervention of the State in its capacity as a protector of the weaker sectors of society flows from the logic of necessity.

If we once accept the position that the weak require protection, then it appears to me that there are three ways of providing such protection. The first is the classical pattern of State intervention—legislation, political and bureaucratic controls. The second is a recent development: an attempt of the weaker sections to organise themselves for self-protection. Trade unions were the first example of this, where workers were not satisfied with State protection but sought their own organisational mechanism for self-protection. Consumers have begun to organise themselves—the voice of Ralph Nader crusading for the right of consumers against the rapacities of big business; a group of Dutch housewives organising themselves into consumer societies for ensuring the quality of milk and butter; the spectacle of Mrs. Mrinal Gore brandishing her rolling pin and leading masses of Bombay citizens to protest against rising prices. The environment is also beginning to assert itself. Public spirited citizens are raising public consciousness on the problems of pollution. Environmental protection societies are being established. I remember the running battle which we had with the citizens of Chembur near Bombay voicing their protest against the nitric acid fumes of the Trombay Fertiliser Plant.

What about the shareholders? They have not found it so easy to organise themselves and the odd shareholder who puts an awkward questions at an annual general meeting is considered to be a crank. But let it not be forgotten that the shareholders exercise the ultimate power, the power to buy or sell the shares. And it is that which reflects the health and good management of the company.

So these are the two means of protection—State intervention of self-protection. What is the third? It is my main case and an appeal to all distinguished entrepreneurs and managers from all over the world.

The true answer to the problem does not lie in the protection provided by public authority or by the weaker sections themselves. Modern managements must seek to provide the protections. It must be an essential part of corporate and business strategy to ensure a fair deal to the worker, a fair deal to the consumer, a respect for the environment, and high integrity of management which is the only true protection to the shareholder. I find that some business-men seem to feel that they discharge social responsibilities by utilising profits and reserves for the creation of charitable trusts, educational foundations, and social welfare work. I have nothing against this, although it is sometimes necessary to examine the motivations involved, which more likely than not, are a means of reducing tax burdens. But such so-called "progressive" mea-sures are no substitute for the in-built protections which managements must provide to the critical interests involved. It is my belief that the only answer to excessive State interference or to what we call changing public policies or the frustrations of weaker interests who seek self-protection is for us as mana-gers to accept these responsibilities as an intrinsic part of modern business policy. It is a heartening sign that such a realisation has begun to dawn but it is important that the true motivation for such an approach should not be that we are under pressure to do it. It should be accepted as normal. There used to be an old-fashioned concept called "goodwill". I believe that this concept has in our times taken on a new and qualitatively more significant meaning.

The Public Interest

We have been considering so far the interests of specific groups which the State considers its duty to protect. These interest groups are clearly indentifi-able and their problems and aspirations can be assessed. A much wider con-cept has now to be examined—what is described under the generic term of "the public interest". All States and societies desire to evolve certain patterns and ways of life. They have goals and objectives. In some cases, particularly in societies which have planned economies, these goals and objectives are speci-fically listed, but even in societies which believe in free enterprise and do not adopt national developmental plans, the overall objectives of public policy and what consequently constitutes public interest are to be found in the manifestoes of political parties which are placed before electorates for their choice. The public interest in this sense can cover a very wide variety of aspirations—the generation of employment opportunities, the development of backward regions, self-sufficiency in production, the fostering of science and technology, import substitution and the earning of foreign exchange. It is clear that the public interests as contained in these subjectives would vary considerably from society to society, depending upon local conditions and what is more, they will inevitably change during the process of development. Thus for example, a country which has an adverse balance of trade may seek in the public interest to follow a strong policy of import substitution and ex-port promotion, but if the situation changes and the same country finds that it has redressed the adverse balance and is now accumulating foreign exchange reserves, it would naturally and once again in the public interest liberalise imports and perhaps withdraw excessive incentives to exports. The public interest in a country gravely short of labour would dictate a policy of capital intensive industries and vice versa, as is the case in most developing countries, where there are large masses of unemployed people, a programme of labour intensive industries is virtually inevitable.

The public interest as thus conceived by public authorities would be reflected in measures of State policy which would seek quite naturally to provide the incentives for the achievement of these public interests and impediments and disincentives to activities which are not conducive to their realisation. Once again I would like to pose this question to all distinguished managers: "Is it necessary for us to leave this matter only to the State? It is not conceivable that an understanding and appreciation of public interests could and indeed should influence the formulation of the corporate strategies of business enterprises?" Some years ago I had the occasion of making a survey of the activities of foreign multinational corporations working in India in a particular segment of industry. An interesting exercise was conducted. On the one hand we identified and listed a series of objectives which in the opinion of public authorities constituted the public interests in this particular economic area. Thereafter we examined the operations and activities of the foreign companies evaluating them in the light of the public interest objectives. A most interesting result emerged. We found that several companies were working in total harmony with the objectives of public interests, many were neutral and some were unfortunately positively hostile to the national objectives. I put it to you as a proposition that it would be a most salutory practice for business enterprises to conduct on themeselves a self-evaluation in terms of this kind of exercise. The results may be found to be quite illuminating and I hope that it would influence the preparation of corporate business plans.

The Tax Gatherers' Intervention

I have discussed so far public policies intended to be of a protectionist nature. There is another angle to State intervention and public policy which has nothing to do with protection. The State wants money. Resources are required for running modern States and taxation is one of the elementary ways of mobilising such resources. Further, economic logic would indicate that one can only tax those who have surpluses. The structure of personal income taxes is thus based on the progression principle. The taxation of business is a sore point and most entrepreneurs and managers find it difficult to reconcile themselves to parting with a substantial percentage of what they consider to be their hard-earned profits. I have heard businessmen who throw up their hands in despair and ask "what is the good of making profits if these are taken away by the State?" And so they find devious means of evading the tax gatherer and perhaps the most profitable profession in the world is that of the tax consultant. Or alternatively, they seek to create lobbies to exercise influence on the politicians and bureaucrats in order to soften the blow. Very often the nature of lobbying takes the form of "if you have to tax, please tax him and not me."

I am afraid that owners and managers are fighting a losing battle. If there is one aspect of changing public policies which we have to recognise, it is the transformation of the State from a neutral law and order institution to a welfare and developmental institution. That means that far more resources are required by modern States than were ever called for in the past. One would however like to make two propositions. The first proposition is addressed to State authorities. Yes, of course, taxation is inevitable but do State authorities consider with the utmost care the economic consequences of a tax policy? It cannot be in the public interest that business enterprises should be taxed out of existence. There is need for realisation on the part of the State that enterprises can only survive and grow on the basis of reasonable surpluses. The second proposition is addressed to enterprises and their owners and managers. It is old-fashioned and illogical to review taxation as an exaction. Once it is recognised that there is need for the public authority to develop an infrastructure, to provide conditions of stability and peace, to create educated and trained cadres, to build systems of power and communications, then possibly business enterprises will realise that they themselves could possibly not exist without such a backup support. In short, why should business enterprises not consider their tax contributions to the public exchequer as an investment and indeed as a very necessary investment for their own survival? The contributions made by business enterprise to the State in the form of taxes are to some extent payments made to a contractor who is providing basic facilities. It is from this line of argument that I suggest the concept that taxation must be viewed as an investment. No doubt, one could ask, how well does the State use the resources and how economical or productive is this form of investment? Thereby hangs another tale and perhaps one which could reasonably be the subject of another World Management Congress.

The State as a Businessman

Quite apart from the role which public authority plays as a protector and as a tax gatherer, a major development has occurred in recent decades. The State which started off by controlling and regulating private business enterprise and levying contributions from their surpluses now asks itself: "Why I should not go into business myself?" And so we witness the growth and expansion of public enterprises which represent the State as a businessman. Perhaps no other recent development has so alarmed the private sector as the substantial growth of public enterprise all over the world. It is a mistaken notion to believe that public enterprises are some manifestation of purely socialist policies. Even in the traditional bastions of the private enterprise system there has been a phenomenal growth of public enterprise activity as we see in Britain, Western Europe, Japan and the U.S.A. One cannot forget that the most spectacular event of the 20th century, the landing of a man on the moon, was a triumph of American public enterprise.

The reasons why the State seeks direct participation in business activities are diverse; it may be for strategic reasons; it may be because certain aspects of the economy are so vital that it would be dangerous to leave them in private hands; it may be because the magnitude of investment involved particularly in infrastructural industries is beyond the capability of private entrepreneurs. There are also cases where public enterprises are created purely because a private company is on the verge of collapse and is taken over for rehabilitation. It could also be that the growth of public enterprise is a part of a national developmental philosophy as is the case in many developing countries. Whatever the origins and rationale of the emergence of public enterprises, the fact remains that it exists and is expanding. The fact remains that most economies of the world are today what are described as "mixed economies". This provides, I believe, a new challenge to the world management movement and the question which requires answer is: "How does one ensure that public enterprises are run with the highest standards of professional management?" It is really very unfortunate that the alarmist view taken by private industry about the growth of public enterprises is tending to build a dividing wall between the two. Instead of a cooperative and mutually supportive atmosphere, there are elements which seek to create confrontation and antagonisms between the public and private sectors. One tends to highlight the worst aspects of the other. In the context of changing public policies, there is grave need for finding a *modus vivendi* between the two major instruments of development in a mixed economy. I do not believe that either one could be professionally healthy if the other is professionally sick. It is a matter of great encouragement to note that in this World Management Congress there has been a cooperative partnership between public and private enterprise management.

In the last analysis there is, I believe, no reason to fear changing public policies. We, of the world of management, ourselves have constantly preached that healthy enterprises and healthy organisations of any kind can only retain their health if they are dynamic in character and if their policies and strategies change with the times. In industry this would be considered a creative and innovative spirit. Why then should we deny public authorities the same privilege of changing public policies? The real answer lies in this: changing public policies must be matched by changing management policies. There must arise in due course a sense of mutual interdependence between public policies and management policies and the old atmosphere of fear, suspicion, mistrust and confrontation must give way to a new spirit of cooperative endeavour. If for no other reason, let managements take heed of this for their very survival.

9. Interim Report on Transfer, Adaptation and Exchange of Management Know-how*

W.J. de Vries and Hugo Bosch

Mr. W.J. de Vries is the Vice-President of the European Foundation for Management Development (EFMD) and President of its Dutch Chapter. He is also Chairman of the CECIOS Working Committee on the Transfer and Adaptation of Management Know-how. Mr. de Vries worked with the Royal Dutch/Shell Group, during 1948–77 and was its Deputy Group Personnel Coordinator from 1969 onwards.

Prof. Bosch is Professor of Management at the Interuniversity Interfaculty of Management at Delft and Professor of Industrial Organisation at the Technical University at Delft. His research activities include professionalisation of management consultants (and management) transfer and adaptation of management know-how and technology, code of conduct for NMC's, etc.

History of CECIOS

CECIOS (abbreviation for Comite European de Conseil International pour l'Organisation Scientifique) was founded in Rome in 1953 as a region of CIOS. The latter was founded by a group of industrialists in Paris in 1926. The CIOS coordinates the international activities of some 40 national management associations all over the world. CECIOS' tasks aim at the coordination of the international activities of the management associations in Europe.

Scope and Objectives

CECIOS is a corporate legal entity, an association of national management organisations in Europe concerned with the development and dissemination of the body of knowledge on the theory and practice of management.
The general purpose of CECIOS is
— To foster on the European level the development of effective management

*Presented on behalf of the CECIOS Working Committee on Transfer and Adaptation of Management Know-how

as a key contribution to human fulfilment and the better utilisation of resources;
— To channel the presentation of views of practicing managers to other international bodies.

Activities

Congresses

Every three years one of the CIOS regions organises a World Management Congress. If CECIOS does not organise a congress itself, it contributes to these congresses through studies on issues like:
— Professional management with special reference to codes of conduct;
— Transfer of management know-how;
— Transfer of technology.

In cooperation with other European associations, CECIOS organises at times conferences on topical issues for practicing managers.

Board Room Meetings

For some years now CECIOS has been active in the promotion of discussion forums for top management. The aim is to provide an opportunity for leading personalities from top management levels in various European countries to get together for a day and to inform them, by means of an up-to-date topic, about management practice in large undertakings.

Working Committees

Within CECIOS, working committees consisting of practising managers are now continually active in the study of:

Professional Management
Objective:
— Endorsing the basic CIOS statement on professional management stated in Caracas 1975;
— Elaborating these per region, especially with regard to standards of competence and behaviour;
promoting these views to the general public.

Transfer and Adaptation of Technology
Objective:
— Investigating the conditions and possibilities of the exchange of technology between countries of different economic and social level.

Transfer and Adaptation of Management Know-how
Objective:
— Studying the way in which transfer of management know-how takes place between industrialised and less-industrialised countries.

With these studies CECIOS aims at assisting professional managers in the execution of their tasks as well as making them conscious of their role within their organisation and society in general.

Introduction

CECIOS (European Council of Management) is of the opinion that in view of the rapidly increasing financial, social and commercial relationship between the industrialised and less-industrialised countries of the world, studies regarding the transfer and adaptation of technology are of the greatest importance for both "givers" and "receivers". The transfer and adaptation of management know-how is an essential requirement to facilitate the transfer of technology.

During the CECIOS Assembly Meeting of November 1956 it was decided to nominate European Working Committees to study the above-mentioned subjects. The basis of the Working Committee on Transfer and Adaptation of Management Know-how was formulated as follows:

1) To define the concept "transfer of management know-how";

2) To collect cases from Europe and to analyse possibilities and limitations both from "givers" and "receivers";

3) To submit an interim report for the 18th CIOS Congress in New Delhi in December 1978; and

4) To study whether the subject can be the main theme of the 19th CIOS Congress in 1981.

A European Working Committee was appointed consisting of consultants and managers working in the field of transfer and adaptation of management know-how.

The Working Committee was formed by:

Mr. W.J. de Vries, Chairman   The Netherlands
   European Foundation for Management Development, Brussels
Prof. H. Bosch   The Netherlands
   Inter-universitarian Graduate School of Management, Delft
Mr. O. Eikeri   Norway
   Norwegian National Committee of Scientific Management, Oslo
Mr. E. Iatridis   Greece
   Business Organisation and Management Training,
   Amsterdam—Buitenveldert
Prof. Dr L. Kympers   Belgium
   NV Bekaert SA, Zwevegem
Mr. K. Loew   Germany
   Rationalisierungs-Kuratorium der Deutschen Wirtschaft,
   Landesgruppe Hessen
Mr. K.F.J. Niebling   The Netherlands
   Shell International Petroleum Co., The Hague

Dr. R. Rinne   Germany
  Klockner Industrie Anlagen GmbH, Duisburg
Mr. H. Stettbacher   Switzerland
  ICME, Business Consultants Zurich
Mr. Ph. Nind   England
  Foundation for Management Education, London

Observer:
Dr. J. Eekels   The Netherlands
  Cindu, Key & Kramer NV, Uithroon, Observer on behalf of the
  CECIOS Working Committee on Transfer of Technology
Mr. H.P. Bruin (CECIOS Secretariat) replaced by Mr L. Bouwens

The theme of the 18th CIOS Congress: "Management Perspectives for Economic Growth and Human Welfare", offered an excellent opportunity to present a pilot study regarding the transfer and adaptation of management know-how.

However such a pilot study can only be considered as a first investigation: To gain an insight in the whole problem a study on a world-wide basis would be required. The scheme in figure 1 also gives an indication of the complexity of the total problem of the industrialisation process.

The Working Committee Members have tried to define the concept of transfer of management know-how and to collect the experiences of a number of European organisations involved in the transfer of management and managers to less industrialised countries. This implies that it has not been possible to incorporate in the study the views of the receivers. It would be beneficial if all CIOS regions would be involved in such studies during the period 1978–1981. Only world-wide conclusions and recommendations would give acceptable answers which would then guarantee a balanced two-way traffic between givers and receivers.

Transfer of Management Know-how in Relation to Transfer of Technology

For the transfer of a certain product or process technology from one country to another country with a different culture and infrastructure the receiving organisation needs appropriate management know-how to adapt the new technology and to get it working. Therefore transfer of management know-how recently became a fashionable subject.

It is generally used in connection with less-industrialised countries. This subject is to a certain extent controversial as it is politically influenced which then might affect the dialogue between givers and receivers.

The industrialisation process of the less-industrialised countries can be discerned in general in four levels as depicted in the model of figure 1.

General concept

In order to be as specific as possible during the pilot study the Committee has restricted the concept for the time being to "those aspects of management know-how which are required to manage (a part of) an industrial enterprise or another organisation in order to achieve (economic) results."

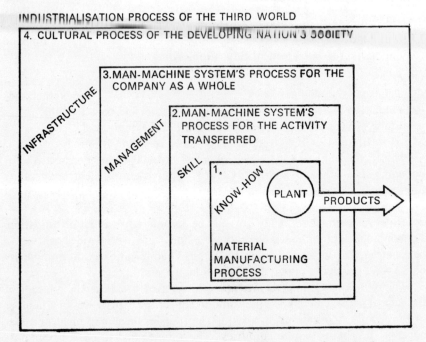

Figure 1. Reference : *Report*, Working Committee on Transfer Technology.
Dr. Eekels and Dr. P.M. Rudhart.

Concept of "transfer and adaptation"

Not long ago, "transfer" of management know-how was regarded as a process like sending a message from a receiver. "Adaptation" was added later, because one became conscious of the fact that the message from the "sender's" end had often to be "translated" into an understandable message at the "receiver's" end. Partly as a result of our study it can be concluded that it will be necessary to regard the process as a learning process in which a two-way communication takes place. The term of "transfer and adaptation" should rather be replaced by "exchange".

Concept of "management know-how"

In order to carry out the study, the Working Committee had to agree on a concept of management, a summary of which is given below. In general, know-how consists of a combination of knowledge and skill which can be acquired by formal education, training and experience. Probably know-how will only lead to useful results if it is applied with the right attitude and has been adapted properly to the specific culture and infrastructure. Our Committee distinguishes—for operational reasons—the following five aspects:

— Know-how to apply a number of management methods and techniques properly (see Questions, Essential aspects of management—1.1.);
— Know-how to pay due regard to social aspects of management with respect to both internal and external relationships;
— Know-how to apply systematically the various phases of the management process;
— Know-how to get one or more levels of management, such as the strategic, the structural and the operational management level, functioning well;
— Know-how to reap benefits from specific knowledge in one or more of the functional area, such as production, marketing, finance, personnel, etc.

Method of Survey

Considering the fact that the Working Committee should stress the practical experiences of organisations regarding the transfer of management know-how it was decided to set up an inquiry followed by several follow-up visits. Likewise a literature survey should take place.

The questionnaire

Each committee member selected names and addresses of institutions involved with the transfer of management know-how. A questionnaire was compiled and mailed to the addresses gathered. The respective committee members mailed questionnaires in their own countries. Although the number of responses was not as high as expected, some useful pointers were collected. It turned out to be useful to make a distinction between:
— Companies with only one or more temporary establishments in less-industrialised countries (CTE);
— Companies with at least one permanent establishment in less-industrialised countries (CPE);
— Educational institutions (EI).

In total 42 useful answers were received from European companies or institutions which were active in some way or another in the transfer and adaptations of management know-how. Of these 42 companies, 24 had permanent establishments, 12 had only temporary establishments in less-industrialised countries and six respondents were educational institutions.

Question 1

Do you transfer managers (for upper and middle management) from Europe to less-industrialised countries?

Question 2

Number of managers transferred since a date to be specified by you........
managers transferred since the year of.........
(The numbers mentioned of managers transferred as well as the years mentioned, differ enormously.)

	Answer received	Yes	No
CTE	12	12	—
CPE	24	24	—
EI	6	—	6
TOTAL	42	36	6

Question 3
Average period during which the managers are working in one position in less-industrialised countries

.... years

Weighed average of the period of CTE's: 2, 3 years
Weighed average of the period of CPE's: 3, 3 years

Regarding the period mentioned there was a remarkable difference between CTE's and CPE's.

— In CTE's the average period ranged from 1 to 4, 5 years.
— in CPE's the average period ranged from 1 to 10 years.

Question 4
What kind of managers do you transfer?

........% General managers   (G)
........% in the commercial area (e.g., sales, finance, purchase)   (C)
........% in the technical area (e.g., production, maintenance, research)   (T)
........% in the administrative area   (A)
........% others   (O)

Status of percentage regarding managers transferred in relation with the area:

	G	C	T	A	O
CTE	10	22	44	16	8
CPE	17	11	67	4	—
TOTAL	14	16	55	10	4

Comment: It is remarkable to see the high number of managers trained technically.

Question 5
How is the know-how of European managers normally transferred to managers of less-industrialised countries?

a ☐ the Europeans have local counterparts

b ☐ the Europeans have to select their future local successors

c ☐ other means of transfer, please specify:
. . . .

d ☐ at present there is no intention to transfer the know-how

	a	b	d
CTE'S	8	4	3
CPE'S	16	9	4

Question 6
To which countries do you send managers?
. . . .
(A large number of countries was mentioned: 62.)

Question 7
Do you educate managers from developing countries in your own country?

	Number of answers	Yes	No
CTE'S	11	7	4
CPE'S	24	22	2
EI	6	3	3
TOTAL	41	32	9

Question 8
Number of managers trained by you since a date to be specified by you
. . . . managers trained
since the year of. . . . .
(The number of managers trained as well as the years mentioned covered a great range.)

Question 9
Average period during which the managers are trained. . . . . months
Weighed average of the period of CTE's: 4, 9 months
Weighed average of the period of CPE's: 7, 7 months

Question 10
From which countries do the trainees come ?
(A great number of countries was mentioned.)

Question 11
What kind of managers do you train?
........% General managers   (G)
........% in the commercial area (e.g., sales, finance, purchase)   (C)
........% in the technical area (e.g., production, maintenance, research) (T)
........% in the administrative area   (A)
Status of percentages regarding managers transferred in relation to their area:

	G	C	T	A
CTE	15	28	49	8
CPE	10	9	74	7
Total	13	18	61	8

Comment : Seeing this high number of managers trained in technical areas
            further analysis is required whether they are trained in manage-
            ment as well.

Question 12
How do you train managers ?
........% in classroom in your own company   (1)
........% in classroom in other companies or institutions   (2)
........% on the job in your own company   (3)
........% on the job in other companies   (4)
Status of percentages which indicates how the managers are trained:

	1	2	3	4
CTE	6	30	38	25
CPE	13	12	62	13
Total	10	21	50	19

Question 13
What is the educational and professional background of the trainees ?
........% high school
........% university
_____
   100%
........% no professional experience
........% 1-2
........% 2-5

........% 5-10 years professional experience
........% 10 and more
_____
100%

Status in percentages regarding educational background of trainees:

	High School	University
CTE's	17	83
CPE's	44	56

Status in percentages regarding professional background of trainees:

	No prof. experience	1-2 year	2-5	5-10	10 and more year	Total
CTE	8	4	26	37	3	100 %
CPE	12	13	29	25	21	100 %

Question 14

Do you consult the management of companies in less-industrialised countries?

	Yes	No
CTE'S	10	7
CPE'S	21	3

Comment: Universities and educational institutions answered this question in the negative.

Question 15

Are these normally the same companies as those to which you transfer managers (question 1) or from which you educate managers (question 7) ?

	Yes	No	Fifty/Fifty
CTE'S	8	—	1
CPE'S	17	1	1

Follow-up Visits

During the follow-up visits to important companies and institutions it was confirmed that management know-how is transferred from Europe to developing countries.

There is, however, very little cooperation between the different agents of transfer ("givers") and there is very little exchange of experience. It seems, therefore, that the issue could benefit very much from the elaboration of a theoretical background.

Literature Survey

In this paragraph only a short survey is presented of literature which is specific for the transfer and adaptation of management know-how. There exists for example, a considerable amount of literature about transfer of knowledge in the form of learning processes and (management) consultation. Also literature exists about transfer (and adaptation) of technology with an emphasis on the problems of the less industrialised countries. Of course, many books have been written about management and a few about the concept "management know-how".

The extensive empirical study of Neghandi and Prasad published in the book *The Frightening Angels* forms the most quoted literature. Their comparative management study uses as a model:

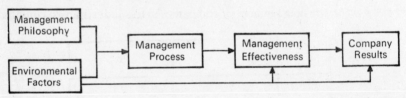

Other interesting studies have been and are being carried out at the European Institute for Advanced Studies in Management at Brussels by Hofsted, Galbraith and Edstrom. The aim of a large research project is to get an insight in the influence of certain environmental (cultural) factors on management behaviour.

Other literature is the result of experiences with management development at large multinational companies. Also management problems involved with the design, the realisation and starting up of turnkey projects have been described in professional articles. Descriptions were found in studies carried out in Ghana, Korea, Mexico, Taiwan.

Regarding the subject of transfer and adaptation of management know-how the Committee recommends the following literature:

Books:
— Neghandi, A.R. and S.B. Prasad. *The Frightening Angels*, Kent State University, 1975.
— Kubr, M. ed., *Management Consulting*: *A Guide to the Profession*, ILO, Geneva, 1976.
— Twis, Brian. *Managing Technological Innovation*, Longman, London-New York, 1974/1976.
— Freeman, Chr. *The Economics of Industrial Innovation*, Penguin, Manchester, 1974.

Research papers:
— Hofsted, G. Many recent working papers on comparisons of several factors between 40 countries, European Institute for Advanced Studies in Management, Brussels.
— Boseman. F.G., Transfer of management process: a case study of industrial enterprises in Mexico, Kent State University, 1972.
— Chen, Ting-Ko, Management transfer, practice and performance—an empirical study in Taiwan, University of Michigan, 1973.
— Restrepo, C.B., The transfer of management technology to a less-developed country : a case study of a border industrialisation program in Mexico, University of Nebraska, 1975.
— Yun, Chul Koo, Transfer of American management know-how to foreign environments: applying managerial budgeting system in Korea, University of Michigan, 1973.
— Roudiani, M., Transfer of management methods across cultures : an empirical approach to determine possibilities and problems, Indiana University, 1970.
   (His study refers to a case of a transfer from the U.S.A. to the U.K.)
— Rath, H.J., An evalution of management techniques used in the international transfer of the production know-how of the Litton LN—3 inertial navigation system, University of California, L.A., 1972.
Articles:
— Galbraith, Jay and Edstrom, A., International transfer of managers; some important policy considerations, *Columbia Journal of World Bus.*, 1976.
— Holand, Susan, S., Exchange of people among international companies : problems and benefits, *Annuals*, AAPS, 424, 1976.

Findings of the Working Committee

Due to the low response to our questionnaires our finding can be given only in a qualitative manner. Nevertheless, taking our own experience into consideration, we can generalise the following results.

Multinational companies

Most of the large multinational companies have well developed systems to train their future managers from the beginning. Quite a few companies conduct so-called trainee-programmes for university graduates. Normally the trainees are given the opportunity to work for two years in several crucial departments. From time to time they are trained in theoretical courses. After termination of the programme they are regarded as a management reserve. This programme is implemented not only in the parent company but also in the larger affiliates.

At a higher level, managers from the parent company work for a limited period in an affiliate and vice versa. The centralised controlling system within large multinational firms additionally contributes to a steady flow of management know-how to the affiliates.

However, this transfer of Western management know-how to less-industrialised countries normally is limited to the range of the multinational firm itself. A dissemination effect to other companies in the less-industrialised countries can only develop if the managers give notice and change to other firms. This, however, is not very frequent, since the employment conditions in the multinational firm tend to be more favourable.

Joint ventures of medium-sized enterprises

There is a tendency that European medium-sized enterprises are interested to establish joint ventures in the Third World. Partners in the less-industrialised countries may either be private investors or public organisations, e.g., development corporations or banks. There are several types of such joint ventures which can be characterised by the objectives pursued by the European investors:

— Transfer of production into countries with low labour cost (e.g., clothing, shoes, mechine-tools, optical instruments, electronic parts);
— Processing of raw materials for export (e.g., sawmill and vaneering mill, rubber articles, cotton spinning, weaving mill, vegetable drying, plantation for medical plants);
— Opening up new markets in relatively high developed countries (e.g., pre-cast concrete parts, brewery, machine-tools, plastics processing, service stations for vehicles).

This kind of joint venture often is promoted by the European or International Development Bank. Management know-how has to come from the European partners who mostly send part of their own staff to the newly created firm, especially the technical manager. Training in Europe normally is only done for specialised operators, rarely for managers from the less industrialised countries. The experience is that part of the managers, especially financial and marketing managers, are either local staff right from the beginning, or local staff is gradually replacing European managers.

In order to evaluate this way of transfer of management know-how it must be taken into consideration that the "givers" in these cases are medium-sized firms. Their own management frequently works on the base of experience and not all of them are capable to transfer know-how of modern management techniques. There is also a natural lack of teaching experience.

Contractors of turnkey projects

Many supply contracts for turnkey plants today cannot be signed unless the general contractor is ready to offer management assistance for a limited period of two to five years, sometimes even longer. In these cases the general contractor:

— Recruits managers for the newly created firm, who are either seconded by friendly companies for a limited period or must be selected on the European labour market;

— Selects local personnel who later shall replace the European managers;
— Trains these future local managers on the spot and in Europe and sends them to training courses in Europe;
— Consults the local management.

These methods often are the only way to implement capital intensive industries in less-industralised countries. Since in many cases these industries are fully or partly financed by government agencies of less-industrialised countries, there are cases in which the local managers-to-be are transferred to other government owned companies where they are needed even more.

Though this is a disadvantage for the firm in question it can represent a favourable dissemination of know-how for the country.

It should be pointed out that firms who act as general contractors are mostly engineering companies whose main business is not management consulting or training. Thus there is a danger that these tasks may not be handled in the optimal way. It should also be considered that clients of turnkey projects sometimes still underestimate the importance of management training and hesitate to allocate the necessary financial means. There is, however, a general tendency towards laying special emphasis on management and training. If there are enough finances, general contractors can improve their services by either creating a special department or by cooperating with management consultants.

Management consultants

There are well-established management consultants who expand their business to developing countries in order to assure the management of newly created industries. In the ideal case they also carry out training for operating personnel. The normal steps for a management consultant—either an independent firm or a general contractors firm—to intervene in managing a new company in a less-industrialised country are:

— Study the professional capabilities in the country in question;
— Establish the organisation plan and job descriptions;
— Define which positions are to be held by expatriates and which by local managers;
— Define the period of transition from the expatriates to local staff;
— Establish a long-range programme both for theoretical and practical training;
— Select candidates for training;
— Support expatriate staff to the new plant;
— Execute or supervise training before and after the start-up of production;
— Give advice to the management of the new plant.

In these tasks they have to cooperate closely with the general contractor or the client's technical consultant and they have to have good contacts with

European plants who produce the products in question. These plants are absolutely necessary for organising the practical part of management training, and it may be difficult for management consultants to establish the right contacts.

Since management training for less-industrialised countries is a relatively new business, new firms offering this service frequently turn out to be incompetent.

Management research and training institutes and universities

Education in Europe in management as a separate discipline started only 10 to 20 years ago not even in all countries. At some technical universities and colleges, undergraduate courses were given in industrial engineering. At universities, faculties of economic developed management courses with an emphasis on accounting, marketing and finance. The teaching of management aspects as faculties like psychology and sociology started later.

The pace of development of management education in the countries in Europe has not been the same. Which means, that some countries are still ahead of others. Two types of education can be distinguished, i.e., undergraduate/graduate courses and—in an increasing number—post-experience courses.

Only recently a few academic institutions started management courses especially designed for people of less-industrialised countries. As most of these courses have to be given in English, (or Spanish), this limits the choice of management teachers to those who have a real command of one of these languages.

In a few cases, universities and management training institutes in Europe are assisting with the setting up of training programmes or even institutes in less-industrialised countries. Some exchange programmes exist for students between universities in Europe and the Third World.

As far as management research is concerned, many faculties of universities in Europe carry out a wide spectrum of specific research projects with respect to Third World problems. Little coordination, however, takes place and the number of institutes which do research, for instance, on such topics as the influence of cultural differences on management behaviour is small.

Publicly financed institutions (also ILO)

Both the European governments and international organisations have established services which are active in management training and general training for less-industrialised countries. In some countries these services are partly financed by private donors. In the Netherlands for instance, hundreds of (future) managers from less-industrialised countries have followed three to nine months' management courses at a score of institutes which are heavily subsidised by the government.

Disregarding those agencies which just allocate finances to the projects of research institutes, which invite tenders for management consultants, or which contribute financial means to joint ventures of medium sized enterprises there are institutions which organise management courses for executives or future executives of less-industrialised countries. These courses are only part of their programme which includes all kinds of training for a most varied range of professions.

Further remarks

Management training includes both theoretical training and practical work in companies whose business is similar to the manager's professional activity.

The degree of success of these courses—like many other courses organised independently from the employer—is influenced by;
— Uncertainty whether the right candidates are selected for training;
— Uncertainty whether the persons trained stay with their jobs and thus are able to utilise their newly acquired knowledge.

Preliminary Conclusions

On this basis of the pilot study and the short survey of literature, the Working Committee came to the following preliminary conclusions:

Difficulties involved with research in this field ,

With the transfer and adaptation of management know-how there are many internal and external factors and variables which might affect the success of the transfer. It is almost impossible to define the conditions, the variables and the effects in such a precise way that accurate descriptions of actual cases and situations—let alone measurements—can be made. The number of possible interrelations between the numerous factors is extremely high and in many cases it is almost impossible to determine what the causes and what the effects are.

Need for proper management of the transfer and adaptation of technology

To get a new process or product technology working, local management should acquire sufficient know-how to adapt both the new technology and the local conditions in order to strike a proper balance. A person with experience from an industrialised country can supply knowledge about the specific technology. A person from the less-industrialised country can supply knowledge about the local culture and infrastructure. Only by cooperation one can hope to arrive at proper results!

Institutional vehicles for the transfer of management know-how

From the pilot study it can be concluded that from Europe management know-how is transferred by the following types of organisations:
— Multinational companies
— Joint ventures of medium-sized enterprises

— General contractors of turnkey projects
— Management consultants
— Management research institutes and universities
— Management training centres
— Public authorities and publicly financed institutions active in technical assistance.

Methods of exchange of know-how

Know-how is transferred through books, articles and other written material or by personal contacts during congresses, conferences, etc. Organised transfer mainly takes place through courses, through training on the job or by combinations thereof.

So far as *courses* are concerned, many special courses are given in Europe for (future) managers in less-industrialised countries. In many of these courses, the technical side plays an important role. There is a tendency that in future more European educational institutions will run management courses abroad or will assist with such courses in less-industrialised countries.

As far as *training on the job* is concerned, there is also a tendency from training in Europe towards training in new industries established in the less-industrialised world. If in a certain region the industrialisation process gets its momentum, more opportunities for training on the job are provided for people of the region itself. Such training is less costly, gives less language problems and is less disruptive for family life. It may decrease, however, the opportunities for job rotation and the internationalisation of management development. Also restrictions from governments with respect to working permits for foreign managers decreases the chances for a proper international exchange of management know-how.

Future Studies and Discussions at New Delhi

As has already mentioned it belongs to the tasks of the CECIOS Working Committee to submit an interim report in New Delhi and to study whether the subject can be the main theme of the CIOS Congress in 1981. In order to form a better founded opinion on this last question, the Working Committee hopes to get some interesting responses at New Delhi during the discussions about the four questions, which are submitted hereafter in this report.

So far our Committee has only scratched the surface and has only looked at some activities which take place in seven north-western European countries with respect to transfer of management know-how. In order to complete the picture far more information has to be gathered both in European as well as in other countries. And not only the viewpoints from the "givers" end but also from the "receivers" end have to be studied. A theme for the CIOS Congress in 1981 might be:

Exchange of management know-how between countries of different cultures in different stages of industrial development

During the period from 1978 to 1981 several studies should be carried out in various regions of CIOS by both research people and practising managers in preparation for a successful CIOS Congress in 1981.

Questions
— From the CECIOS Working Committee on the Transfer and Adaptation of Management Know-how:

1. *Essential aspects of management*
   Management in industrialised countries covers a number of aspects which we have tried to describe below. Please mention which of these aspects are lacking or are difficult to apply in less industrialised countries as regards:
1.1. Management methods and techniques
..   investment planning
..   financial budgeting
..   organisation methods
..   man-power training
..   computerisation
..   network technique
..   quality control, etc.
1.2. Social aspects
..   internal relations, i.e., leadership, management styles, etc.
..   external relations with government, trade unions, etc.
1.3. Phases of the systematical application of the management process
..   analysis
..   decision-making
..   planning
..   organising
..   staffing
..   leading
..   controlling
1.4. Levels of management
..   strategic
..   structural (also called organisational or administrative)
..   operational
1.5. Functional management
..   production
..   marketing
..   finance
..   personnel, etc.

2. *How to acquire management know-how*

2.1. Which would in your opinion be the most appropriate way to acquire those aspects of management you mentioned in your answer to question 1, and which role can be played by industrialised countries? It might be necessary to restrict the discussion to only a few major aspects of management.

Possible ways of transfer and adaptation;

.. by courses in industrialised countries

.. by courses in less-industrialised countries

.. by practice (on the job-training) in industrialised countries

.. by practice (on the job-training) in less-industrialised countries

.. by other ways

2.2. Which problems do you expect to encounter by using these possible ways and how could these problems be handled?

3. *Results of management know-how*

3.1. Is the average European manager capable of transferring his knowledge to nationals of your country? (those who train in Europe and those who train outside Europe)

3.2. How is the performance of managers in your country who have been trained in Europe?

4. *Future studies*

So far, the CECIOS Working Committee on the Transfer and Adaptation of Management Know-how has only made a descriptive pilot study on the ways transfer takes place from Europe to less-industrialised countries. Do you judge it useful—in preparation for the CIOS Congress in 1981—to extend this study on world-wide basis in which also the views from organisations in less-industrialised countries are incorporated?

Have you any suggestions by whom and how such studies should be undertaken?

10. Entrepreneurship

Duk Choong Kim

Dr. Kim is President of the Daewoo Industrial Co. Ltd., and the Korea Capital Corporation. He is Chairman of the International Cooperative Committee of the Korean Chambers of Commerce. Dr. Kim, who is a Director and Member of a host of other Korean organisations, has served as an adviser to his government on economics and educational reform.

Since I do not claim to be a management theorist, this presentation on entrepreneurship is mainly based upon my personal experience and undocumented observations of entrepreneurs.

Matching with the theme: "Management Perspective for Economic Growth and Human Welfare", my observation begins with a brief discussion of entrepreneurship in relation to economic development. Then, a Korean case of entrepreneurship will be examined. And, finally, I will discuss the challenges and tasks facing the entrepreneurs of today in view of the ever changing international business environment.

Entrepreneurship and Economic Development

Schumpeter, in his classic *Capitalism, Socialism and Democracy*, spoke of the function of the entrepreneur as follows:

> ...the function of entrepreneurs is to reform or revolutionise the pattern of production by exploiting an invention or, more generally, an untried technological possibility for producing a new commodity or producing an old one in a new way, by opening up a new source of supply of materials or a new outlet for products, by reorganising an industry and so on.

He further pointed out that the entrepreneur is the catalytic agent that makes any free economic system grow and prosper. As an economist-entrepreneurial manager, I completely concur.

The industrial progress and vigour of a free economy depend first on its entrepreneurial ability to find, develop, and utilise natural, financial, and human resources effectively. A meaningful understanding of the dynamic growth of any economy thus necessitates substantial attention to the roles of entrepreneurs and their activities. The success story of recent Korean economic growth is not an exception since the industrial growth has largely come in the private sector.

A recent government statistics indicates that Korea's real private non-agricultural gross domestic product grew at a compound rate of over thirteen per cent per annum from the early sixties. A study on the Korean entrepreneurship found that this extraordinary economic growth of Korea is manifest in a concomitant blossoming of entrepreneurial activity [1]. The study further noted the following:

> ...the net volume of entrepreneurial activities from 1961 to 1976 was more than six times that of all preceding Korean economic history. In world history, there are only a handful of cases of sustained entrepreneurial expansions of this magnitude. If four years is an economic sprint and the half-century expansions of the U.S. and Japan are marathons, then Korean entrepreneurs may be said to be in the running for a world record in the middle distances.

In order to examine the rigours of Korean entrepreneurs within a more limited actual setting, the case of Daewoo Industrial Co. in Seoul will be presented. The company was selected as a case for discussion because the success story of the company represents "New Generation" entrepreneurship in Korea.

A "New Generation" Korean Entrepreneurship: A Case of Daewoo Industrial Co.

Just ten years ago, with little more than courage and initiative, Daewoo launched as just another textile exporter in Korea. But in that short span of ten years it has rocketed into the position of one of Asia's leaders in world trade.

Daewoo's phenomenal growth in sales, capital and profits may only be described as a record among records. Sales alone increased from a mere U.S. $580,000 in 1967 to an expected U.S. $2 billion in 1978. Capital increased from slightly over $10,000 in 1967 to more than $92 million in 1978, solidifying the company's position as one of the largest and most diversified general trading companies in Korea. With the continuons and tireless drive for growth and expansion through corporate multinationalisation, Daewoo was recently listed by *Fortune* magazine as one of the top 500 international companies in sales volume just after successfully closing the first decade of its history.

Korea aims at $12.5 billion in exports and $1,064 in per capita national income in 1978, the significant year in which Daewoo will start the second decade of developments. Daewoo is planning to consolidate the foundation for its continuous growth as an international corporation. It plans to export $1 billion worth of its diversified products in 1978, up to 100 per cent over 1977, and to increase the share of heavy and chemical industry products to 50 per cent of the export target. This means that Daewoo will account for 8.1 per cent of the $12.5 billion export goal and 10 per cent of the heavy and chemical industry product export goal of the nation in 1978. Daewoo has also taken active part in technology export mainly in the form of industrial plants exports to other less-industrialised countries.

As a general trading company, Daewoo is also strengthening the import business, which is now drawing the government's attention under its import liberation policy, in order to supply foreign products and raw materials at lower prices to Korea. The development of natural resources in foreign countries is being carried out in such a manner as to ensure a smooth supply of materials to Korea in the face of resource nationalism and to help develop the economies of the host countries.

The marketing strategy toward less-industrialised countries is shifting from the past simple sales activities to active participation in the economic development of these countries through joint ventures, establishment of local corporations and technical and financial support. This will help expand the export market in depth for Daewoo products in these countries and develop local economies.

In the development of new products, emphasis is being put on technology-intensive items bearing high value added. This requires Daewoo to provide financial and technological support to the manufacturing firms of the country which are in want of money and technology and modernised equipment. This is helping integrate production lines of the country's industry in the direction toward a better international competitiveness. In short, Daewoo is pursuing corporate multinationalisation even further with increased host-country orientation.

How can we explain this remarkable growth of Daewoo? What is the prime mover for this growth in this short span of time? When venture capitalists decide whether or not to make an investment in a new organisation, it is known that 90 per cent of their decisions are being made on their evaluation of the man who will be in charge of the new business, the entrepreneur—because the single most important variable in the sucess of any new venture is the entrepreneur [2]. By definition, any single-factor explanation of corporate growth is partial, but if one wishes to focus on prime factor then entrepreneurship is a likely candidate. In this sense, it can be said that only entrepreneurship may be the prime mover for the phenomenal growth of Daewoo.

Entrepreneurship behind Daewoo's vigour and commitment to outward looking expansion is well exemplified in the words of Sydney Rolfe.

In the late 18th century the originator of one of the great British trading companies waded ashore in what was then British Guinea with a pack of goods on his back to sell to the natives. His venture illustrates two principles which are still in force for the multinational company and a third principle (the colonial pattern) which is dying. The first two principles are that you must go where the market is in order to do business and that in doing so you must get your feet wet [3].

In this connection, it is interesting to note that the president of Daewoo was the first Korean businessman who visited Lagos, Africa for export marketing there, when most Korean businessmen are domestically oriented.

For its international orientation, Daewoo is frequently cited as a symbol of a "new generation" entrepreneurship in Korea. The company name itself incorporates its international orientation. Daewoo means in Korean "the great universe". By adopting an early stage of corporate multinationalisation scheme, together with the dynamic ideas of growth and international perspective, Daewoo could become Asia's leaders in world trade as we can infer from the opinion of Endel Kolde

> The trade linkage of the multinational corporation differs in one respect from the classic notion of foreign trade. It is not trade among independents or unrelated residents; all these trading units are harnessed to the same ultimate objective; to serve the corporate interest, whatever its definition in any particular firm. Thus, it remains intra-company despite being inter-nation, i.e., internal from the viewpoint of the firm as a totality but external for all the nations whose boundaries are traversed by the trade. It goes beyond the scope of any individual nation. Such intra-company international trade opens many new possibilities [4].

Although there may be other entrepreneurial factors behind the success story of Daewoo, the multinationalisation approach taken by it has played a significant contribution to its achievement in international trade.

Multinational entrepreneurs with international outlook take the initiative in combining natural, human, financial resources, and technology in different countries in order to produce goods and services for sale in local and international markets. The strategic decisions which have resulted from the exercise of multinational entrepreneurship in Daewoo include answers to the following key questions: Where in the world are our best markets? How about sources of raw materials, equipments, and production technology? In short, Daewoo is abandoning a binational strategy for a multinational strategy. Hence, the multinational enterprise system of Daewoo becomes more integrated in production, marketing, finance, technology and management internationally. For all of these, entrepreneurial orientation was changed from ethnocentric orientation to geocentric orientation by following policies which are world oriented.

I want to emphasise one very important point from my personal observations: an idea and a little capital do not ensure a successful entrepreneur. Hard work, self-confidence, goal and action orientation, systematic risk-taking attitude, creativity and adaptability are all necessary ingredients for a successful entrepreneurship.

Concluding Remarks

The influence of multinational corporations on the economies of less-industrialised countries as host countries is currently a popular subject of arguments. The discussions frequently revolve around the extensive international activities of major multinationals the implications being that corporate multinationalisation is the special and peculiar province of industrialised countries especially the big multinationals in the U.S.A. and Europe.

However, as this case presentation argues, multinationalisation of exporting firms in less-industrialised countries is not only a feasible proposition but also it can be a valuable approach in solving some of unique exporting problems of those countries. There is widespread agreement that multinationals have superiority in promoting exports since those firms by their very nature have greater access to market information, distribution channels, and marketing skills for export markets than do one-country-plus export market type of enterprise. This inherent superiority of multinational firms mainly arises from their simultaneous operational capabilities in many different national environments.

For a capable entrepreneur, these international entrepreneurs are those individuals who successfully conceive of, organise and start new business ventures, and manage them through their initial struggle for survival. Accordingly, entrepreneurs, unlike professional managers, are faced with one of a high degree of uncertainty. It seems to me that the task and uncertainty facing entrepreneurs of today is even more awesome than in the past mainly because of the exceeding rigorous competition in the domestic market as well as in world's market place. However, I don't think it is an insuperable obstacle to success for a hard-working devoted entrepreneur.

REFERENCES

1. Jones, Leroy, P. and Sakong II, *Government and Entrepreneurship in Eoconomic Development: The Korean Case*, Working Paper 7802, Korea Development Institute, Feb., 1978, p. VI-1.
2. Swayne, Charles and Williams, Tucker, *The Effective Entrepreneur*, New Jersey: General Learning Press, 1973, p. 4.
3. Rolfe, Sidney E., *The Multinational Corporation*, New York: The Foreign Policy Association Inc., Headline Series No. 199, Feb., 1970, p. 10.
4. Kolde, Endel J., *Working Papers on the Organisation and Behavior of the Multinational Firm*, Seattle: Graduate School of Business Administration, University of Washington, 1972, p. 11–15.

11. Entrepreneurship

Paul Appell

Mr. Appell is President of the French Management Association, Paris.

I am going to highlight the problem which we now have in France and the adjoining countries, and that problem is extremely urgent because we must build up our economy so much in order to be able to buy what Korea is going to deliver to us in the next few years. We have a lot of regulations imposed by the Government. My Government in France has already controlled over 40 per cent of the national products and we have a lot of regulations. We have lived under a price control for the last 35 years. We have a social regulation practically in all fields. We have consumer protection quite developed and we have also ecology. Of course, all these are good for obvious reasons. But altogether we find ourselves in a situation of being in the middle of a tactical manoeuvre because everytime we move, we find some regulation in our way. That certainly poses a large problem to the entrepreneur. And we have to adjust ourselves.

I am struck by the fact that the question is not what entrepreneurs are going to do to adjust themselves to the outside world, but what the outside world is going to do to adjust itself to the entrepreneurs. And I wonder if it is a very realistic situation, I think we have to meet the demands of the people, the demands of our own country. And now we not only have a big change in the ever-increasing Government regulation practically in all western countries, but we also have a change in what the people want. Well, it is a fact that once the people have got enough money and wealth and live comfortably, they ask for something else. They demand for security, more consideration, and interest in their jobs, etc. It is something extremely important, because when the new demands which are purely qualitative, are not satisfied the people stop working. That is why they are asking for reduced time of work. That is why they are asking for more vacation. That is why they are asking for more education. I do not blame them. But we must accept the fact that when we succeed in giving the people more money or more qualitative goods or more qualitative satisfaction, they quite normally ask for more.

102

One must also take into account the fact that information, not only information in business but general information, especially through media like T.V., has completely changed the point of view of the people. They have now the same information as you have everyday; practically all the people in France receive the same information at the same time because the same piece of information is transmitted on T.V. So you cannot pretend to be better informed than the worker in your factory. So the question of information is really a new problem and you must accept the fact that it is entirely a different situation now, entirely different from what it was 15 years ago when people got information only through a newspaper.

Therefore, we have to accept that there is a big change now. In fact, there are two big changes: One is the change in Government regulation and the other is the change in people's attitudes towards work. Now they want the work to be gratifying, they want the work to be interesting, they want a work in which they can develop their own qualities and faculties. That trend has come to stay. And that obliges us to consider the role of an entrepreneur with a new perspective.

The first problem is the selection of an entrepreneur. Who is going to be the entrepreneur in the next 10 or 20 years? Well, when I was a young engineer, a suitable entrepreneur was one who had the technical know-how and a bit of financial knowledge. That was practically all. But now the people have to have a good sociological and psychological approach, because they are going to act not only through the market, through their technical knowledge, but they have to act inside the market, that is, they have to work with the people working in the company. They have to know the wishes and expectations of the people working inside the company. And if we do not do that, we will face problems. The problem of the Americans now is their decreasing productivity. It is a very important manifestation of that trend. So the first problem is the selection of the manager, of the entrepreneur, their education and also the way to appreciate their performance. We can no longer appreciate the performance of the manager only by economical results.

Up to now practically all controls were aimed at developing economical control. Now we have the problem of how to control the social situation inside the company. The French Government has imposed upon us what we call a social budget; that means every year we have to give quite a lot of figures about social phenomena like turnover, absenteeism, accidents, etc. That means now the man in charge of a factory has to be responsible both for economic and social results. That is a big change, as all the engineers, all the people, from the universities have not been trained in this direction. So really we have a large educational problem as far as managers are concerned, and the problem of developing new methods of controlling our company.

Well, that is not the only problem we have. Unions have been mentioned which is another important area. In Europe, unions are very important. In

France we have five different unions in cooperation with each other. Unions are very important and they are protected by law. We have to deal with them. A manager must be able to understand what their policies are, the way they handle their problems, because it is part of the day to day routine. The problem is further complicated sometimes by the unions themselves. Unions are not what they used to be 30 years ago. Thirty years ago it was quite a simple thing. But they are much more complicated now; they have the same market problem as we have in the company; they are not too clear as to what they are really going to do, because it is not easy for a union to come out clearly with what it wants. Asking for qualitative improvement of a thing is entirely a different matter.

Then we have also the same problem with the press. For instance, we had two years ago a public inquiry into the way a private enterprise should be reported. We had a big report made by the minister on enterprise reform, which proposed, I think, 35 different propositions for new laws concerning the way an enterprise should be run. It was proposed that if the managers are unable to run an enterprise, then the people and the administration should tell them how to do it. We went too far in that direction. People realise it now that an enterprise should be permitted to be run by the people who work within, without external interference. Yet, the temptation to step in and run the business is still very great for the administration.

To overcome management problems, as I have inferred already, new managers have to be trained for a wider spectrum of techniques. Not merely managerial techniques, but also sociological and psychological techniques.

It is very important that workers in an enterprise should have freedom to express their opinions on their work, during working hours. It has been found that when people express themselves on the job, what they say is extremely positive. They take a lot of interest and initiative, contributing many constructive suggestions and points of view.

The economic and social aspects of each problem need to be considered. Each economic problem has social consequences and there is no social measure which has no economic cost. So we must learn to integrate these two aspects of a problem.

In conclusion, I would like to state that we must realise one thing in the years to come. Earlier we thought that the problem was only of how to create wealth; then came the problem of redistribution of that wealth. Now after attaining a certain level of riches, the problem is of how to motivate the people further. I think therefore the problem for the entrepreneur, in the years to come, is really to adjust himself to the new demands of the outside world. This is a big lesson we have learnt in France during the last 10 years.

12. Behavioural Expectations from Managers

B. van Vloten

Mr. B. van Vloten, whose industrial career spans a quarter century, is President of the European Council of Management (CECIOS). He is Vice-President of CIOS—World Council of Management, and of NIVE, Netherlands Management Association; President of the Royal Netherlands Society of Forestry; and ex-President of the Netherlands Federation of Professional Soccer.

At the Caracas CIOS Congress a report on professional management was presented. This report and its recommendations were accepted by the CIOS Assembly held at the occasion of the Congress. The recommendations asked to promote the development and acceptance of Standards of Managerial Competence and Behaviour and to nominate regional and national working committees for these purposes. This report was prepared by a CECIOS Working Committee on behalf of CIOS. The CIOS Assembly asked CECIOS to continue its work and to prepare another report on the same topic for the 18th CIOS Congress in New Delhi. CECIOS accepted this challenge and installed a new Working Committee. At the instigation of this Committee, national committees in some European countries have carried out studies along the line of the Caracas proposals. Among others, in the Netherlands, two working committees were installed, one on Managerial Competence and the other on Managerial Behaviour.

One Dutch Working Committee on Managerial Competence took as the starting point the following questions:

1) What are the substantial changes in the function of the general manager in these days?

2) What is to be understood by the notion "general manager"?

3) Which competence consisting of knowledge, skills and attitude must the general manager possess as a consequence of the development of his function?

The Working Committee first formulated some of the recent substantial changes in the field of operation of the general manager. Financial/econo-

105

mic, technological changes and economic and socio-cultural changes were listed as having an internal or external impact on management.

Further, the Working Committee described the position of the general manager in his organisation. The Working Committee emphasised the necessity of steering qualities more than the need for an absolute leader. The definition of the managerial task which resulted from the foregoing is as follows. It belongs to the task of the general manager:
— To clarify in a continuous process the objectives of his organisation, to put them up for discussion and to see that they are laid down;
— To promote that the objectives of the organisation are realised by managing the organisation leaning on an effective way of decision-making, which is controlled by him;
— To harmonise the interests of all the groups involved in the functioning of the organisation.

The Dutch Working Committee could in principle agree with the conclusions of the Report on Professional Management of Caracas 1975 provided that it is accepted that the primary aim of any organisation is to fulfil a social need. The Dutch Committee was of the opinion that the so-called internal aim of any organisation namely to assure its own survival is derived from its fulfilment of a social need.

The Dutch report ends with a chapter in which the Standards of Competence are formulated. The Working Committee remarks that knowledge can be acquired, that skills need some natural aptitude but can be trained and that attitude depends on the behavioural qualities and inclinations of the manager which in a way can be developed but not acquired. The Dutch Working Committee on Managerial Behaviour has based its study on the British "Code of best practice incorporating the Code of Conduct with supporting guides to good management practice". According to the Dutch concept for a code the general manager:
— Shall not abuse his authority or position;
— Shall act according to the laws—and in the spirit of the laws—applicable to his organisation;
— Shall act in his function according to this code and the guides to good managing practice belonging to it.

The guides refer to general management as such, and its relation to the organisation, the collaborators, the suppliers, the consumers and the environment. The Working Committee remarks that the draft code represents an effort to lay down rules and norms to be accepted by the majority of the general managers in the Netherlands.

The Working Committee refers in its introduction to the draft code to the problem of the sanction on infringement. How to bind general managers? Is this possible on a voluntary basis? Comparisons are made with other groups of professionals with a code. On the one hand the membership of such professional groups implies acceptance of the code and on the other hand the membership can be a guarantee for certain standards of quality.

The CECIOS Working Committee has made an attempt to combine national results of studies on both items: managerial competence and managerial behaviour. As the CECIOS report shows only a few countries have followed the recommendations of the Caracas report to form national committees. Therefore the Working Committee has used a questionnaire to collect information from individual general managers on certain aspects of management. Outside Europe the questionnaire has also been sent to PACCIOS, AAMOCIOS and Dr. Koontz, the chancellor of the International Academy of Management.

To integrate the answers received from the CECIOS member organisations was already quite a task. The answers confirmed the statement of conclusions and recommendations prepared for the CIOS Congress in Caracas 1975: The function of the manager is accepted as part of the social system. Further professional training has been qualified as one of the most important means to improve the public understanding of the managerial function, task and responsibility. The acceptance of a Standard of Competence is therefore considered of great importance.

Here again the requirements for a Code of Competence are specified:

1) Knowledge which can be acquired in a learning process: economic, legal, social, political, cultural and technological facts and developments.

2) Skills: think and speak in a clear and purposeful way, recognise and select main facts from unimportant informations, arrive at logical conclusions, lead, motivate, absorb the impact of failures, etc.

3) Attitude: conduct, morale, way of thinking. In the Swiss report the element "attitude" refers to perseverance, charisma, capacity to carry stress, fairness, adaptability, creativity, courage to take decisions, willingness to accept responsibility, confidence in oneself, determination for continuous training. It is the least accessible for a learning process, but by the same token it is considered to be of increasing importance thus deserving full attention of those engaged in the field of training of managers.

In the context of attitude and skills the China Productivity Center speaks of intuition, wisdom, coherency, which can hardly be learned through training.

One of the conclusions is that the way of approaching these problems by different people does not differ too much. The philosophy however which underlies the formulation of norms and values may differ greatly according to the diverse cultural backgrounds of the different people.

Therefore I put the question before you: If we want to elaborate rules or standards of competence and behaviour, should we not limit this work to smaller territories, for instance territories with the same cultural background?

Or should we aim at standards on a worldwide scale with such a built-in flexibility that each culture can insert its own norms and values?

My next question is: What could be the use of worldwide standards with a built-in flexibility?

If you agree that we have to limit our work to territories with the same cultural background, is it nevertheless possible for CIOS to draw up a general framework, in which each cultural territory can fill in its own standards based on its own norms and values? If we believe in the profession "manager", because management is a key-function in this world, it seems necessary to demonstrate that it is a profession which implies that there must be some basic universal criteria. Like for other professions the profession of manager should be made recognisable not only for managers themselves but also and specifically for the public at large.

This implies that those basic universal criteria should be determined.

It is stated in the CECIOS report that any code of conduct needs to undergo continuous adaptation to new circumstances and changing values.

Static codes of conduct would even appear dangerous in our fast changing times where demands from suppliers of goods and services, suppliers of capital, labour, consumers and environments alter ever faster. Managers cannot be bound by exact rules. Man himself has an innate sense of freedom. But on the other hand it is clear that it is not the purpose of a code of conduct to completely tie down management. As long as a code of conduct for managers reflects the real intentions, it will be a help to improve the image of the manager which according to the CECIOS report is often vague and ambiguous and rather uncertain.

However many codes of conduct we develop, however many image promoting techniques we develop, unless our action is starting from a positive attitude, for which "personality" and "maturity" are important, we are building an outer shell.

Since our Congress in Munich in 1972 we have been studying "professional management" on a worldwide basis. The CECIOS report recommends to continue our study on a regional basis. Personally, as I said before, I would strongly recommend to consider whether those studies should be carried out on even smaller scales.

At the end we can then try to compare the criteria laid down in smaller scale studies and try to find common denominators for universal use.

Codes of competence and codes of conduct can assist us but they can never replace the inner richness from which all our actions should flow.

It is a privilege for all of us to be in the country of India, known for its search for truth and inner peace and for its techniques of reflection. Let us, professional managers, listen to what this country can teach us!

13. Report of the Working Committee of CECIOS on Professional Management on behalf of CIOS

B. van Vloten

1. CARACAS CONGRESS 1975, OUR MANDATE

Statement of Conclusions and Recommendations of the Caracas Report

1) Management is a continuing social process leading to the accomplishment of the objectives of organisations.

2) Organisations can be publicly or privately owned, with or without profit as an objective.

3) The internal (individual) aim of any organisation is its own survival. The external (social) aim is to fulfil a social need.

4) (a) The function (role) of the manager is to lead and represent the organisation.

   (b) His task is continually to define the objectives of the organisation in a changing environment with a view to its aims.

   (c) His work is to lead the organisation towards attainment of the objectives balancing and harmonising the needs and interests of the different vital relations of the organisation. These vital relations are those with
   — suppliers of good and services,
   — suppliers of capital,
   — labour,
   — consumers,
   — the environment.

5) The right of the manager is to demand from each vital relation its stipulated contribution to the organisation.

6) The responsibility of the manager is to ensure that each of the vital relations gets its fair and appropriate share in relation to its relative contribution to the organisation.

7) The managerial function is increasingly being fulfilled professionally through:
— The application of generalised and systematic knowledge;
— Orientation to community interest;
— High degree of self-control with regard to competence and behaviour.

8) Management will be regarded as a profession according to sociological norms when it has strong professional associations enforcing with sanctions, generally accepted standards of competence and behaviour. There are the beginnings of a movement towards this.

9) The CIOS Working Committee on Professional Management recommended the CIOS Assembly of November 4, 1975 to adopt the statement of conclusions as laid down in the report of the Committee prepared for the 17th CIOS World Management Congress at Caracas and to decide:
— To further the development of their appropriate Member Organisations into professional associations;
— To promote the development and acceptance of standards of managerial competence;
— To promote the development and acceptance of standards of managerial behaviour;
— To nominate Regional and National Working Committees for these purposes.

CIOS Assembly Meeting on November 4, 1975

During the CIOS Assembly Meeting on November 4, 1975 the first report on Professional Management was accepted and supported by CIOS.

The presentation of the report during the CIOS Congress turned out to be the start to many a lively discussions. In view of this the CIOS Assembly asked CECIOS to continue the stimulating and coordinating task and prepare another report on the topic for the 18th CIOS Congress in New Delhi, December 1978.

CECIOS Assembly on December 9, 1975

The CECIOS Assembly on December 9, 1975 accepted the above request and on behalf of CIOS it nominated a Working Committee. The task of this Committee was formulated as follows:
— Promote that on an European and world scale National Committees be formed;
— Promote that these National Committees give publicity to the Caracas Report and further enlarge upon it;
— Work out further the eight conclusions reached in Caracas and indicate the general lines of development of
— Standards of Competence; and
— Standards of Behaviour.

— Coordinate the results of the National Committees and feed the results of coordination back to them.

— Prepare a report for the 18th CIOS Congress in New Delhi, which should reflect both the work of National Committees and that of the CIOS Working Committee reinstalled in Caracas.

Before Caracas 1975

On March 29, 1973 the CECIOS Board decided to stimulate each National Organisation to start activities aimed at the promotion of the study of Professional Management. As a basis for a discussion on this topic it was suggested to take the original speech of Sir Frederick Catherwood held in Munich during the 16th Congress and the speech he held during the 3rd Davos Symposium. The title of his speech in Munich was "Responsibilities toward society and Government in an Institutionalised environment". In Davos he further defined the topic of Professional Management. During the 3rd Davos Symposium a working group of managers developed a first tentative declaration, which was also recommended to be part of the papers necessary to start the CECIOS discussion. This first tentative declaration reads as follows:

a) The purpose of professional business management is to serve its customers, investors, employees and the communities in which it operates and to reconcile their different interests.

b) 1) Management must serve the *customer*. It must satisfy the needs of the customer and give him the best value. Competition between one business and another is the most common method of making sure that customers receive the best value and widest choice.

Management must aim to turn new ideas and advances in technology into economic products and services.

2) Management must serve the *investor* by giving him a higher rate of return on investment than the rate of interest on loans to government. Such higher rate is necessary to include a risk premium above the cost of capital.

Management is a trustee for the shareholders.

3) Management must serve the *employees* since, in free societies, no one will accept leadership from those who do not care for their interests.

It must make the optimum use of the knowledge and resources under its control. It must push back the frontiers of knowledge in management and technology.

It must ensure that its enterprise pays its due share of taxation to the community to enable it to fulfil its tasks.

Management should also make available its knowledge and experience to the community.

c) Management reaches these objectives through the company. It is therefore necessary to safeguard the long range existence of the company.

That long range existence cannot be guaranteed without sufficient profits. Company profits therefore are the necessary means to enable management to serve customers, investors, employees and communities.

The members of CECIOS studied the above mentioned first tentative declaration together with the speeches of Sir Frederick Catherwood and on the basis of the first tentative answers of the CECIOS members the CECIOS Assembly decided on October 18, 1973 to nominate a special Working Committee which should:

1) Lead the studies on Professional Management entrusted to CECIOS by CIOS;
2) Investigate the possibilities of sounding out the first results of the study during the 4th EMF Symposium (February 1974);
3) Coordinate all activities in this field, including those of the other regions of CIOS.
4) Prepare a report for the 17th CIOS Congress in Caracas, November 1975.

In the beginning of 1974 sufficient material was available on the topic of Professional Management for cooperation between CECIOS and EMF to be further worked out in a joint activity. The idea behind this joint activity was that the cooperation with the EMF would offer a chance of sounding out the first findings of the Committee among a large audience of practising managers.

The results of the joint activity with the EMF and other material provided by the members, enabled the Committee on Professional Management on its working meeting on May 31, 1974 to conclude the following:

1) That the study and promotion of a code of conduct is an integral part of a wider study, Professional Management;
2) That important aspects of the study of a code of conduct can only be dealt with adequately after having studied the position, task, responsibility and competence of the professional manager;
3) That, the study of Professional Management should comprise the study of the following elements;

Society: responsibility of manager toward it; tasks of managers in it

Manager: definition of task, position, responsibility from this study will follow;
— Standards of competence;
. now: subjective legitimation;
. future: objective legitimation;
— Standards of behaviour;
. few enforceable headlines;
. many guidelines of good practice.

Sanctions: desirability/need

During the CIOS Management Board Meeting in Auckland on October 26, 1974 the CECIOS region reported upon the meeting on Professional Management which took place in Athens, in October 1974. AAMOCIOS reported that in some National Organisations the study of Professional Management had been started. This warranted CIOS to give a further mandate to CECIOS to prepare the presentation of a report on Professional Management for the 17th CIOS Congress in Caracas, CECIOS would aim at including in this report the views of managers and management organisations from as many CIOS Member-Organisations as possible.

To give the study a more academic backing and to be able to present a more worldwide view, the Committee decided to send a questionnaire to all Fellows of the International Academy of Management, among whom are found high-ranking top managers and professors of management.

In the course of 1975 a report on the total study was composed and presented during the 17th CIOS World Management Congress in Caracas. The final report contained the statement of conclusions and recommendations.

After Caracas 1975

Working Committee on August 24, 1977
CECIOS decided to install a new Working Committee on Professional Management. The first meeting of this Working Committee after the presentation of the report in Caracas, in November 1975, took place on August 24, 1977.

The Working Committee formulated its aims as follows:
 1) To clarify the role of the manager in present day society, and
 2) To influence the public understanding of that role.

The Working Committee decided to compose and distribute a questionnaire in order to acquire from the answers a better insight of the work already done in this field.

CECIOS Assembly Meeting on October 21, 1977
— Some CECIOS Member-Organisations reported to have formed or to be in the process of forming National Committees for the study of Professional Management; other Member-Organisations promised material contributions. It regarded: Belgium, France, Germany, Greece, Norway, Spain, Switzerland and the Netherlands.
— The CECIOS Assembly decided to ask the Committee to present a report on its findings during the CIOS Congress 1978.

Working Committee Meeting on October 21, 1977
The Meeting considered the draft questionnaire and decided that:
— Information should be obtained from each country;
— To send each CECIOS Member-Organisation a number of questionnaires for distribution;
— Each country should collect the information.

Working Committee Meeting on March 16, 1978

It was felt that the answers on the questionnaires from the different nations cannot be taken one by one. There is an interdependence between the answers. To come to a good result, which means an integration of the national activities, it was decided that:

— Each Committee Member should be responsible for compiling a national report on the basis of answers received from his country;
— The national reports should be mailed to the central secretariat together with the respective completed questionnaires;
— The secretariat should distribute the national reports to the Committee Members;
— To invite Committee Members to study the national answers on two questions and to give a summary of all these answers;
— A total draft report based on the aforementioned material should be considered on the meeting of the Working Committee on August 29, 1978.

Working Committee Meeting, on August 29, 1978

The Working Committee Meeting on August 29, 1978 discussed the subject, amended the Draft Report and approved the Report finally, including the summary of the answers as set forth under the questionnaire.

Activities in other CIOS Regions

Considering the fact that the CIOS Working Committee on Professional Management executed its task on behalf of CIOS questionnaire were also mailed to:

PACCIOS,

AAMOCIOS,

Dr. H. Koontz,

(Chancellor of the International Academy of Management).

Answers were received from the Australian Institute of Management and the China Productivity Centre, Taiwan.

The Questionnaire

Status of received answers to the questionnaire

Organisation/Country	Answers received
AAMOCIOS	6
The Netherlands	15
Belgium	9
France	17
Germany	4
Switzerland	7
	58

Question 1

Is Professional Management studied in your country, e.g., through Working Committees as suggested in the Caracas Conclusion, item 9?

Answer to question 1

From the answers received it is obvious that Professional Management is studied in the countries involved. It is, however, notable that of the answers received from France over 43 per cent deny that Professional Management is studied in France.

As far as can be deducted from the answers received, Working Committees as suggested in the Caracas Conclusion, item 9, have only been set up in the Netherlands, Germany, Switzerland, New South Wales and Tasmania.

Question 2

Is there a generally accepted definition in your country of "manager"?
(In some countries "manager/management" does not apply to non-profit organisations.)

Answer to question 2

The majority of the answers received from all countries involved makes it obvious that there is no generally accepted definition of "manager" in these countries. From many of the answers it is, however, also obvious that a kind of general notion, however vague about what a manager is, is gradually developing in the countries concerned.

Question 3

There are several levels of management, top, middle and lower. The CECIOS Committee drafted a matrix suggesting some skills necessary for managers. Give your own estimate in percentages of the amount of time/energy/application of a manager on a certain level?

Answer to question 3

Management/ Managers	Strategic skills	Organisational skills	Social skills	Negotiating skills
Top				
Middle				
Lower				

One could derive internationally—as far as the participating countries are concerned—an overall understanding that the matrix applied to clarify the relations between the various skills used and the appropriate management levels is sufficient for the purpose to enlighten the mutual dependence.

It is obvious, and the answers received confirm this conclusion, that top management spends most time and energy on following strategic aims and exercising strategic skills, whereas organisational and social skills are above all applied by the medium and lower levels. Negotiating skills are either attached by equal percentages to all three categories of managers or with a light increase to top management. It is also obvious that professional skills, should they be taken into consideration, predominate at the middle and lower management levels.

The following matrix gives a median of the individual answers:

Management/ Managers	Strategic skills	Organisational skills	Social skills	Negotiating skills
Top	40	18	19	21
Middle	16	38	25	19
Lower	7	29	42	21

The individual answers showed rather important differences.
Critics of this matrix system mention that:
— Operational skills should be used instead of social and negotiating ones by stressing the point that the three main tasks of management are strategic, organisational and operational;
— Strategic and organisational skills form one group of skills which is being overlapped by the social and negotiating skills;
— Negotiating skills do not fit in the range: planning, organising, leading and control.
— Leadership with lower and middle management depends relatively more strongly on other skills than those mentioned in the matrix;
— A parameter of professional skills is missed in the matrix. The impact of professional skills is higher in lower levels.

Question 4
Would you add elements to the matrix? For what reason?

Answer to question 4
Supplementary remarks to be added in the matrix as requested by respondents:
— Skills in public affairs;
— Operational skills;
— Political skills (predominant role of the government in the western hemisphere);
— Delegation and motivation;
— Marketing ability and product know-how especially for lower and middle management;

— Financial and economic skills;
— Technical skills;
— Controlling skills;
— Verbal skills;
— Entrepreneurial skills.

Question 5

a) Is the function of the manager in your country accepted as a part of the societal (social) system?

b) If not, what is the public image of managers in your country, their task, their responsibility?

Answer to question 5

(*a*) In spite of the fact that the majority of the answers to this question were positive, the respondents judged it necessary to give a description of the public image of the manager.

In all countries where this survey took place, the majority accepted the function of the manager as a part of the societal (social) system. Several respondents indicated that the manager is part of his organisation, and that this organisation is part of the societal system.

Additional comment: The image of the manager is often vague, ambiguous and rather uncertain. Whenever an opinion is stated same is at best: "qualified", in the worst: "bad" and this situation is not improving.

The manager is considered, unless in exceptional cases, as the representative in the enterprise of capital and by such right, as having a power not shared with others.

Often a lack of knowledge about the exact function of the manager—because his function is not explained is, without any doubt, the cause of this image. A more sincere and more objective communication and a more truthful dialogue within and outside the enterprise might contribute to improve this image.

Answer to question 5

(*b*) In general the description of the public image of the manager tends to a technocratical person who is rather "defensive" and "profit conscious". Often he is considered the representative of the capital interests. In several countries however there is an improvement of this image.

Additional comment: The image is unfavourable to the extent that the manager is often considered as a technocrat serving capital.

Here again we have to consider the cause as being the lack of knowledge about the function of the manager, whose action is restricted to the success of the enterprise and the way in which he exercises his power.

Can we hope for an improvement of the image of the manager, both within the enterprise and among the public, as long as there is no consensus on the purpose of the enterprise?

Question 6

Can you indicate through an order of preference how managers can best improve the public understanding of their functions, task and responsibility (see Caracas Conclusions, item 9)?
— Professional training;
— Acceptance of a code of conduct;
— Acceptance of a standard of competence;
— Public service;
— Professional public relation activities;
— Others?

Answer to question 6

From the answers it appears that a basic professional training related to standards of competence can best improve the public understanding of the role of the manager.

Furthermore, the code of conduct and the public service are indicated as means to improve the understanding. And it is clear that public relation activities are continuously necessary as support.

Additional comment: There exists a near unanimous opinion that the manager should have made diversified studies at university-level, with a basic professional training. In short, a good manager must be a man of a general and superior formation, with a scientific mind.

In addition thereto an experienced in command and with respect to operational activities is indispensable in different sectors in order to know the tools and the people.

Finally, it is by giving proof of professional experience, by accepting to comply with a code of professional competence and by participating in activities for the public good outside their own professional jobs, that managers have the biggest chance to improve the understanding of their function by the public and thereby to improve their image.

Question 7

a) What would be in your opinion the requirement of the professional training of a manager?
b) Would you expect standards of competence to be drafted and accepted in your country?

Answer to question 7 (a)

1) Answers to question 5 have confirmed the Statement of Conclusions and Recommendations prepared for the CIOS Congress 1975: The function of the manager is accepted as part of the social system. In the answers to the questionnaires, question 6 on professional training has been qualified as one of the most important means to improve the public understanding of their function, task and responsibility (see comment on answers to question 6) with a view to better social service to be rendered by the manager, the acceptance of a

standard of competence ranks less high for this purpose.

2) The national reports commenting on the answers to the questionnaires received mainly focus on continuity of professional training of a manager. This can well be justified when looking at what is being expected from the manager as regards his skills. A German and a Swiss study on professional training of managers analyse these requirements as follows:

— Knowledge (learnable: economic, legal, social, political, cultural and technology, facts and developments);
— Attitude (conduct, morale, way of thinking);
— Skills (knowledge plus attitude plus exercise) allowing to think and speak in a clear and purposeful way to recognise and select main facts from unimportant information, to arrive at logical conclusions, to lead, to motivate, to absorb the induct of failures; etc.

The element "attitude" refers to perseverance, charisma, capacity to carry stress, fairness, adaptability, creativity, courage to take decisions, willingness to accept responsibility, confidence in oneself, determination for continuous training. It is the least accessible for a learning process but by the same token it is considered to be of increasing importance (Swiss group), thus deserving a full effort to achieve penetration of this field by professional training of managers.

Many reports to management educationary institutions. However, the objectives quoted for such schooling are limited to some items which are easily accessible to university training, whether postgraduate or post-experience. We find that it would certainly be possible to include some neglected further elements into the programmes of management educationary institutions and suggest that the Regional Organisations of CIOS encourage their National Member-Organisations to take up contact with management educationary institutions with a view to define some less accessible areas which could be added to their training programmes.

To the extent that the elements quoted cannot be learnt at any kind of school, the manager is left alone with himself and self-education is expected. Continuous exercise is to be considered as the only source of improvements. "Continuous development" is one of the comments received from The Netherlands answering question 7 of the CECIOS questionnaire. The Belgian National Report underlines that for a manager "to maintain himself some time in permanent education during the whole of his career as manager" is a must. One of the German questionnaires returned refers to "updating the knowledge". The questionnaire returned by the China Productivity Centre, Taiwan, points out to intuition, wisdom and inherency and confirms that these can hardly be trained. This is even more absolute than what was stated above on the elements "attitude" which is the least accessible of all for a learning process.

When in the Swiss national answer to the questionnaire reference is made not only to "continuous self-education" but also to "contrasting and well-developed and continuously pursued hobby interests", this suggestion can well be justified because it sharpens some of the most important characteristics of "attitude" quoted above: perseverance, creativity, adaptability, confidence in oneself, determination of continuous training. This may be one of the answers on how to achieve training in the least accessible area "attitude"

3) Many of the answers to question 7 refer to "thinking in specific social system terms", "interrelations between business and the society", "more emphasis on the social and political environment", "social skills" and "know-how about functioning of society". This reference is predominant in the answers received from the Netherlands. We have quoted a choice of relevant answers in order to give the flavour of this abstract element in the best possible way. The subject will require a lot of emphasis in the future work on professional management.

Answer to question 7 (b)
1) Considering the above analysis of the answers to the first part of question 7 and the quite theoretical and abstract qualification of many elements of professional skills of a manager, it is not surprising that the answers to the second part of question 7 are very much withholding, the possibility of a standard to be more than a guideline is being questioned (Belgium), they are difficult to specify (the Netherlands), because standard of competence cannot be measured. Its performance is considered to be easier in big corporations and advanced medium size companies than in small firms (Switzerland).

2) It is generally recognised that a competence profile for a manager is difficult to be established. For gaining more insight, the German Member-Organisation of CECIOS suggests to collect information on employment profiles and criteria in literature and contracting trade and technical associations and enterprises.

Question 8
Does a code of conduct for individual managers exist in your country?
If yes: can it be enforced?
If not: why does it not exist? Is it desirable in your country?

Answer to question 8
1) A code of conduct has been introduced by BIM in Great Britain and it has special sanctions for its enforcement. In West Germany a code is in discussion. Australia reports that they do have a code which will be enforced through sanctions.

From other countries the answers are rather open-ended and withholding. Again with respect to code of conduct it is suggested to qualify it as a guideline only. In the Netherlands, a Dutch version of the British BIM code has been drafted but answers from this country to the questionnaire tend to support a guideline function only.

An enforceable code would also not be acceptable in Belgium where one answer mentioned the danger of oligarchy in case of an enforceable code.

Scepticism is being shared by the Swiss group which suggests putting all the more emphasis on standards of competence.

2) The aspect is different when looking at a situation assuming that a code of conduct would already exist. This analysis can be made because the French translation of the questionnaire modified this question.

Whether *firms* would adhere to such code or not has been answered in an affirmative way (two-third of the answers) both in Belgium and in France attributing equal importance to the responsibility towards the various "stakeholders".

The question whether *individuals* would adhere has received a four to one voting in favour. General management being exposed to a separate question in this French questionnaire is less positive: the answers reflect a very affirmative picture with respect to the responsibility vis-a-vis the enterprise, the shareholders and the banks, while a code requiring responsibilities towards suppliers, customers, consumers, personnel and nation would be adhered to by only half of the answers while the other half would be against such adherence.

A Belgian questionnaire comments that we live in fragile times with erratic developments and it would be mistaking the situation by settling with a collection of rigid regulations of the kind of a code of conduct. However, an earlier Swiss report had underlined that any code needs to undergo continuous development because of circumstances changing continuously.

NEW DELHI 1978, OUR RECOMMENDATIONS

The answers to question 5 confirm that the image of the manager is not favourable. A vague, ambiguous and uncertain understanding is responsible for this detrimental situation. We are *even* faced with the fact that the term "manager" is in no way an established notion.

This state of things invites—no, compels—to continue the work and study regarding professional management.

This work and study should be concentrated on the following subjects:
— To create more clearness about the term manager by further development of the definition of standards of competence and of behaviour;
— To establish suggestions as how to improve competence and behaviour, some suggestions being given in the answer to question 7;
— To make a project on an image building publicity policy.

Furthermore the Working Committee on Professional Management recommends the CIOS Assembly:
— To ask not only CECIOS but all regions to install a Working Committee on Professional Management. Each Regional Working Committee should stimulate the nomination of National Working Committees which members should preferably be elected from management and science and each Regional Working Committee should in the first place report to its own members;

— To ask CECIOS to provide the other regions with appropriate literature about standards of behaviour in order to facilitate the studies in this field;
— To invite each Regional Working Committee to give information about the progress at the CIOS Assembly of 1981.

Members of CIOS Working Committee on Professional Management
Mr. B. van Vloten (chairman),
President CECIOS,
The Netherlands.

Mr. M.P. Bloemsma,
Chairman, Management Board Harten Holding,
The Netherlands,

Prof. Dr. H. Buntinx replaced by Mr. S. van Munster
Centre for Efficiency and Management,
Belgium.

Dr. V. Heuss,
Escher Wyss AG,
Switzerland.

Mr. K. Loew replaced by Mr. W. Limp,
RKW Rationalisierungs Kuratorium der Deutschen
Writschaft,
Germany.

Mr. R. Nicolas,
Associate General Manager, Galeries Lafayette,
France.

Prof. Dr. H. Ruhle von Lilienstern,
RKW Rationalisierungs Kuratorium der Deutschen,
Writschaft,
Germany.

Mr. Y. Turpin,
Consultant VECTEUR,
France.

Mr. H.P. Bruia replaced by Mr. L. Bouwens,
Secretary, CECIOS.

14. Behavioural Expectations from Managers

M.C. Schubert

Mrs. Schubert is Trade Relations Director for the Shell Companies in Malaysia. She has been Chairman of the Malaysian Institute of Management for the past two years, is a Fellow of the Institute, and Member-at-large of the CIOS Board. Mrs. Schubert is also a Fellow of the Institute of Public Relations, Malaysia, and is its Vice-President. She is a Member of the Private Sector Consultative Committee for Malaysia and Chairman of the Manpower and Training Panel.

I come from a small country Malaysia, which has very few claims to fame. But one of them is that we provide one of the few remaining places left in the world as the habitat of the turtle. I said one of the few. They come every year to nest on our east coast. So, having had the advantage of studying this somewhat curious species, my observation is that the only way the turtle makes progress is to stick out its head. And the subject I have been asked to speak on today is so characteristically fashionable that it has been spoken on a thousand times before. I have, therefore, decided to try to emulate the turtle of my country and stick out my head just a little and gradually. I begin with the theme.

I was somewhat intrigued by the title "Behavioural Expectations from Managers". As this is India where the English language is treated with a great deal more respect and used far more conspicuously than it is today in the country of its origin, I dismiss any idea that the proposition was not intended as is stated and, therefore, I will give it the full presentational force.

What I think is implied is that the expectations are imposed in today's climate of opinion upon managers, almost as an external requirement, even a demand. While I think we are very much aware that corporate policy and corporate behaviour today is subject to intense scrutiny and debate and what seems often to be a questioning of the essential integrity of business as various social pressure groups become positively strident in their protest and in their censure and the politician and the civic leaders in their very earnest concern, the citizen groups tend to join in the chorus. So, I can quite see how that presentational form came to be included in the title. The response of management, as you have seen from my predecessor's observations, has been in some cases perhaps a little hasty. I have codified the codes of conduct for managerial behaviour. We have not been the only ones. Respected organisations like the United Nations or the ILO or the OECD have been busying themselves writing guidelines for the conduct of multinationals. And it seems extremely fashionable and so perhaps the first opportunity for the turtle to protrude its head.

The first thing I would like to say is that I find nothing new in this and nothing to debate. I do not regard these codes as a product of a sweet mentality. The old adage that honest trading makes good business is still fairly well entrenched. The vast majority of managers that I have met at the personal level, perhaps because I can talk with those dedicated people who run the CIOS, have again all been people of the highest integrity and people whom I could respect. My own organisation, a year ago, published its own general statement of business principles. It contains absolutely nothing new. It merely lays down the philosophy and the practices that I have grown up with as a young girl ever since I joined the company.

So, I conclude that our newly minted codes of conduct are making explicit that justice should be seen to be done probably more so for the benefit of the world, what has always for the practising managers, the responsible practising managers, been implicit. If this is so, I make the further point that these codes are empirical, they are based on managerial experience from within, they are not probably handed down by a superior moral authority in the community. What has really happened is that we have reached a point in the evolution of the managerial profession as a profession where we are already unable to codify established behavioural norms. While we first began to think of ourselves as a profession, we naturally concentrated upon the skills, knowledge, techniques which go into the technical preparations of the management and which lay down what has earlier been called the standards of competence that make for managerial proficiency. The attempt to do the same for behavioural standards has indeed come later with the effect, to my mind, of underpinning our technical proficiency, with a strong sense of vocation and that sense of vocation is particularly needed to meet the very critical challenges of the modern world. In order that these codes be effective, they have to be matched by changes and developments in our actual behavioural modes. And this is the subject to which I am going to address myself most.

Again, behavioural expectations upon the individual are not new. A long time ago, in another country, Sir Francis Bacon said: "I hold every man debtor to his profession where too he should strive to be an ornament thereof." To be an ornament to your profession in the sixteenth century when men lived to the concept of honour probably meant an elegance of behaviour and propriety of conduct.

Unfortunately, when we came to the beginning of management in the

19th century, we did not look upon it as yet as a profession. I would make the distinction that the hypocoristic oaths accompanied the beginnings of medicines. In that they had the advantage over us and we went through a period of Mckenziean horror as we exploited labour in the 19th century. By the way, we still have not left this habit. People do not realise that we do mature and with maturity comes greater responsibility. It was in fact, precisely when we became conscious of professionalism that we had to be giving up self-discipline. The authority of role and status by itself confers power and it can sometimes be unbridled power. But when it is supplemented by that other authority of knowledge and competence, then there is a professional self-respect which imposes the most exacting standards in the world, which are the standards which you set for yourself.

Now, I am not trying to make out that in the modern world, managers have not reverted to practices which are unprofessional. We have been dubbed by two peculiar big vices that, I think, are unfortunately endemic in business. I refer to the vices of greed and lust for power. I say endemic because one relates to the profit motive and the other is unfortunately a product of the organisational setting particularly of the hierarchical kind. There is, however, yet again another difference in the 20th century. And this is the present influence of the mass media. Greed and power-play has gone on as long as mankind existed. But today we live in a world of instant communication with the result that a misdemeanour committed on one side of the globe is flashed immediately along the headlines of the press and is given worldwide publicity. The other effect of this is that it calls the piccadiloes, the aberrations, the downright sins of a company, again half-way round the world, and they can reflect on the corporate recitations of a whole group of companies. For instance, if one multinational receives adverse publicity, then the whole of the multinational corps stands condemned.

I have to admit here that one of the repercussions hit me on the platform at the very start of today's assembly. The management will always be served by the few and so we have had what Mr. Drucker just described in rather the same terms as a moral revulsion. And certainly one, sometimes, has the feeling that management today has been brought into the fine line of society's expectation and that it will only legitimise itself on the ability to meet that representation. The total will, therefore, now make out a little more and I wish to question how effective the codes of conduct alone can be.

First of all, unfortunately, they have a tendency to be somewhat negative in emphasis in their response to moral revulsion. Rather like the law which seems to be made for the criminals, the codes of conduct are often framed with managerial delinquents in mind. Of course, they are also positive and they offer guidelines for uplifting behavioural standards in general. But here we immediately enter into the sort of cultural difficulty the previous speaker referred to and which drove him to the conclusion that we shall confine this to the small group. A view with which I do not agree.

As soon as you begin to spell out the specific, you get into different value systems. So, we take very frankly first the concept of integrity. The fundamental concept is a worldwide one. But it is capable of subtle differences in implementation and the legalistic mind of the West lays further claims in honouring the contract. But there has to be a contract signed, sealed and delivered. The countries which originated the term "a gentleman's agreement" have either run out of gentlemen or they have abandoned the concept that a man's word is a bond. Now, in the East, we still work to the order of trust and the handshake. In fact, you can get a situation in my country, where in a Chinese firm a man who works withuot a written contract, will work longer hours than the statutory requirement, for less than the standard rates of pay. But this is because he has implicit confidence in that his employer, when the rewards come ultimately, they will be shared out honourably. Now, in this sort of conduct, the westerner's insistence on black letter law and his almost obsession with fine prints can sometimes cause a static effect, because it would seem to imply a lack of the proper trust that is seen in the East, the spirit of true partnership.

Let us take another delicate area: Scruples. Scruples often vary. The westerners will shun personal relationship in, and sometimes, out of the office for fear of losing the cherished objectivity. But in the East, the fraternitism and nepotism are still integral parts of the system and unshamedly so. Where one group reads nepotism, the other group reads genesis, for which he has a right and proper regard.

Traditionally, here, business may be conducted along a very complex network of contacts, personal relationships, godfathers, cousin brothers and whom you know. And for this, is required a little social lubrication, I think, euphemistically so called, which is nothing but graft. And then the political payments are in most managerial codes. But they may be the indispensable norm in a country in which you are required to operate and without which you would not survive to operate long. The last example we had of this was the country of which we could then say "When in Rome, etc...." And the purist, of course, in this situation may decide to stick to his principles and withdraw. Others choose to adapt. Whatever we can do, however, in terms of a code for managers, I think what we perhaps should do, is take the highest in present standards of practice and try to apply these.

In other words, try to standardise the practice by gaining an acceptance and a commitment to the conduct and underlying the philosophy involved. But again as implementation is difficult, sanctions are difficult and these were often elusive, especially where there were cultural barriers. And the manuals in my country, the sophisticated manuals of sales managers, have had no effect whatsoever on the local procurements and marketing matters which continue to ply despite what the manual says. And while the advertisers may have been ousted by the computer, the indigenous methods of keeping the book are adhered to have a greater force than what the computer prescribes.

Lastly, and this is my viewpoint, because I want to leave the code of conduct behind, I believe that a code of conduct is only the minimum. The great jurist Edmund Burke has said: "It is not what the law tells me I must do, but what reason, justice and humanity tell me that I should do." I, therefore, would like to look at aspects of behaviour in managers where we might improve our performance against the newer, wider imperatives of social responsibility in today's world. The world is changing and these forces change the managers. But again I would maintain that there has been a record of spontaneous responsiveness to these outer changes. We are trying to inject a greater sense of purpose and ethics into the profession, because we ourselves have come to a height of consciousness, a social justice, not because entirely of external pressures. I do not believe, in other words, in selling ourselves cheap. The people are in the habit of talking about managers as if they are not a part of the society. We are just as much a part of the society as the politician, as the civil servant, or as the skilled worker. And we identify with social issues. In fact, if you want to make it clear, it is not a part of our job to monitor social changes and the environment for business practices. We may be the first to know and detect when there are emerging priorities and new value systems which have to be answered.

The greatest managers I know have been distinguished by the fact that they are average not at the levels of techniques in sciences, but at the philosophical level. They are by nature thinkers and they too have contributed to the progress of human ideas, and they too can therefore be safely assumed to ensure that these ideas will be translated into the work. I have one specific argument to support me here. Nobody has researched human behaviour as deeply and as conscientiously as the management proponents of the behavioural sciences which base their studies on the occupational workplace. And because we have studied behaviour, I think, we are well down the road of trying to make a conscious effort to influence behaviour in the corporate sector.

But there are a lot of behavioural challenges, new ones, and which are not easy. I do not think that such was our intent, but I am not sure that we have yet developed the social technology to stand up to these challenges. Very briefly, therefore, I think there are three levels. They are of course within the organisation.

The first level is where management styles are adapting to the precepts of the behavioural sciences which advocate some more open society; where the whole of the organisation is being influenced by the general trend in the community towards more humanistic and democratic values; where there is a shift from organisational relevance to personal relevance; and where the focus is on the human individual, his aspirations, his needs for fulfilment, his sense of significance as a human being.

At the second level are the demands of the community, managers today being accountable for the quality of life and for the payments of corporate citizenship. In fact, the criteria today is not just rigorous standards of performance against efficiency and profitability. The new criteria for business proficiency is also social performance and we have an obligation, I think, to build in ways of monitoring this and guarantee a social audit on our social performance.

The third level is the demand of a wider world community, because the world is becoming interdependent and we cannot ignore the global problems before us because they threaten the survival of our civilisation. With the joint pruning of technology, we have still not been able to tackle first the population problem and so there is an increase in more and more mouths to feed alongside the unrelenting pressure of poverty. We shall have to narrow the gap between the developed and the developing regions, I would suggest that problems that are global in scope require a global approach, and that alone will help us in solving these problems. In other words, if we really believe that our objective is the betterment of the world, we need to inject our expertise where it is most needed, which may be outside our particular scope or field. That will require, however, more intricate personal skills, more skills with new relationships and greater cultural sensitivity than we can possibly possess.

Behaviour and the attempt to influence behaviour is a very subtle area. Technology can be transferred easily because technology is neutral. But behaviour is culturally determined. In here, I have a knowledge bin, into which there is also an attitude bin made up of all the conditioning and the programming that went to produce this individual before you with lots of prejudices, historical and social, emotionalism and value systems that I find very hard to emancipate from. And all we do with the code of conduct is prescriptive. We must do this, we should do the other, we are not doing this, and so on. But against this, there is the traditional, cultural conditioning which differentiates us all because we do belong to very different cultural settings.

Now, let us take the organisation. Native authority, as it used to be, we were told, should now lead to participative controls in management and intellectually we may all agree to this. But, we know that management has a very strong idiosyncrasy traditionally. The early models of managers began as owner-managers. He had absolute power. He issued his instructions with the force of a thunderbolt, jarring the whole organisation and galvanising the people into hasty, not always well-directed, efforts. This was power. Sometimes it had a charisma. Sometimes it produced the tyrant. But I do not think we have forgotten that authority does also imply power and where you get the owner-manager replaced by the professional, you still have an hierarchy with all its subtle nuances of status and control which gives a rather unbridled expression to a personality. We have the delightful story today whether the ball should be yellow or should be green and we all recognise the sycophancy and in similar situations, I think, the outcome is to recognise behavioural sciences, we will recognise organisational bullying; we will recognise the power game; we will recognise the sort of man who sacrifices his family and builds up his outfit in a pursuit of aggression and ambition.

The turtle now wishes, to stick its neck out into another delicate area of behavioural response—to the advent of another curious species—women into the organisational world. I do think that this is going to need some change of behaviour on the part of men, because you are up against an unknown and unfamiliar entity. I declare, at the outset, that I am not an exponent of women's lib, but I do know that I, still, am regarded as somewhat of a corporate sweet rather than as a manager, and I am rather tired, for instance, of being constantly referred to as a woman manager. Why not as just a manager? It is not the exclusive domain of man. And, the same goes for *lady* doctors, *women* lawyers, etc. I have yet to find out why some of the ladies and other women in professions always attract the adjectives. Now, we have been given an entry to business and management. But it is a very qualified one. We tend to end up with managerial practices in terminal jobs, computing the pay rolls of our company boys and are not always given the career development jobs given to a man. And this is because chauvinism is often unconscious and a lot of you gentlemen may be chauvinists without realising it. May I highlight some of the possible rationalisations? Why don't you invest money in the training of women? It is said: "She is a diminishing asset, because she will grow up and get married or she will grow up and have children, or she will have divided loyalties and she will have babies and this will be a permanent disability instead of a temporary inconvenience. Women are not mobile, there will be trouble, they will not be accepted, they are too frail. A man may have a nervous breakdown but he will not ask for three months (maternity) leave. She is emotional." Oh no! I disagree. My colleagues are emotional. They lose their temper at least once a week on the hour, every hour; and it is an emotion of a different kind. These are frivolous arguments and there is a great deal of misplaced chivalry. And, what is more, I think, the performance is judged by the irrelevant criteria like your personal circumstances, which I mentioned a moment ago, instead of the actual performance. And, on the other side of the coin, women who cannot rid themselves of the subservience that is outmoded, are still to be seen. They have before them their ancestors, who still pay too much deference to the male in a situation where there should have been equality. If women are going to retain subservience then they should keep it at home where they have a respected place as wife and mother. They should not exchange the subservience in a company where they will not have that respected role. Similarly, of course, I condemn the use of any feminine weapons, tears or emotional blackmail.

Finally, in the area of social responsibility, as I see it, multinationals who are in battle should welcome investigations. They are still, to my mind, the most effective vehicles for the mobility of capital and expertise and they have the longest experience as being guests in foreign countries. And I think they should develop some maturity in interpersonal relationship which should stand them in good stead. They should also have by and large a very good record as an employer setting the pace in salaries, training, development and the like.

I do not believe that social responsibility ends with regulations that you have to conform to. I think it is a matter here of new relationships. So often now, we hear about the public and the private sector having come together. This means not just negotiating; it means developing a new type of relationship. But we do not prepare people for the culturally sensitive areas. We give them powerful skills and techniques. On the technical side of management, we don't. Perhaps there may not be the time on how to approach the relationship. We take a reservoir engineer and ask him to negotiate with a national oil company. Reservoir engineers are brilliant. Their minds are brilliant, 12,000 feet below the ground. But if you put them up against the national oil corporation, they have to acquire political heads, commercial heads as well as excellent technical heads and many of them succeed in doing it. But at the same time, you have to be very careful, particularly when you cross the cultural barriers. It is so often assumed that because a manager succeeds in his own country, he will be automatically guaranteed success in another.

We have a fruit in my country called dullian. It is so delicious, but it has a very obnoxious aroma. We brought in an eminent social scientist who went to stay in one of the hotels and I went to pick him up one day. There was a huge notice "No dullians allowed in this hotel." He greeted me with saying, who are the dullians? Now, there you have an example of how automatically the values of your own society are imposed on a different one. I have had to explain many times to the westerners many such things. The greeting that our Prime Minister gives is not a sign of recalcitrance. It is half the *salam* according to his own custom and the *salam* is essentially a very gentle movement. But we have, I think, to have a transnational and a transcultural curiosity and an interest in other countries and people in order to succeed, because we are differentiated and we are going to come up against new groupings all the time.

Business is increasingly international, conducted across national boundaries. The international nature of business has to be conducted in what is often an intensely nationalistic climate. And you have, therefore, a situation of a foreigner in another country—as you may be the foreigner at the express invitation, if not the incentive, by the host Government—when he actually takes the form of an individual, he becomes a focus of resentment. The resentment may centre on the issue of dependence. The resentment may be in having to import expertise not available at home. It may just be a cultural gap that divides the two. If it is an expertise gap, the new breed of experts do not always realise how formidable their expertise may seem to the inexperienced nationals of the host country and if they flaunt it too obviously then this will make the national reach for his own superior ground, which is political power. Because here we have the central issue of power and capability: Governments have the power, because no longer do the international companies have a prescriptive right to operate in other countries except by invitation, and yet they have the capability that results in their being invited in.

They begin as welcome invaders but the minute they get in, they often feel that they can only be welcome if they cease to be foreign and cease to be private. The transfer of technology can be again bedevilled if there is not the necessary humility. The application of logic in a situation of emotion can often come through as arrogance rather than humility.

I hope I have given enough indication of where, I think, are the real behavioural challenges. It is a very deep and a very complex subject. But, I sincerely believe that management is a profession that spans the world. We have a common language. We are codifying our philosophy so that we might come to a commitment and acceptance of a fundamental set of values. I think this is the way in which the global problems of this world have a chance of being solved. But it will require, to my mind, positive action.

May I give you a delightful story? It is the story of a farmyard where all the animals got together and decided to give the farmer a present. The chicken did most of the talking and he suggested that for the rest of the farmer's life they should give him bacon and eggs for breakfast. They called all the animals together and the chicken got up very excitedly to announce their decision. Then the pig, who was a slow thinker, suddenly approached and said, "Just a moment, taking an egg, it is all very well for you, you are participating, but I am involved."

Management and Technology

15. Management and Technology

Jermen M. Gvishiani*

Dr. Jermen M. Gvishiani is Chairman of the U.S.S.R. Scientific Council on the Social, Economic and Ideological Problems of Scientific and Technological Revolution; Chairman of the Committee for Systems Analysis at the Presidium of the U.S.S.R. Academy of Sciences; Chairman of the Council of the International Institute for Applied Systems Analysis; and a member of the Advisory Committee on the Application of Science and Technology to Development of the U.S.S.R.

Dr. Gvishiani is a member of the Royal Swedish Engineering Academy, Member of the Academy of Management, U.S.A., and Member of the International Management Association. His interests include philosophical and sociological problems in the theory of management and social organisation, and systems analysis. He is the author of about 250 scientific books and papers.

Scientific and Technological Progress in the Modern World

The last quarter of the twentieth century will go down in history as an epoch of rapid changes in the material and spiritual life of people, the changes that are caused by the progress of science and technology. The scientific and technological revolution increasingly enhances its effect on the development of human society and opens up new avenues for its prosperity.

The scientific and technological revolution is a multifacet process with a variety of revolutionary transformations and qualitatively new phenomena both in the system of science and technology themselves and their interaction with different spheres of society's development.

Naturally, the essence of the scientific and technological revolution does not come to just a number of discoveries or trends in scientific and technological progress, no matter how great and significant they may be. It consists in the restructuring of the entire technical base and technology: from the

*Paper presented on behalf of Dr. Gvishiani, by Dr. Boris Milner, Deputy Director, Institute for Systems Study, Moscow.

utilisation of raw materials and energy to the system of machinery, forms of organisation and management, the place and role of man in the process of production. The scientific and technological revolution creates the prerequisite for unification into a single system of the major forms of human activity: science—theoretical cognition of the laws governing nature and society; technology—complex of material means and experiences for transformation of nature; production—process of creation of material wealth; management—means of rational integration of expedient practical actions in achievement of production and other goals.

We are witnesses of the actual transformation of science into the leading element of the productive forces. It means that the unity of theoretical cognition and production activity becomes the powerful force of production. Creation of new materials and energy sources, appearance of new types of production activity, radical changes in the traditional technological processes—these are the factors that begin to play a most important role in technology. It becomes particularly evident in the new approaches to utilisation of natural resources.

Changes that are revolutionary indeed are taking place in the social structure as well as the material and technical basis of production. Due to such innovations as computer-based production and management, invention of devices capable of performing not only mechanical but also logical operations, man's labour functions in many cases are undergoing radical changes too. And, finally, management is becoming one of the major types of activity closely connected with the key spheres of society's life.

In the most general way one may say that the scientific and technological revolution constitutes a major qualitative transformation of the productive forces, the transformation of science into a direct productive force and, correspondingly, a revolutionary change in the material and technical basis of national production— its content and form—as well as in the character of the division of labour in society. These processes influence all the spheres of life including education, mode of life, culture and human psychology. While exerting a growing influence on the socio-economic development of society, the scientific and technological revolution itself is conditioned by a certain level of this development. It became possible only due to a high degree of socialisation of production.

Exerting the ever increasing influence on the further development of human society, the scientific and technological revolution engenders at the same time new, as yet unknown social problems that can be solved only through science-based management of the socio-economic processes of human life.

Never before in the history of human society did problems so critical for the destiny of human civilisation come to the foreground. Never before has man possessed such powerful means of mass destruction as now. Never before have people expressed such deep concern whether there are sufficient natural resources to meet the needs of the rapidly growing population of the planet. Never before has human impact on the environment been so strong. Never before has the total relationship between man and biosphere; society and nature caused so much anxiety as now—in the last quarter of the twentieth century.

Establishment of a lasting peace and equitable international relations, provision of natural resources for the future functioning of the world economy, protection of the natural environment, elimination of the most dangerous disease, the conquering of space and utilisation of the world ocean resources, reproduction of population, integrated regional development, long-term planning—these are real and serious problems the solution of which, to a great extent, will affect not only the welfare of the present and future generations but also the destiny of modern civilisation.

One of the most critical and, in a certain sense, "representative" global problems of the present time are the problems of the natural environment and the natural resources of our planet.

In order to understand the new meaning of the current stage in the relationship between society and nature, the new ecological situation should be analysed not only in its scientific and technological aspects but also in the context of the whole political and socio-economic picture of the contemporary world.

For many centuries humanity acted on the assumption that natural resources are inexhaustible, constantly increasing its impact on nature.

The optimistic view on the infinite capacities of nature's mechanism of "self-purifications" was formed at a time when man was not aware of the implications of his interference in the natural processes because man knew considerably less of the world he lived in.

At present it is becoming quite obvious that the increase in the world population, the speedy growth of cities and large industrial complexes, the higher educational and cultural level of people, and other factors lead not only to greater intensity and scale of human impact on the natural environment but also to a change in the character of man's interference in natural processes and, consequently, in the character of implications of that interference. Today the man-made technological impact on nature has achieved a level of intensity comparable to that of the natural forces themselves. There is a potential threat of the irreversible changes in the earth's ecosphere, the upsetting of the main mechanisms of life support systems on our planet, and a danger of damaging the natural conditions of existence for the generations to come.

Therefore control and management of the earth's ecosphere has become a most essential factor. In this connection one must be fully aware that nowadays each national economy has not only its "own" natural environment to consider—as has been the case so far—but in some very important respects it must consider the entire ecosphere of the earth. In other words, it is actually plugged in the natural physical system of a complex and higher structural level.

Global problems are connected with the development of mankind as a whole. They cannot be solved by effort of one State or a group of States but call for a united action on the part of governments and peoples of all countries.

Of equal importance is another aspect. The transient character and the ever-increasing rate of the processes of the scientific and technological revolution as well as the irreversible nature of some implications make these global problems even more critical and urge their reasonable solution. One has to be aware of all that to be able to take the appropriate measures in order to prevent the negative or, possibly, disastrous implications.

Besides making an objective evaluation of the changes that occur in the conditions of human life and continue research into natural phenomena, it is necessary to study the interaction between man and nature, as well as the socio-economic aspects in the development of human society. It is the socio-economic sphere that contains the most pressing problems of our time. It is an undeniable fact, as is undeniable the assertion that the essential condition for a successful solution of global development problems is detente, in the interests of our planet's population, so that wars and conflicts among countries might be prevented.

Systems Approach—Instrument of Scientific Knowledge and Management

The emergence of global problems objectively presupposes elaboration of a new, adequate methodology for their solution. The traditional mode of development of scientific knowledge proves to be inadequate for a comprehensive analysis of the ongoing processes and creation of mechanisms for their management. Global problems require new analytical tools.

The advance of science and technology that brought about these problems has at the same time equipped man with new instruments of their solution—in particular, a totality of methodological principles that became known as a systems approach and systems analysis.

The large scale and complexity of the objects of management, the closer interdependence of heterogeneous factors—economic, social, ecological and technological—the considerably faster rates of the continuing processes give first priority in scientific cognition to the systems concept, imply comprehensive and objective investigation of new problems.

The latest development of research gives reason to treat the systems approach as a methodology and instrument of scientific knowledge. It is:
— An approach based on the necessity to define as explicitly and comprehensively as possible the desired goals, when any system is regarded as a mechanism for their achievement;
— An approach oriented at identifying all the relationships and interactions

of phenomena, involving the application of logical, mathematical, computer and organisational modelling;

— An approach providing for formulation and assessment of alternative ways of achieving the goals, as well as assessment of the long-range effects of each alternative;

— An approach based on the interdisciplinary judgement and evaluation of the decisions to be taken;

— An approach aimed at organic combination, coordination and integration of various types of activity both in research and implementation.

A systems approach to natural and social phenomena implies a comprehensive analysis of social implications of scientific and technological progress. The systems approach based on the methodological principles of complex system management allows not only to form an integral picture of the relationship between the scientific and technological progress, on the one hand, and development of man and society, on the other, but also serves as a practical tool of optimising the management of the scientific and technological progress in their interests.

Global problems of common concern are characterised by the high degree of complexity and scale as well as dependence on a multitude of factors: natural, technological, economic, social, cultural, etc. Hence it is evident that these problems must be comprehensively analysed and treated as systems with all the interrelations and interactions. The conclusions of the analysis formulated in the language of theory should be also translated into the language of managerial practice to provide for scientific organisation of human activity.

One of the most important principles underlying the optimal organisation of human activity is comprehensiveness of management that implies integration of systems approach and scientific management to make it a unified and well-structured new theory. It is the systems approach to management that is called to ensure that the entire management system be regarded as a comprehensive integral entity taking into account a widest variety of feedback loops and long-term effects of control actions.

It implies that the systems approach to management is an essential methodological reserve of higher effectiveness of human activity in various spheres, including science and technology. The modern scientific and technological progress, its current stage in particular, differs qualitatively from the earlier modes of development of the productive forces which occurred largely as a result of spontaneously accumulated production experience, without any direct relation to basic science.

Nowadays management of the scientific and technological progress can and must employ the modern quantitative methods, objective evaluation, mathematical modelling, mathematical statistics in the analysis of the controlled processes, and the production-economic complexes.

Systems analysis contains a very important tool of studying and managing the global processes in society's development, i.e., modelling. Modelling in modern research increasingly becomes a universal means of investigating complex systems that either cannot be investigated directly by traditional tools or cannot be investigated at all. Modelling facilitates comprehension of the problem, unification of the conceptual framework, elaboration of standard research procedures and formalisation of the scientific language.

Global development modelling presupposes elaboration of a certain conceptual framework, a methodological approach to modelling global processes —ecological, economic, political—as integrated processes resulting in the change of social relations.

A valid global model for an effective analysis of alternative ways of social development may be built only on the assumption that provides for a constructive solution of the fundamental problems of today—preservation of peace and acceleration of social progress, elimination of poverty and all forms of social inequality.

Global modelling is an analytical tool of comprehensive investigation of possible global development alternatives and appropriate decision-making. It is more correct therefore to regard global modelling as designing man-machine interaction systems for the analysis of global development processes. In these systems all the non-formalised operations are performed by man, and a huge amount of routine work by computer.

An essential component of man-machine interaction systems is mathematical global development models *per se*. Their improvement and application require an in-depth analysis of such methodological problems of formalised description as principles and techniques of mathematical description and analysis of global systems; optimisation of computing techniques oriented at large-scale problems with non-linear relationships, problem identification, sensitivity analysis of output versus input, accuracy of parameter definition, multi-attribute optimisation, organisation of decision-maker/model interaction.

Evaluating the state-of-the-art in global modelling one may come to the conclusion that global modelling concentrates more on problem identification than elaboration of methods of their solution. One can assert, however, that global modelling based on the scientific theory of social development is undoubtedly becoming a valid instrument of knowledge, the application of which will lead to a more profound understanding of the specific regularities and their mechanisms in society's development. It is also going to provide an insight into a likely future situation and thereby improve the quality of planning and management decisions taken today.

Management of Scientific and Technological Progress

The above section of the report deals with the feasibility of managing the processes in society's development. The same applies to the management of the scientific and technological progress.

Since management in its most general sense is a goal-oriented influence on a certain object or process, the designing of a management system should be preceded by a clear-cut definition of goals.

Man represents the highest value and his welfare is the goal of history. With respect to man, science and technology perform an instrumental function. Therefore the major goal of managing the scientific and technological progress should be creation of favourable conditions for full satisfaction of human material and spiritual needs. This general goal encompasses sub-goals, such as:

— Facilitation of man's manual labour and harmonisations in his physical development;
— Minimisation of elementary, routine operations in the sphere of brain work;
— Improvement of the conditions of human life;
— Reduction of the working hours.

Another major goal in the management of the scientific and technological progress is minimisation of its negative implications. Management is confronted with a new important problem—that of eliminating the negative tendencies that threaten the very fundamentals of human existence.

The way to achievement of this goal will always be laden with serious problems. Many of its negative implications caused by implementation of scientific discoveries do not become evident at once. Information with respect to these implications often comes through feedback channels too late, i.e., when the changes are already irreversible.

In these conditions there should be higher standards set for the methods of forecasting. N. Wiener wrote that the retribution for errors in forecasting of technological change was bad enough already but it would increase manifold when automation gained scope.

This statement acquires even greater significance since the system of management of technological change operates under uncertainty and rules out any deterministic type of control.

One of the most important management tasks is regulating the rates of technological change. It is wrong to believe that these rates should always be maximised. They should be correlated with availability of the natural resources, the state of the ecological system and feasibility of implementing the achievements of science and technology at a given stage. In other words, the rates should be optimal.

The range of problems propounded by the scientific and technological revolution is characterised by width and variety. The conscious and purposeful management of this process requires a profound and comprehensive analysis of the current trends in technological change, formulation of a scientifically sound policy and organisational steps providing for the most favourable conditions for implementation of the scientific and technological achievements in the interests of socio-economic progress.

The scientific and technological progress in the U.S.S.R. is closely connected with the radical socio-economic changes. It is always aimed at consolidating the material and technical basis of communism, raising the people's living and cultural standards. These goals are stated in the U.S.S.R. Constitution and the Programme of the Communist Party of the Soviet Union.

From the very first days of its existence of Soviet State got down to elaborating a scientific and technological strategy. It was developed under the guidance of V.I. Lenin who attached great importance to this effort. Worthy of note is the fact that the fundamental principles underlying this policy have not undergone any major changes up to the present time. Their objective and expendient nature was confirmed by practice. These principles are:

— Orientation at socio-economic goals and consideration of the related implications of technological change;
— Concentration of effort on key issues of development;
— planned nature of the contemplated measures;
— Integrated development of science and engineering regarded as a complex interaction of the system elements "education-research-development-application-consumption";
— Evaluation of the effectiveness of scientific, technological and organisational decisions and their long-term effects in the light of entire society's interests;
— Observance of a balanced structure of R&D and industrial application, correlated with the specific historical conditions, with main accent on basic research;
— Strive for development of the country's own scientific and engineering potential, with due consideration of the international character of knowledge-producing activity, i.e., orientation at feasible and mutually-beneficial cooperation.

The implementation of the scientific-technical policy is impossible without a solid scientific basis, the creation of which has been the focal point of the Soviet State since the first years of its inception.

At present the network of R&D institutions of the U.S.S.R. is composed of 5500 establishments including 2300 research institutions and laboratories whose activity embraces practically all fields of modern science and engineering.

These organisations employ 1.3 million scientists (including the teaching staff) that account for 25 per cent of the total number of scientists in the world. Altogether more than 4 million people are involved in research and research-supporting activities. That exceeds the number of people employed by any key sector of material production.

The system of science management and planning as well as industrial implementation of R&D results in national economy has been functioning successfully. At its top level is the Supreme Soviet and the Council of Ministers of the U.S.S.R. The presidium of the U.S.S.R. Academy of Sciences determines the main directions of the basic research and estimates the expected results. The State Committee for Science and Technology coordinates and streamlines the applied research and development of new technology. The State Planning Committee does the planning with respect to industrial application of new technologies and marketing the new products.

The administrative system also encompasses several specialised bodies— among them State Committee of the U.S.S.R. for standardisation for matters of inventions and discoveries, the administrative organs of sectoral and regional branches of the Academy of Sciences, scientific councils (associations) for various sciences and disciplines, ministries and regional administrative bodies.

A tangible contribution to the accelerating of the progress of science and technology is consistent introduction in the management of science and technology of the goal-oriented approach, i.e., application of systems principles in this sphere of activity. In general terms this approach can be defined as programme-related decision-making which implies consistent decision-making and implementation across all the stages of the general cycle of investigating a complex problem: goal-setting, elaboration of a programme of action, resource and manpower allocation, assignment of personnel, evaluation of the outcome. The above said approach is employed in the process of defining the entire system of plans where five-year and annual plans are not regarded as independent directives but constitute the consecutive stages of implementation of the long-term objectives.

Goal-orientation is inherent in socialist planning as it stems from the unity of goals and objectives of economic development based on the socialist forms of ownership.

Programme planning is carried out at all stages of socialist construction. From the very start long-term plans were contemplated as programmes. The distinctive features of programme approach were most fully realised in GOELRO (plan for electrification of the country) elaborated under the guidance of V.I. Lenin. This plan may be rightly called a programme.

The elements of programme approach existed in the plans of industrialisation, technological re-equipment of the national economy ensuring economic independence of the country. They could also be observed when development of such regions as the North and the Far East was undertaken, in exploration of space, utilisation of atomic energy, etc. Greater emphasis on programmes has been put in the years of the ninth and tenth five-year plan periods in the light of decisions adopted by the twenty-fourth and twenty-fifth congresses of the Communist Party of the Soviet Union. It is a current practice now to develop integrated national economic programmes aimed at solution of major problems in the most important spheres of society's activity, including integrated furtherance of the scientific and technological progress.

The integrated programmes as a means of solving some of the major problems provide for integration of the techniques and forms of plan elaboration with the methods of managing its implementation. Programmes are looked upon as organic harmonisation of the programme target with organisational steps and management mechanisms.

Management of science and engineering is one of the widest spheres of application of the goal-oriented approach. The mechanisms of formulating various level programmes in this field have already been developed.

In the U.S.S.R. an unprecedented document has been produced—"The Integrated Programmes of Scientific-technical Progress and its Socio-economic Implications for 1976–1990", put together by highly qualified Soviet experts. It contains analysis of the most promising lines of development for science and engineering predictions of the likely implications for the next 14 years. The analysis was performed with due account of the needs of national economy and the available resources. The programme served as a basis for a ten-year plan of national economic development. It will be regularly updated.

The programme provides a basis for elaboration of integrated programmes for the development of the specialised fields of scientific and technological progress, such as the all-round mechanisation of labour, minimisation of manual labour in industry, space research, development of computer techniques, utilisation of the world ocean resources, etc. These programmes also bear a predictive and analytical character.

In this connection it is worth pointing out that lately integrated programmes for tackling specific problems of science and technology are being elaborated on a national scale. About 200 of similar programmes were included in the tenth five-year plan.

Each programme is a complex of measures relating to production, R&D and economy harmonised with respect to resources, manpower and term of completion. In aggregate form, these measures provide for the achievement of the set goals.

These integrated programmes differ basically from the coordinating plans employed earlier in that they are oriented at obtaining practical results from introduction in the national economy of the scientific and technological achievements and results of the completed R&D projects. The programme is a plan-governed directive document covering all the stages of the creative process: research, development, pilot engineering and industrial implementation of the R&D results. Worthy of note is the fact that the result-orientation does not belittle the value of the underlying basic research which is duly represented in the programmes.

Scientific guidance of basic research in the U.S.S.R., the unified scientific-technical policy of the Soviet State provide for the streamlined and effective utilisation of the scientific-technical potential of the country. The soundness of the R&D policy is confirmed by the results achieved by our science and economy. Among the universally recognised achievements are: solution of social problems, space research, nuclear power plants and other very important fields of knowledge.

One can refer in particular to the fact that in the years 1955–1975 intensive factors of development accounted for almost half the increase in the product output. In 1969–1976, 80 per cent of the increase in the national revenue resulted from higher labour productivity (43 per cent due to higher engineering level and 37 per cent to better training and skills). By 1975 (compared with 1940) the volume of industrial production had increased 17-fold.

International Cooperation in the Field of Science and Technology

Possessing a powerful scientific, technological and economic potential, and equipped with all that is necessary to solve most sophisticated problems in science and technology, the Soviet Union has been steadily pursuing a policy of developing business contacts with all the States ready for mutually beneficial cooperation. The vast experience accumulated by the U.S.S.R. confirms that the socialist planned economy is proof against the market fluctuations and thereby permits a stable long-term basis for external relations. It creates a solid foundation for the development of international scientific-technical cooperation.

The difference in ideologies and social systems between socialist and capitalist countries do not constitute any obstacle for establishing and developing their business relations in this field provided these relations are based on the principles of sovereignty, equality, non-interference in the internal affairs, and mutual benefit.

The U.S.S.R. takes an active part in any international organisations, programmes and events related to application of science and technology for the development purposes, constantly comes out with initiatives directed at creating favourable conditions for scientific, technological and economic cooperation among all countries.

The specific nature of scientific-technical interaction between the U.S.S.R. and other countries is the wide employment of intergovernmental and interdepartmental agreements, long-term programmes with clearly defined socioeconomic goals. Cooperation is effected in almost all the fields of science and technology on the basis of more than 330 agreements covering over 4300 problems and subjects.

A striking example of mutually beneficial cooperation in science and engineering is collaboration of socialist countries within the framework of the Council for Mutual Economic Assistance (CMEA). In establishing a basis for their relations, the CMEA countries acted on the assumption that integration is more effective for economies of the same level of development. It does not mean specialisation of individual countries only on the production processes and activities that are in their command at the present moment, but orientation at developing an identical and progressive economic structure. The Soviet Union has rendered substantial assistance to other economies by effecting (mainly gratis) technology transfers, manpower training (on all levels) in keeping with the requirements of modern socialist economy.

Scientific and technical cooperation between the U.S.S.R. and other

CMEA countries is effected on a multilateral and bilateral basis. The Comprehensive Program for Socialist Economic Integration for the years 1976–1980 adopted by the CMEA member-states includes 17 intersectoral comprehensive problems. The CMEA member-states jointly tackle over 3200 problems and subjects.

An impressive illustration of the effectiveness of the scientific-technical cooperation based on socialist principles is the result of the joint CMEA programme "Interkosmos" (joint space research) which gives the Czechoslovak Socialist Republic, The Polish Peoples Republic, The German Democratic Republic and other member-countries an opportunity of launching their scientists into space for research and engineering experiments and thereby joining the ranks of the cosmic States.

The economic relations based on the mutual benefit, equality, respect, sovereignty are established between the U.S.S.R. and young developing States. For the developing countries the scientific and technological progress opens up new prospects of development. It can considerably influence their status in the world economic system. There emerge new real opportunities for eliminating the gap between the levels of development of the developed and developing countries. In order to achieve that, however, one has to overcome serious difficulties connected, in particular, with the lack in the developing countries of their own scientific and technological potential. The developing countries account for a mere 4 per cent of the total expenditures (taken on a global scale) on R&D, and for 6 per cent on personnel.

In view of the above, an essential component of the cooperation between the U.S.S.R. and the developing countries is assistance rendered with the aim of strengthening the scientific and technological potential. The U.S.S.R. takes an active part in the shaping of the educational system, construction of the higher-learning establishments, and secondary schools, vocational training centres, institutes and technical schools. In cooperation with the U.S.S.R. over 170 undertakings have been and are being completed in various countries.

Besides, tens of thousands of specialists from the developing countries have been trained in the Soviet Union's educational establishments. Their training programmes take cognizance of the specific problems of the countries they come from.

The U.S.S.R. makes a tangible contribution to the economic development of these countries. Emphasis is placed on the acceleration of the ongoing process of their industrialisation. About 90 per cent of the total volume of the Soviet economic and technical assistance to the developing countries fall on the development of the material production sphere, where almost three quarters are the energetics and industry. The U.S.S.R. participates in the construction of the major industrial complexes in the key industries of the economy.

Mass technology transfers, their adjustment to the specific local conditions and applications to the national economy are a most important element of the cooperation between the U.S.S.R. and the developing countries. The construction with the Soviet assistance of a large number of key projects, results in a considerably higher level of employment of the population, increases the ranks of the working class and skilled manpower in the developing countries. For the period of cooperation between the U.S.S.R. and the developing countries about 400 thousand workers and technicians have been trained in the process of construction and operation of the complexes.

By the present time, stable and lasting scientific-technical relations have been established within the framework of intergovernmental agreements with various developing countries: Algeria, Argentina, Bolivia, Guinea, India, Columbia, Morocco, Mexico, Syria. In specialised areas of science and technology contacts are established with government agencies and research institutions of Brazil, Peru, Singapore, Sri Lanka, etc.

The U.S.S.R. has concluded intergovernmental agreements on mutually beneficial scientific, technological and economic collaboration with the majority of the developed capitalist countries as well. Under and outside these agreements Soviet government agencies conclude agreements on scientific-technical cooperation with research institutions and corporations. Naturally, the forms and methods of scientific-technical cooperation between the U.S.S.R. and other countries depend to a considerable extent on the terms and conditions offered by the partners.

The Soviet Union, its government agencies, research and public organisations are members of more than 550 international organisations, 340 of which are concerned with investigation and solution of economic, scientific and engineering problems. The U.S.S.R. takes an active part in the activities of the central and regional organs of the United Nations and its specialised agencies. Soviet scientists and specialists participate in the programmes of UNESCO, WHO, UNIDO, UNEP, WMO, etc., and exchange information in the process of such international meetings. The Soviet Union annually plays host to about 100 international congresses, conferences, symposia and seminars related to science and technology.

Science and technology are a powerful means of cognition and transformation of the world. They are capable of tackling the most sophisticated problems faced by humanity. The prerequisite of solving these problems in the conditions of the contemporary scientific and technological revolution is unification of effort on the basis of multilateral international cooperation of intergovernmental character. It corresponds with the interest of all the countries of the world, socialist and capitalist, developed and developing. Successful achievement of this goal requires first of all political consensus of all the States.

Strengthening of the international scientific-technical cooperation must become an essential factor in stepping up the socio-economic progress of the entire human society.

16. Management and Technology

Guido Brunner*

Dr. Brunner is a member of the Executive of the FDP (German Liberal Party) since 1975. Dr. Brunner has served his government in various capacities, notably in the field of foreign affairs, since 1955.

Our present theme is Management and Technology. You are managers—on all sorts of scales—or you would not be here. I am also a manager on a broad and political scale involving both technology and its impact. So let me begin with a particular definition of technology. Technology is the body of usefully applicable knowledge. As such, it belongs, in some sort, to all of us and in some sort, to those who have laboured to produce it. Indeed, the balance between these two belongings determines a whole complex of law and practice which could well be the subject of a whole congress in itself. And it is at once clear that the management of this useful knowledge that we call technology involves its acquisition, its distribution and its exploitation or application—just as with any other more conventional commodity. So that gives us already a framework for discussion.

Even though much has been written on the importance of technology, it is still quite difficult to grasp the overwhelming nature of its impact on our lives. In large areas of the world, everything has been refashioned by man using his tools and his intelligence—every tree, every crop plant (and we have seen spectacular recent changes in this country)—every beast of the field—a good many lakes and some mountains, quite aside from all that we wear, eat and use.

The effect of this has been, taken over all, to raise standards of living to an extraordinary extent, if at variable rates and in various ways at different times and places. It has, in particular, given us our modern transport and communication system. Indeed, without them we would not be gathered here.

*Presented on behalf of Dr. Brunner by Dr. Raymond K. Appleyard, Director-General, Scientific and Technical Information and Information Management Commission of the European Communities.

However, let us not forget that, with them, we are condemned to one world of fierce commercial and industrial competition, whether we like it or not. And it is this real, technological still evolving world that we have to manage between us: a world of three elements; living and natural phenomena of which the most obvious and useful are all around us—sun, wind, rain and wave (all of which interest the European Commissioner for energy); human desires, phenomena and needs; and that accumulation of technology which has made the world today what it is and with which we must shape tomorrow. Among these, I would accord place of pride to human needs—and to human understanding of human needs. To that we should dedicate our thoughts and our theme.

To the economist, the development and application of new technology is self-evidently a major source of new wealth. But, today, we must place some reserves on this bland declaration. Do those who may feel they have lost their work to machines, the "technologically dispossessed", feel the same? Or, do those whose work has become a machine-governed repetition of intolerable boredom voice the same feeling? Are the great dust bowls and deserts created by the exaggerated impact of agricultural technology a form of wealth? What of hundreds of thousands of tons of oil on once beautiful beaches? What of the dead, maimed or sick from certain pollution accidents or—in far greater numbers—from the automobile? The list is long and it is easy enough for everyone to construct his own. The lesson is short. Certainly, on balance, new technology is a—one might say *the*—great source of new wealth, *but only if it is correctly managed*—and correctly managed at every level. Nor can we, any of us, in one world, isolate ourselves from each others' triumphs and disasters: the proper management of technology is a worldwide necessity in which the public interest and the citizens have as much concern, and as much need for education as the engineer, the entrepreneur and the worker. What is involved in the management of this complex process? Let us take first the application of new knowledge. The origin of new innovation may occasionally be a need or even an accident; but the overall progress depends upon fundamental research, upon the free, enquiring intelligence which is one of the glories of the human spirit. Of this, I say to my friends and colleagues, more particularly in governments and in education: manage it well! Preserve its scale, scope and freedom, continue to nourish it with bright young minds; see that society uses well its practitioners where their youthful bloom of originality is over—and how better than by retraining them as industrial managers?—and see that we all—all parts of the globe—share in the great intellectual adventure. This last is important. Because fundamental research is, almost by definition, open and published, it is tempting to "leave it to George", to let others do it and one should benefit from the results.

This policy may occasionally seem to offer certain short-term economies and advantages. But, in the long run, it will guarantee a lack in knowledge and an absence of necessary trained minds and technologies. More so, it impoverishes fundamental research itself, for here is an area, above all, in which the interplay of radically different ways of looking at the same thing have immense value. It is no accident that some of the most remarkable developments in modern mathematics came from the combinations of Western minds with those from our host country, India.

Beyond fundamental research we have, the more or less applied, shading into development and the process of new innovation itself. Here new criteria, not directly pertinent to fundamental research, enter progressively—feasibility and utility (a word I prefer to profitability). And the overall task of technology management is clear: it is, first, to cause a hundred flowers to bloom; to be sure that all the new original findings are known, are accessible, are actively scrutinised for useability—an activity which is today being revolutionised by the computer and transport revolution, by the modern data base, by workshops and clubs of all kinds, very often international, and by the new mini journals; and one which every manager of science, technology and innovation would do well to reflect.

Because we cannot afford to do everything, the counterpart of this broad sowing of seed and encouragement of "points of departure" is, of course, a progressively critical view with progressively more severe criteria for their development stage by stage towards real products and services; and it is certainly at this stage already that the public interest must begin to take a hand, either in the criteria whether or not to go forward and in which direction, or, if the matter directly concerns the public interest, as it does in the case of health technology, by directly, intervening in tests of feasibility, tests of performance, analysis of cost and benefit.

Nor can we afford, as managers, to neglect that other fruitful source of innovation: know-how developed on the spot, in the factory or field, and leading to an improved process. Industrially, this remains a highly important branch of technological innovation and we do well, in the public area, to see that it is stimulated and rewarded. The problem, for example, of the employee's rights to inventions is very variously handled in different countries and regions.

Now, we have our new technology, we know it is feasible and what it might well cost. What about its proper application? What about its conversion, through the process of innovation, into new products, processes and services? Here too, the management problem is easier to identify and pin down than to resolve.

Some recent writers have strongly contrasted 'market pull' and 'technology push' as stimuli for innovation. Such a contrast seems to me to be wrong. Neither 'market pull' nor 'technology push' is the driving force but the marriage of the two at the hands of a suitable entrepreneur is — and this is as true for a radically new product as for a minor improvement devised by a charge-hand for an assembly line.

Innovation or technology application decisions are thus crucial, complex and difficult. They have all one further point in common: the element of risk. So, quite apart from selective orientation of innovation in the direction that the higher managerial strategy wishes to see, there is a general need for all of us to encourage and support these innovative risk takers.

Now the real risk taker or entrepreneur in an innovative application of technology may be a small new business, or a small or medium enterprise reoriented, or he may be a point of growth—at any level—within a large well-established company. Again, I submit to you that the problem is always the same and is double: first, to provide him with all the specialised services, advice and information he needs without stifling his initiative and necessary degree of independence. Second, to ensure that if his gamble comes off, he receives rewards commensurate with the risks of failure. These two principles have many ramifications: the first bears particularly upon the internal structure of large companies and upon both private and public services available to small ones; the second bears upon the taxation system and government financial policies, especially in many western countries. But employee invention laws do not fall outside it. Above all, we shall only find the necessary risk-takers, at all levels, in societies which believe in themselves and inculcate a certain spirit of adventure in the education and training of their young.

Both very large companies and, above all, governments, will wish to orient innovation and the new applications of technology along lines which correspond with their general strategies, but without trying to organise innovative decisions in detail from the top down in a way which human nature simply does not permit. We have, for example, an energy strategy in Europe and we would like to see the correct choices made among new technologies, nuclear and others, to solve our very serious problems. This kind of situation leads to a most important and difficult principle in the choice and application of technology and the question of risks and risk takers. Particularly for large-scale innovations, but to some extent at all levels, the risks and potential benefits do not fall on the same group. When this is so, whether it is the population living near a power plant or the workers in the next room, it is essential and a matter of common responsibility that the non-involved put-at-risk be consulted and heard. This needful responsibility is why I have recently held public hearings on the future benefits and risks of nuclear energy in Europe: a most rewarding exercise, I might add.

Let us turn, then, to the question of choice of technology within a general strategy. The very idea of choice implies alternatives really available and comparisons between them, itself requiring a capacity for sober analysis and judgement. Therefore, all who must choose technologies for innovation need to equip themselves or those around them with the proper capacity for analysis. And all should remember that the public and its interest may well be involved and make the necessary preparations, also sometimes educative, for this.

If you will permit another general view of things, it is far from certain that

the new technology we have adopted and applied over the last many decades
will serve us as well over the decades to come. We have concentrated upon
hardware production and often upon what I would call brute-force chemical
or mechanical methods. But we are clearly coming to the limit of these. We
have been a phase where much innovation—especially in technologically advanced countries—has been directed to the reduction of labour costs and so
has given rise to a population of technologically dispossessed as well as to a
certain resentment which does nothing to help the process of science and
adaptation as whole. Perhaps, on both grounds, we need now a new thrust,
in science, in technology, in innovation, to a gentler, more humane way that
could lead us to a more human and cultivated world. That would be my
hope. Its realisation may depend much upon what you actually do.

A word—which should be unnecessary—to all managers but specially to
those in developing countries. By marrying 'technology push' and 'market
pull' you choose a technology for a need or problem and apply it. Choose
the appropriate technology. It is not always the most glamorous—often not.
But glamour costs money: better that it be the simplest and most elegant that
will do the job. Amid supersonic jets, hovertrains, Wankel engines and the
rest, I cannot resist reminding you that the bicycle remains the most efficient
means of transport known to men.

Nor should one be in too much hurry to choose. On one side, time spent
in analysis, in comparisons, in feasibility studies, in pilot and demonstration
projects, is rarely wasted. On the other side, everything has its time. Nowhere
is this more true than in medical research, which provides first rate examples
of this particular management problem on a global or near global scale. It
has looked for years as if we were on the verge of a major breakthrough in
curing cancer. But, really, we are still in the phase of keeping many balls in
the air and of testing, unglamorously and painfully, feasibility and prospects,
before putting great resources behind any one approach. Feasibility testing is
an early step in the innovation process, and many inventions which reach that
stage still fall by the wayside later. It is also a stage in that process of technology transfer which has been responsible for many misunderstandings and is
the last subject with which I propose to deal.

Technology transfer occurs when a body of knowledge developed by one
group of persons in one place is applied by another elsewhere. It is often
taken to mean transfer of technology from advanced to developing countries.
But every manager should be aware that it also means transfer from the laboratory to the factory floor or even between enterprises or sub-enterprises—
and that the problems are not dissimilar. Nor are they less vital, for technology is only useful when correctly applied by innovation, so technology transfer is vital to our story. It will be reviewed at length later in this session, so I
shall confine myself to pointing out certain principles that underpin all three
kinds of technology transfer in all their diversity.

First, it can only occur between a willing donor and a recipient. Even the not-invented-here syndrome is enough to stop it. So is the feeling by an enterprise that it may be expropriated or made over-dependent. Why this need for willingness, not to say enthusiasm? Because we are not dealing with a mere purchase of hardware, but with a risky transfer of skills, with training men, with adapting people and conditions. That takes time and what is in reality, whatever it may be called on paper, a joint venture. I commend this notion of joint venture to all our colleagues and authorities and especially to those who, at the interface between developed and developing countries, are in a position to create conditions and machinery which facilitate them. We are developing some special machinery for this within Europe, but we should all look equally at the wider horizons.

I won't try to teach you your business, but do insist that the business—and a very serious one—of the public authorities is to get the legal framework right, be it competition and monopoly rules, patent law, codes of conduct (which are only useful if they have a positive result) or whatever.

Yesterday's technology has shaped our world. Today's will shape all our tomorrows and can bring new real wealth, real values and humanity to mankind—if we manage it right. In that connection and to reassert that humanity is paramount in these discussions, I recap a very old and wise text on management itself: men who can manage men will always manage men who can manage machines.

17. Appropriate Technology

George McRobie

Mr. McRobie is Chairman of the Intermediate Technology Development Group Ltd., London. He has been associated with the SIET, Hyderabad, during 1965-68, as a consultant. His experience in small-scale, capital-saving technologies for rural communities has been utilised by many nations.

Introduction

Today it is impossible to ignore the fact that the conventional capital and energy intensive technologies, which still form the main currency of aid and development programmes, are by no means always in harmony with the needs and aspirations of poor cauntries. This is most obvious in relation to employment.

Taking developing countries as a whole, the ILO estimate that about 40 per cent of a total workforce of some 700,000,000 are unemployed or under-employed—working at levels of activity that condemn people to poverty. More than three-quarters of the 280,000,000 in this poverty trap live in rural areas where seasonal unemployment is often extreme. This results in mass migration from the rural areas to the cities, many of which already pose insoluble social, economic and environmental problems.

Large scale, capital intensive technologies aggravate these problems. Being city centred, they are in the wrong place; the kind of goods they produce are generally of the wrong kind to meet the needs of the poor; and being capital intensive and labour saving, they cannot provide jobs on anything like the scale required (no one ever earned a living, learned new skills or became self-reliant by having his labour 'saved'). It is, of course, not only employment that is at stake; capital intensive technologies also make demands upon special types of infrastructure facilities, shape educational standards and norms, influence consumption patterns and life styles, and dictate import requirements. Technology is neither economically nor culturally neutral.

It was for these reasons that the late Dr. Schumacher argued that the choice of technologies was the most critical choice confronting any developing country.

Dr. E.F. Schumacher's advocacy of an intermediate technology that would be more appropriate to the needs and resources of poor people in poor countries is now widely familiar. Its essence is that the capital intensive, increasingly complex and costly technologies of the rich countries are generally inappropriate for the poor, and especially for rural communities. To meet *their* needs, a new technology must be discovered or devised: one that lies, so to speak, between the sickle and the combine harvester and is small, simple and cheap enough to harmonise with local human and material resources. The convictions that informed Schumacher and his supporters may be summed up as follows:

a) The source and centre of rural poverty lies primarily in the rural areas of poor countries which tend to be bypassed by aid and development as currently practised.

b) The rural areas will continue to be bypassed and unemployment, as well as the flood of migration into cities, will continue to grow unless efficient small-scale technologies are made available with assistance in their use.

c) The donor countries and agencies do not at present possess the necessary organised knowledge of adapted appropriate technologies, and communications, to be able to assist effectively in rural development on the scale required.

d) In matters of development, there is a problem of choosing the right level of technology to fit the given circumstances: in other words, there is a *choice* of technology and it cannot be assumed that the level of technology used by affluent societies is the only possible level, let alone that it is necessarily the best for poor countries.

e) The technologies most likely to be appropriate for development in conditions of poverty would be, in a sense, intermediate between, to speak symbolically, the hoe and the tractor or the *panga* and the combine harvester.

In insisting on *technological choice*, we make a clear distinction between science on the one hand, and technology on the other; between scientific knowledge and its applications. The knowledge of scientific laws, of materials and methods is, in a sense, absolute, as one could hardly talk of intermediate knowledge or intermediate science. But the *application* of the best knowledge can take many different forms and can lead to many different types of technology and modes of operation. It is here that the need for and the possibility of intelligent choice enters. Different economic and social conditions demand different applications. It is therefore a complete misunderstanding and often a wilful misrepresentation when people accuse the proponents of intermediate technology development of wishing to withhold sophisticated capital intensive, labour saving 'advanced technologies' from poor societies or of offering intermediate technology as the only mode of production to be considered. No one would deny that there are conditions in which the most sophisticated technology is the most appropriate and that there are other conditions in which an intermediate technology is the most appropriate. However, as long as an intermediate technology does not exist or is inaccessible because of lack of knowledge and communication, the people in the latter condition have no useful choice. Either they do nothing at all or they do the wrong things by trying to use an inappropriate technology and then the result is negative.

To give more concreteness to the concept of intermediate technology, we would emphasise four criteria: smallness, simplicity, capital cheapness, and non-violence. Even if it may be impossible for all four criteria to be satisfied in every case, any one of them, or any combination of them, will be of value.

These principles go against the conventional trend of technological and organisational development which is towards ever larger scale units. This is said to be justified by the economies of scale. Large scale production units, however, tend to create many sociological, ecological, and resource problems, the burden of which normally has to be carried by the community at large and does not enter into the unit's cost calculation. Even from a narrow economic point of view, large units are economical only when certain conditions are satisfied—high market density and/or highly efficient reliable low cost transport system, skill in large-scale administration, management, buying, selling, and so on. When these conditions are not satisfied, so-called economies of scale become illusory. In any case, large scale tends to act as a principle of exclusion: only people who are already rich and powerful can embark on new productive enterprises. The small man is excluded and reduced to the position of a job seeker and when there are not enough jobs provided by the rich and powerful, he has no reasonable possibility of becoming productive. Smallness is, in fact, a pre-condition for rural development and it is now becoming increasingly relevant from other points of view: social, ecological, and in terms of resources.

Much the same applies to simplicity and capital saving. It does not take great technological creativity to take a further step in the direction of complexity, capital intensity, and giantism. The suggestion to engage the best of modern knowledge and intelligence in the search for smallness, simplicity and capital saving almost invariably meets the argument in the first instance that it cannot be done, or, if it were done, it would prove to be totally uneconomic. In this matter, prejudices and untested presuppositions are very deeply posted. There is now accumulating evidence that it can be done, but it requires a more creative and original research development effort than is normally forthcoming.

The principle of non-violence refers to modes of production which respect ecological principles and strive to work with nature instead of attempting to force their way through natural systems in the conviction that unintended damage and unforeseen side-effects can always be undone by the further applications of violence. Generally, one problem is solved by creating several new ones. Poor societies cannot afford this kind of violence and it is doubtful whether the rich societies can afford it much longer.

It has become increasingly obvious that as far as employment, and especially rural employment, are concerned, the application of these principles is the only feasible course of action. If developing countries are not offered a range of choices in technology, or if they are persuaded that no such choices exist or can be created, then there is no hope for the mass of rural and urban poor; and this can be illustrated by the following example, used by Dr. Schumacher:

"According to my estimates, there is in India an immediate need for something like 50 million jobs though others put it as high as 80 million. If we agree that people cannot do productive work unless they have some capital—in the form of equipment—and also some working capital, how much can be afforded for each job? Now, if it costs £10 to establish a job, you need £500 million for 50 million jobs. If it costs £100 to establish a job, you need £5,000 million. And if it costs £5,000 per job, which is what it would cost, say, in Britain, to set up 50 million jobs, you require £250,000 million. Now, the national income of India is about £15,000 million a year, so the first question is how much can you afford for each job, and the second question is how much time do you have to do it in. Let us say you want 50 million jobs in ten years. What proportion of national income (which I identified as about £15,000 million) can one reasonably expect to be available for the establishment of this capital fund for job creation? I would say, without going into any details, you are lucky if you can make it 5 per cent. Therefore, if you have 5 per cent of £15,000 million for ten years, you have a total of £7,500 million for the establishment of jobs. If you want 50 million jobs in these ten years, you can afford to spend an average of £150 per work place, at that level of capital investment per work place, in other words, you could afford to set up 5 million work places a year. Let us assume, however, that you say: 'No, £150 is too mean. It will not buy more than a set of tools, we want £1,500 per work place.' Then you cannot have 5 million new jobs a year, but only half a million. And if you say: 'Only the best is good enough. We all want to be little Americans right away, that means £5,000 per work place', then you cannot have half a million new jobs a year, let alone 5 million, but only about 170,000. Now, you have, no doubt, noticed already that I have simplified this matter very much because in ten years with investment on jobs, you would have an increase in the national income, but I have left out the increase in the population, and I would suggest that these two factors cancel one another in their effect on my calculation."

Appropriate Technologies in Practice

There is now a growing body of literature of case studies of appropriate technologies under actual operating conditions. The following examples illustrate what has been and is being done by the way of scaling down and adapting technologies in a number of industries where the intermediate level of technology was formerly unknown or did not exist.

Construction and Building Materials

In the construction industries, recent work by the ILO has shown that intermediate technologies in road building are feasible and competitive with conventional capital intensive methods. The ILO team has been closely concerned with the excellent earth roads being constructed in Kenya under the Rural Access Roads Pragramme.

Highly efficient, small-scale brickworks have been designed and are in operation in several African countries. A typical modern brick factory in an industrialised country produces over a million bricks a week. The mini-brickworks, which is either hand operated or uses very simple machinery, produces some ten thousand bricks a day. Capital costs per work place in the small unit are about £400 as against some £40,000 in a large modern brickworks. In small units, very large saving on fuel costs are possible by air drying the bricks before firing, and local production virtually eliminates transport costs. Such brickworks established by ITDG consultants during the past few years now create employment for over a thousand people. The IT unit responsible for developing and installing mini-brickworks has also recently developed an on-site method of making fibre reinforced corrugated roofing sheets using cement and a variety of fibres. These cost an average of about one quarter of important roofing sheets.

Cement

Mini cement plants in China, where 50 per cent of the total output of 39 million tons of cement is made in small-scale vertical shaft kilns, have recently been described in some detail. The same author in *Rural Industrialisation in China* (Harvard University Press, 1977) also describes many plants in China for chemical fertiliser, farm machinery and engineering, iron and steel, and paper. A considerable amount of work has been done in India on such mini-cement plants, and the Appropriate Technology Development Association, Lucknow, is in the course of implementing a pilot commercial project for a 25-ton a day vertical shaft kiln making Portland cement. The feasibility study indicates a capital cost of about half that of the large-scale technology per unit of production capacity; lower-scale requirements for installation and much more rapid installation (about a quarter of the gestation period required for a large-scale plant); lower transport and distribution costs; lower quality of fuel required; and, in addition to the wide dispersal of small scale units in rural areas, the utilisation of small deposits of calcareous materials which otherwise remain unused.

Alternatives to cement, based on lime, brick dust, and other local raw materials have also been developed in India; this mortar is suitable for many kinds of construction required in rural areas. Development work is still proceeding, but it is already certain that this alternative to cement can be produced cheaply and in small quantities. A pilot plant is currently being erected in Tanzania.

Sugar

Mini sugar plants are already well established in India where there are some 2,500 units in a number of different States. These units produce about half a million tons of sugar out of a total national output of about $5\frac{1}{2}$ million tons. About 30 new units a year are being installed. For the same investment as is required for a modern sugar mill, it is possible to erect some fifty mini sugar plants, which produce $2\frac{1}{2}$ times the output of the large mill, and employ eleven times more people. While the mini mill is technically less efficient than the large-scale mill, its locational advantages make it an economic proposition for many entrepreneurs.

Two aspects of the mini sugar plant deserve special mention. One is that the plant is capable of being fitted into an existing mixed agricultural pattern. One such plant recently visited by the author in India filled the gap that otherwise existed between two paddy cropping seasons. The sugar mill began operation in November, a few weeks after the end of the paddy season, and continued through until May, shortly before the start of the next paddy season. The plant had virtually wiped out local seasonal unemployment, which had formerly driven many young people into the cities.

The second point relates to the identification of improvements required to bring the mini sugar plants up to the level of technical efficiency of the large plants. Work done by the PRAI in India has identified the precise points in the operation where the small mill loses out to the large, and development work is now in hand to make good these deficiencies. The mini sugar mill is a good example of the technology intermediate between the village level sugar processing and the large-scale modern mill based on a plantation economy.

Cotton Spinning

A similar gap is now being filled in cotton textiles. The textile industry is the second largest employer of labour in India after agriculture. Until about 1900, the industry was localised in villages and a few urban areas. With the advent of mechanised large-scale technology, this highly flourishing and prosperous local industry disappeared and the impact was far greater on the spinning than on weaving; so much so that by 1940, spinning in villages had virtually disappeared except for subsidised hand spinning under the Khadi Programme.

A decentralised handloom weaving industry still produces nearly 50 per cent of the total cloth of India and employs seven million people as against one million employed in large mills, but the handloom weaver has to depend entirely on yarn produced by large mills and he pays up to 30 per cent more for the same yarn as the large weaving mills use.

A programme for the decentralisation of spinning is now being implemented by the Appropriate Technology Development Association of India. Preliminary trials indicate that a 1,200 spindle capacity can be made viable in a rural area as against a 21,000 spindle minimum capacity for a large-scale mill, at a substantially lower capital cost per unit of output and with considerably greater employment. Under this programme, 12-spindle spinning frames operated either by mechanical or pedal power have been made and tested. These will be used by villagers and a central service centre will carry out supporting function, such as centralised purchasing of cotton, respinning and reweaving processes, training and development, and marketing.

Soap

The development of the soap industry in Ghana provides another example of how productivity and income can be raised through an intermediate technology. As in so many other instances, the 'law of the disappearing middle' operates in the soap industry in Ghana. The advanced technology (of Lever Bros. Ghana Ltd.) has a production capacity of about 38,000 tons a year, or about half the national demand. At the other extreme, there are hundreds of cottage industry soap boilers making soap in 50-gallon oil drums, each producing about one ton a week. The Technology Consultancy Centre of the University of Science and Technology, Kumasi, set out to demonstrate that an intermediate soap plant much simpler than the large-scale industry but far better than the cottage industry could be viable. This would enable individuals, partnerships or cooperatives to meet more of the demand that exists in the country.

Several one-ton-per-day plants were designed and have been constructed and are now operating in different parts of the country. Indigenous supplies of caustic soda were developed from the byproduct of a local factory. Experiments are going on with a view to finding alternatives to palm oil, which is in short supply in some areas.

Mini-hydro

Energy from renewable resources is now receiving widespread attention and must receive much more if the ultimate violence of nuclear power is to be avoided. Here is an example from Pakistan where in the Swat District a number of villages are now getting their power for lighting from mini-hydro units. The developments described are part of the work programme of the Appropriate Technology Development Organisation, Pakistan:

"The micro-hydel units consist of an electric generator, which is at present imported, and a water wheel which is made either of PVC or steel pipes. A 10 kilowatt generator costs the State 9,500 rupees and a PVC water wheel costs 450 rupees. The civil work, including the digging of the power channel, excavation of the power house site, and construction of the power house itself is done by the local people. In Sultanabad in Gilgit, a cooperative society has already been formed and others are in the process of formation.

The share of cost of electrification borne by the State for a 10 kilowatt installation is 9,500 rupees for the generator plus 450 to 900 rupees for the water wheel. Thus the maximum cost for a 10 kilowatt installation as borne by the

State is only about 10,000 rupees. This gives a per kilowatt installation charge of about 1,000 rupees in contrast with 35,000 rupees per kilowatt if the work is done on the basis of conventional methods which, of course, involve imports. Moreover the State has to bear huge recurring expenditures on maintenance. Under the ATDO Programme this is done by the people themselves.

An arrangement has now been made with the commercial banks that areas which require electrification, where hydroelectric potential exists, can obtain loans from the banks through cooperative societies for procuring a generator and water wheel. The installation of distribution facilities and house wiring is all done by local people through their associations or cooperative societies. The University of Engineering and Technology in Lahore has now been funded to develop 5, 10 and 50 kilowatt generators so that the import of these items can be eliminated."

The Philips pilot plant

Finally, there is the case—unique rather than representative—of the Philips pilot plant in Utrecht. The pilot plant aims to act as a centre for information and assistance for developing countries. It sees as its object the adaptation of know-how available at the company headquarters in the matter of products and production methods in such a way that:
— The required equipment and its operation will be simple wherever possible and adapted to small production series;
— The maintenance of the equipment used will be as simple as possible;
— The necessary tools and auxiliary equipment will, as far as possible, be available locally or at least it must be possible to make them from locally available materials;
— The amount of capital used will be kept as low as possible.

These requirements have, in turn, necessitated the creation of a pilot plant with facilities for development, assembly, the transfer of know-how, and for service and follow-up.

The Growth of A.T. Centres

During the past few years, there has been a rapid increase in the number of units, both in the rich and poor countries, concentrating on the various aspects of intermediate technology. A recent guide published by the Commonwealth Secretariat in London lists well over a hundred organisations which are partly or wholly working on small-scale low cost technologies, the great bulk of these being in developing countries. It should be added that almost without exception, they are of relatively recent origin, lacking in funds and resources, and, although a few enjoy some government financial support, they are mostly isolated from the mainstream of development activities within their own countries. (India is a recent exception.) But a number of them, in spite of their modest beginnings, have already developed impressive work programmes and the following examples will serve to illustrate how much can be done with relatively insignificant external support.

The *Technology Consultancy Centre* in Kumasi, Ghana, provides a link between the technical and scientific expertise of the University of Science and Technology in Kumasi and government agencies and local entrepreneurs and craftsmen. With a staff of fourteen, the TCC draws on the expertise of about thirty senior university staff and its work falls roughly into three categories:

a) *Technical and commercial advice to business and government:* This has included advice on the manufacture of gunpowder, rubber mouldings, wood and coconut charcoal, leather goods, envelopes, sugar, blackboard chalk, kaolin, shoes, tonic drinks, jams and preserves, glues, lost wax brass casting, bead making, oil palm cultivation, and weaving. It has also undertaken the chemical analysis of soap, glue, bleach, alcohol, latex fluid, cassava starch, seashells, and caustic soda.

b) *Development and testing of new products:* A pedal driven rice thrasher, baby incubator, traffic lights, pyrolitic converter to produce fuel oil and combustible gas, as well as charcoal from charcoal raw material (this in collaboration with the Georgia Institute of Technology); bullock carts, irrigation pumps, ploughs and cultivators, wood fired (and electric) soap and caustic soda plants, dryers for cassava, pepper and spent brewers' grain.

c) *Production units attached to the TCC:* A unit making steel bolts employing 15 trainees and producing 30,000 bolts for local sale in 1975–76; construction of soap and caustic soda plants, rice thrashers, bullock carts, gate hinges, replacement plough shears, saw benches, water tanks, hose, charcoal stoves; a weaving unit employing seven weavers; animal feed from dried brewers' grain using screw press and solar drying, producing two tons per week; and a soap pilot plant which produced 108,000 bars in 1975–76.

In the next five years, the TCC plans to turn increasingly to agriculture and to the rural areas, setting up two demonstration/training workshops away from the university to train local craftsmen and introduce new product, and two other offices to provide extension advice to small entrepreneurs. They plan to increase the involvement of university staff from ten to fifty per cent of staff members. Young graduates are being trained as project managers to act as links between the experts and the university and individual business and craftsmen who have sought advice.

Basic village technology is well represented by the Village Technology Unit run by UNICEF in Nairobi. This unit has a staff of three engineers along with local artisans. It concentrates on housing, sanitation, water supplies, food production and processing, and energy use. It propagates the idea of appropriate technology among national and community leaders, trains Kenyan village polytechnic instructors, and artisans from Kenya and elsewhere in the construction and use of A.T. equipment. It is also helping to set up village technology units in three other centres in Kenya. It can provide an extension service on A.T. to any project: for example, the improvement of traditional granaries in Uganda or water supply for a town in Kenya. It develops, adapts and tests equipment and does acceptance trials in villages. It exhibits over fifty items of A.T. hardware at its base in Nairobi, including a foot-vice, oil drum forge, solar steam cooker and solar water heater, charcoal cooler, improved stoves and ovens, grain storage bins, windmills, water pumps, food smoker, cement jars, hydraulic ram pumps and a sheller for groundnut and dried legumes.

Much more ambitious programmes dealing with more complex technologies have been developed in Pakistan and India. In Pakistan, the Appropriate Technology Development Organisation is a government unit within the Ministry of Finance's Planning and Development Division. The unit has in hand some forty projects in various stages ranging through research and development, field testing, social acceptance, economic evaluation and extension. Its minihydro (or micro-hydel) scheme has already been noted earlier. Other activities, where successful results have been achieved, include low-cost building, under-soil irrigation, the development of local gas plants, windmills for water supply and irrigation, utilisation of local iron ore for production of iron for locally fabricated plants, and vegetable and fruit dehydration.

The work programme of the Appropriate Technology Development Association of India covers a wide range of technologies, some highly sophisticated. A summary is given as follows:

a) Scaling Down of Large-Scale Technology
   (i) cement making
   (ii) paper making
   (iii) cotton spinning
   (iv) jute spinning and weaving
   (v) wool spinning
   (vi) chemical fertiliser manufacture
   (vii) improving the efficiency of mini sugar technology by:
       —manufacture of liquid sugar from molasses
       —plate evaporation
       —screw press for higher extraction

b) Scaling-up of Village Technologies
   (i) handloom weaving
   (ii) blacksmithing
   (iii) carpentry
   (iv) extraction of vegetable oil
   (v) village pottery, both red clay and white ware
   (vi) village tanning and shoe making
   (vii) rice milling

c) Home Living and Community Technology
   (i) village power pool
   (ii) village sewer disposal system and environmental sanitation

    (iii) village transport

    (iv) bio-gas

    (v) solar cookers

    (vi) animal husbandry

    (vii) social forestry and forest based industries

The method of approach involves four stages. The first is a survey and analytic study to establish the potential for a village industry pilot plant project. Secondly, there is the preparation and implementation of the pilot plant project. Thirdly, the diffusion of the industrial package tested in the second stage. And fourthly, the hardware development directed at improving and upgrading the technology thus established in the field. Reference has already been made to the work of the ATDO on sugar, cement and textiles.

There is also a growing number of organisations in the rich countries which aim to mobilise information on appropriate technologies, undertake field testing, and assist with the practical application of results. These include the ITDG in London, the Brace Research Institute in Canada, the TOOL Organisation in the Netherlands, VITA and the Georgia Institute of Technology in the U.S.A., and very recently Appropriate Technology International. There is thus at least a foundation of an international infrastructure for the development and promotion of appropriate technologies; and what is needed is not a control system of any kind, but a strengthening of its infrastructure.

Conclusion

But there remains an enormous gap between intention and implementation. It is agreed that there must be rural development and involvement of the whole population; it is agreed that there must be innumerable small activities all over the place instead of just a few gigantic projects in a few big cities; it is agreed that the technology must fit the actual conditions of the developing country that imports it. All this is easily granted, but how is it to be done? If most of the aid is government-to-government, how can it break down into thousands upon thousands of small activities involving millions of people? Governmental bureaucracies, no matter how efficient, can never handle more than a modest number of projects, and if the bureaucracies are enlarged to handle more they almost inevitably become unworkable. The same applies to the great international agencies, which also have to work through the governments of the developing countries.

In short, while the intentions of aid have changed and are changing, the administrative structures and methods still have to be adapted, if the existing gap between intention and implementation is to be closed. It is here that the voluntary agencies and private industry come in.

Voluntary agencies already have very large number of devoted men and women "in the field", several hundreds of thousands of them. These people are sharing the burdens of poverty with the local population; they do not claim the privileges of government emissaries or officials; they come, and they are prepared to stay many years, unlike short-term volunteers or visiting experts.

The task of the future, as we see it, is two-fold, to develop new methods of cooperation between governmental and non-governmental, voluntary agencies and private industry; and, second, by means of such cooperation or by other means, greatly to increase the effectiveness of the voluntary effort: and that is where private industry can help.

Voluntary agencies have frequently been criticised for being unbusiness-like and ineffective, more often than not by themselves. There have been insistent demands for 'stream-lining' and 'coordination'; but these things are easier said than done, and there is a real danger that coordination may mean nothing but the setting up of more committees to cause delays, strangle initiative, and kill enthusiasm. It is not surprising that the demand for coordination arouses the antagonism of field workers, who know more about the difficulties and frustrations of development work than the coordinators back home and realise how much depends on their own spontaneous devotion and initiative. All the same, the voluntary organisations are by no means deficient in the power of self-criticism, and they are looking for ways and means of improving the effectiveness of their efforts. If "coordination" is not the right answer, what is?

Instead of the idea of coordination we would propose the idea of infra-structure. In many developing countries there are literally hundreds of groups of voluntary workers working in relative isolation, each on its own small project, almost like subsistence farmers. The resources at the disposal of each of them are normally extremely limited. "It's the poor that helps the poor" true enough; but the limitation of resources does not apply merely to money; it also applies to know-how and everything else. Like subsistence farmers, the voluntary field workers are generally too much on their own, lacking an effective infrastructure of facilities. Here is a group struggling with a technical problem which others have solved long ago; owing to an almost total lack of communications, they are in complete ignorance of the solutions found elsewhere. The same mistakes are made over and over again; the same inventions have to be made over and over again; there is no cumulative process leading from strength to strength but, instead, a thousand-fold starting again from zero. In short, there is a lack of infrastructure, and just as subsistence farmers cannot help themselves effectively, no matter how hard they work, until someone creates for them an infrastructure of communication, transport, education and research, so the development work carried on by voluntary organisations needs to be given an infrastructure of facilities of an analogous kind.

Let us see what this would mean at least in rough outline. There should be a "focal point", politically and religiously neutral, to fulfil at least four functions:

1) The function of communications to enable each field worker or group

of field workers to know what other work is going on in the geographical or 'functional' territory in which they are working, so as to facilitate the direct exchange of information.

2) The function of information brokerage to assemble on a systematic basis and to disseminate relevant information on appropriate technologies for developing countries, particularly on low-cost methods relating to building, water and power, crop storage, processing, small-scale manufacturing, health services, and so forth. Here, the essence of the matter is not to try and hold all the information in one centre but to hold 'information on information' or 'know-how on know-how'.

3) The function of 'feedback', that is to say, the transmission of research problems from the field workers in developing countries to research establishments (including university departments, specialised institutions, business firms, etc.) in the advanced countries, wherever the facilities exist for these problems to be effectively dealt with.

4) The function of creating or coordinating 'substructures', that is to say, 'action groups'. Such 'action group'—some of which, as mentioned above, have already been brought into existence by ITDG—will be autonomous, voluntary groups, involving the administrative, the business, and the intellectual institutions of the developing country in question. They would aim to be in touch with all field workers operating in the country, to facilitate communications and the exchange of information. They would also be able to act as "verification centres" to test and prove new methods, materials, and equipment which, having been provided by advanced countries, appear for application but may need modification to fit specific local conditions.

We are not, of course, arguing that private industry has no direct role in the development and promotion of appropriate technologies: of course it has. But certainly experience in the U.K. is showing that big industry does not always find it easy, for technical, philosophical and administrative reasons, to involve itself directly in such work. For example, take what is happening in Britain now, where a growing number of large firms are becoming concerned about the growth of long-term unemployment in the localities where they are operating—and in many cases the firms themselves are aggravating unemployment by closing down factories or 'rationalising' people out of work. In several instances already, such firms (and others) are helping to set up 'local enterprise trusts' (or sub-structures as described above) which in turn are taking on the tasks of creating and fostering small enterprises. This is how, I believe, a growing number of large enterprises will discharge their obligations to society in the future. The four criteria of guidelines that motivate most of those who are concerned with appropriate technology—smallness, simplicity, capital saving, and non-violence and which we suggest as guidelines for new technological research and development, may not appeal to everyone. What can be said in their favour is they have arisen out of actual work, not out of theorising. Experience shows that wherever one can achieve smallness, simplicity, capital saving and non-violence, or indeed any one of these, new possibilities are created for people, singly or collectively, to help themselves. Also, the patterns that result from such technologies are more humane, more ecological, less dependent on fossil fuels, and closer to real human needs than the patterns or lifestyles created by technologies that go for giantism, complexity, capital intensity, and violence. At the very least, we in the rich countries, should be concerned to ensure that as far as possible we offer *choices* of technologies to people in developing countries so that *they* can choose which they prefer. It would be less than honest to pretend that no such choices exist or that our scientific and engineering capacity cannot devise them; the more so as a growing body of opinion in the rich countries is beginning to question whether the technological structures we have created in industry and agriculture and, therefore, our own lifestyles, are sustainable.

REFERENCES

Employment, Growth and Basic Needs, ILO, Geneva, 1976.

E.F. Schumacher. *The Problem of Unemployment in India*, address at Conference of the India Development Group, U.K., June 1971.

See, for example, the following annotated bibliographies, Marilyn Carr. *Economically Appropriate Technologies for Developing Countries*, IT Publications, London, 1976; Gareth Jenkins. *Non-Agricultural Choice of Technique*, Institute of Commonwealth Studies, Oxford, 1975; and David French. *Appropriate Technology in Social Context*, U.S.A.I.D., Washington, 1977.

See D. Lal. *Men or Machines*, ILO, Geneva, 1978; G. Irvine. *Roads & Redistribution*, ILO, Geneva 1973; M. Allal, G.A. Edmonds, A. Bhalla. *Manual for Planning of Labour Intensive Road Construction*, ILO, Geneva, 1977.

Cradley Heath. *Report on the Activities of the Building Materials Workshop*, IT Publications, London, 1978.

Jon Sigurdson. *Small Scale Cement Plants*, IT Publications, London, 1977; *Rural Industrialisation in China*, Harvard University Press, 1977.

Appropriate Technology Development Association, India. *Annual Progress Report*, Lucknow, 1978.

Unpublished report, I.T.D.G., London.

J. van den Brink and F. Menkenveld in *Appropriate Technology*, A Studium Generale Course, The Technical University of Eindhoven, 1977.

18. Management and Appropriate Technology

Y. Nayudamma

Prof. Nayudamma is Distinguished Scientist, Central Leather Research Institute, Madras. A pioneer in leather research in India, Dr. Nayudamma was earlier Director of the CLRI, Madras; Secretary to the Government of India in the Department of Science and Technology; and Director General CSIR.

Introduction

Appropriate Technology (AT) is a term that has been much used and abused. It means many things to many men. There is much controversy, confusion and conceptual chaos with "elements of religious revival and a strange mixture of Marxism, Puritanism and something called Buddhist (or Gandhian) economics" (W. Rybezynyki). For many, the important question is "will this solve our problems or not? If the answer is yes—hooray! If no—the hell with it!

Is it appropriate to ask "Is Appropriate Technology an appropriate topic for discussion by the World Management Congress?" The answer is yes. Why? The word 'appropriate' connotes choices and choices are made by management. Choices also imply there is freedom and knowledge to choose. It is important for the management to study in depth several issues in making hard technological choices.

For a country like India it is all the more appropriate because of the emphasis placed by the Government about rural development. In fact, the word 'appropriate' appears to have emanated from India in 1964 though started of as 'intermediate' by Schumacher while he was consultant to the Government of India.

An attempt is made here to define the terms; set boundary conditions for technology issues, interrelations and interactions; the factors that govern or impede choices; criteria for appropriateness and the role of management to arrive at appropriate technology.

Definitions

Several terms are used loosely clouding the definition of appropriate

168

technology. Our initial task therefore is unhappily one of definition.

Science: is to know, acquire and accumulate knowledge. To be interested in science is like falling in love for the first time. The essence of science is scientific method and a curious, critical, creative mind.

Technique: is a tool, machine, method, skill, a process for solving a problem. Technique differs from technology in that it is independent of social, political environment. Choice of techniques is different from choice of technologies.

Management: is a set of precepts and practices used in production and distribution geared to profit or efficiency and affected by societal values.

Technology: A spectrum or system covering techniques, management; both hardware and software, integrated, organised and orchestrated dictated by economic, social and cultural values. Technology chain covers supply, service and linkages, from an idea to final product, a service through extension and social technology. Technology affects and gets affected by society.

The "dimension" of technology system covers organisation (centralised or decentralised); scale of operation (small or large); factoral inputs (capital or labour intensive); intensity and efficiency of utilisation of resources (heavy and light); level (modern and traditional); science base (sophisticated or simple) and state of art (advanced, intermediate or primitive) (P. DeForest, 1978).

The 'categories' of technology system would then be high, low, intermediate, mixed, dual and alternative technologies.

Technology Issues

Technology is mankind's main enterprise: making a massive impact on our outlook, life styles, social, political and economic structures.

Technology is usingology: using knowledge to produce goods, offer services and meet the present and potential human needs. Needs differ from wants. Basic needs of people come first.

Technology increases output: A twist in technology will increase output for a given input. Financial flow should be coupled with technology flow.

Technology is specific: Resources, people, skills, culture and need specific.

Technology is problem-solving capability: Increased skills and problem-solving capability of people, make them an asset not a liability. Technology is not for making 'poor wealthy' but 'poor productive'.

Technology is for people: To catch the fish the bait must be attractive to the fish and so technology should be coupled with social technology. People differ and so do their needs, and values, and so technologies differ.

Technology needs social control: If technology is to serve people, people should be involved and should control it. People should have ability and knowledge to control and a thirst to absorb and utilise technology.

Technology is a change agent: Technology brings about changes in attitudes, values and life styles of people.

Technology is a resource: Technology has a cost, life cycle, long gestation period, involving risks, transferable, marketable and negotiable. Therefore technical literacy is crucial for bargaining, particularly when it is common knowledge that technology knowledge and use is available with only a small group of nations and TNCs that exercise cumulative hierarchical control.

Technology is indigenous and imported: Importing technology without the ability to assimilate it or generating indigenous technology without making use of what exists in the world are inefficient and expensive.

However technology import, used as a short cut allows only ready made technology applied to an existing environment (Mathias, 1977) resulting in imitative growth patterns, undesirable modes of consumerism, not based on real actual social needs, disrupts traditional knowledge, alienates workers and undermines the confidence of local innovators, bringing a culture to treat "what is rural is bad, what is urban is good and what is foreign is best." Import should be to complement and supplement indigenous competence which is essential if only to assess what to import.

Technology is a tool for development: Technology has been used and abused more and more for material gain, acquisition, consumption and consumerism. It is said "poverty is the carcass of such wealth acquisition" and underdevelopment is a consequence of disparity and domination. It is the height of obscenity for one half of world's scientific research to devise measures for the destruction of mankind.

A genuine concern for the billion poor and for the liberation of all men from want, exploitation and alienation calls for alternative development and alternative technologies. Development is development of man—his resourcefulness as his best resource and to be self-competent, and live in harmony with his environment. It is an endogenous, man-centred, need-based, self-reliant, eco-sound development.

Technology and social values: Life is worth living. Worth depends upon values and values define quality of life. "We are what we value that which we value moves us into action."

To live with a sense of values of human dignity is the greatest value. Dignity comes from self-competence, self-confidence and self-reliance. Thus self-reliance becomes a focal social value.

Technology is organically linked with human rights, justice, peace, harmony, security, disarmament, sovereignty, etc.

Technology is self-reliant: Self-reliance is a social value, a human right, a basic need and the very core of man-centred development. Self-reliant development requires self-reliant technology. Resourcefulness coupled with problem-solving capability is self-reliant technology.

Self-reliance is not autarchy or self sufficiency. It implies an in-built preference for developing indigenous technology competence; the wisdom to use knowledge; the ability to discern and autonomous decision making.

Appropriate Technology

Technology is to produce good services to meet the societal goals and needs with the given societal resource endowments including competence.

A priori, all technologies are appropriate to fulfil a need in a particular context. It 'depends' upon the place, resources, time and choices.

Appropriate choice: The word appropriate implies a choice; choice implies there are a number of choices and further the right, freedom and capacity, to collect full information, assess, discriminate and make a choice to adapt and apply it to a given social, cultural and environmental conditions in a dynamic setting.

Choice is not a simple primrose technology path. It may be multiple technology paths from traditional to sophisticated. Advanced technologies are not necessarily equated to latest technologies from advanced countries. They can be modern and labour intensive; modern and capital-intensive using imported or indigenous technologies (G. Ranis, 1978). Similarly simple technology is not necessarily old technology. Any fool can make something complicated but it makes a genius to simplify.

Choice is also not in terms of technology alternatives but more importantly in terms of product alternatives to serve the same purpose.

Product alternatives depend upon the choice of life styles which in turn depend upon social values.

The good life of 'new age' with all its affluence and material acquisition begins to look like a colossal aggregate of junk, full of stress and strain. This is reflected by the need for new technologies like transcendental meditation, organic foods, etc. This is also one of the reasons why advanced countries are talking about appropriate technologies.

Not only do values differ from society to society but values are often in conflict. The choice is thus deeply embedded in the political process. There is not much of a choice really—all decisions are basically social and political.

Cockhman and Ridgeway (1977) argue that A.T. is at best irrelevant and at worst a shield for dangerous and reactionary politics. Technology exists as a reflection of the existing social, political and economic systems.

Appropriate referents and adjectives: Appropriate can be measured only in relation to specific social, economic and cultural referents. This is reflected and categorised in the several adjectives attached to technology (van Brakel, 1978). For example:

a) Economic, political: appropriate, adequate, convenient, correct, optimum adapted, mixed, dual, pluralistic;

b) Production factors: labour intensive, low capital, capital saving, low cost intermediate, small scale, small capacity;

c) Humanistic values: rural, survival, self-help, barefoot, Third World; peoples: indigenous;

d) Seeking new: alternative, alternate, radical, liberatory, progressive;

e) Socially desirable and non-polluting: soft, clean, economic; and

f) Man-centred: self-reliant technologies.

Such an array of adjectives only go to show, different ideas of social, political life entail different technologies for their realisation. But given a number of boundary conditions and specified goals, one should be in a position to choose the correct or appropriate technology system. But what are these boundary conditions and can they be changed? What are the social goals and who sets these goals?

Criteria: Choice implies criteria. A long list of criteria have been presented by a number of workers in the field. Robin Clarke and David Dickson set out 35 criteria for soft technology alone. UN agencies and World Bank have their own set of criteria. But basically these criteria relate to techno-economic, ecological, socio-political and psycho-sociological aspects and intended mainly for developing nations. The criteria suggested are:

a) Development goals (humanistic, employment, use of local resources, skills; reduced inequalities, basic needs; quality of life, ecological, non-violent to man and nature.)

b) Resource endowments (local capabilities, water, energy natural resources, etc.)

c) Conditions of application (local and foreign markets; climate, environment, social structure, traditions, cultural background, system approach).

Factors influencing choice (Fouad, 1978) are:
— To produce a product, choices among techniques at several steps are available and exercised;
— Output:

a) Quality: inexpensive plastic sandals require capital and science based industry while expensive leather will do with labour intensive methods.

b) Scale of operation, size of market: It is large-scale enterprise that calls for capital intensive production techniques rather than modern technology requiring large scale enterprise. In fact, modern technology actually increases the small producers' competitiveness.

c) Product mix: we may select labour intensive products; not labour intensive methods;
— Economic efficiency, profitability and factor prices: A substantial degree of substitutability between capital and labour is indicated;
— Adaption to local conditions;
— Direct and indirect employment;
— Total social cost analysis putting technology decisions into a context of social values;
— Market demand and supply.

In free enterprise, A.T. is viewed simply as the technology that would be chosen in an idealised market and if inappropriate technology exists, it must be because of some imperfections in the markets due to monopoly, oligopoly or political intervention (Harvey Brooks, 1978). The function is to maximise profits on the principle of standing up to the emery wheel of competition, in the framework of equal opportunity. In reality we live in an unequal world with unequal opportunities. The present emphasis is shifting from a private profit maximisation to social development optimum, e.g., basic needs etc.

Factors impeding appropriate choice: Communication gap; lack of technology information and ability to assess and bargain; existence of monopolies; restrictions on markets; factor price distortions; going in for prestige projects; national and international development policies, and programmes, etc.

Do criteria differ? For example:

Developing (LDCs) and advanced countries: If the present day technologies are blamed for the imbalances in the world, will the countries that have advanced through such technologies abandon them?

The technology reference frame for advanced countries is based on the facts that: (1) labour is scarce, (2) population has its basic needs fulfilled and so the consumption can only be stimulated by sophistication, rapid obsolescence and variety, irrespective of their social value; complex and expensive goods despite wastage of resources, (3) highly competitive economy, (4) the defence needs, and (5) free enterprise and profit motive (Herrera, 1977).

The reference frame for developing countries is very different and hence the criteria would vary.

Technology that is good for the rich may not be appropriate for the poor. This applies for people within the country (the elite and the masses) or for rich and poor countries.

Public and private enterprise: The private enterprise is expected to work for profit and the public enterprise is to pursue socially responsible, maximising the use of resources and development of local potentialities. Personal profit versus social good is the criteria, for private or public enterprise.

Rural and urban: Technology appropriateness loses its rationale unless it is oriented to rural needs as most people live in rural areas in LDCs. The rural poor: artisan, small land holder, landless poor, seasonal labourer, share cropper are untouched by modern technology—agro-forest-animal based industries techniques that reduce drudgery, increase returns; improved tools; weaving in modern methods into traditional tapestry is the crying need. That rural technology is low or intermediate technology is highly inacceptable. We need sophisticated technology to survey national resources, or to reach the masses, or for educational satellite, or for even building a simple wind mill.

Big versus small: Here is a clear case of what is utterly inappropriate when people talk about small is beautiful and big is beastly or ugly. Centralised management and decentralised production could be big and small at the same time.

In short, appropriateness 'depends'. However it is the bungling of not appreciating what is appropriate that leads to the misery of many people.

A.T. is basically Technology Assessment + Social Choice (NSF—Integrative Design Associates, 1976).

Put it in another way, A.T. is technology with common sense and a grasp of fitness for the task (Lovins, 1978). However, common sense is not that common and neither is appropriateness.

The emphasis really is on human capacity the capacity to ask the right question. Asking the right question is the best protection against being given the wrong answer.

The right question is—what does one want? A.T. will then mean the technology best adapted to get us where we want to go.

New Sciences and Alternative Technologies

The way science and technology has been generated and used, has only led to increased disparities, wants, production explosion, pollution and depletion of resources. The new quest for new science arises from the new awareness that man's inner needs and social values are as great as his outer requirements and acceptance of the fact, the world is evolving towards a plurality of civilisations, to meet different societal values; needing new sciences and alternative technologies, as the old ones are inadequate.

Why do we have new mathematics? Why not have new sciences? Instead of science for science's sake—why not if only to an extent "science for the sake of societal values?" This results in alternative technologies.

Alternative technology is a concept, not a dogma. It is not intermediate, appropriate, rural, scale down or small technology.

Alternative technology (Nayudamma, 1978) is at the heart of the development process—to mitigate man's misery; to remove or reduce poverty; to provide gainful employment to raise productivity and production of man, making him an asset and not a liability; to meet his basic needs; to improve quality of life and to make him self-reliant. Alternative technology is to mobilise and optimise the use of natural and human resources; to liberate people from the drudgery of degrading and heavy work. Such a technology should suit the local resources, skills, culture and needs of the people with less capital, energy, pollution and less centralisation and more labour-intensive and decentralised agro-forest-animal and their waste based industries. It may require little skills or modification of existing skills; improving traditional skills and tools; weaving modern technology into traditional tapestry and using sophisticated technology wherever required. Such an alternative technology is a new technology —a new basket woven with low and high, traditional and modern technologies and is relevant to local resources and people's needs and priorities.

Several industries like footwear, leather goods, paper, oil and other agro-industries could be run by centralised management and decentralised production utilising a blend of modern tools and traditional skills.

In such a system, the technologies and technologists will be more readily utilised within the country. This would further mean less brain-drain and less import of technology. Further the traditional skilled workers could be brought into the mainstream, increasing total productivity and gainful employment.

For such technologies, self-help is the foundation; indigenous technology, competence; local problem-solving capability; and resourcefulness of man and his enterprising attitudes are essential ingredients. This becomes clear when you ask yourself: Why does a Punjabi prosper no matter where he is?

Management's Role

From this account the role of management becomes clear. The management must first recognise the significance of the terms 'appropriate and technology'; societal goals and technology needs.

The management should have an appreciation of technology indicators and social indicators and relationship between the two, to arrive at appropriate technology. Such an appreciation would help to give specific weightage and identify appropriate technologies for heavy/light, large/small, rural/urban centralised/decentralised and for meeting basic needs of the poor.

To utilise existing technology knowledge or to create new or alternative technologies, the management should have adequate indigenous technical literacy and competence to search for, collect, assess and select appropriate or alternative technologies, alternative sources (natural and foreign); unpackaging technology package; adaption and diffusion of technologies; ability to negotiate; technology assessment and forecasting and develop indigenous technologies.

In India industry exists in large, medium, small, tiny and cottage traditional and modern sectors. The needs, demands, and technology absorbing capacity at these different levels differ. How to weave in modern technology into traditional tapestry to increase productivity, to reduce drudgery and to provide gainful employment, require close study by the management. Certain industries are amenable for development in small scale sector, e.g., subcontracting 'farming out' or 'assembly' or 'science and skill based' industry—the management should provide technology backing, quality control, design and development and other components to make them succeed.

The job of the management is to study the systems and sub-systems of technology flow from the generator to the user. Training programmes for changing attitudes, values, scientific temper, motivations in the direction of technology effectiveness, entrepreneurship and productive efficiency would help.

It is the job of the management to help the decision makers in defining the technology goals, needs, policies and setting up appropriate institutions; structures and linkages for technology generation, acquisition, adaption, transfer and utilisation of technology. Management is to see that rational choices are made from out of several techno-economic options and not at the advice of an astrologer.

If technology is for people, the demand for it must be created and nurtured. Management should strive for technology consumerism raising the technology absorbing capacity of people, releasing their resourcefulness and entrepreneurial attitudes.

Conclusion

Appropriate technology is essentially technology assessment coupled with social choice.

For assessment and making a choice, knowledge and competence are needed. It is not only choice among existing products, processes and techniques but also search for new products and alternative technologies. The choice is a social, political choice. The emphasis is on human capacity to ask the right questions, to select and manage the most suitable mix, to maximisation of societal goals, given the societal resource endowments.

19. Management and Technology

Raymond K. Appleyard

Dr. Appleyard is Director-General of the Scientific and Technical Information and Information Management of European Communities, Belgium. A biophysicist of international repute, Dr. Appleyard specialises in Molecular Biology, and has several publications to his credit.

I take technology to be those results of science and research which are useable in the economic sense. Thus research results may pass into or out of the category of technology by change in the environment of economic pressures, interests and markets without themselves necessarily being different or changed.

So, looked at from this economic point of view, there are just two problems for any country or enterprise: to acquire the technology it needs in the correct quality and quantity; and to use it effectively.

Of course, these two processes are inextricably linked, but I believe there are three comments that should be made on their relationship:

— The first is that useability must dominate acquisition (which is never cheap in real cost);
— The second is that improved products, processes and services are the criteria of success;
— The third is that the whole must conform to the overall strategy, whether for a country, a ministry or a firm: it is not so different.

It is all very different from pure science, which is in many respects the mother of everything, but which must be left free to follow its own insatiable curiosity and is universal and universally available. We are not, alas, discussing here the glories of the human spirit but the realities of an economic world.

Let us be clear from the start of our discussion that the acquisition and use of a new technology is and will always be complex, expensive, and risky, and that, particularly at the stage of putting it to work and converting it to new products and services by the process of innovation.

Governments and public authorities act upon the process in two very different ways:

177

— By direct specific support of individual *projects* or *funds* (and the two are themselves very different);

— By so-called non-specific horizontal measures—those which determine the environment within which decisions about technological innovation are taken: taxes, patent laws and the like.

I shall not say very much about technological projects in government. Outside wartime or military affairs, they are subject to well-known difficulties, some or all of which apply in most parts of the world. For example, it is extremely difficult to carry out project work and work designed to be tightly cost-beneficial or profitable with government staff under most statutes for those currently in use. It is also difficult to contract out, to judge contractants, to follow them up; and the choice of a contractant for a big job makes one friend and many enemies.

Needed, in fact, is a hard-nosed hard-fisted outfit hidebound by no rules, not to be blinded by technical excuses; the usual solution is the para-governmental agency and may be this is the best that can be done. But this amounts to no more than creating a new enterprise in the public sector and it needs watching.

Let me, therefore, concentrate upon the horizontal measures which are of considerable interest, for they all hinge around the question, what makes people tick?

The first and most obvious way to attract technology and turn it into profitable and useful innovations is certainly to have a prosperous, expanding economy. This sounds trivial; and certainly it is easier advice to give than to carry out. But it is important that it be said, for it is 80 per cent of the battle; and the precise difficulty which many of the advanced industrial countries face in innovation is that of having economies which, for the moment are stagnant, combined with a social conscience which determines them not to let a part of their people become poorer. No room is left to reward adequately the successful taker of risks, that is the innovating entrepreneur. So perhaps that is why some developing countries appear to the visiting European to be choc-a-bloc with innovators.

Within the general economic possibilities, what does the process of technological innovation comprise?

First, availability of the technology in the form of invention.

Second, a need or market to which it can be usefully or profitably applied.

Third, resources in men, money, and so on to transform the technology into a productive process and mount the production.

Fourth, an individual or a group of persons capable of taking the decision to exploit the invention and of following this decision through. I call this the entrepreneur, whether it is within a small private company, a big multinational or a government. Government actions and practices affect all these stages of innovation.

Let us look first at the supply of technology. Most of it—most new useable inventions come from deliberate organised research and development in governmental or industrial laboratories; but not all! Some of it is improved know-how found on the factory floor; and both the government and enterprises can, and do, act to stimulate this by systems of rewards whether legally imposed or not.

Industrial research should and usually does have the advantage, of being closely integrated with the strategy of the eventual producer, but faces the problem of "spin-off" inventions. It poses a nice problem to governments, of how to encourage it along the lines they would like to see in their respective countries without weakening the direct links to eventual production. The obvious general method, almost universally applied, is to consider that R&D is a legitimate expenditure for deduction before profit: it is indeed a direct investment in the future. Within this general view, practices differ widely, particularly as regards capital expenditure on R&D as distinct from running costs. Some countries (notably, I believe, India and Sweden) offer further encouragement by allowing a write-off of more than 100 per cent—say 130 per cent—of R&D expenditures.

Depending on tax rates and profits, this makes a useful extra subsidy, but my impression is that it does not do very much really to alter the amount of R&D decided and carried out. Note that it does not help the newborn company or one which is not making a profit to be detaxed.

Governmental research and development *per se* is never so integrated. It usually relates to a perceived need, but not that of a producer. So there is almost invariably a real problem of setting it into exploitation, because a further partner is needed. The number of devices employed to do this is legion. The government may contract out the R&D to an eventual producer. It may set up its own organisation to screen the inventions available and act as middleman (with or without substantial financial resources) to bring them to exploitation. It will, in any case, usually open its technology to industrialists for exploitation under licence; and the conditions for such licence are a permanent source of controversy: industry likes—or would like—exclusive licences and feels that, if these are not available, it is unreasonable to put in the money and effort to go into production. Government is restricted by political doctrines about monopoly, and by the need to treat all firms fairly and alike and prefers non-exclusive licensing.

Practice is variable: the argument will continue a long time.

Even within private companies, the problem of optimising their R&D activities and meshing them closely with other elements of company strategy is a far from trivial management problem. If it is not faced, much R&D effort may be wasted. Some useful new approaches do exist here: there is one large European company which is prepared to allocate quite a reasonable internal budget, say 10,000 dollars, to anybody within certain of its divisions who has an idea for R&D that would be useful and is able to interest a member of the R&D staff in carrying it out.

This is direct linkage of R&D to its market: or direct market pull rather than technology push with a vengeance.

A second approach to such stimulation is an indirect one, by the offer of prizes or awards. This is generally cheaper than supporting the development of technology directly: it promotes competition and can focus much effort on selected targets. Examples of this kind of approach are the Queen's Awards in the United Kingdom and certain awards for energy conservation in France; but others abound.

Certainly, one of the most powerful environmental influences upon the development of technology and upon inventivity is that of the patent law and its application. Specialists write volumes on this, so you cannot expect it to be treated in depth in one brief paragraph. Yet the situation merits close attention:

— On the one side, it is a vast, world-wide system, heavy and slow to change;
— On the other side, some parts of the world use other, if partially equivalent systems;
— Reforms and developments exist or are in the air: for example, in Europe we have created the European patent and licence office, which much simplifies the simultaneous taking out of patents in several countries of this region. This will doubtless be followed before long by the European Community patent, which will in effect unify patent law in the nine countries of the EEC and modify, not just the taking out of patents, but their legal effect.

What I would urge is that all concerned remember the fundamental basis of the patent: it is a sort of contract between society and the inventor whereby society concedes to the inventor an exclusivity in the use of his invention for sufficiently long periods (another controversial point) to ensure rewards by exploitation, in return for public disclosure in detail of the invention. It is a fair bargain. If it is tampered with seriously, so that inventive R&D does not have and is not seen to have its rights and rewards clearly, legally and stably established, one of two things will happen. Either invention and industrial R&D will just dry up, or its results will be held as secret know-how by those who acquire them, so giving rise to much wasteful duplication of scarce and skilled effort and much restricting and reducing useful exploitations and innovations. In the advanced technological area we are today seeing a concrete and widespread example of trouble of this kind. Computer software is, in general, not protectable by patent, because it is a form of writing. So it is subject to copyright rather than patent law. But copyright fails to protect it, because trivial changes can always be made without essential alteration in a programme; and this already gives rise, in some countries, to the effects I have described.

For many years, the focus of discussion in the patent world has been the exclusive legal rights conferred. Recently, we have seen the beginnings of a swing back to recognition of the remarkable importance and utility of patents as a source of current technological information. No enterprise and no government interested in technology should neglect this or the virtues of having enough people trained in making use of it.

New technology may come, as I have described, from within a firm or within a country. Even within a firm the difficulties of transforming it into new production are enormous: psychological, departmental and financial barriers abound. This is one meaning of the phrase "technology transfer". The other meaning is transfer between countries and between cultures. All countries export and import technology, but its importation is particularly important as a source for late developing countries. Although the whole subject is dealt with in another session of our congress, it requires a word here on government responsibility in the matter. You cannot legislate or compel this process into being. You cannot even do that much directly by intergovernmental agreement because most of the inventions are not in the hands of government. Indeed, ultimately, the research-maker/inventor is about the least compellable man in the world. Nor can you just, for the most part, buy it. Successful technology transfer is a continuing joint operation by the donor and the receiver on which both must work hard, into which both must put substantial resources. Therefore both must see an advantage in the operation —as in any other reasonable contractual arrangement. What governments can do, is to make agreements and arrangements which foster and protect under international or intergovernmental law and authority, those joint ventures which are the necessary and primary vehicle for technology transfer. We in Europe are a potential technology exporter (we import it, too) and I should very much hope that in future negotiations and discussions, for example in those leading to a renewal of the Lome Convention, adequate thought would be given to the creation of joint legal frameworks and umbrellas to facilitate and protect joint ventures and projects and the corresponding structures.

If the technology is there, and the need or market visible, the next thing needed by the innovator is resources in men and in money. Governments have some responsibility in respect of both, although more particularly in respect of the supply of trained manpower. True, many of the needed skills are and must be acquired or adapted on the job. But industry can only do its best with the raw material presented to it; and this means schooling, encouragement, standards at all sorts of ways and in all sorts of levels. I will limit myself here to two or three points only.

The problem is universal: if late developing countries do not, as yet, have enough skills to go round, industrially advanced countries often turn out to have the wrong pool of them. Perhaps that is why, against a background of very high unemployment, you cannot in Europe get or keep a computer analyst or programmer for love or money: well, certainly not for money.

Basic skills acquired in the schooling years last a lifetime—provided they are broadly drawn. Highly specialised ones don't, at the present rate of technological change. Perhaps, then, we are tackling it wrong: perhaps what we need is to inculcate in people a basic skill for adaptation and change—and let them take the most specialised aptitudes one after another all life long by continuous life-time education just as much as by full-time schooling.

Next, the whole business of new invention, new technology, and its exploitation depends on a few crazy people. They are not really crazy—just crazy, nice or enthusiastic. But they must exist. And this propensity to take risks—in a good cause—and to throw the whole of oneself into a project, has deep natural and educational roots. I don't want to pursue that line of thought further: but it is one which educationalists of many regions and cultures should be asked to ponder.

Money supply for technological innovation usually means the capital to get going and to cover the initial running costs and losses. But it is often not realised how long it takes, not just to bring something new into production but into the market and to the stage of profit in the sense of net positive cash flow: eight to ten years for a new drug: almost 30 years for the nuclear reactor industry.

So we have here the classical combination of long-delayed potential gains and high, including technological risks, in a world in which capital in all countries is short, because of a general pressure of expectations—and even conscience—upon resources for consumption. This situation is complicated further by management practice. It is as true for branch banks as for senior executives in big multinationals, as for officials in many branches of many governments that they are usually in office for three, five or seven years. In the public sectors, budgets are always tight; in the private sectors, profit centres are largely judged on quantitative financial criteria. So why take risks and incur outgoings for the reward of the successor (if it works) or his criticisms (if it fails). In short, our excellent management practice of moving people around at intervals shorter than exploitation times carries a built-in disadvantage for the allocation of resources to technological innovation. And please believe me when I say I am not suggesting that the lifetime-security bureaucrat—is the ideal solution: I am one myself !

All this suggests that, even where central government has considerable responsibility for innovation (or the central company board)—special arrangements need to be made to favour innovative projects with their particular features or risks.

Two or three features of the contemporary scene devolve from this: one is the "new venture group" or similar approach of the large company, which helps *inter alia*, to avoid new internal enterprises becoming snarled up between established department competences. Another is the rise of so-called venture capital companies, usually sponsored by banks and deliberately engaged in high-risk investment. A third, which is beginning to be explored, is the control (via detaxation) of the reinvestment of company profits.

It is often argued that the most direct and immediate influence of public authorities upon technological development is through their purchases and their great—often preponderant—purchasing power. But when one examines this argument closely, it is not so simple. The argument really derives from military experience. But the military side of life is quite unique:

— Defence was probably the first and remains one of the overwhelmingly important responsibilities of government; and where government is the great purchaser;
— It has always depended for its success upon technological advance or at least up-to-dateness, ever since orders went out to spare Archimedes at the fall of Syracuse or Hannibal found that the Indian elephant was better than the African—and long before that;
— It is the classic area where dependence upon others is unacceptable and the domestic technology must be pushed as an integral part of the defence effort.

In other areas, the picture is less clear, and the job of the government purchaser must in principle be to obtain the best goods or services for the least expenditure of the public funds. If he accepts this principle, how can he go out and purchase new, untried, initially expensive innovation? If he abandons the basic principle, upon what does he stand? We have here a delicate and difficult management problem which has, I think, only been solved so far through special and limited schemes, such as that of the United Kingdom, for purchase of a limited initial production of a new product as a deliberate instrument for fostering industrial innovation, not connected with government purchasing in its ordinary daily functions.

A major problem for technology users—indeed for all industrial innovators—is adequate information:

— What is the state of the technology?
— What are the technological alternatives?
— Who holds them?
— How tested and tried is the proposed device?
— What are the existing products on the market, what do they cost, who provides them?
— What markets exist for the new invention and where?
— What are the pertinent regulations, at home and abroad? (And so on and so forth.)

Where does the entrepreneur—be he public official or private company—go for all this information and more in the few days sometimes available before a decision on a technological innovation is needed? Human nature being what it is, the nearest and easiest source often predominates, but is not nearly so often the best or most reliable: at least one should try to make comparisons with what the travelling salesman claims!

Fortunately, a substantial technological advance in the world is changing entirely the handling of information: I mean the systematically collected and arranged bank of data held in the computer and often accessible by direct dialogue, the so-called on-line mode. We are only near the beginning of this development and already the industrialist who can easily and quickly interrogate the big and the specialised data banks relative to his problem has an immense advantage over the one who cannot. Yet this form of interrogation, because computer-held data bases come in all styles and all languages—both natural and machine, remains a task for trained and specialised personnel which the small, new or developing company certainly cannot afford. There is therefore a role to be played in all countries by industrial advisory and information services which can be based, as far as acquiring factual information is concerned, upon rather small units.

We are conducting a considerable effort in the European Communities towards the liberalisation and facilitation of this trade—for information is a commodity—within Western Europe, notably through our Euronet data transmission network; and we are glad to share our experience and cooperate closely with anyone else interested.

So much for preliminary factual information. But it isn't really much use to you without evaluating it. Indeed, without some evaluation and interpretation, one can easily drown in a morass of information without acquiring any real knowledge at all; and this distinction, made notably by Mr. Piganol, is of great importance. Available objective consultant expertise is the key here, and all public authorities have a very serious responsibility to do more about it in the technological area. God knows, they all do more than enough in the relatively dismal area of economics!

Their need ranges from highly expert state-of-the-art reviews written so that the industrialist or non-expert technologist can understand them to the availability of dollar-a-year men on tap to give advice.

We need some imagination in this area—and not just from technological innovators but from organisers in the public service.

A great deal of the world's useable technology resides today or passes through the hands of large companies—and it makes no difference to my argument whether these are private or state-owned. Quite aside from the exploitation of the technology they have developed under licence—whether because it does not suit their strategy to exploit it by their own production or for other reasons—there is considerable technological exchange between them and their subcontractors who are often smaller companies with a narrower technological base, and often, especially among their suppliers, potential or actual technological innovators. Much technology can pass in this way from large to small, even if it is only through the establishment of standards and norms to be met or surpassed, and this makes it of some importance to have a clear doctrine in the matter on the part of public authorities and the established rules of law.

All in all, technology and its exploitation, innovation, the creation of new products and services is as complex as human nature itself on which it closely depends. Government or public authority has many opportunities to influence both its scale and its direction.

But above all, if I may draw one single lesson from this whole complicated and interlocking web of factors, it is the need for public policy to be consistent: consistent in time, consistent between policies, and for governments to establish satisfactory machinery to that effect.

20. Public Policies on Technology

B.J. Shahaney

Brigadier Shahaney (Retd.) is Secretary to the Government of India, in charge of Technical Development in the Ministry of Industry. A tele-communication engineer by training, Brig. Shahaney has been closely associated with the advancement of the management movement in India for a long period.

The substantial contribution of technology as an instrument for accelerating economic development, social justice and self-reliance is by now well recognised. In this direction, India has moved a long way in the establishment of an industrial and technological base during the last three decades of planned development.

In the early stages of our development, it was inevitable that we should have inducted a substantial dose of foreign technical know-how in various disciplines—material, product, project and system—to the extent of even import of complete projects and systems on a turnkey basis through package transfers. With the increasing output of technical manpower in the country, the process of depackaging of technological composite got accelerated, assisted by a parallel and concurrent growth of infrastructure in the shape of R&D institutions, design and engineering consultancy organisations, specialised firms in civil constructions—erection and commissioning, technical training institutions and related organisational framework. This has resulted in considerable development of technological capability and potential in the country in design, engineering, manufacture, fabrication, erection and commissioning of industrial projects and systems. A vivid example of this capability is the many advanced industrial plants being built almost entirely with local inputs at prices which compare favourably with those in developed countries, the stimulation of indigenous inputs and innovations, the export from the country of complete sugar plants, cement plants, coke ovens, thermal power stations and a number of other products. The direction of technology is no longer unidirectional, the country has started exporting it as is evidenced by

186

over hundred joint ventures operated by Indian entrepreneurs in countries abroad. In areas like metallurgy and mining, oil drilling and exploration, petro-chemicals and fertilisers, the gaps in capability are getting narrowed. The most spectacular national achievements in nuclear, space and complex defence fields, owe in no small measure to the development of industrial technology and research in the country.

In historical perspective, notwithstanding the considerable progress made, the technological growth in the country over the last 30 years has had its measure of problems, and distortions owing to the limitations of as yet undeveloped domestic demand, operations in sheltered market situations and other cognate factors. Stemming out of these and other considerations, there have been problems pertaining to modernisation, industrial productivity and stagnation of technologies in certain sectors. Many of our plants are 15 to 20 years old, if not more. Also there have been through the earlier induction of technology and multiplicity of standards, proliferations of designs and consequential problems of maintenance and spare parts. Ahead of us lies a more different and difficult phase with its unique challenges and opportunities in developing capabilities for new products based not only on our experiences of the last 30 years, both in science and technology and in industry, but also keeping in view our national objectives and priorities.

Learning from the lessons of the past, it would be fair to state that the competence and industrial potential already generated will now permit the country to diagnose and trouble-shoot the basic technological problems and to avoid mistakes of the past through a coordinated and proper technological approach. We have been attempting, of late, a critical review of technological development, its status in important sectors and technological requirements—guidelines for development and acquisition of relevant technology, adaptation of technology to maximise the use of indigenous inputs like equipment, raw materials and human resources, horizontal transfer of technology including its spread effect in development of ancillary and small-scale units, science and technology infrastructure including coordination with national planning and linkages at macro and micro levels, the role of design and consultancy organisations, standards, documentation and information services, monitoring and other allied matters. This has thrown up a number of issues of both policy and planning. I would like to make a brief reference to a few important concepts and issues that have come up in this appraisal, the new policy direction and the new tasks that face the country and the management.

The first lesson to be learnt is, I think, that without viable R&D capability of its own, a developing country is ill-fitted to know what technologies developed exist elsewhere or to evaluate and make selection for import, much less to absorb and adapt it after import. A strong infrastructure of R&D activity and technological capability is thus necessary even to be an intelligent buyer of technology from elsewhere. Our National Committee on Science and Technology is currently engaged in an attempt at analysing these problems and in evolving a framework of policies and programmes of R&D for meeting socio-economic objectives in the Indian context. Also there can be no substitute to close involvement of user industries, R&D, design and consultancy organisations, academic institutions, etc., right from the initial stage of the country's technological effort.

Keeping in view the well-developed technological infrastructure, Government's policies lay stress on full scope being given to the development of indigenous technology and the development of industries in India based on indigenous technology as far as possible. It is, however, essential that development of technology within the country is responsive to the objectives of efficient production of increasing quantities of goods that society urgently needs and operations in the competitive market situations. This concept of technological self-reliance does not, however, mean self-sufficiency. Indeed, no country in the world can be self-sufficient. Rediscovering knowledge or technology that exists already can be a costly and time-consuming process. Also, time and again, we find that in a particular product, a single large company is well established because of its lead in technology and a strong manufacturing and marketing base. Generation of effective competition by a suitable Indian party is retarded in some situations because foreign collaboration is not permitted due to indigenous technology being available. While on purely technical grounds the technology developed in the country may be suitable but for a variety of reasons, which are not merely technical, it has been found that in practice new firms do not come up. The result is not only that the country faces scarcity of the product in question accompanied by a rise in prices but simultaneously the privileged position of the existing company is strengthened and seller's market situation perpetuated. We have therefore to bear in mind that at a given point of time and in a given field, there is a trade-off between possession of indigenous technology and rapid economic development. However, where foreign collaboration is so permitted, there could be a cut-off point thereafter to enable indigenous technology to take over depending upon its suitability. Obviously, the medicine prescribed should not kill the patient but is to be decided on merits as a treatment for development of judicious competition which, in turn, will have other beneficial spin-off effects in technological and quality upgradation, productivity improvements, price stability and in "looking-up" to the customer instead of the customer knocking at the doors of the industry.

Similarly, in some cases of large sized projects involving systems oriented technology with wide variety of unit processes/operations involved in the total activity, the Government has permitted on merits back-up services being obtained from suitable consultancy organisation abroad through a prime consultant in the country for execution of projects with desired efficiencies and yields and other efficiency parameters.

What is, however, important is that even where technology is imported for a variety of reasons, it is necessary that we keep pace with the indigenous effort and in assimilation and absorption of technologies imported. A number of such technologies have been absorbed and even in some cases exported, but there is still scope for generating necessary software in organisations and in companies and systemisation of doing things incorporating the means of assimilating technologies.

In such a picture, one would find a variety of situations ranging from cases where technologies should be imported or adapted considerably domestically with the aim of strengthening national economic and technological capacity. The machinery of transfer and the criteria for selection and development may differ from one case to another and hence the need to recognise that transfer of technology has naturally different aspects and different forms. In this, however, we have to appreciate a number of important points. Firstly, in our concepts of technology upgradation or induction of newer technology in a number of areas, the technological options to be worthwhile would have to consider other interrelated and interacting areas and their possible upgradation, to ensure an effective blending and operation of the system as a whole. Secondly, technology which is directly relevant to the needs of industrial development, is best generated as close to the production process as possible and the best motivation for this is operations in a competitive market situation. We will have also to bear in mind that industrial research is not merely a matter of research in or by the industry. This has to be carried out in a framework involving considerable linkages and overheads of a technological nature. This includes not only production and marketing, but also information and documentation servicing, standards and standardisation, specialised testing, human and presentational aspects for optimum equipment-operator interaction, etc.

In our reviews, a number of federations and industry associations, distinguished representatives from abroad and the units in the industry from time to time have made suggestions on matters relating to foreign investment, export obligation, royalty payments, periods of foreign collaboration agreements, easing of controls and procedures, etc. Managers trained and brought up to believe that efficiency is the major goal have often voiced their feelings that completion of the procedure becomes more important than completing the task. I agree that procedural formalities and bureaucratic delays must be reduced to the absolute essential. This, you will also agree, includes companies as well. In this direction, certain streamlining of procedures has already been effected and emphasis given to time-targeted disposal of applications within the framework of policy guidelines. More can and should be done. It must not be forgotten, however, that from the very beginning and until recently, planning in India was faced with a constraint in the form of foreign exchange and balance of payment problems. It is to the credit of managements that in some areas a number of companies relied on research, design and development to develop products based on materials available in the country which otherwise would not have seen the light of day. It is possible that it is through Government policies on import substitution and self-reliance that the Indian engineering and chemical industries, for example, have grown to the level and broadened as they have. The scene some years back reflected large companies being found to dominate markets for consumer items and other not so priority items with reliance on trade and brand names for capturing the domestic market. The policy lays stress on quality rather than on brand names and larger companies to enter more sophis- ticated areas.

In the Industrial Policy Statement announced in December, 1977, Govern- ment has clarified its policy regarding participation of foreign investment in India's industrial development and the acquisition of technology necessary for India's industrial development which could be allowed only in such areas which are determined by the Government of India to be of national interest. To guide entrepreneurs, Government issues an illustrative list of industries where foreign collaboration, financial or technical, is ordinarily not consider- ed necessary. For all approved foreign investments, there will be complete freedom in remittances of profits, royalties, dividends as well as repatriation of capital subject, of course, to rules and regulations common for all. As a rule, majority interests in promotion and effective control should be in Indian hands though Government may make exceptions in highly export-oriented and or in sophisticated technology areas.

In regard to export obligations and duration of agreements, in the past it was quite common to impose export obligations on projects involving foreign collaboration to ensure a foreign exchange balance of payments. This policy has now undergone a major change. Export obligations are now imposed where the industry is being permitted mainly for export production or, in appropriate cases, for testing the competitiveness and quality of products. The argument advanced for longer duration of agreements is that collaboration is akin to a "marriage" and it should not end in a "divorce" all too soon or in all cases, keeping in view that technology is on the move all the time. This and other matters are currently under the examination of the Government although there are examples where the Government has, on merits, already permitted a number of agreements for longer duration or have extended agreements which have been in use for over 15 years. On the other hand, the industry would have to lay rightful emphasis on the twin package of appropriateness of technology and their preparedness as recipient.

The tasks ahead have acquired new dimensions with increasing emphasis on self-reliance in developing the production of goods on the basis of capital saving production, the social priorities and other economic dictates. These will be technical know-how requirements for maximising use of raw material re- sources and setting up of resource-based industries which provide value addi- tion, fight pollution, conserve material and energy, improve agricultural and industrial productivity and improve social welfare. In some of these areas, we would have to further reinforce our indigenous technological capabilities by placing renewed emphasis on the development of industrial technology and research within the country through adequate allocation of resources and coordination of actions based on forecast of technologies. In fact, a number of studies exist giving detailed diagnosis of technological status of various industries, the gaps that exist and requirements of innovation both in the short and long term.

At micro levels we find that odds are often loaded against indigenous technology for a variety of reasons, some valid and some stemming out of apprehensions that technology is not proven. Yet, there are a number of industries where indigenous technology has proved its mettle as also there are some specific cases where foreign collaborations have not given the desired benefits. What is perhaps more important is the management and managerial attitudes. You have also to bear in mind that production planners abroad used to manufacturing say at least 500 tractors a day, are somewhat at bay if only 500 tractors are to be made in a month. This requires massive exercises in process replanning and re-tooling. Certainly, for competitive prices and assured quality a large volume of production becomes necessary in some sectors. The demand pattern in the country in the context of social and economic growth will undergo a change thereby generating larger purchasing power and demand in the country. Industry has a role to play in this. However, it should be remembered that relevance in the Indian context may simultaneously call for establishment of mini-sized units—be they steel, cement or paper—to exploit the limited material resources and consumption in some parts of the country, to use wastes/scrap and to generate better employment.

Another important key challenge area, in my opinion, is the need to increasingly develop within the companies, software capability in design and in providing technology and other support to assist in decentralised operations. Government has permitted import of designs and drawings as well as other facilities under various schemes like the Technology Development Fund Scheme. Whereas, there are some fine examples of units making use of such facilities and having generated the requisite technological capability in their companies, yet there is considerable scope for this capability to be developed further. The technology gap between the parent firms and sub-contractors in the ancillary and small-scale unit would require to be narrowed through technological and other assistance extended by the former. This is of particular significance with the small-scale units playing an important role in the economy.

Lastly, I would like to stress the need for further increasing the technology awareness in our managers and the requirement of training and re-training of managers and supervisors for obsolescence in people can be more costly than obsolescence and equipment or technology.

To conclude, we have before us a number of perspectives for economic growth and human welfare. In moulding the shape and prosperity of our operations in the future years the role of technology as a stimulant has added emphasis including necessary interactions with environment in the attainment of our social and other objectives. The goals, philosophies and systems of management would further require to be reoriented in this direction.

21. Management of Research and Development

T. Thomas

Mr. Thomas is Chairman of Hindustan Lever Ltd., since 1973. A chemical engineer by training, Mr. Thomas is a past President of the Bombay Chamber of Commerce and Industry, and is presently a member of the General Committee. He is also a member of the Managing Committee of the Associated Chambers of Commerce and Industry and a member of the Indian National Committee of the International Chamber of Commerce.

Introduction

Management of R&D, like the management of any other activity, is to some extent dependent on environmental factors. My observations are primarily based on experience of managing R&D in India; but I trust that they will have relevance in several other countries, especially those which are similarly placed as India.

This paper deals with R&D on a national or organisational scale and some of the views expressed here may not apply to R&D work by individuals or very small groups.

I have divided this discussion into three parts:

1) The importance of management in R&D.
2) Basic principles of managing R&D.
3) Some suggestions regarding management of R&D in India.

IMPORTANCE OF MANAGEMENT IN R&D

R&D resources, like all other resources of a nation or a business, can with advantage be subject to some principles of management. However, R&D has two distinct characteristics which make it difficult to manage. Firstly, in spite of all modern methods, it involves a certain measure of sheer faith in ideas and people involved. This places limitations on the degree to which it can be managed. Secondly, it usually calls for some tolerance of creative individualism which cannot always be subjected to the normal principles of management. Because of these two reasons, there is often a temptation for nations and business organisations to let the R&D activity go unmanaged. Ironically, the danger of this happening is greater if the R&D activity initially produces some spectacular achievement. Thereafter, it considers itself above normal disciplines and develops a tendency to become more like a prima donna and the community around it becomes increasingly reluctant even to suggest any form of management for fear of upsetting the prima donna. Even organisations which are otherwise very well managed tend to fall into this trap occasionally. Yet, it is very important that the R&D activity, despite its unique nature, is managed like any other resource of an organisation for the following reasons:

1) Whether it is a country or an individual business, its long term ability to keep pace with others and, more so, to overtake others will depend on its innovative skills. And the single largest source of innovation is R&D. Therefore, managing the R&D resource is as crucial to success as managing finances or human beings.

2) In the modern world, R&D is more of a team effort than the effort of brilliant individuals. Where people work together, the need for, and the benefits of, applying principles of management become more real.

3) R&D is becoming more sophisticated and therefore more expensive as years go by. This again makes it important to subject it to the principles of management; otherwise it can become a serious liability.

4) As the main resource in R&D is people, the result of an unmanaged group effort can be aimless demoralisation and setback. Demoralised and non-achieving R&D is, in my opinion, worse than having no R&D because the former has a debilitating influence on the whole organisation. Management of R&D is necessary to avoid this danger.

The comparative lack of achievement in R&D in a country like India is, at least partly, due to the lack of applying some of the principles of management which are described hereafter.

PRINCIPLES OF MANAGING R&D

1) Linkage to the User versus Scientific Freedom

Innovation is very often the response to a demand from an actual or potential user. Furthermore, any innovation becomes useful only to the extent to which the user accepts it and finds it worthwhile. Therefore, one of the first principles of managing R&D is to ensure that there is a strong linkage to the user.

Such a linkage to the user will provide for clearer objectives for R&D which is very essential. Otherwise it is possible that at the end of considerable R&D work the result may not be what the user needed. Scientists tend to get carried away sometimes by a series of mirages of ideas and could get lost.

Equally well the resources for R&D has to come from some user ultimately.

If there is a linkage to the user, it is more likely that the resources will be provided on a continuing and even increasing scale, if the R&D is found to be useful.

A major reason for the non-achievement of a lot of R&D work is due to isolation from the user.

On the other hand, one has to be careful how the linkage with the user operates in practice. Very often, the user is not a scientist and has a much shorter time horizon in mind. He may not be able to see all potentialities of a piece of work or all the problems associated with it. If he is allowed to bull-doze the scientists, very soon the R&D work will become devoid of its 'R' part and develop itself into mere short-term developmental or application work.

Therefore, one of the crucial and delicate aspects of managing R&D is to strike a judicious balance between linkage with the user and maintenance of scientific freedom.

A practical method of doing this is to involve the user in the planning and the progress review of R&D work, but in the actual administration of R&D. The scientists will prepare long term plans as well as proposals for R&D projects to be undertaken which, in their view, will further the interests of the user. As part of this planning, they should spell out: (a) the objective of each project, (b) the estimated resource requirement, (c) the expected benefits quantified, (d) the estimated time required for completion, and (e) the probability of success.

The plan can then be studied by the user and can form the basis of discussion between the scientists and the user. As a result of this discussion, which is usually a process of mutual education, an agreed R&D programme can be evolved. Once such a programme is agreed, the scientist is committed to the targets and the user is committed to support the programme.

Along with the programme, a system of review will also be agreed upon. The frequency of review will depend on the nature of the work. It can be quarterly, half-yearly or annual, but the dangers of too frequent review are to be avoided because scientific work can be disturbed by too frequent review by non-scientists. Of course, internal review procedures in the R&D set-up itself, as described later, should be instituted to prevent the other danger of too much time interval between external reviews.

2) Basic Work versus Project Work

In my experience, another delicate balance which has to be achieved and maintained in R&D work is that between what may be termed as 'Basic Work' and 'Project Work'. Basic work is meant to extend the frontiers of scientific knowledge in any given field, e.g., (a) the behaviour of particles in suspension, or (b) identification of trace chemicals in a mass. Project work would be to apply existing or new basic scientific knowledge in a user situation, e.g., to use the basic work mentioned above in the prevention of redeposition of soil particles on fabrics during the washing process, or the removal of trace chemicals which are identified in the basic work.

For the good scientist, basic work is more interesting and satisfying. It also establishes and sustains his credentials among the scientific community. Therefore, there will be a natural tendency especially among good scientists to concentrate on basic work, and perhaps, even look with disdain at applied project work. On the other hand, until basic work is utilised at least partly in project work, which will have some interest for the user of R&D, the sustenance and support of R&D could become less certain. Furthermore it is only through such applications for the benefit of the user that R&D will gain acceptability and esteem among the wider community in any organisation.

But there is also the danger that when applications of R&D produce results and that part of R&D therefore gets glamourised by wider sections in an organisation, the management of R&D is tempted to swing the pendulum too far in favour of applied research. This will probably yield results in the short term. But it cannot be sustained for long periods because, in the longer term, all R&D has to have its moorings in basic work which cannot be easily borrowed. It is the basic work which produces the understanding and extension of knowledge. Even as we apply the knowledge, it gets dated and more knowledge has to be created.

Therefore, within any sizeable R&D group, there has to be a special effort by the management to stimulate and maintain a balance between basic work and applied work. Any attempt to apply a 'stop-go' system to either part of R&D work will only retard progress. The exact proportions of basic and applied work will depend on: (a) scientific capabilities and facilities available, (b) possibility of borrowing basic or applied work, and (c) size of resources and commitment of the user. Those who are responsible for management of R&D have to encourage the user to recognise the need for basic work and at the same time enable the scientists to extend basic work into applied projects without losing the flair for basic work.

3) Management of the Scientists

As in all creative functions, the most important resource in R&D is the scientist. Therefore, a very important part of the management of R&D is an understanding management of the scientist himself. In this connection I would like to make the following observations:

a) Training and development of research scientists

This is an aspect to which very little attention is normally paid probably because no one can train a scientist except another scientist, and as they tend to be individualistic there is no attempt to recognise the need for formal training. However, R&D management can recognise certain principles with regard to the development of the scientist.

i) There is need to recognise that after obtaining a doctorate it takes a few more years for a person to acquire the skills of a research scientist. One has to provide the time and facility for the young scientist to practise his research skills for a period of two or three years before one should expect any significant results from his work. However, during this period he should be provided guidance and pacing by other scientists who are more experienced in R&D.

ii) It is necessary that the scientist is given some scope for the free run of his own creative inclinations, however much these may differ from the objectives of the user of R&D. One way of providing this freedom is to allow a small portion (say 10–15 per cent) of the total R&D budget to be spent on projects chosen by the scientists as their own interests which may not necessarily coincide with the perceived interests of the user. The very existence of such a provision, even if it is not fully utilised by the scientists, gives them a sense of freedom which is very crucial in the sustenance of their creativity.

iii) It is necessary for the longer term development of the scientist that he is exposed to new challenges. There is always the danger that after working in a relatively narrow field for several years, some scientists could become stale. Those in charge of managing scientists have to watch out for symptoms of such staleness—e.g., declaration in generation of ideas, reluctance to try new avenues, etc. As the staleness begins to show, it may be necessary to provide a fresh set of challenges by assigning new projects or shifting the interest from applied to basic work or vice versa.

iv) An important element in the training and development of scientists is to provide opportunities for individuals to present their findings to scientific peers periodically, for attracting comments and suggestions. Interdisciplinary seminars of this type help the scientist to clarify his own thinking and can also provide the necessary correctives as well as confidence to further his work.

Finally, there is the need for scientists to pace themselves within their own R&D group, as well as outside. Development of scientists requires their having to discuss, compare and compete with scientists outside their own organisations. It also means international pacing because there can be similar or related pieces of R&D going on simultaneously in different parts of the world. One of the major drawbacks of Indian national scientific effort has been the minimal importance given to flow of scientists to and from this country. Those who go out seem to prefer to stay out and we do not encourage any one else to come in either. This has not benefited the development of our scientists who largely tend to remain in what has increasingly become a 'semi-closed' scientific society for science which we have built up in India.

b) Organising scientists for R&D

Successfully scientific research calls for a combination of skills for the scientist. He has to be creative and generate ideas. He has to be entrepreneurial and take certain risks. He has to manage specific project on which he is engaged in terms of planning resource needs and the programme of work, and then reviewing the progress. He has to be a sponsor of his own work and seek and gain acceptance for his work. He has to be an antenna and collect all the information and data relevant to his specific work.

Each of these functions calls for different typical characteristics. The creative scientist has to be technically strong with a flair for the unconventional. The entrepreneurial scientist has to be aggressive with a broad vision. The project-manager scientist has to be well organised and sensitive to people and plans. The sponsor scientist seeking acceptance has to be mature and less aggressive. The antennal scientist has to be a communicative and friendly person who likes to attend seminars and conventions.

Now it is unlikely that we would find all these characteristics in the full or required measure in any one scientist. Therefore we should seek to identify the strengths of individual scientists in these different aspects and bring them together in teams so that different members of the team will bring in these characteristics, and thereby create an effective team. Fortunately, most R&D work today is teamwork and therefore it is possible for those in charge of managing R&D to try and create such teams rather than pay no attention to match functional needs against individual characteristics.

Apart from the internal organisation of the R&D team as discussed above, there is also a need to organise the linkage between the R&D team and the user. It is useful to designate certain individual senior scientists as the contact for specified users so that over a period of time a client relationship is built up without disturbing the internal structure of the R&D activity. While the R&D activity is organised according to scientific disciplines such as chemistry, physics, biology, etc., the user groups may be organised into business groups with diverse commercial interest. The reconciliation of these two organisations is best achieved through a matrix management of the type mentioned here. If a formal arrangement is not provided for this, the communications and relationships between the clients' group and the R&D groups could become confused and less effective.

c) *Ageing of scientists and maintenance of prime*

Unlike in many other professions, with notable exceptions, there seems to be a problem of premature ageing of scientists. They have a period of initial development, then some hesitant starts, followed by a period of blooming into creativity. This stage may occur in the thirties or forties in most cases. But it will be unwise for those who manage science to expect that this period of commendable creativity will continue to be at a peak till the scientist retires. At some stage or other, it will begin to taper off. This could be due to the physical ageing of the scientist himself. It could be due to pressures of a growing family and the consequent vicissitudes, especially in a country like India, where financial rewards are extremely meagre and therefore economic insecurity is a nagging problem which becomes more acute as one gets older. This economic frustration is even greater for Indian scientists because most of them have had some international exposure and have a fair idea of their own value in the international job market. Furthermore, many of them find that they cannot give their children the kind of education which they themselves received a generation ago, because unwisely our economic system has kept down the resources of employed professionals, whilst traders and others can enjoy unlimited incomes.

Even in other circumstances, most scientists do pass their peak performance and start on a decline at some stage. It is very important that those who manage R&D should recognise this as a problem and realign the functions of the scientist in such a way that there is an increasing proportion of non-creative functions in his total responsibility. In fact, it is perhaps at this stage that a scientist can best be shifted to management of R&D as distinct from actual R&D. There are also some scientists who are entrepreneurial and communicative, who can be given opportunities to migrate into technical development or even commercial functions.

The most important considerations to be kept in view are that: (a) the individual scientists is not allowed to go into a steeply declining phase because it can have a demoralising effect not only on him but on others around him, and (b) in any given group of R&D scientists, there should be no accumulation of scientists who have passed their prime. This danger exists especially where a larger number of scientists started at the same time as the R&D lab started. They could all age together and become a collection of aged scientists. The problem is made more acute in a country like India where there are very few alternative outlets for such people. Therefore, those who manage R&D have to be specially vigilant to ensure that there is a flow out of the group that actually carries out R&D and there is a constant flow in of younger scientists so that the group continues to be stimulated and will never pass the prime.

4) Accountability

A crucial component of any management system is accountability for results. In spite of all its unique characteristics and in some ways because of them, it is necessary and possible to have a system of accountability among scientists.

The Project Planning system described earlier provides for accountability through review with the user of progress against agreed targets of achievement, resource allocation and time horizons. This can indeed be a very effective instrument of control.

In addition it is possible to institute an overall cost-benefit analysis of R&D in an organisation on a quantified financial basis. As the establishment of R&D and the actual utilisation of its results will take some years, perhaps such a cost-benefit analysis should be instituted only after the initial five years of an R&D establishment. But thereafter, it can be a regular annual feature.

One of the practical ways of quantifying the benefits is to place a value on each new product or process developed by R&D. For example, in the case of new processes and products a credit of 4 per cent of sales value can be taken for 14 years (which is normal life of a patent in India) and in the case of cost saving arising from R&D, the credit of the actual cost savings may be taken for three years.

If the benefits on the above basis exceed the costs by a significant margin, the R&D is producing an acceptable result. In this calculation the other benefits of having an R&D group within an organisation are excluded because without the basic justification in terms of cost-benefit, the other benefits by themselves could be misleading and sometimes imaginary.

Many scientists are initially inclined to look upon such a system of accountability through cost-benefit analysis to be too much of an infringement on their freedom. However, fortunately this assessment can be done for the group as a whole without disturbing the individuals or sub-groups. Once the analysis is available and suitable action is taken to achieve an acceptable cost-benefit ratio, thereafter the scientists themselves begin to see in this system the merit of expressing their contribution to the organisation in terms which are more easily communicated and understood by the rest of the organisation. This gives them more confidence in their own work and to demand more resources from the users.

5) Upgrading of other Functions in the Organisation

For the successful operation of R&D within an organisation it is necessary to ensure that other functions within the organisation are upgraded and geared to utilise the fruits of R&D and also to stimulate R&D with new problems and challenges. In a business organisation for instance, it is essential to ensure that R&D finds a sufficiently competent and sophisticated delivery system on the technical side of the business (i.e., production and maintenance). Equally well it is necessary to upgrade marketing skills to be capable of increasing with the R&D as well as technological skills. There are organisations where R&D is either isolated from or well ahead of the other sides of the business. It is frustrating for R&D and wasteful for the organisation not to correct this imbalance. It is often the responsibility of those who manage R&D to bring about a gradual upliftment of skills in other parts of the organisation—and this has to be done without causing offence.

6) Long Range Direction

Unlike many other activities within an organisation, R&D has a longer time horizon. Therefore there is greater need to plan for the longer term with regard to the direction as well as the provision of resources for R&D. Again, unlike some other activities, R&D is a constantly evolving activity. New disciplines and new knowledge keep extending the scope of R&D. In some ways, having an R&D unit can be like riding a tiger unless one has clear long term directions, because in the short term it is very difficult to get off or to change course dramatically without doing a great deal of damage to the whole R&D structure.

It is useful therefore, to have a long range plan evolved for R&D by a group consisting of senior operating executives in the organisation as well as those who manage R&D. Such a plan is useful also to assess the resources both in terms of scientists and capital equipment required for the future growth of R&D. Like all other activities we cannot expect R&D remain static. It has either to grow or to decline. And it is better to let it grow according to a plan rather than by chance. Hence the importance of long term direction and planning.

SOME SUGGESTIONS FOR REVITALISING INDIAN R&D

Expenditure on R&D and related activities in India has risen steadily from about Rs. 29 crores in 1958–59 to Rs. 344 crores in 1974–75. This is a twelve-fold increase in 16 years. As a percentage of GNP, the increase has been from 0.23 per cent to 0.54 per cent in this period. Of this expenditure, only 10 per cent is incurred in the private sector and 90 per cent is accounted for by Central and State government.

There are about 1,20,000 persons engaged in R&D establishments in India. Of these, only 10,000 are in private sector, with the remaining 1,10,000 engaged in R&D establishments of the government.

Now let us see what we as a country have to show by way of results. It is difficult to assess precisely the impact of R&D on a national scale. But some measure of this can be provided by: (a) the number of patents taken by Indian R&D workers, and (b) the value of production from processes licensed by NRDC which is the licensing agent for all government sector R&D labs. It should be clearly noted that this does not include or reflect the achievements in the fields of agriculture, defence, sciences, etc. These indices will measure mainly industrial applications. Even so, it can provide an indication of achievement. During the period 1959–74, out of a total number of 54,000 patents taken in India, only 6,800 were in the name of Indians. Out of a total of 28,000 patents which were in force in 1974, only 3,000 were in the name of Indians and the remaining 25,000 were taken by foreign nationals. Furthermore, the number of applications for patents made every year by Indians as well as foreigners has actually gone down from 4,500 in 1959 to 3,400 in 1974. Thus, in terms of patents, progress has been disappointing.

The value of goods produced on the basis of processes licensed by NRDC is estimated to be a meagre Rs. 18 crores in 1974–75.

It is evident, therefore, that while the expenditure of resources for R&D has been steadily growing in India, there has been no commensurate growth in benefits. And I submit that one of the major causes for this non-achievement on a national scale is the lack of management of R&D in the government sector. The following steps may improve the situation:

1) Selective R&D

It would be far better for our country to concentrate our R&D resources in selected major areas of national importance than to dissipate available resources on a large number of items. Even the management of national R&D is made unwieldy by the large number of directions in which R&D has been taken. As a result, sometimes vital areas are neglected.

The highest national priorities are perhaps to be assigned for R&D on population control and for agriculture, especially in items like pulses and oil seed. It will be of great advantage to devote massive resources to a few areas of this type. Concentration of resources in selected areas will be more productive than effort thinly spread over many areas.

This may involve scaling down some of the existing R&D which has been unproductive. This should be done on a planned basis by retraining the scientists wherever possible or moving them away into other productive activities.

2) Linkage with the User

The greatest weakness of R&D in India is the lack of linkage with the user in most of the government sector R&D. This has to be corrected urgently, and I would recommend the following method:

Each national laboratory should be told that over the next five years the finding of their R&D budget will increasingly have to come from clients in industry or other agencies. In the first year 20 per cent of the budget should come from these sources and gradually over the five years this percentage should increase to say 60 per cent of their budget. Only 40 per cent of their budget will then be funded by Government. This would be for conducting basic research and to carry out R&D for which there may be no immediate customers.

The above arrangement will provide a challenge to those responsible for managing the R&D to produce results. Equally well, the R&D scientists will also derive much greater satisfaction as their work will be related, at least in some measure, to the needs of clients who are willing to finance the work.

On the other hand, the users who finance the R&D projects will involve themselves more closely with R&D and facilitate the actual utilisation of R&D findings for which they are paying.

This arrangement would require that each R&D establishment should enjoy a certain degree of independence and should be freed from bureaucratic controls and political interferences.

3) Private Sector and R&D

In the countries where R&D has made the greatest contributions to the welfare of its population, some of the best R&D is done in the private sector. Unfortunately in India, this very effective medium for sponsoring R&D has been largely immobilised as evidenced by the fact that only 10 per cent of the R&D in the country is accounted for by private sector. The major reasons are:

a) Growth and profitability of private sector companies are constantly questioned and criticised by a vocal and influential section of politicians. As a result, although Indian private companies are very small compared to their international counterparts, they are deprived of achieving the levels of size and profitability that can support substantive R&D over long periods.

b) Even when an Indian private sector company evolves a process or product through its own R&D, there is no assurance at all that the company can get an industrial licence or clearance under various other enactments like Monopolies & Restrictive Trade Practices Act and Foreign Exchange Regulation Act, to take up a manufacturing venture based on its R&D.

As a result there is no incentive for Indian companies to do basic R&D. It is essential that our laws and regulations are suitably modified to remove these impediments so that the private sector can play a more positive role in exploiting R&D in a more substantive manner and thereby reduce our dependence either on imported technology or on obsolete processes which make us less competitive in world markets. It will stimulate the search for growth through excellence in industry and lift it from the present somewhat retarded (by international standards) state.

4) Humility to Borrow and Adapt

Perhaps as a reaction to the colonial domination to which we were subjected for centuries, we have developed almost an obsession for self-sufficiency which we tend to equate with independence. Whilst such self-sufficiency in items like essential food articles, defence, etc., is necessary, it is against our interests to seek self-sufficiency in science and technology. Some of the most prosperous and independent countries are the most interdependent. One of the ingredients of Japan's success has been its ability to accept that other countries were ahead of it in technology and that it would happily buy it, assimilate it, build on it and even try to resell it. In India we have been placing too much emphasis for too long on rediscovering the wheel. Science has no national frontiers and those who put up frontiers will only shut out something. The stage has been reached when Indian capabilities can afford to open the doors to the inflow of science and technology from abroad. This requires a measure of humility and confidence especially at the highest level of both politicians and scientists.

5) International Contacts

Because of our foreign exchange stringency in the past, Indian scientists have very limited opportunities for going abroad to spend any time in laboratories there. Nor are our laboratories able to invite and remunerate any foreign scientist to come and work here for any period. Such international stimulation is vital in R&D.

What is even more disturbing is the fact that unlike in the '50s and '60s when a large number of Indians went to R&D works, especially to the U.S.A., and returned to pursue an R&D career in India, today the number is dwindling. Firstly, Indians can no longer get such generous terms for working in the U.S. universities as they used to. Secondly, a diminishing proportion of those who are able to go to advanced countries seems to be coming back, because the disparities both in rewards and R&D facilities have widened considerably over the years. Thus, we are losing the infusion of international R&D which used to take place through our own people as well.

Whether we like it or not, most of the R&D and technology in western countries (which are well ahead of the Eastern Block in this respect) are developed by large private sector corporations which have the resources and the management to conduct successful R&D. As a part of our country's general apathy to such large enterprises, this source of R&D flow into India is also diminishing.

In my opinion, there is a need to realise this gradual conversion of India into a closed society as far as R&D is concerned and to reverse this trend. If we do not reverse the current trend, the consequences will be serious in the next decade or two when we will become increasingly dependent on import of technology, which is often obsolete and will at the same time be nurturing a non-achieving bureaucracy-ridden public sector R&D. Now we have enough foreign exchange resources, as well as scientific reserves to encourage greater international contacts in R&D and technology.

Conclusion

R&D, whether on the national scale or at the organisational level, can, with advantage, be subject to the principles of management. However, it involves taking into account certain specific characteristics of science and scientists who are to be managed. This paper has described some principles that may be adopted and has attempted to make some suggestions as to how some of these may be applied on a national scale in India where R&D is, in some ways, at a historic cross-road between becoming a springboard or continuing to be largely bureaucratically dampened.

22. Management of Research and Development

A. Hamilton

Mr. Hamilton is Regional Director (Far East) of the Dunlop Overseas Group since 1975 and a Director of Dunlop International Ltd. He joined Dunlop in 1951 in the Finance Division and later became Finance Director, Japan. In 1965, he became Managing Director of Dunlop, New Zealand. From 1968, he was Planning Executive concerned with strategic planning group, and was appointed General Purchasing Manager of Dunlop's Materials Supply Division. His managerial experience of over 25 years covers finance, corporate management, purchasing and research and development.

Introduction

There are at least three sure ways of losing money; women, gambling and R&D; of these, women are the most pleasant, R&D the most certain.

More sober reflections, however, suggest that without activities aimed at technical change business will decay and eventually die. My own company, Dunlop, without technical change, would still be manufacturing only a rather inadequate cycle tyre.

Accepting therefore, that industry needs some R&D effort, this paper will seek to suggest how resources might be allocated to R&D and within the R&D activity. I will also discuss ways of monitoring R&D performance against its cost.

But first, a definition of R&D. Research covers all activity aimed at advancing the threshold of knowledge while Development is the process that converts new ideas into commercial success. In a manufacturing business, therefore, R&D includes everything except expenditure on process control and technical service.

Allocation of Resources to R&D

1) The amount of money that a business should allocate to R&D is debatable. There are complex accounting calculations that seek to relate expenditure to the life cycle of a product but although R&D is about ensuring

the continuity of a business, such calculations contain too many pitfalls to be very helpful.

2) It will be of more practical use to ask how much a business can afford to spend. This approach should enable you to fix broad lower and upper limits to R&D expenditure. The lower limit could be set by arguing that little meaningful R&D could be accomplished with fewer than four people employed in this activity. In the U.K., the overall cost of employing four people would be about £40,000 or 2 per cent of the turnover of a business with annual sales of £2 million. Probably therefore, businesses with sales below £2 million could not afford its own R&D department. (Bear in mind however, that it is possible to contract out specific R&D work and this *could* be within the financial capability of a very small business.)

Determining the upper limit will depend on a number of factors. Firstly, perhaps, is the overall strategy of the company which will set the pace and direction of business. Secondly, you must consider the type of industry you are in and whether this is one that is subject to rapid technical change. In the U.K., industries such as aerospace, electronics and telecommunications are in a period of very rapid development and the rate of their R&D expenditure reflects this.

EXHIBIT 1

R&D Expenditure in the U.K. as Percentage of Turnover (1968)

	%
Aerospace	21
Electronics and telecommunications	12
Industrial engines	6
Pharmaceuticals and toiletries	5
Instrument engineering	3
Plastics	3
Machine tools	2.5
All manufacturing	1.8
Textiles, clothing, leather and footwear	0.4
Food, drink and tobacco	0.3

You will see that at the bottom end of the scale some activities attract only very low levels of R&D expenditure in relation to turnover, e.g., textiles, clothing, food and drink.

A further guide to what you should spend is to have regard to what your competitors are doing—do not assume they have got it right but do not ignore what they are doing either.

In the final analysis, of course, you can only budget to spend what you can afford and if you cannot afford to keep up with technical change in your industry and with what competitors are actually spending in terms of hard cash (not just a percentage on sales), your company may not survive.

3) I might just digress at this point to draw your attention to questions of scale.

One often reads these days that bigness (in business) is not always best and indeed there has been some substantial criticism of big businesses in general and of the multinational company in particular. One of the advantages of bigness, of course, is that the big business can afford to allocate large sums of cash to R&D. The company itself, of course, gains but so do the rest of us, by the sale of know-how through licensing, etc. And in this way, technology is transferred from big companies to small ones at a price they can afford and from developed countries and developing ones on a similar basis. (There is an interesting distinction to be made between large scale R&D and innovation, the latter often being best nurtured in very small scale businesses.)

Allocation of Resources within R&D

1) Having arrived at a view on what your total R&D budget is to be, the next question must be—how much of it should be spent on research and how much on development? In making this decision it is wise to bear in mind that R&D is not the only way to effect the change that your company's strategy may dictate. Indeed, if you are seeking completely new products or to move into new industries it may be cheaper and more expeditious to achieve this by buying the know-how or buying or merging with another company.

But to return to the allocation of resources between research and development—to some extent these are philosophical questions and subject to a wide range of answers. In my opinion however, the bulk of the R&D expenditure incurred by most industrial companies comes under the heading of Development (and it will be recalled I defined this earlier as the process whereby new ideas are turned into commercially successful products.)

2) Research as such, or the extension of the frontiers of knowledge for its own sake, is often best left to the universities and research institutes, although most companies would probably want to try to keep up-to-date in their basic technology, e.g., Dunlop in polymer science. Businesses will also want to have the basic research facilities to cope with the research needs of bringing innovations through the development stage to commercial success.

Monitoring R&D Expenditure

1) As regards the research part of R&D, which in most cases I have suggested, should be a small part of the total R&D expenditure. I know of no way to plan either the projects that should be launched or one's performance against any preconceived financial or other norm. You have, I suppose, to rely on experience or "feel".

2) For development expenditure within the R&D budget, however, there are some well established methods of allocating resources over

EXHIBIT 2

RESEARCH AND DEVELOPMENT

Major Products		Technical Objective	Estimated Date of Transfer to Production	Expenditure		Commercial Benefits
Project No.	Project Name			Revenue	Capital	
				£000's		
1.	Production of Product "A"	A simplified process for making this product directly from the rubber compound and textile components thus eliminating the numerous intermediate fabrication steps presently used.	Available end 1979	Cumulative to: 1977		Elimination of the numerous intermediate fabrication operations giving more efficient utilisation of labour and factory space. Direct labour savings of £200,000 p.a. based on present output would result from the use of the technique for all U.K. production. In practice phased introduction would occur.
				170	8	
				Latest Estimate: 1978		
				95	50*	
				1979		
				110	—	
				1980		
				—	—	
				1981		
				—	—	
				Post: 1981		
				—	—	
				375	58	

*Pilot Plant

individual development projects, and of monitoring results. Development projects *do have* quantifiable objectives and *do cost* estimable sums of money and efforts to relate the desired goal to the cost of reaching it are worth making. There are a variety of methods but in my own company we use the type of project analysis illustrated in Exhibit 2.

I would make one or two observations on this method:

a) The dates on which progress towards success is to be reviewed should be determined at the start of the project and adhered to—rather like a critical path analysis. This is not an easy task, but essential.

b) Having said that, you must expect the unexpected—there is no way of planning development progress with certainty but experience will come with practice.

c) Remember that in the early stages of most development projects, the costs tend to be minimal. So do not stifle new ideas by too rigorous an analysis too early.

d) The number of attractive projects awaiting development will have a bearing on how you allocate resources to them and indeed if staff shortages or lack of facilities is the only bottleneck, there may be a case for increasing these. In this situation, a ranking of projects in a matrix in which strategic importance is measured against the likelihood of (R&D) success may be worthwhile.

Strategic Importance

		Low	Medium	High
	Low			
Likelihood of Success	Medium			
	High			

Summary

1) The allocation of resources to R&D should take heed of the nature of the business, its strategy, the rate of technological change, the action of competitors and your own company's ability to pay. In-house R&D may not be the best or only way to meet R&D needs.

2) The allocation of resources between R&D should probably give the bulk to development projects, but making sure research effort is adequate to preserve the basic technologies of the business, to produce new knowledge necessary to complete individual development projects and, hopefully, to spur some innovation.

3) Monitoring research expenditure is not easy but there are successful methods for analysing performance on individual development projects, and some pitfalls.

4) A method of ranking competing development projects is worthy of adoption.

23. Report of the CECIOS Working Committee on Transfer of Technology

Otmar Franz

Dr. Franz leads the team that presents the CECIOS Report at the 18th CIOS Congress.

Preface

Towards the end of 1976, CECIOS established a Working Committee on Transfer of Technology in order to prepare a CECIOS contribution on this subject for the CIOS World Management Congress of December 1978 in New Delhi. Similar Working Committees were established for the subjects "Transfer of Management Know-how" and "Professional Management".

The Working Committee on Transfer of Technology consisted of:
— Dr. A. Pedinelli, Italy—President
— Mr. M. Dubois, deputy B. Reumaux, France
— Dr. J. Eekels, Netherlands
— Dr. P.M. Rudhart, Germany
— Prof. Dr. H. Ruhle von Lilienstern, deputy Dipl.
  Kfm. H. Degenhard, Germany
— Dipl. Ing. G. Schmidt, Germany
— Mr. H.P. Bruin, CECIOS Secretary, replaced by Mr. L. Bouwens.

The plenary Working Committee assembled five times, but a number of intermediate working sessions were held too, where a few members met to discuss particular items. The Working Committee maintained contact with the other two Working Committees, especially with the Working Committee on Transfer of Management Know-how, for which a special liaison officer was appointed (Dr. J. Eekels).

From the very beginning the Working Committee was convinced of the necessity to focus its contribution on the problems of technology transfer to less industrialised nations and it was aware of the complexity of its field of investigation.

The latter consideration caused the Working Committee to devote attention to a methodological description and clarification of its subject area. This

211

resulted in a recommendation to pay special attention to problems connected with the man-machine systems and with the infrastructural aspects of newly transferred technologies.

Between these centres of attention lies the very important area of management know-how. An explicit treatment of this level was reserved for the Working Committee on Transfer of Management Know-how, but inevitably this aspect had to be touched upon in the Working Committee's own contributions too.

The methodological basis is to be found in the introductory paper by Eekels and Rudhart. How the other papers fit into the Working Committee's philosophy is indicated in the Final Remarks of this introductory article.

The Working Committee wishes to acknowledge the valuable help it received from many authorities, institutions, companies and individual persons. Without their help the results presented, however imperfect, we feel they may be, would not have been possible.

The Hague, November 14, 1978

CECIOS, EUROPEAN COUNCIL OF MANAGEMENT

B. van Vloten
President

Introduction

Technology Transfer (TT) has recently become a very modish subject to which many books, papers, seminars and congresses are devoted.

The term is often used in connection with developing Third World nations, and is understood to be a more comprehensive concept than, for example, licensing or exportation of technical products or production equipment to those countries.

It is heavily loaded with social and political controversies within the increasing North-South and West-East dialogue; these sometimes lead to communication derangements in that dialogue. Moreover, the field turns out to be very complicated with many different entries.

The CECIOS Working Party on TT, therefore, cannot and will not try to deliver an all including treatment of this subject. We will, by means of limited methodological analysis, give a systematic survey on the different problem fields of international TT.

Such a systematic approach will aid to position the other CECIOS papers delivered on TT during this CIOS World Congress. Its second, more general aim is to show the plurality of different problems and solutions within TT to managers and officials who are working in this important field of international cooperation.

Philosophy

The difficulties start already with definition of TT. Etymologically, technology means science of technique or science of engineering, and in certain languages the equivalent word still has that restricted meaning. But in American practice, for example, the term technology has reference to both the technical science and its application in real production and the use of technical products.

Technology Transfer as it is understood here certainly does not restrict itself to the transfer of a body of science even not so, if this body of knowledge takes the form of technical know-how. Know-how is a potential. It must be made to work if we want to speak of successful TT. The mere erection of a workshop or plant in another country does not already constitute real TT. This workshop or plant must be made to work. And it must be made to work successfully both in the technical and in the economical sense. Therefore, we want to define TT as "a process of transferring know-how from a giver to a receiver, leading to a further process of developing a new technology within the receiver's socio-technical-economical system." This definition does not exclude that giver and receiver reside in one country nor does it exclude that the receiver party is a subsidiary or affiliate of the giver party. It does exclude, however, any transfer of mere knowledge that is not really made operational for the receiver.

Any transaction that has not been enforced by either the giver's or the receiver's side should be advantageous in one or the other aspect for all parties concerned. Let us take the very simple example of the sale of a product or equipment. This provides the manufacturer or/and seller with income and it provides the buyer with a means to fulfil a need through the use of this good —presuming that it is able to fulfil the necessary functions.

However, this world is not built of advantages only. All actions and consequently all transactions are directed towards certain desired effects, but they are inevitably accompanied by more or less serious side effects. Sometimes these do not seriously harm either party, but in many cases they harm either the giver of technology (in which case we speak of rebounce) or the receiver or even the third parties.

These side effects can be of economy, of environmental, of social or of political nature. In the modern, complicated and strongly interrelated world, everything influences everything.

It is, however, impossible to take everything into account when we design an action like, for example, TT. Here lies the big problem: which specification and boundaries of the giver and receiver system should be taken into account when technology is transferred between a giver and a receiver. There have been made many serious mistakes in TT by considering a too narrow or too vast sector of the socio-technological-economical system of the technology receiver. But also on the giver's side, there are problems of system, definition, i.e., in assessing possible rebounce consequence. In order to solve these problems, we want to use the system's approach to define the objects, the ways and means and the different aspects of TT.

Objects of TT to Developing Countries

In general, the objects of TT can be of hardware and software character; they can relate either to the economic sector (industry, craft, agriculture, etc.) or to the infrastructural sector of the receiver's system. In detail, those objects can be:

a) New products either to be imported, to be assembled, to be manufactured or even to be developed in the receiver country;

b) New industrial or agricultural procedures (uses, application, methods) improving the economic development of the receiver country;

c) New material elements of the infrastructure of the receiver country, like new roads, harbours, airports, power stations, hospitals and schools;

d) New socio-cultural procedures improving the infrastructure of the receiver country, like new methods of medical care or education.

Interrelated Fields of TT within the Receiver's System

As mentioned before, it is the aim of successful TT that finally a comprehensive new technology "works" in the receiver country. This means that a number of interrelated processes have been initiated by the original transfer process between giver and receiver. Let us illustrate this by considering a mature TT project where a plant, a manufacturing unit for a new product, has been built in a developing country. It doesn't make any difference whether this plant is operated by a private or a state-owned company.

Now, in general, four levels or fields of technological development can be discerned as depicted in the model Fig. 1.

These more or less hierarchically ordered processes or levels are:

1) The nucleus is, in general, the technical installation, the plant. Energy, raw materials and human working power are "fed into it" and consumer goods or technical equipments turn out. This is the material manufacturing process: level 1.

2) This material process is part of a more encompassing process: the functioning of the man-machine system, e.g., the organisational framework to operate the transferred technological hardware. This level 2 includes level 1.

3) These activities (including a plant and the people to operate it) must be harmoniously incorporated in the development of the total enterprise as a socio-technical system. This third level includes level 1 and level 2.

4) Finally, the total entrepreneurial and economic activity should go in line with the socio-cultural development of the country in which this techno-economical development takes place. The country should develop transportation and market possibilities to absorb at least part of the output of the new plant and it should provide the new technical and economical sub-systems, the plants and companies with the material and non-material infrastructural framework, like the necessary administration, housing, medical care, education, etc.

The question of adaptation and compatibility between these four levels is

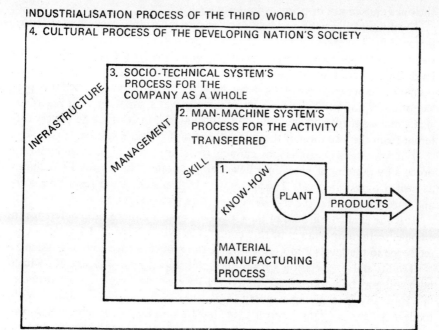

Figure 1. Reference : *Report*, Working Committee on Transfer of Technology,
Dr. Eekels and Dr. P.M. Rudhart.

of utmost importance. However, this essential part of TT does not necessarily develop from the more limited process (1) to the more encompassing one (4). The reverse way is also impossible. The levels/processes are interrelated. One thing is sure: to neglect one of these levels of TT will, in the long run, ruin each and every TT project. A great difficulty, if not the greatest one, is the fact that the more encompassing the process is (the more it is depicted towards the outside of the model) the more it is directorised by socio-cultural parameters, which are very difficult to control.

The lower level processes (depicted towards the centre of the model) are more characterised by technological parameters with far more possibilities of control.

In each of the rectangles of the model, representing the TT process, a *key word* is inserted, pertaining to the respective level of TT.

For the material manufacturing process, the key word is "know-how" in the traditional sense of technical know-how. For the man-machine systems level the key word is "skill". For the company as a whole, the key word is "management".

For the developing society of the receiver's country, the key word is "infrastructure", both in its material and socio-cultural form (hardware) and software. Of course, other key words can be of relevance, too, but we feel that the ones chosen are of primary importance.

Traditional licensing restricts itself to the innermost process of TT, the material level of erecting a plant and setting up a manufacturing process. In these cases it has been always silently presumed that at the receiver's side the levels 2 to 4 were more or less equivalent to similar levels in the giver's environment. Experience has taught us, however, that in many cases this presumption is not valid. In most cases the receiver's situation with regard to skills, management and material and non-material infrastructure is very different from the situation of those levels within the giver's system.

For successful TT it is not enough to set up a material manufacturing process by building a plant in a developing country. Successful TT includes as well progress in levels 2 to 4—mostly by transfer of the respective soft- and hardware besides the transfer of the pure technology.

It is the explicit purpose of the CECIOS contribution to this conference to emphasise the importance of this comprehensive concept of TT with special reference to the levels 2 to 4 as shown in the model of the receiver's system.

Traditional exportation of products, of blueprints—(licensing)—which both still may be important elements of TT were quite simple actions between one company in a giving country to another in a receiving country. With modern TT not only the receiver's side has become a more encompassing system to be envisaged but also the giver's side of the stage has become much more complex. So, national or international agencies for TT are being involved; companies, both at the giver's and the receiver's side of TT often cooperate on a national or even international level; consequently nearly every company can participate in the process of TT. With these enlarged possibilities of TT, however, the possibilities and even dangers of rebounce for an entire industrial branch or the whole giver's country have to be taken seriously into account. It is often difficult to establish the delicate balance between short term advantages for a single company transferring a technology with remarkable economic benefits for itself and the possible long term disadvantages for the whole economic system at the giver's end.

So, the concept of TT finally ends up in the task of balancing the systems of the giver's and receiver's country as well in technical, economical, social and, last not least, political respects.

Ways and Means of TT

The objects of TT, discussed as before, can be interpreted as purposes which may be attained with different means. These instruments of TT can be combined in various ways. According to the distinction of TT objects in hardware and software the ways and means of TT can also be divided into hardware related and software related instruments.

Some important instruments of TT from industrial to developing countries (and—in the long run—vice versa, too) are:

— Export of consumer goods, industrial products and installations;

— Investments in form of joint ventures, mergers and acquisitions;
— Maintenance of industrial and infrastructural installations;
— Consulting and engineering;
— Training, education, and upgrading.

Aspects of TT

Technology transfer has to be studied and can be effected by realising a number of different aspects.

It is not the same, whether TT
— Is primarily done under technical, legal, social, political or economical aspects;
— Is a private (profit) or a public (more or less non-profit) matter;
— Is accomplished on national or international level.

A Three Dimensional Matrix of TT

The above discussed objects, ways and means and aspects of TT can be combined into a cube as shown in Fig. 2, representing the systematic three-dimensional approach to the problems and solutions of TT. Each of the three visible sides of that cube represents a specific problems' and solutions' area and thus this figure gives an idea of the enormous complexity of our subject. It also makes clear that a comprehensive treatment of the vast subject TT is an immense, interdisciplinary task to be fulfilled by economists, engineers, lawyers, social scientists and politicians in close cooperation.

Final Remarks

These methodological remarks on TT were induced by the CECIOS Working Committee, "Transfer of Technology". They were intended as a systematic basis or framework of the other papers representing the CECIOS input to this congress' sub-theme "Transfer of Technology".

If we try to position these papers by use of Fig. 2 shown here we come to the following results: The contribution of the CECIOS Working Committee on Professional Management focusses on management in general and especially on the profile and image of the individual manager. So, it lies more or less outside the scope of the subject TT.

The contribution of the CECIOS Working Committee on Transfer and Adaptation of Management Know-how, however, touches some important questions in the field of TT, because its work focusses on level 3 in Fig. 1 (Management) which is one of the necessary levels of successful TT in a developing country.

The papers of Dr. Pedinelli, Dr. Franz and Mr. Dubois were written within the scope of the CECIOS Working Committee on TT. So, there are many interrelations between these contributions and the three-dimensional system of TT, developed above. In fact, each of these papers concentrates on one of the three surfaces of the cube shown in Fig. 2: Dr. Pedinelli

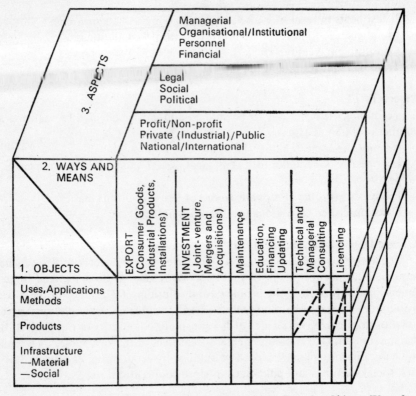

Figure 2. The Three-dimensional Matrix of Technology Transfer: Objects, Ways & Means and Aspects of TT.

pays special attention to certain aspects of TT, Dr. Franz to certain ways and means and Mr. Dubois to the infrastructural level as a certain object of TT.

All CECIOS contributions, however, try to pay attention to several viewpoints of the complex system of modern, comprehensive, international TT.

The CECIOS Working Committee on TT has collected and consulted a number of relevant publications in the field of TT. A survey of this literature is available on request to organisations and individuals interested.

24. Transfer of Technology

Otmar Franz

Dr. Franz is President of the Klockner Industrie-Anlagen GmbH, Germany. He is a vice-president of CECIOS (European Management Council) and member of the board of several leading international industrial organisations.

It is a great honour for me to express my opinion on international technology transfer to experts on this subject from the so-called giver- and, receiver-countries. I personally don't like this distinction. In my opinion, the transfer of technology is not a one-way-road. All of us are givers and receivers of technology.

Let me start by referring to a recent discussion on our subject which I had by chance with Dr. Gewalt, director of the world-famous Duisburg Zoological Gardens, being together with him in a plane on a flight to East Africa.

He definitely stuck to his opinion that the industrialisation of developing countries is a severe fault. He even doesn't like those being concerned with the building-up of industrial plants, power stations, streets and harbours, thus changing so-called natural paradises into modern industrially developed areas.

This very serious and famous scientist, of course, feels particularly responsible for wild animals and untouched nature in African, Asian and South American countries. In fact, the animals in those regions may live a better life in savage, untouched nature without industry, power stations, hospitals, school, etc. For human beings, however, in my opinion it's far away from paradise, to live underfed and without work and education.

You will agree that industrialisation on the basis of careful and responsible technology transfer is a means to increase economic development and human welfare and helps to solve, or even to avoid conflicts within and between our countries.

Travelling, however, in Africa, Asia and South America, talking with managers, officials and politicians in these countries and looking at many industrial ruins destroying nature and social structures without ever reaching production and thus without creating employment and income benefits, you may ask indeed whether transfer of technology is always reasonable.

I do not intend to bother you with lots of definitions and theoretical reflections. Nor do I like to report on mistakes which have been made in the transfer of technology. I prefer to concentrate on elaborating a bit on a modern instrument of technology transfer between countries of unequal technological development, granting advantage in the long run not only to the giving and receiving partners but also contributing to development and stabilisation of the world economy as a whole.

"The design, engineering, financing, delivery, erection and start-up of turnkey industrial plants, called general contracting."

For the export-bound, highly industrialised countries as well as for the developing countries this field of international business activity has gained tremendous importance. It has attracted special attention within the frame of the intensifying socio-economic and political North-South and West-East dialogue on development aid, exploitation of raw materials and industrialisation.

The general contracting of industrial installation offers remarkable advantages—under the conditions, of course, that the general contractor and his technical and economic partners meet high quality standards in terms of technological, economical and managerial performance.

General contracting of modern industrial installations, including the whole range of services from the original design to the final successful start-up of a plant, definitely enlarges the scope of traditional technology transfer by offering a complete package of highly specialised services:

1) Reliable technical and economic feasibility studies, taking into account the technological demand of the client, considering the stage of industrialisation and transtructure as well as the market potential and the educational standards in his country.

2) Planning and engineering of technologically and economically favourable industrial plants.

3) Delivery and erection of the turnkey plant. Besides, the direct transfer of technological knowledge is passed indirectly to the client incorporated in the technical goods and procedures handed over to him.

4) Technical assistance by formation and training of local personnel and management.

5) Putting into operation of the plant and technical assistance in the start-up period.

Evidently such a turnkey project including machinery, installations and buildings as well as the respective technical know-how to use them is a comprehensive instrument of international technology transfer. It offers the possibility to transmit the whole range of technological hardware and software combining the export of technical items, consulting, engineering, training and maintenance services; it comprises many suitable ways and means of modern technology transfer. A practical example, how my company is realising transfer of technology from industrialised countries to developing countries being of advantage for all partners concerned will be elaborated in detail in my speech on December 6, 1978.

Based on this practical example I should like to present to you 10 theses on the transfer of technology which may guide us in our following discussion.

1) Transfer of technology is advantageous for all partners involved if the special situation of the company and the socio-economic situation and future development of the countries concerned are carefully taken into account and appropriate technologies and all necessary services are offered.

2) Transfer of technology is most successfully effected by private enterprises. Governments, administrations and international organisations can assist and should help setting the framework but should not replace the daring and ingenious private inventor, innovator and general contractor.

3) Reasonable transfer of technologies is advantageous for the company transferring the technology contributing to cover the high cost of inventions and developing new processes and allowing further growth. New investments in advanced technologies are possible.

4) Reasonable transfer of technology is advantageous for the company receiving the technology avoiding high cost and time for invention and developing of own technologies.

5) Transfer of technology from industrialised to developing countries effects positively growth, employment and welfare of the industrialised countries. Transfer of technology can lead to growing markets.

6) Transfer of technology leads to economic growth and social progress in the developing countries. It may contribute to more employment, better housing, nutrition, education and medical care.

7) Transfer of technology may enable the developing countries to better exploit their specific resources, reducing the cost for exploration and beneficiation of raw materials and deferring the limits of growth for all countries.

8) Transfer of technology can contribute to change developing countries from mere raw material suppliers to industrialised countries thus becoming more important partners in international trade. Increasing world trade could lead to more liberalism in international trade being advantageous for all partners.

9) Transfer of technology may help to overcome international prejudice and to create understanding between partners and countries of unequal development.

10) World-wide transfer of technology is one of the great challenges of our time. By practising it in partnership we can contribute to solve international problems and to build up a better world for our children.

25. Technology Transfer and
Aid to Development

Antonio Pedinelli*

Dr. Pedinelli is Chairman of CNOS (Associazione per la Promozione del Management a della Tecnica, Rome) and to Tecnoservizis. He is a member of several international committees on R&D, technology transfer, etc.

The introduction of new technologies into developing countries occurs through what today is known as "technology transfer". This can be carried out either by investment or by appropriately training workers, technicians and managers. However apart from the transfer of equipment (hardware)—no longer considered sufficient—it also includes the transfer of plans, information and knowledge (software) as well as of abilities and skills aimed at preparing the receiver to set up a local innovative process. This transfer of managerial capacities places the LDC in a position to control the new technologies introduced and also to develop its own technological conscience.

Technology transfer can thus be seen as a cultural phenomena, i.e., as an actual process of communication not only of hardware and software but also of a whole series of messages, from one culture to another. This involves the interaction of different forms of culture, from educational policies to patterns of scientific thinking. The social, as well as the economic impact is hence significant.

Opinion is now widespread that the countries of the Third World should start by "standing on their own feet" and only later resort to outside aid. In fact the technological advancement of such countries initially requires a study of their characteristics and aptitudes in order to identify, understand and evaluate local technological conditions in terms not only of the reference points and basic structures for a fruitful insertion of new technologies, but also in terms of the country's capabilities of stimulating research within the country itself. Often the traditional technologies and practices used in agri-

*This article was presented by the author as member of the CECIOS Working Committee on Transfer of Technology.

culture, construction and other crafts are valuable sources of knowledge and involve educational capabilities and entrepreneurial and innovative spirit which cannot and must not be readily ignored.

It is important to underline that a society's propensity to assimilate technological change depends in part on its capacity to adapt technology to its own specific conditions but principally on its capacity to adapt itself to the needs of technology. One cannot be considered without the other and in fact it is far better to stimulate the country towards a process of innovation and self sustained growth rather than trying to adapt the technologies to the conditions of the receiver.

In fact the introduction of technologies that are too violent for a system of the traditional type and which do not take into account the precise socio-economic repercussions could entail the risk of destroying florid activities valuable to the country. An example of this was the introduction into a Middle East country of a plastic shoe manufacturing factory utilising western technology. The outcome was a saturated market, with the consequent ruin of many craftsmen and no substantial advantage to production. Similarly the introduction of European carpet weaving machines ruined a florid and well-known handicraft in North Africa.

In addition to the paralysing effect of imported technology on local techniques account must be taken of the lack of flexibility of the modern sophisticated technologies with regard to the use of raw materials, to conditions and methods of production and to the product type which do not permit either modifications or adjustments. These very technologies often impose high dimensional thresholds for the domestic markets of a number of countries in the Third World. This is particularly serious for those countries that wish to follow a well-balanced development without major jolts or upsets, whose markets are of a moderate size and who enjoy regular expansion.

Recently two textile factories have been set up in Tanzania. One is based on technologies developed in an advanced country and required a fairly high level of investment. It employs 1000 well-qualified persons many of whom had to be recruited from overseas. Spare parts have to be purchased from abroad and it is most improbable that, in the short run, such sophisticated machinery can be manufactured locally. The other factory called for lower investments, employs 3000 people, all of whom are natives of Tanzania, and provides work for craftsmen both in the mechanical and in the textile sector.

From a strictly return-on-investment evaluation both projects appear to be valid, but a closer look at their impact on society shows that the former offers a much lower stimulus to the local economy due to its limited ties with other activities and to its limited impact on instruction, since the skilled personnel involved are relatively few. The second project, however, represents a far more stimulating involvement.

A further handicap is represented by the costs of technology, which are not always readily estimable and are often the bone of contempt between those who grant and those who purchase technology. In particular the LDC's feel that technology, as a cultural asset, should be substantially free and available to all, when in fact it is a very costly asset. Apart from the investment layout, the cost of transferring technology includes those for generating it and for keeping it up-to-date as well as transfer costs, personnel training, etc. Furthermore large-size plants in particular call for a combination of investment in costly infrastructures which must be borne by the receiving country.

It is thus evident that the introduction of technologies may create serious problems and therefore it would be much better to conduct case by case evaluations considering such factors as:
— The advantages offered by the new technology compared to the traditional process;
— Which of the available technologies best adapts itself to the conditions of the country in relation to the socio-economic structure, costs, productive factors, etc.;
— The possibility of adapting the technology, either directly or through research, to be conducted in the country or elsewhere;
— The burdens that the technology involves (licences on patents and know-how and their related limitations);
— The economic and social cost-benefit ratio;
— The problem of skills and of how the country is placed to provide them;
— The availability of capital;
— The existence or lack of infrastructures and of subsidiary activities;
— The capacity to stimulate other local undertakings;
— The effects on imports and exports.

Appropriate Technologies

The appropriate technologies, undoubtedly originate in the industrialised countries, and are subsequently transferred to the developing countries. This process of technological transfer cannot, however, be viewed and carried out (as is often the case) in light of R. Vernon's international product cycle theory. The reason for this is that we are no longer dealing with technologies developed in advanced countries and which, no longer satisfying their economic situation, have been replaced by higher productivity technologies. Logically the practicability of this "technology transfer", which uses innovations developed world-wide and adapted, that is appropriate to the conditions and objectives of the socio-economic growth of the developing countries, must be valued under a series of factors and limitations.

This process implies both the use of existing technical-scientific know-how which could give rise to appropriate technologies and the setting up of new guidelines for R&D (particularly in the public sector).

It can therefore be upheld that the concept of "appropriate" technology should initially be seen from the angle of appropriate sectors, by which is implied product types whose production processes are appropriate to the socio-economic conditions of the Third World.

An "appropriate technology" (a term that in itself includes the more limited concepts of "intermediate technology", "low-cost technology" and "soft technology") is hence one that is capable of meeting the needs and the technical capabilities of the country that adopts it. In other words, a technology is appropriate if the people of a country feel its need, are able to use and develop it, and find it suitable and profitable to their way of life. The "appropriateness" of a technology cannot, however, be evaluated in abstract terms, but necessitates a clear indication of the criteria selected (social, economic, political and cultural) in relation to a precise historic context.

In developing countries and, in particular, in those that have no available strategic mining resources, appropriate technologies should be characterised by:

a) Low capital intensity compared to labour,

b) Decentralisation into small productive units spread throughout the territory,

c) Upgrading of local human and natural resources,

d) Saving of scarce raw materials,

e) Energy saving (via a non-conventional, non-decentralised energy producing system),

f) Stimulating rural development via a widespread agro-industrial system,

g) Respect of the environmental, natural and cultural conditions of the country concerned.

These criteria aim at providing an answer to some of the main bottlenecks in the development of the Third World, starting from the shortage of capital and of qualified labour. At the same time it is necessary to exploit the human and natural potential without depressing local cultural values thus contributing to the spreading of technical know-how and stimulating innovation and local entrepreneurship.

Despite continued debates on this subject, little has effectively been done to set up appropriate technologies in the developing countries. The OECD has estimated that approximately only 5 million dollars a year are spent on R&D for appropriate technologies against a layout of 60,000 million dollars for the conventional forms. Examples of the former are to be found in agriculture, energy, construction and civil engineering, crafts, services, etc. In fact the developing countries have studied and created small sugar refineries; huskers for farm products and other simple agricultural machines: brickyards, small spinning and weaving machines; local chemical production (caustic soda products and soap)—wood and sugar cane derivatives (charcoal, gas, methanol, acetic acid, etc.); non-conventional energy sources—wind (for pumps and mills), solar (for domestic water animal refuse derivatives), methane (for energy and manure); and systems for the collection and distribution of rainwater.

The above technologies in general, favouring the decentralisation of production lines and services, promote local employment and reduce the transportation costs of raw materials and finished products. Also, compared to conventional technologies, investment costs are low and labour employment is higher.

However, even though these technologies were introduced on the basis of the results of research work, several failures have occurred. An example of this was in the production of methane from fermenting cow manure. The plant in fact showed some faults, due mainly to the fact that an insufficient amount of R&D was carried out on the methods of adapting the technology to the effective situation. Technical assistance and trouble shooting is thus of primary importance in the introductory phase of any new appropriate technology.

Appropriate technologies give rise to relatively inexpensive plants but demand ample diffusion. Thus total costs are high and comparable to those of the large productive systems. These latter are undoubtedly more spectacular and offer more impressive and exhilarating solutions, also they are easier to administer since they consist mainly of strictly codified hardware and software. On the other hand practically nothing has been done with these to identify a system capable of reconciling efficiency, small dimensions and technical simplicity.

If appropriate technologies are to contribute substantially to the employment problem in the Third World their application must be extended also to the services sector. To this extent a great amount of research has yet to be carried out. In fact their success or failure, in both industrialised and Third World countries, depends on a profound modification in the orientation of scientific and technological policies. It must be realised that up to now these policies have favoured an overcentralisation of the economy and have accepted a given power structure. This major change in scientific and technological policies must also be reflected in a change in economic and social policies as well, thus permitting a direct involvement and participation of each individual in the decision-making process.

To consider appropriate technologies as the only alternative to the traditional ones, would not only be unjustified but also unrealistic. On the contrary we believe that the fundamental objective is to follow an appropriate set of technologies starting from an approach that we can define as *technological pluralism* in order to thus underline the relationship between appropriate and traditional technologies (in particular the large-scale and capital-intensive ones).

A pluralistic strategy can be achieved both among and within the various sectors by pointing out the different technological solutions possible within a single sector and by defining those sectors particularly suitable, in each territorial land-improvement area, to the introduction of such appropriate technologies. Individual sectors or specific production processes particularly suitable to appropriate technologies are, for example, the building materials or local raw materials sectors or else the recycling processes. On the other hand, even in certain sectors like the steel industry, space exists for different technological solutions: the traditional capital-intensive plants can be integrated with others capable of supplying high quality goods via more flexible process, or even with other smaller decentralised scrap recovery and recycling plants.

Thus it is only within a set of pluralistic limits that the appropriate technologies find their true existence. Not only, but they must also have a high scientific and technological content which means that their development must be research-intensive.

Finally, an appropriate technology should try to avoid complex, over-automated systems of control and should whenever possible split such control systems into sub-systems so that automation be best integrated with human work, thus facilitating the identification of possible breakdowns, and their repair. At the same time, with respect to job organisation, each individual should be assigned to more intelligent and less parcelled work.

Thought must also be given to spare parts, which should be readily obtainable and possibly manufactured locally, as well as to the necessary infrastructures, not only productive, commercial and organisational, but also educational. Indeed, it is not only the workers who need to be educated, but also the students, if they are required to play a future role in the development of appropriate technologies. Moreover, a whole web of innovators and entrepreneurs must be woven around these technologies, if they are not to remain, as is the case with imported technologies, something static or rigid. It is in this perspective that we think of appropriate technologies as an instrument to allow a truly autonomous development of the countries of the Third World.

26. A Key Support for Accelerating the Development of Human Capabilities

Michael M. Dubois*

Mr. Dubois is Director of EUREQUIP, a consulting firm of France, operating in 50 countries.

My only aim is to present to you my own contribution on a very specific subject, that is "Technology Transfer—A Key Support for Accelerating the Development of Human Capabilities".

It is a vast and important subject and I am only going to develop some key concepts.

In fact, these concepts are the result of fifteen years of experience on this subject, as my own company and myself have been active in this field in forty-five developed and developing countries.

First of all, we consider that the transfer of technology is not a reason in itself, however, we very often observe that this is the way in which this is understood. This is the reason why I will pose a first key question which I will try to answer.

Why Does a Country Ask for a Technology Transfer?

From our viewpoint, we consider that a country or an organisation calls for a technology transfer to widen the scope of its performance and its capacities, in order to be able to improve and optimise, for the sake of its people, the exploitation of its natural resources or other genuine resources and doing so, to face the growing needs of its population.

These needs range from better nutrition, better health care, to better living conditions, in a word, everything linked to the material living conditions, but also, and with the same emphasis, for a better education.

This last point is obviously a very important one if we consider that it is through education that present situations can evolve to the human goals we have been referring to, either directly or indirectly.

*This article was presented by the author as member of the CECIOS Working Committee on Transfer of Technology.

So, the technology transfer has a key role which is to train the people to the point where they are able to be industrially creative and through this innovation to build, themselves, their own new models for reference.

This important statement drives us to formulate a new concept "the Industrial Mastery".

From Technology Transfer to Industrial Mastery

If we agree fundamentally on the statement we have just formulated, and for many years we have been pushing in this direction in all the operations of technology transfer we have been concerned with, we must observe the evolution of the concept of technology transfer and its application and then analyse how the technology transfer serves both material improvement and educational evolution of the concerned population.

The technology transfer may be defined in three main aspects:

a) The right to do   = patents and licences
b) The means to do = equipment and machines
c) The ability to do = behaviours, knowledge and skills of the people operating the investment

Therefore, if we consider the various aspects of technology transfer, we can observe four important aspects:

a) Political
b) Technical
c) Legal and financial
d) Human

All of these aspects are very much linked together, they are interdependent. However, we are going to concentrate on the human aspect of technology transfer which is the purpose of our reflexion today.

This specific aspect can be clearly defined as an exceptional meeting of two different technological cultures, the culture of the sender and the culture of the receiver.

We can then observe the different steps which the meeting of various technological cultures has provoked in the last twenty years.

From the stage of acceding to products, the different countries can now accede to a production technology and today some of them are capable of acceding to industrial mastery and even to the design capability.

Let us take a closer look at these last two steps.

The new concept of industrial mastery shows that the Turnkey approach, Product-in-hand approach, Market-in-hand approach are the natural results of the evolution of the previous conception.

First of all, there must be the production. Then, when the elementary stages of production have been acquired, there must be efficient production (productivity). Another step will be taken when profitability becomes imperative. During this step, we discover that production is not the only function in a profitable company or profitable unit, (but also sales and marketing, supplies, maintenance, finance, etc.). Step after step the company advances towards industrial mastery.

Industrial mastery which is not only the manufacturing of products and their sales, whether nationally or internationally, but also, and may be mainly, the possibility of having the new organisation work with the same efficiency under all of its aspects, not only in operations but also in corporate management.

We may then understand that the new organisation will be an exceptional set-up in order to develop the education of the people concerned by the functioning of the whole organisation and to prepare them for the ultimate step which consists of knowing how to evolve themselves with little outside help; of knowing how to improve and innovate; of knowing how to invent new products and production methods; of knowing how to enter new markets and eventually of knowing how to transfer all of this industrial knowledge to others.

Then, we can say that every technology transfer must aim at the progress of the industrial mastery of the receiver. This will either bring into action new techniques or new developments making the already existing technologies more efficient, or will contribute to the widening of the scope of existing activities.

A final objective is that the technology transfer will be the root of genuine innovation. If technology transfer definitely needs a real support by the local culture, it has, on the other hand, an obvious accelerating effect in the spiral of the development of human capabilities.

The "T" Method

Of course, such an approach may appear very idealistic and one may feel that the concepts which we have been developing here must be very difficult to implement in a real situation. In fact, effective methods exist in order to use the technology transfer as a real motor in the development of education.

One of these effective methods is the "T" Method. It is a succession of steps which organise all the elements and techniques bringing progressively, the organisation, then the related persons to human and managerial effectiveness.

Preliminary survey

Survey of the primary characteristics of the sending and receiving companies and of their countries, cultures, available manpower, training facilities and industrial structures.

Transfer leaders

Selection and training of transfer leaders coming from either the sending or receiving companies.

Planning

Design of a plan for all human and managerial aspects of the technology transfer.

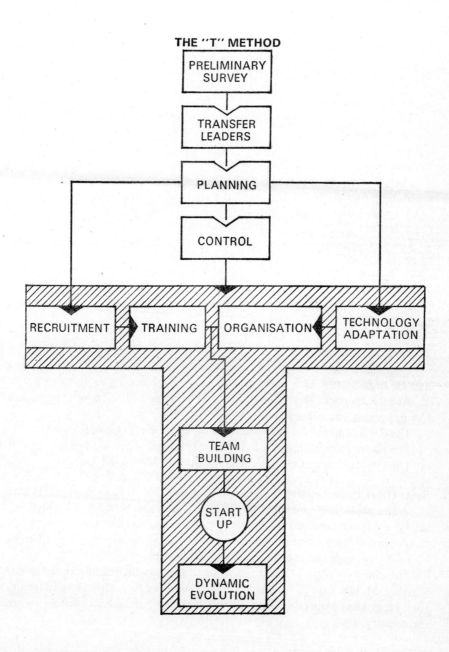

Control

Measurement of progress and decision on corrective actions whenever necessary.

Recruitment

Location of manpower sources, then selection and recruitment based on tests, interviews, observations in real or mock-up situations.

Technology adaptation

Adaptation of the technology and human tasks to the industrial culture of the receiving country.

Training

Choice of training methods and means adapted to the trainees. Careful scheduling, preparation, diffusion and control of the training.

Organisations

Design of an organisational structure and definition of career paths adapted to the country.

Team building

Creation of an effective team by coaching the personnel in the real situation.

Dynamic development

Permanent monitoring and improvement of the efficiency of the people and the organisation after the start-up.

As an example of the "T" Method and in order to illustrate it, we would like to present you some cases:

— The development of a uranium mine in Niger: the SOMAIR case;

— The path to autonomy of a liquefied natural gas plant in Algeria;

— The CAMEL case (Compagnie Algerienne de Methane Liquide).

Some Other Paths Leading to Industrial Mastery

While presenting and illustrating these two cases using the "T" Method, we have only emphasised one of the paths leading to industrial mastery. In fact, many other paths lead to industrial mastery, mainly through different education systems and the ways of combining them.

The chart on page 233 presents some of these paths leading to industrial mastery. Middle term (less than five years) and long term (from five to twenty years) approaches will contribute actively to develop industrial mastery within the country.

a) The middle term approach

Because of the evident reasons of inactivity on behalf of these outside

VARIOUS PATHS LEADING TO INDUSTRIAL MASTERY

MIDDLE TERM PROGRESS SYSTEM DIRECTLY CONNECTED WITH THE COMPANY	NATIONAL INTERNAL PATH	• Recruitment of the best adapted nationals, coming out of the education systems in the country or from abroad • Organised training effort in the company in relation with the "cascade training systems" (following the descending hierarchy).	LONG TERM : To widen the national paths by : • Better adaptation of men in function of industrial development objectives • Better adaptation of technologies to national realities
	EXTERNAL PATH : INTERNATIONAL INDUSTRIAL COOPERATION	• Choice of one or several senders. Organisation of transfer or industrial mastery • Intervention of a pedagogical and operational technical assistance	
LONG TERM : PROGRESS SYSTEM RELATED TO EDUCATION SYSTEMS	NATIONAL INTERNAL PATH	• Research of synergies with the objectives of the development plan • Better knowledge of student "sources" notably among the working population • Adaptation of education systems to the two elements noted above • Preparation of future managers to their role of instructor in the company • Amelioration of the relations between the education system and the company • Control of results and permanent amelioration of the system	
	EXTERNAL PATH : INTERNATIONAL UNIVERSITY COOPERATION	• Choice of an associated education system in an industrialised country • Implementation of transfer. . Adaptation of programmes and methods • Intervention of professors coming from industrialised countries	
LONG TERM : PROGRESS SYSTEM RELATED TO TECHNICAL CENTRES	NATIONAL INTERNAL PATH	• Critical study of results obtained with imported technologies • Precise description of national economical characteristics which can influence the choice of technologies • Research of adaptations and slight ameliorations of imported technologies	
	EXTERNAL PATH : INTERNATIONAL SCIENTIFIC COOPERATION	• Choice of one or several associated technical centres • Implementations of a cross-fertilisation plan • Elaboration of common research programmes • Engage research specialists. Progress in the technologies adapted to the conditions of the country	

systems, education, technical centres, the middle term problems must be resolved by the company itself, accepting these systems as they are and trying to make the most of them.

The company can then choose one or the other of two paths:

A national internal path, combining the recruitment of the best adapted candidates—who are either free on coming out of the existing education systems, or having returned to their country after having followed an education or having worked in an industrialised country, with a huge organised effort in internal training using the existing sources of technology: similar plants, technical centres, management centres.

The new or growing company is transformed, at least partly, into a school of application, in which each manager is responsible for training his own group, using the skilled workers as the first trainees, then eventually as the instructors.

This path is indispensable in order to realise an amalgam of man and knowledge of the company and requires the total involvement of everyone, but there are three limits:

i) The first one is the very conception of their role by the national managers. These, who have only just come out of their schools, have rarely been oriented towards pedagogy and therefore are very little open and prepared to an active role in education.

ii) The second is the necessary workload, which is difficult to change in a working company.

iii) The third is the complexity of the technologies used, which, to a certain point, are non-existent in the country.

This is why it is often necessary to use an external path, with assistance from abroad, and using the resources in experience and men from one or several industrialised countries.

This second path can be subdivided into two: one which privileges the transfer of industrial mastery to nationals from ascending structures to be chosen, and the other which privileges the technical assistance, this means the intervention of expatriates participating in an operational role in the national company, to which they are already habituated in their own country.

The external path allows a surplus of technology in the environment of the company. This must be relayed by an internal path in order to realise a complete technological osmosis, and not only the juxtaposition of two different cultures which are totally ignorant of each other.

b) The long term approach

The long term actions are interesting for the complete technological structure of the country, as well as the company, therefore calling for both education system and technical centres.

These last two components can evolve themselves at middle term, but can only progress for the companies, and therefore the economy, at long term.

In each case, it is possible to distinguish an internal path, as with the company, which is national, and an external path of international cooperation whether this is by the universities or science.

Naturally, the progress of education systems and technical centres can only transmit industrial mastery where there is sufficiently satisfying synergies between companies, education systems and technical centres.

It is then possible to imagine a long term enrichening of the company which receives:

— On one hand, men prepared for the company, capable of relaying the expatriates, even the rare specialists;
— And on the other hand, the technologies which are most adapted to the realities rather than the imported technologies.

Conclusions

From our point of view, "Technology Transfer, A Key Support for Accelerating the Development of Human Capabilities" is a fascinating subject for reflexion and dynamic actions. We consider that in our short expose, we are far from having treated the subject in all of its facets. However, we consider that this is probably one of the most important subjects for the next twenty years.

If we try to formulate some conclusion, we could say that any industrial investment cannot be considered only through its immediate and material outputs; it must be seen as an essential support for the progress of men; for the progress of their education; for the development of their knowledge and skills, for assisting their march to creative autonomy, through a real industrial mastery.

Technology transfer can be the worst thing for nationals if the transfer is done in such a way that it is brutal and not adapted. On the contrary, technology transfer can be the most profitable operation for the nationals in terms of development of their own capabilities if this necessity of human development is taken as a first objective—the expected economic outputs will then appear as a direct consequence.

Receivers have the responsibility of choosing the right approach for receiving the technology—Senders have their own responsibility as well in developing human capabilities.

Both sender and receiver must take into account, with the same emphasis, their willingness to develop the men and then the fantastic difference between success and failure will appear clearly.

27. Transfer of Technology

Peter M. Rudhart

Dr. Rudhart is Controller, Machine Tool Division (National and International Operations) of Klockner & Co., Germany. He is a member of the CECIOS Working Committee on Transfer of Technology and has considerable international experience in this area.

I present the final report on the findings of the CECIOS Working Committee, named Transfer of Technology. This committee had been established in 1977 and it was done in order to prepare a CIOS contribution specially for this congress and for further congresses of CIOS and its regional councils. Similar working committees have been established for the themes "Transfer of Management Know-how and Professional Management". This working committee consisting of managers from France, Germany, Italy and the Netherlands, including Dr. Pedinelli, Mr. Dubois and myself, as you can see from the Congress papers, intended to reach mainly three aims, to do a little job to solve these problems.

The first thing was to study the present state of the practice and theory, which involves a lot of literature study and to talk to managers busy in this field. Our second task was, or is, to elaborate a systematic survey of problems and solution areas to probably make a check list for everyone who works in this field. I would later on give some examples on this. And our third task which has not been completed yet is to collect case studies and examples of successes and failures of technology transfer and possibly develop and elaborate some recommendations for the so-called givers and receivers. I do not like this distinction too much because in the long run we are all givers and all receivers; but at the moment the flow of technology or technological information is of course more from the side of the industrialised countries to the side of the developing countries.

Very soon we became aware of the enormous complexity of this subject, especially when, of course, concentrating on technology transfer from industrialised to the developing countries. But encouraged by the President and the Board of CIOS and the healthy support of the CIOS Secretariate, this task has been nearly completed.

Before pointing out and showing some of the findings, let me clearly state that we do not believe to have found final solutions, that we do not want to teach anybody how to transfer technology. We hope, however, that work may contribute a little to clear up the present North-South and East-West dialogue on successful technology transfer which is, in fact, one of the great questions of the time.

Reporting to an audience of experienced managers from the so-called giver and receiver countries, there is no need for a definition of international technology transfer nor to stress its importance for economic growth and human welfare nor to mention it—it is a well-known problem. Technology transfer has become a very important and modest subject. And on these three issues— the definition, the importance and the main problems—a general agreement has been reached in theory and practice, as we found out.

As for the definition, I suppose we all agree that the technology transfer means the process of transferring technological hardware and software which means machines and the know-how to operate them from one company, one country or one society to another, especially from the industrialised to the developing countries. That is our subject for today. As for the importance, I may say, evidently technology transfer is the means of economic growth and human welfare, at least for economic growth, in both parts in the giver countries and the receiver countries. And the third, for the problems, I think the agreement is reached also. The major concern is the adaptation of the transfer of technology to the socio-economic system of the receiver country or vice versa and I have just mentioned the key words. Dr. Pedinelli has mentioned appropriate technology, soft technology, intermediate technology.

Well, based on these widely accepted agreements on definition, importance and major problem areas, we found it unnecessary and inadequate to adjust another definition or general remarks to the great amount of excellent papers and books available on this subject. From our host country, India, for example, Mr. Tata has delivered an interesting paper on the practice of technology transfer in Asia to the delegates of the Asian Association of Management Organizations last year. So, according to our tasks stated above, the working committee decided to elaborate the radical framework on TT, but don't be afraid, it should at the same time allow practical application for managers and officials working in the field of technology transfer which means to be a check list, to ask for problems and solutions.

This subject, technology transfer, shows an extremely fast growing complexity, as I mentioned before, and as has been mentioned here before. Two examples: Technology transfer is no longer just a matter within one company transforming, for example the R&D results of the scientists into products ready for being marketed. Today, technology transfer is accomplished between different companies, between whole industries within one country and, of course, between different economies and countries. This means the macroeconomic level of technology level, the small, narrow level, has grown to a technology transfer on a macro-economic level; national transfer has widened to international transfer.

Secondly, technology transfer no longer happens just between one ingenious technical inventor and one risk-bearing inventor on the other side who will market its products. Today, everybody receives directly or indirectly technical know-how included in the products he can buy. This means, besides the direct, just bilateral technology transfer, for example, by selling blueprint or granting a licence from company A to company B, there is vast indirect multiple distribution of know-how all over the world hardly to be controlled by the original inventor. So this just gives a short idea of the complexity of this subject.

In conclusion I would like to say: The work of our committee was meant for both sides—the donors and the recipients, or the giver and the receiver countries. We from our side have learnt a lot while studying the complex subject of technology transfer. If our findings and recommendations are of help to you too, we would feel rewarded for our work.

28. Ownership, Control and Technology Transfer via Multinational Corporation

Paulo Mattos de Lemos

Prof. Lemos is Professor of Management and Head of the Graduate Management Programme of the COPPEAD, Universiade Federal do Rio de Janeiro, Brazil. A well-known consultant, his special interests are Management Applications of Multivariate Statistics, Decision Analysis and Forecasting.

Summary

The last decade has been witnessing a growing concern over the role of multinational corporations in the economic development of recipient countries by their governments and private domestic business.

This paper intends to provide a contribution to the debate about the regulation of the activities of multinational corporations in relation to technology transfer.

We selectedly review the literature on foreign direct investment and introduce a behavioural model for multinational corporations facing the decision among alternative strategies of international operations, regarding exports, sale of technology and direct investment.

Based on this model we make some inferences on the expected types of response by multinational corporations to the regulations imposed by host Governments, such as regulatory constraints on repatriation of profits, on payments for technology transfer and on the operation of the subsidiary by the parent company.

We finally examine some data on flows of foreign direct investment, conventional return and payments for technology transfer in the light of our model.

Introduction

This paper examines the aggregate trends in time of conventional returns to direct investment and of technology transfer payments from U.S. subsidiaries to their parents, in the light of the concept of Optimal Degree of Ownership.

Section (1) reviews the concept of optimal degree of ownership of a subsidiary, from the point of view of the parent company.

Section (2) presents what seems to be the most interesting trends on the data on conventional returns and technology transfer payments from U.S. subsidiaries to their parent companies between 1963 and 1972*.

Finally, section (3) examines these trends in the light of the concept of optimal degree of ownership.

1) A Review of the Concept of Optimal Degree of Ownership

The concept Optimal Degree of Ownership derived from a contracting costs view of foreign direct investment, has been proposed before [1] as a contribution towards a better understanding of the economic rationale associated with direct investment/licensing decisions.

In the previous article it is argued that the conventional industrial organisation view—explicitly suggested by Caves [2] and implicitly by Hymer [3], Dunning [4], Vernon [5] and Knickerbocker [6]—on foreign direct investment does not suffice for a full understanding of the economic rationale associated with the direct investment/licensing decision because it does not examine the specific problems associated with the market intermediation of the commodity know-how.

The degrees of uncertainty and informational asymmetry which characterise the sale of know-how may prevent the establishment of the complete contingent claims contract necessary to the transaction. The likelihood of a situation of small numbers** in exchange being obtained, as a result of an incomplete short term renegotiable contract, may prevent the establishment of the succession of incomplete contracts necessary to the transaction.

The higher the levels of uncertainty and informational asymmetry, which characterise the specific sale of know-how, the higher the transactional cost associated with the establishment of the complete contingent claims contract necessary to the transaction. The higher the likelihood of being obtained in small numbers the higher the transactional cost associated with the establishment of the successions of incomplete contracts necessary to the transaction.

Hence, the higher the levels of uncertainty, informational asymmetry and likelihood of small numbers, which characterise the specific sale of know-how, the higher the incentive to have this transaction shifted away from the market place towards an internal organisation.

From the point of view of a parent company there will be an optimal degree of ownership of a subsidiary which will depend on the degrees of

---

*Source: Teplin, M.F.—*U.S. International Transactions in Royalties and Fees: Survey of Current Business*, U.S. Department of Commerce, Washington D.C., 1973.

**Designation given by Williamson [7] to situations when the balance of bargaining power is altered as a result of a short term contract.

uncertainty and informational asymmetry and on the likelihood of small numbers conditions associated with licensing the know-how.

The optimal degree of the ownership would result from the comparison between the contracting costs associated with obtaining the desired level of control over the stream of monopoly rents on the know-how advantage through licensing, through full ownership of a subsidiary or through some combination of partial ownership with licensing.

The optimal degree of ownership of subsidiary from the parent's point of view should be, therefore, expected to vary across countries and across industries within a country—even abstracting from regulatory and political risks differentials—to the extent that the degrees of uncertainty and informational asymmetry and the likelihood of small members associated with the rate of know-how vary across countries and across industries within a country. The pure licensing case, for example, would occur when for the specific activity, industry and country the optimal degree of ownership of subsidiary were 0 per cent.

2) Trends in Time of Conventional Returns and Payments for Technology Transfer: Empirical Highlights

Official statistics classify payments for technology transfer in two categories: royalties and administration fees.

A clear conceptual distinction exists between those payments for technology transfer and the so-called conventional returns on direct investment, which involve interests and dividend payments and remittance of profits from subsidiaries of multinational corporations to their parents.

Conventional returns versus total payments for technology transfer

Table 1 shows the value of total U.S. direct investment abroad, the conventional returns on direct investments, the total U.S. income from technology transfer, the total technology transfer payments from U.S. subsidiaries (defined as the ones at least 50 per cent owned by their parents) and total technology transfer payments from non-U.S. subsidiaries for the 10 year period, 1963–1972. Annual and average (for the 10 year period) rates of growth as well as the corresponding standard deviations were calculated and are also presented. From the reading of Table 1 one can observe that:

i) Total technology transfer payments have grown faster than conventional returns on direct investment;

ii) Technology transfer payments from U.S. subsidiaries have grown much faster than technology transfer payments from non-U.S. subsidiaries;

iii) Technology transfer payments from non-subsidiaries have grown approximately as fast as conventional returns on direct investment.

iv) From the variables shown in Table 1, direct investment is the only one which can be said to be following a rather stable pattern of growth (mean 9.8 per cent; standard deviation 0.9 per cent).

Table 1

CONVENTIONAL RETURNS VERSUS PAYMENTS FOR TECHNOLOGY TRANSFER ($ MILLION)

	(1) U.S. Direct Inv. (beginning of year)		(2) Conventional Returns		(3)=(4)+(5) Total Technology Transfer Payments		(4) Tech. Tr. Payments for U.S. subs.		(5) Tech. Tr. Payments for non-subs.	
Year	Amount	%Change	Amount	%Change	Amount	%Change	Amount	%Change	Amount	%Change
1963	37,226	—	3,134	—	933	—	660	—	273	—
1964	40,686	9.3	3,670	17.1	1,057	13.3	756	14.5	301	10.3
1965	44,386	9.1	3,963	8.0	1,259	19.1	924	22.2	335	11.3
1966	49,328	11.1	4,045	2.1	1,383	9.8	1,030	11.5	353	5.4
1967	54,771	11.0	4,518	11.7	1,534	10.9	1,136	10.3	398	12.7
1968	59,486	8.6	4,973	10.1	1,798	17.2	1,246	9.7	552	38.7
1969	64,983	9.2	5,658	13.8	1,894	5.3	1,393	11.8	501	−10.2
1970	71,016	9.3	6,001	6.1	2,203	16.3	1,620	16.3	588	16.4
1971	78,178	10.1	7,295	21.6	2,491	13.1	1,865	15.1	626	7.3
1972	86,198	10.2	8,004	9.7	2,760	10.8	2,090	11.2	670	7.0
Av. rate of growth	—	9.8	—	11.1	—	12.9	—	13.6	—	11.0
Std. dev.	—	0.9	—	5.8	—	4.6	—	3.5	—	12.8

Conventional versus effective rates of return

Table 2 presents the U.S. direct investment figures (column 1), the conventional returns on direct investment (column 2), the payments for technology transfer (column 4), and the total income from U.S. subsidiaries (defined as conventional returns plus technology transfer payments from U.S. subsidiaries to their parents—column 5) for the world as a whole and for the period 1963–1972.

What we choose to call "conventional" and "effective" annual rates of return are calculated for the purpose of comparison and appear in column 3 and 6 respectively.

Conventional rates are defined as conventional returns in year t divided by direct investment in year t. Effective rates are defined as total income from subsidiaries (conventional returns plus technology transfer payments) in year t divided by direct investment in year t. We would not strongly support the theoretical appropriateness of these measures of profitability. Rather we simply hope that by having calculated means and standard deviations for a series of 10 data points, we are able to at least attenuate the problems of matching returns against investment at any single year as a measure of profitability.

It is interesting to observe the high degree of stability of both conventional (mean 8.7; standard deviation 0.42) and effective (mean 10.8; standard deviation 0.54) rates during the period. Technology transfer payments "allowed for", on average, an additional 2.1 per cent return on direct investment of U.S. multinational corporations abroad.

Conventional versus effective rates for Latin America

Similar to Table 2 for the World as a whole, Table 3 shows the figures of U.S. direct investment in Latin America (column 1), the conventional returns (column 2), the payments for technology transfer (column 4) and the total income from U.S. subsidiaries (conventional returns plus technology transfer payments—column 5) for that region of the world for the same period 1963–1972.

Table 2
CONVENTIONAL VERSUS EFFECTIVE RATES OF RETURN FOR THE WORLD AS A WHOLE ($ MILLION)

	(1)	(2)	(3)=(2)/(1)	(4)	(5)=(4)+(2)	(6)=(5)/(1)
Year	Direct Investment	Conventional Returns	Conventional Rate of Return (%)	Tech. Transfer Payments	Total Income	Effective Rate of Return (%)
1963	37,226	3,134	8.4	660	3,794	10.2
1964	40,686	3,670	9.0	756	4,426	10.8
1965	44,386	3,963	8.9	924	4,887	11.0
1966	49,328	4,045	8.2	1,030	5,075	10.3
1967	54,771	4,518	8.2	1,136	5,654	10.3
1968	59,486	4,973	8.4	1,246	6,219	10.5
1969	64,983	5,658	8.7	1,393	7,051	10.8
1970	71,016	6,001	8.5	1,620	7,621	10.7
1971	78,178	7,295	9.3	1,865	9,160	11.7
1972	86,198	8,004	9.3	2,090	10,094	11.7
Mean	—		8.7	—	—	10.8
Std. dev.	—		0.42	—	—	0.54

Conventional and effective rates of return are again calculated and are shown in columns 3 and 6, respectively.

It is interesting to observe that for Latin America effective rates seem to present a more stable pattern (mean 12.8 per cent; standard deviation 1.5 per cent) than conventional rates (mean 10.7 per cent; standard deviation 1.6 per cent). Technology transfer payments "allowed for", on average, an additional 2.1 per cent return on investment of U.S. multinational corporations in Latin America.

Conventional versus effective rates in Japan

Similarly to Table 2 for the World as a whole and Table 3 for Latin America, Table 4 shows the figures of U.S. direct investment in Japan

Table 3
CONVENTIONAL AND EFFECTIVE RATES OF RETURN FOR LATIN AMERICA ($ MILLION)

Year	(1) Direct Investment	(2) Conventional Return	(3)=(2)/(1) Conventional Rate of Return (%)	(4) Tech. Transfer Payments	(5)=(4)+(2) Total Income	(6)=(5)/(1) Effective Rate of Return (%)
1963	8,424	956	11.3	136	1,092	13.0
1964	8,662	1,011	11.7	148	1,159	13.4
1965	8,894	995	11.2	174	1,169	13.1
1966	9,391	1,113	11.8	176	1,289	13.7
1967	8,826	1,190	12.1	192	1,382	14.0
1968	10,265	1,218	11.9	226	1,444	14.1
1969	11,033	1,277	11.6	245	1,522	13.8
1970	11,694	1,057	9.0	264	1,321	11.3
1971	12,252	1,130	9.2	281	1,411	11.5
1972	12,982	962	7.4	272	1,234	9.5
Mean	—	—	10.7	—	—	12.8
Std. dev.	—	—	1.6	—	—	1.5

(column 1), as well as the conventional returns (column 2), the payments for technology transfer (column 4) and the total income from U.S. subsidiaries (conventional returns plus technology transfer payments—column 5) for that country for the period 1967–71. (The data for the whole period 1963–1972 was not available in the sources used, Teplin and Sanvincente).

Conventional and effective rates of return were again calculated and are shown in columns 3 and 6, respectively.

It is interesting to observe that, for Japan, effective rates seem to present just a slightly more stable pattern (mean 13.3 per cent; standard deviation 1.66 per cent) than conventional rates (mean 8.4 per cent; standard deviation 1.21 per cent). Technology transfer payments "allowed for", on average, an additional 4.9 per cent return on investment of U.S. multinational corporations in Japan during the period under consideration.

Conventional versus effective rates: comparing between Japan and the World as a whole, Latin America and the World as a whole and Japan and Latin America.

Table 5 shows the calculated averages and standard deviations for conventional and effective annual rates of return for the World as a whole, Japan and Latin America.

i) *Comparison between World and Japan:* While conventional rates do not significantly differ (8.4 per cent for Japan and 8.6 per cent for World), the average effective rate for Japan (13.3 per cent) is substantially higher than for the World as a whole (10.8 per cent).

Table 4
CONVENTIONAL VERSUS EFFECTIVE RATES OF RETURN FOR JAPAN ($ MILLION)

Year	(1) Direct Investment	(2) Conventional Returns	(3)=(2)/(1) Conventional Rate of Return (%)	(4) Tech. Transfer Payments	(5)=(4)+(2) Total Income	(6)=(5)/(1) Effective Rate of Return (%)
1967	756	53	7.0	33	86	11.4
1968	870	63	7.2	41	104	11.9
1969	1,050	95	9.0	51	146	13.9
1970	1,244	110	8.8	66	176	14.1
1971	1,423	139	9.8	80	219	15.4
Mean	—	—	8.4	—	—	13.3
Std. dev.	—	—	1.21	—	—	1.66

Table 5
CONVENTIONAL VERSUS EFFECTIVE RATES FOR THE WORLD AS A WHOLE, LATIN AMERICA AND JAPAN—MEAN AND STANDARD DEVIATIONS CALCULATED FOR THE PERIOD, 1967–1971

Region	World		Latin America		Japan	
Rate	Mean	Std. dev.	Mean	Std. dev.	Mean	Std. dev.
Conventional	8.6	.42	10.8	1.53	8.4	1.21
Effective	10.8	.54	13.0	1.41	13.3	1.66

ii) *Comparison between World and Latin America:* On grounds of, perhaps, political risks differentials it is not surprising to observe that the average conventional rate of return in Latin America (10.8 per cent) is higher than for the world as a whole (8.6 per cent). However, it is interesting to observe that for the period 1967–1971, technology transfer payments allowed for an additional 2.2 per cent return on investment of U.S. multinational corporations both in Latin America and in the World as a whole. Note that this equality also holds for the period 1963–1972 (2.1 per cent for both Latin America and World as a whole).

Conclusion

The trends on the data on conventional returns and on payments for technology transfer from U.S. subsidiaries in Japan, Latin America and the World as a whole to their parents for the period 1963–1972 seem to be consistent with two major implications of the Optimal Degree of Ownership view of the World, namely:

a) Abstracting from political risk and regulatory differentials, the Optimal Degree of Ownership of a subsidiary from the parent's point of view should be expected to vary across countries and across industries within a country, to the extent that the degrees of uncertainty and informational asymmetry and the likelihood of small numbers associated with the sale of know-how also vary across countries and across industries within a country.

b) Regulatory limits on profit repatriation and on the degree of ownership of a subsidiary tend to force the multinational firm to alter its optimal ownership solution. The force change in the optimal ownership position will affect both, the real flow of technology transfer and the extent to which the nominal flow of payments reflects the real flow of technology transfer.

REFERENCES

1. Sotelino, F.B. *The Optimal Degree of Ownership of a Subsidiary Helpful Concept?*—Relatorio de Pesquisa s/no., COPPEAD/UFRJ, 1978.
2. Caves, R.E. *International Corporations: The Industrial Economics of Foreign Investment*—Economica, Feb. 1971.
3. Hymer, S.H. *The International Operations of National Firms*: A Study of Direct Investment, MIT, 1966.
4. Dunning, J.H. *Studies in International Investment*, Allen and Unwin, London, 1970.
5. Vernon, R. *Sovereignty at Bay—The Multinational Spread of U.S. Enterprise*, Basic Books, New York, 1971.
6. Knickerbocker, F.T. *Oligopolistic Reaction and Multinational Enterprise*, Harvard University, Boston, 1973.
7. Williamson, D.E. *Markets and Hierarquies: Analysis and Antitrust Implications*, Free Press, New York, 1975.

Management of Development for Human Welfare

29. Management of Development for Human Welfare

George Fernandes

Mr. George Fernandes, is Union Minister for Industries, India. A well-known and active trade union leader, Mr. Fernandes has been at the forefront of Indian political life for a long time.

The Conference has a very interesting theme: "Management of Development for Human Welfare". I presume all of us have been concerned with management of development for human welfare in some form or the other because I like to believe that except for such elements as are classified anti-social, the rest of us are always concerned with human welfare, and no matter what position one occupies and in what station one is placed at a particular point of time, one is always concerned with human welfare and all activity invariably points in that direction.

A few days ago I was addressing a different group of people which included managers, and the theme was about hope, "Hope for Mankind". And I was to make a point that most of the time one man's hope generally becomes another man's despair, one experiences it everywhere, in any situation; in personal life, in the lives of nations. One hopes for victory which is another man's defeat, one hopes for success which is another man's failure. So invariably one man's hope is related with despair of someone else. And I was wondering as to how one could get out of that kind of a situation and make things different. The same thought is in my mind when I think of management of development for human welfare, not for the same reason, because I do not believe that development for human welfare can at all mean deprivation of a certain segment of the people. In other words, I do not believe it is necessary to divide humanity into two parts, and think of someone's welfare as someone else's deprivation. But I thought that, may be, this is the forum where one should really get into this point. I wonder whether at least in our own country, what happens in India with its 630 million people. I note that you have delegates from a large number of countries, but we pro-

251

duce thirteen million people every year at the moment. So what happens in this country has a bearing not only to the welfare of the people of this country but it has a bearing on the welfare of humanity elsewhere also. So, putting oneself in the position where one is concerned with development, where one is concerned with human welfare in one's own country, one wonders whether we have a situation here where development for human welfare can mean different things to different men. I notice that we are discussing management of various services in today's session which concerns housing, health, civic services, and so on—management of all these as a part of the total concept of management. I hope it will be possible for us to discuss this in a concrete form and not in an abstract form. It could be an excellent theorising on this subject, for instance, how to provide houses to everyone in this country, how to provide medicare to everyone in this country, how to provide excellent education to everyone in this country. Therefore, it could be real, good, theorising on this subject, and a certain management perspective on providing the excellence in everything, could be worked out. But that would be the abstract. Our problems are very concrete, very genuine. Therefore, the question before me is whether it will be possible to apply all our thinking and relate it to the problem as it is, as it exists, as we have inherited it. Some of us who have assembled here may even have contributed to the making of it, not deliberately. But now, having inherited a situation, allowing that situation to continue, to accentuate, in fact is also part of the contribution. But the point is that we have inherited a certain situation and we have problems at various levels. And at the micro-level when we start examining them or at each sectorial level when we start examining them, what kind of a management approach is possible in order to solve the problem, or, in other words, to manage the whole system as we would like to manage it?

I have been trying to popularise the phrase called the 5-star culture. It is related to 5-star hotels. But actually this 5-star culture perhaps brings out in the shortest possible form the kind of contradictions that we face and the kind of management problems that we face. I will explain why. Perhaps someone who runs a 5-star hotel could also be a part of this audience discussing management for human welfare. It costs thousand rupees a day; the tariff I am told is Rs. 490 and given all the other perquisites, all the other expenses that are normally associated with a 490-rupee single occupancy tariff, it amounts to a thousand rupees, howsoever you pay it, for 24 hours. Now this in a country where the per capita income per annum in 1977 was Rs. 1000. And this when from the Planning Commission, from the Government, from the statisticians, from the academicians down, everybody is aware that 300 million people live below the poverty line. And the poverty line in India is not an academic subject. For instance; once I blew my top off when someone said, "there is poverty in the United States also. So what if there is poverty in India, and it takes a long, long, time to do away with it?" There are two different concepts. Poverty has different concepts. It means one thing in

the United States and it is another thing here. Here when one talks of "below the poverty line", it means not being able to spend 10 U.S. cents per day per head. That is the type of poverty that we talk of in India. That is the size of the problem when we talk of living below the poverty line in India—not being able to spend 10 cents per day per head, a little less than a rupee. And this is where human welfare has got to be put in focus:
— A thousand rupees a day in a 5-star hotel;
— A thousand rupees per annum, per capita income;
— And 10 cents per day per head, less than a rupee per day per head, for almost half the people.

Now, what is the management of development for human welfare that we are going to discuss, given these problems? And is our debate, our discussion, and all that we are going to think and plan going to be related to the development of 10 cents per day, the Rs. 1000 per annum, or Rs. 1000 per day on a person?

A very fundamental contradiction! And perhaps none of us is responsible for having created this. That is why I said we have inherited this. But any management perspective will have to take note of these problems and then take a step forward. And that is why I raised this question: If someone hopes, someone else despairs. Therefore, is this human welfare, this development of human welfare concerned with the development of a segment of the population? Or is it concerned with humanity as a whole? And while sitting here in New Delhi where a large number of managers are going to share their experiences from all over the world and where the cream of managers have assembled, when we talk of human welfare, is that human welfare going to encompass every human being within this country at best, or does it preclude some? Or, is there a graded form of management so that each year we lift a certain number of people from a certain state of helplessness to a state of welfare and hope that gradually in times to come everyone will live happily? My submission is that proposition is not going to work in this country.

Dr. George McRobie has presented a paper wherein he talks of the problems of investment for a country like ours. He talks of the total amount of money that will be available, say, in the next five-years or in the next 10 years, if you are going to have even a 10-year or a five-year perspective, to provide jobs to everybody. When we discuss human welfare, we cannot forget the fact that we have 40 million people who are unemployed in this country just now and many more millions who are underemployed. We cannot run away from that problem. What is management of development for human welfare in India which does not take note of those unemployed? It would be totally irrelevant to the problem as it exists.

There has been reference to the new thrust to the industrial policy, for instance, in this country that the new Government has given. The policy that has been much criticised, has also been understood, and I hope, as days go by, it will be better understood. There we talk about three major shifts from the ideals of industrial development as they existed till a year ago. In another fortnight, it will be a year since the new policy has become the Industrial Policy of the country. We decided that we shall move from the urban to the rural, a highly centralised urban to the rural. We decided that we shall move from the large to the small in terms of share investment, in terms of the size, of units that are going to be set up. We decided that we shall move to the extent possible from the machine to the hand. I emphasise to the extent possible, because one can always reduce any proposition to absurdities. Now, this is related, in my view, to human welfare, or development for human welfare.

As I said, in that industrial policy we intend to put man at the centre of things. And the inspiration to put that phrase in came from Mahatma Gandhi, whose observation was that the supreme consideration is man. So, to us, the new industrial policy is oriented towards human welfare or development for human welfare. It is not everything. Human welfare is a much wider term. In fact, the four topics that have been taken up, I find that the various problems which the society faces and the various social problems that one has, are being discussed. But I relate it with my new thrust in the industrial policy. I have had managers, and I have had industrialists and also Government functionaries, very senior Government functionaries, who come and tell me that this whole idea of moving from the large to the small, from the urban to the rural, is going to create problems. And what are the problems? You go to the rural: you do not get clean drinking water; you do not have medicare—not medicare in the sense in which it is understood elsewhere—but you do not have medical facilities; you do not have schools for the education of your children; you do not have housing. The fact is that all these things are there. Everybody in this country drinks water, some form of water. So it is not true that there is no water. Everybody lives. We are very proud of the fact that millions of our children are going to school. And we also have hospitals and dispensaries and health units all over the country. We have them. But somehow the managers, the Government officials, the industrialists, all believe that when we talk of moving to the rural, none of these things exist. In other words, they don't exist to the satisfaction of those who are accustomed to a certain style of life or to certain conditions which are available in the urban areas. Any discussion on the kind of human welfare that encompasses the whole lot of our people, has to take note of the fact that you have divided the society into two, may be three, may be four, different segments.

Some years ago they built houses for top Government functionaries, and perhaps all Government functionaries, right here in Delhi. They were very symbolically named. Very literal translation of the very highly sanskritised names would be difficult for me. But one was called Shan Nagar which meant glory, that all those who live in glory, in real luxury, in luxurious glory, live in Shan Nagar, the highest in the Government in terms of functionaries or in terms of ministers. Ministers, of course, belong to a different category. They cannot be classified. But at the level of managers, at the level of professional managers in the Government—even a civil servant is a manager in the ultimate analysis—there was Shan Nagar. And there was Man Nagar. In other words people to whom you gave respect—next in hierarchy. Then there was Vinay Nagar where man was expected to behave in a certain way. And then finally there was Seva Nagar, the servants. And the Prime Minister of this country named them! *Shan, Man, Vinay* and *Seva!* The point I am making is that when I am today discussing moving into the rural areas, I am taking humanity as a whole, not humanity in a segmented form, in a fragmented form, not in terms of these divisions which, in a certain way, we have inherited for 5000 years and in a certain way we are trying to perpetuate today with—*Shan, Man, Vinay* and *Seva.*

How does one really plan, let us say, housing? Take Bombay. There were 7.8 million people in December last year. Out of these people, 4.8 million were without homes. Recently when I had to take a decision to find a house for the Chairman and Managing Director of one of our own undertakings, a public sector undertaking the cost was Rs. 400 a square foot. Now, where is the management for human development, for human welfare in Bombay City in the area of housing where Rs. 400 per square foot is at one end and 4.8 million people living on pavements and in shanty towns is at the other end? Take education—millions of children in municipal, primary, schools run by local boards, local Government, where the per capita monthly expenditure varies from 50 cents to a dollar, which is what the Government or the local body spends on education. On the other hand there are children going to private and public schools. I am sure I don't have to ask how much it costs. I am not trying to bring out the class distinctions in society. I am only trying to raise the point: What is the management of development for human welfare? Because if it is going to be on the basis of Rs. 500 per month on education for one child and Rs. 5 per month on education for another child then what is the human welfare concept? Is it a concept which says that the divisions must continue, the welfare of society will rest in the perpetuation of this kind of a situation? This is a fundamental question.

I only hope that you won't pass them off by saying that these are philosophical questions, these are not problems of management. The problem of management is that you manage a school with Rs. 500 per month per child efficiently and effectively and you manage a school with Rs. 5 per month per child also efficiently and effectively. If this is the management, then we are on two different wavelengths. Then let us not go into these high-sounding phrases, of development for human welfare, because humanity is humanity, mankind is mankind. We have had enough of divisions. Ideologies will be there. We are not discussing ideologies. People can swear by private enterprise; people can swear by public ownership. We may have different ideological perspectives. We are not discussing that. We are concerned with the theme: Human Welfare. The same analogy applies to medicine; the same applies to hospitals.

I was recently engaged in three political campaigns—one of them proved to be a rather difficult one. There was a case of police firing and there was a case of police beating. And I ad to go to a hospital—not once but twice to the same hospital in a little place called Belthangadi in South Canara in Karnataka. It wasn't a hospital. There was no medicine. There was just nothing. And this is not a hyperbole. There was just nothing. The bedsheets were stinking. They must have been used, for God knows how many patients. They just had no facilities. I could not allow the large number of injured young people go without proper medical attention. I went there and took them out of the hospital. I begged the people there to put them in some private nursing homes, but that was a problem again. In Bombay now the status symbol, I am told, is a place called Jaslok. I would like someone to find out what the bills are. I know, of course, you have the various municipal hospitals where if you don't look down to see where you are walking, you will be walking on people. This is the truth. So what is the management here for human welfare? There is on the one hand a well polished, well cleaned, well oiled, very well managed, everything spick and span, Jaslok, and on the other hand there is Nair Hospital run by the Bombay Municipal Corporation with all its problems and those other public hospitals in the city which in retrospect are also very well managed. Is that all that human welfare is about?

When a manager, when a man from my ministry, from the Industries Department, or when an industrialist, comes and tells me, he cannot go to the rural area, and asks me, "What happens to my family, what happens to my children's education—my children are in school?" I, of course, give answers to these questions. But they are not adequate answers. I am aware of it. I tell the people, if what is available is good enough for people there, then it is jolly well good enough for others. But I know it is not an adequate answer. This is, to me, what human welfare is about. One can always speak in the abstract and make excellent formulations. But one, I believe, needs to get down to brass tacks and really find ways and means of answering these questions. And this pertains not only as I said, to managing the kind of new thrust. Though in the area of industry, I believe, that one will have to, as in the area of agriculture, one will have to create new managerial skills that are attuned, that are related, to the size of the problem as we face it in our country.

I had occasions to address—not occasions but one occasion to address—the All-India Management Conference in Madras some time ago where I raised this point: How to make all that we are trying to do, relevant and related to the man who needs that help, to the man who needs that assistance right down there? In other words, when you put man at the centre of things, how to relate everything to that man, to the problems that beset and confront that man? In my view you just cannot try to compartmentalise human welfare by setting up different segments of society and concerning oneself with the welfare of each segment of society in its own form.

The role of 'manager', has been defined by various people in various ways. Many experts in management are capable of giving excellent definitions which have been memorised by students of management, I am sure. Maximum profit, minimum cost and so on and so forth, and somehow interplay some of these things, about efficiency and all that. Mr. Charat Ram said that I was a trade unionist. Years ago at a meeting of the Productivity Council in Bombay I was faced with this question by an industrialist. He said, "Mr. Fernandes, I have the best factory in town", and he elaborated. He was a very articulate man who could put across his ideas very effectively. He said, "We have lighting by Philips, we have airconditioning by Voltas, we had BECON people come and lay out our whole machinery; our factory is the finest place to work in; it is one of the best anywhere in the world." And he was right. But he said, "The workers are not working, I am not getting anything, they are no different from workers of any other unit." I told him, "you are perfectly right, because you have the best in everything insofar as your factory is concerned; but you seem to forget that your workers come to work on a train where under your own laws, the railway regulations, even animals cannot be sent or cannot be packed in a wagon beyond a certain number —we have rules on how many animals can be put in a freight car—but we do not have rules on how many people can sit in a railway compartment; we simply do not have them. And the workers come packed like sardines. Believe it or not."

You have got to go to Bombay as part of an exercise to see how our suburban railway trains run. In fact, you can see it in Delhi buses. Just go and try and hang on to one of the Delhi buses and you would know. And when a worker comes to work 20 miles, packed in a train with no sitting room, or in a bus in the manner in which he comes here in Delhi, where he has got up in the morning at 4 O'clock because there is no water tap in his house, he has to line up with scores of other people for a drop of water which may or may not come sometimes, where he has to settle the quarrel which his wife has had with the wife of one of his neighbours the previous evening over a bucket of water, and where at the end of the day he has again to go back, to the same kind of shanty town living, then lighting by Philips, airconditioning by Voltas, layout by BECON—the best consultancy perhaps—is not going to give production. Therefore, the more important factor is the motivation. But what does the worker see? What kind of a motivation is being given to that man? Is he being inspired to do something? Or, is he told "Well, here are excellent arrangements, you produce, and for the rest of your life, for the 18 hours of your 24 hours' day, for the greater part of your life—because in my factory you are spending only a small part of your life—for the greater part of your life I don't care what happens to you, you can go to hell." It may not be said in so many words, I know, none would like to say that, but it is there. The worker is also a conscious and thinking human being. Therefore, what kind of motivation does he have?

Ultimately what kind of a motivation are we going to give to people? Because, human welfare will call for a tremendous effort not only by the manager but by the people right down the line. And unless the right kind of motivation is given to the workers, you are not going to achieve anything. As Government we keep discussing this problem; as trade unionists we keep discussing this problem; as managers we keep discussing this problem. And now as a minister I am concerned with all the three and I have got to keep on discussing this problem at all levels. Somewhere along the line I feel that we failed to provide the right kind of motivation which, if I may come back to the point I started from, is related to the kind of culture that we are going to build. The 5-star culture cannot coexist in the given situation, particularly in our country, with the kind of deprivation that you see right around you.

Therefore, in this excellent theme of management of development for human welfare, I hope it will be possible for us to discuss the issue not only in its abstract but in its concrete; by understanding the problem; by putting the spotlight on the problem, and relating to the solutions of the problem; by bringing about where necessary—and in my view it is absolutely necessary—the kind of cultural changes that are also required to bring about human welfare with which all of us are concerned.

30. Management of Development for Human Welfare

Ivan Lansberg Henriquez

Dr. Lansberg heads the largest consortium in Latin America and Spain in the field of insurance and reinsurance. In Venezuela, he is a member of the Board of several firms such as Sears Roebuck, Philips, and Brown Boveri. He is Honorary President of CIOS-World Council of Management of which he was the President during 1972–1975. Dr. Lansberg is also the President of the Institute for Educational Counselling and Institute for Organisational Development.

Management, the Missing Link

As a great Prime Minister of this country, Jawaharlal Nehru, has been reported to complain: "We have had lots of advice from experts on how to make economic plans; but when shall we hear something on how to implement them?" A foreign delegation which visited one of our Latin-American countries, expressed to its President in its farewell visit that: "Seldom have we found a people so brilliant in analysis and so backward in execution." If these complaints can be considered as architypical all over the developing world, as I am sure they can, and if by definition "implementing" and "execution" are no less than synonyms of management, may we quickly agree that management is now standing in the limelight of the world as the missing link in the chain of development for human welfare. Why should I dare to say "missing" link? Has not management been the theme and subject of a growing amount of teaching and speeching, of seminars and congresses, of schools and universities all over the Third World? Is there not an ever increasing flow of thought on the management of change and management of development, and management of society? My question is, if relatively so little has happened: Why?

Why have We Failed?

I am sure that there are many answers, and our first task should be to find them. May I venture a few:

1) Management is a product of the Western Industrialised World, which still seem to be groping to understand it. Even new definitions of management are still coming in. Faddism, managerial "nouveau-mania" is still the order of the day. Just think of OR, MBO, ST, OD, TA, 3-D, only to mention a few.

2) Management "principles", as they were developed in—and for—Western industrialised countries, do not seem transferable to cultures where people have totally different existential assumptions and attitudes. We all know—and Japan has proved this point spectacularly—that effective management of development must start from each nation's own cultural legacy, the identity of which of course must be well understood by the nation itself, which can be at times a difficult requirement indeed!

3) Apart from the cultural aspect, let us remember that existing management knowledge has been generated in relatively structured and stable societies. It was built on the rocks of much more advanced stages of social, economic and political conditions. To walk on these rocks is a different thing than to swim in the rough seas of our developing nations, with their overwhelming problems we all so well know.

4) Management has been mainly developed in private enterprise, and has focussed on responding to its environment, keeping for itself a relative autonomy of action. It has centred more on producing goods and delivering services, on fighting for its revenues, on looking for opportunities. In government we see management mainly concentrating on the maintenance of order and services or on the collection of revenues, rather than on the detection of felt needs. Management for development, on the other hand, seems to require something quite different, about which unfortunately we still know too little. It calls for social creation, a subject on which I hope to elaborate later.

5) Management for Development has many implications and requires capabilities in the all important areas of power and structures.

It calls for special skills in the management of conflict, in the building of trust, in the understanding and management of prejudice and discrimination, in the handling of the sense of bereavement which in most of us is such an important byproduct of change.

We know relatively little about the organisation of systems, which are themselves made up of independent organisations, so the ability to "link" becomes an important requirement in the management for development. Most of the areas I have mentioned here have been quite scantly treated in management literature and training, and the research on their influence on effective management for development has been quite insufficient.

6) Top-leadership in public management is in general, and quite particularly so in developing countries, highly power (i.e., politically) motivated. On the other hand, management as a faculty is more achievement oriented, albeit that power plays an important role in the emotional set-up of most executives. Undoubtedly politicians, who also are good managers, appear to be a

scarce breed indeed. Many seem to accept management as something like an inevitable nuisance. This attitude, which is not uncommon in individuals with a great drive for power, surely has been another barrier in the development of social management.

7) Development itself, as a process, has been taking quite a long time to be understood. As we all know, in the beginning the concept (of development) centred only on economic growth; this simple idea was then successively broadened to include other important factors like skills, motivation for productivity, tools, institutional structures, equity in income distribution, "quality of life" and so on.

Development

However, we have slowly been awakening to a much deeper insight, which in my view has tremendous implications on our thinking about management for development. It is the proposition that the development process itself must be seen as a dynamic social system which, like an ever widening galaxy, is composed of numerous sub-systems in mutual and circular interaction. Apart from the economic system of production and distribution, these sub-systems include systems of values, of world-outlook, of motives and attitudes, of shared knowledge, of kinship and family. And a very fundamental characteristic of authentic development is that it must be self-propelling, that it be capable of generating, managing and controlling its own continuous change for which it must keep ever innovative, as well as structurally strong enough to absorb unceasing tensions. Its political, economic, social and cultural institutions must be able to adapt to ever new impacts. If this deeper understanding of development has taken so much time; and if management in developing countries is so far behind as we have seen, it will be clear that management for development is a very new concept indeed. I venture to say that this concept is destined to be the greatest challenge of our times!

Management versus Ideology

As we all know too well, traditionally change and development have been strongly guided by ideologies. However obsolete we may consider their contents, what gives ideologies of course their power is the passion they engender in people. They provide guidelines for action, and legitimise the exercise of power. Some cynic wrote in a Caracas newspaper that those who lack an ideology betray themselves in that what they really are after is to wield power. But again, in spite of everything, ideologies must, of course, be taken very seriously indeed. They are a bridge between the beliefs and the actions of men and women.

There is one thing about action, which I would wish to underline, as I believe we sometimes tend intellectually to underestimate its effects. Was it not Jean Paul Sartre who advised us that reality is not created, nor do values exist, except through action. Indeed, with values it is as with the traveller in a famous Spanish poem "..there is no road, the road is made whilst you walk" which may be quite a pertinent reminder to management in general, and management for development in particular!

Although management is an important generator of values, of course in no way can it ever become an ideology. It cannot have particular postures on political and social issues, nor will it pretend to explain or legitimise any special perception of social reality.

However, if we ponder over management for social development we find ourselves making inroads into the traditional domains of ideology, as our final purpose after all is the detection and satisfaction of human needs. So, inevitably, issues arise such as how to relate effectively with the community, how to seek political support, how to analyse and comprehend social structures and processes, how to overcome the deeply conditioned mistrust of peasants, or how to organise the poor for participation in making policy decisions which affect their lives. So this is the dilemma: Ideology without management is fatal; on the other hand, if the main purpose of social management is not delivery and maintenance of services, however important that may be, but rather the creation of positive change, necessarily the question arises; what change is positive?

The "trickling-down effect" on which orthodox capitalism has based its hopes, clearly has not performed in the Third World. The mere pace of growth in numbers, of the poor, wipes out most of the effects of the trickling. Social management may present us here with some important remedies, as precisely its purpose is reaching the poor.

Socialism, on the other hand, has been victimised by its rigid centralisation of power, hampering the development of private initiative on all levels, which is a vital requirement in developing countries. Social Management, on the contrary, focuses on all possible ways and means to liberate, integrate, mobilise and channel human energy at all levels towards the satisfaction of individual and collective needs.

So, far from becoming a conflict, the dilemma I have posed between social management and ideology has the potential to turn into a symbiosis, which indeed can be truly constructive.

The Management of Social Development—a New Issue

Although the idea of social management may not be so new at all, what is new is the serious effort we are presently witnessing in building a body of knowledge which can be relevantly applied in the process of development.

In August 1976, the Rockefeller Foundations sponsored a conference in Bellagio, Italy, where about twenty top representatives from the most outstanding Institutes of Management in the developing countries were brought together to share their understanding of the subject, and identify its basic issues. The papers of this conference, which I think was an important breakthrough, were published by the Foundation. Then, in July 1977, another

meeting of minds took place, this time in Caracas and sponsored by IESA where leaders of four major Third World management Institutes came together to share their emerging experiences, and to hasten the knowledge building process to which their institutions were already individually committed.

Professor David C. Korten from Harvard, who has been associated with the Asian Institute of Management in the Philippines, presented at the Caracas meeting an important background paper from which I will draw some ideas as an example of the kind of thinking which is going on in social development management. Korten proposes to put to rest the traditional formal organisational models, which find their sustenance in the Analytic and the Cybernetic paradigmy of decision theory. Analytic organisational thinking—the old way—is of course based on the bureaucratic model, on central control, uniform compliance and a minimisation of adaptive behaviour. Planning and implementation are strictly separated, ends and means are kept apart. We all know what has happened to the analytic paradigm. From its drama Albert O. Hirschman developed his classic: "Principle of the hiding hand" which states that one can never foresee the multitude of barriers to implementation, nor the creative responses by which these barriers can be overcome on the spot through the initiative of implementors. The cybernetic paradigm on the other hand starts from quite different assumptions. It is guided by the realistic observation that individuals in fact "play it by ear", that they make their decisions based on "short-cycle information feedback", seeking to eliminate uncertainty. It focusses on processes, rather than on techniques of decision-making. "The decisions" which emerge from complex social systems are a result of the mutual coping and adaptation of multitudes of decision-makers throughout the system, each attempting to address his or her own definition of organisational and personal purpose within the context of a changing environment." In the cybernetic model, planning and implementation become inseparable parts of an ongoing dynamic process.

Professor Korten's proposition is to come to a synthesis of these two paradigms, for which he proposes the adoption of a "Rational—Adaptive Model of Organisation", which "seeks to improve system-performance by creating problem-solving teams throughout the organisation, and which are able to act within broadly defined policy guidelines to achieve high levels of performance, responsive to local needs." This model, the basic concept of which has been successfully applied in advanced business corporations, combines performance orientation, flexibility, and greater rationality in problem-solving on the spot.

Linkages

Korten's other point I want to mention relates to the great importance of effective linking of local institutions. A major study of Governments in 16 Asian countries carried out by Cornell University has concluded that those

countries which have strong horizontal linkages, combined with effective vertical linkages, are also more likely to have higher agricultural productivity, make better use of improved agricultural technologies, have higher levels of nutrition, health, and education, greater security in rural areas, less rural unemployment and underemployment, more equal income distribution, and lower rates of population growth. The evidence seems then clearly to reveal that the creation of inter-institutional system is a much more central management task than even the planning and implementation of particular projects. Here again, we find ourselves with an amazing lack of research and literature on the subject.

Meta-Management

Out of these kind of ideas has arisen what has been labelled "Meta-Management", where system-management approaches an idea of statesmanship, and on which some literature has come forth from Harvard scholars as well as from the Scandinavian Institutes for Administrative Research.

The fundamental concept of Meta-Management is described as an endeavour toward influencing problem-solving processes within the system rather than an attempt at "finding solutions to problems" on behalf of the system.

In Bellagio, William J. Siffin said some very revealing things about problems. He said that problems are not actually defined—they are stipulated. The question "What is the problem?" can be answered by analysis and deliberation, or by action, or both. When the answer is determined by action more than by analysis, an interesting thing happens: the solution specifies the problem. The problem then becomes that set of conditions that is affected beneficially by the intervention.

Roles of the Social Development Manager

As we can see, the management of social development is turning into an important new field of research and knowledge-building, where the education and training of Development Managers is of course a major issue.

One researcher, John Ickis, has identified the following roles of an effective manager of Social Development: not only must he be a strategist, infuser of values, decision-maker, negotiator, organisation architect and implementor, all of which roles of course are common to most kinds of managers, but additionally to these traditional roles, the Social Development Manager should be an ambassador capable of establishing working linkages with other organisations, a public spokesman who must be able to defend a controversial programme and above all he must be a good interpreter of community aspirations.

Obviously these kinds of roles will require distinctive skills, the training in which has not formed part of our traditional curricula, and thus will need special planning and elaboration.

Leadership

The process of Development taxes its managers with an exceptional demand. They are to be effective catalysts of change, the practising representatives of that very new profession, which is Social Architecture. As such, these managers are to become sowers of new values, transformers of social energy, educators and creators of those new dispositions and virtues, that are required in this cumbersome process.

In his latest book John Kenneth Galbraith focusses on that one characteristic which seems to be the core of every leader, "the willingness to confront unequivocally the major anxiety of their people in their time."

Herein no doubt consists the pervading principle of management of development for human welfare: the detection of deeply felt needs and anxieties must be the overriding priority of its efforts.

It is a great challenge indeed, because this kind of leadership is called for within a most turbulent environment, characterised by ambiguity, uncertainty, complexity and ever present interdependencies.

Human Welfare

But let us return to the basic notions expressed, i.e., that management is a creator and a motor of development, and that authentic development should be seen as a self-propelling self-regulating problem-solving social system. Inevitably, we must now confront the eternal question: "for what?" Here both the theme of our subject today, as well as the general theme of this Congress seem to come to our rescue. They state as the explicit purpose: "for human welfare". No doubt such a lofty goal must be acceptable to all of us, but then of course the problem lies in its qualification. What is human welfare? Is Utopia our purpose? What is Utopia? Is it "the good life"? What is "the good life" to each of us, be it individually or as nation-states? Please bear with me that I am asking these kinds of questions, but I do believe them to be most important indeed. Firstly, because I am quite sure there are many fundamental differences between our personal and collective views on the essence of what human welfare really is about. In the second place because, as Dean Mendoza has put it: "We will never be able to develop a working system for ourselves until we know clearly what we want the system for." Of course we all know this to be an elementary principle of any planning, organisation, any structure or strategy.

Last, but not least, if our goals are unclear, may we not quite easily fall into the trap that "while pursuing the unattainable we make impossible the realisable?" (Robert Ardrey).

So it will be imperative to put boundaries to our lofty purpose, and be as specific as we can possibly be. The discussions in the group sessions on special topics, like Agriculture, Social Services, Urban and Rural Communities, no doubt, will give us such an opportunity.

Psychological Barriers

In the management for development a number of psychological forces are of importance to be understood, as they must be reckoned with as potential barriers in the process of development. Let me touch on a few.

Power: The first one which comes to mind is power. We all remember Lord Acton's famous injunction that it tends to corrupt, and that absolute power even corrupts absolutely. Let us not forget, however, another admonition, just as true as Lord Acton's, which says that "all weakness tends to corrupt, and impotence corrupts absolutely" (Friedenberg). In management for development the point of course is to find peaceful ways and non-violent means to mitigate the defensiveness and resistance commonly expressed by those in power, when it comes to real change in the *status quo*.

Envy: Secondly, I want to touch on a totally different psychological reality, deeply rooted as well in human nature, which is envy. The mere mention of the word is enough to generate immediate rebuttal, and it is hard to bring clear and objective reasoning to bear on the subject. However, there appears to be no greater restraint on innovation, on personal development and on the defence of certain values, than the fear of envy. Although envy probably fulfils some important functions such as facilitating social controls, promoting the pluralisation of power, and in its own way contributing to equity, any excess of it can only succeed in impairing social justice. There seems to be no doubt that societies which have been capable of making real progress are those which were able to mitigate envy, restrain the fear of envy, and soften the impacts of guilt, shame and embarrassment.

Prejudice and discrimination: A third force to reckon within social development is of course the widespread presence of prejudice and discrimination, and it is still an open question to what degree this can be really overcome. We seem to have an imperative need to divide the human race up in "we's" and "they's". It would distract us too much from our subject to elaborate on this, but let us keep in mind that some feeling of solidarity is an obvious condition to be able to work together towards any common purpose. For this we must take stock and understand the ties that bind us. Harvey Hornstein of Columbia University has said it well: "Ultimately human survival will depend upon our wisdom as well as our willingness to transform society by creating social conditions which cause the bonds of *we* to prevail over the barriers of *they*."

Sense of loss: As a fourth and last example of a strong psychological barrier to change I would mention the sense of loss, the anguish of bereavement which accompanies change. Our individuality itself is a confluence of perceptions and emotional attachments to the systems around us. This confluence is what Peter Morris calls a "structure of meaning". When these linkages are cut or manipulated, it is as if the individual himself has been violated. While radicals may seek change and conservatives resist it, in each of us there is a disturbance which encompasses that very ambivalence, the wanting to accept

the new and yet hang on to the old. In this light 'The management of change seems to depend on the articulation of these conflicting impulses, which must be allowed to work themselves out" (Peter Morris).

A Nobel Prize

In 1973, in a CIOS Board Meeting in New York, it was suggested that management should be included as a field in which Nobel Prizes be awarded, be it as an extension of the Economics Prize. It was a great moment indeed for all of us, when this year for the first time in history, a Nobel Prize was conceded to a great scholar of management, Professor Herbert A. Simon of Pittsburgh's Carnegie Mellon University. His classic book *Administrative Behaviour* was cited by the Nobel committee. His theories on the process of decision-making in organisations have much contributed to our deeper understanding of what really moves social systems. I want to take this opportunity, and use of this platform, to express our feeling of immense satisfaction at the outstanding recognition which has been given to management in the person of Professor Simon.

Management—the New Name for Development

Hardly could there have been more timely a recognition, where it has now become clear to us that in the thrust of development for human welfare management indeed has been the missing link, without which development can neither take off, nor progress.

A great Pope has announced to the world that "Development is the New Name for Peace." In that order of thought, may I propose to you that *management is the new name for development*. This is our challenge lying ahead. Let us hope that we and our children will be able to meet it in time, with understanding, courage and perseverance. Never has a task been more urgent.

REFERENCES

Laurence D. Stifel, James S. Coleman and Joseph E. Black (Eds.). *Education and Training for Public Sector Management in Developing Countries*, The Rockefeller Foundation, March 1977.

David C. Korten (Ed.). *Population and Social Development Management: A Challenge for Management Schools. The Population and Social Development Management Center*—IESA, Caracas.

Harvey A. Hornstein. *Cruelty and Kindness*, Prentice-Hall, Inc. 1976.

Bertram M. Gross (Ed.). *Action under Planning*, McGraw-Hill Book Co., 1967.

Peter Morris. *Loss and Change*, Pantheon Books 1974 (Random House,

New York). (See also Book Review by Matthew P. Dumont, *A Theory of Social Behaviour*).

Helmut Schoeck. *Envy*, A Helen and Kurt Wolff Book Harcourt, Brace & World Inc., New York, 1970.

Albert O. Hirschman. *Development Projects Observed*, The Brookings Institute 1967, Washington, D.C.

Ivan Lansberg Henriquez. *Administration y Desarrollo* (Administration and Development), Monte Avila Editores, C.A., Caracas, 1974.

John Kenneth Galbraith. *The Age of Uncertainty*, Houghton Mifflin Co., Boston, 1977.

31. Management of Agriculture

M.S. Swaminathan

Dr. Swaminathan, an eminent agricultural scientist, is the Director General of the Indian Council of Agricultural Research (ICAR). Dr. Swaminathan, who is associated with a host of Indian and international organisations in the field of agricultural research, economics and genetics, was awarded the Ramon Magsaysay Award for Community Leadership in 1971. He was also awarded the Shanti Swarup Bhatnagar Medal for his contribution to the biological sciences in 1961.

Man's desire to have a settled life in place of a nomadic existence gave birth to the process of domestication of crops and animals about 10,000 years ago. Thus began the transition from hunting to farming. The credit for this transition should largely go to women. Many changes in farming technology have taken place over the last 10,000 years. It is, however, of interest that practically no new plants or animals have been added to those identified by the early agriculturists for domestication from among the wild flora and fauna, although attempts are in progress to develop and popularise a man-made cereal "Triticale". Even in fisheries, where man had remained until recently solely a gatherer of the fish produced in nature, there is a growing trend towards the growing of fish. Fish farming based on recent developments in freshwater aquaculture is slowly getting into prominence.

Agriculture moves forward only when a package of economically viable technology is supported by appropriate package of services and public policies which can enable every farmer irrespective of the size of his holding and risk-taking capacity to derive economic benefit from new technology. The art and science of successful agricultural management depend upon: (a) the knowledge base for the optimum use of the available human, sunlight, soilwater, nutrient and air resources, and (b) the ability to generate synergy or multiplier efforts in energy and investment input-output ratios by introducing blends of production and post-harvest technology, services and public policies characterised by a mutually supportive nature. The energy cycle upon which modern agriculture depends is shown in Fig. 1. For good management, there is need for: (a) a clean understanding of the agriculture assets and liabilities of each area, (b) the size of the untapped production reservoir existing in each farming system at current levels of technology, and (c) the constraints responsible for the gap between potential and actual productivity. The preparation of *Agricultural Balance Sheets* which can help to formulate scientific resource utilisation strategies and the organisation of *"gaps/constraints"* and *"malady and remedy"* analyses will have to be undertaken by competent interdisciplinary group. Scientific Agricultural Management needs only a good data base relating to the resource endowments of an area but also a clean understanding of social, cultural economic parameters governing a specific farming system.

Contrasting Trends in the Evolution of World Agriculture

The state of food and agriculture in the world shows two contrasting trends. In one kind of agriculture, larger and larger farms are being farmed by fewer and fewer cultivators. Such farms are highly automated and capital-intensive. Let me cite an illustration. A firm called Superior Farming Company, owned by Texas Oil Company, raises 26 different crops on about 6,000 hectares, with land and equipment worth about Rs. 30 crores. In this agribusiness, an irrigation system, called the drip method, bring individually piped water to every fruit tree and regulates the flow to a trickle, supplying exactly what each tree needs and no more. Under such systems of farming not only is the efficiency of inputs like water and fertiliser high, but labour productivity also is very high. In one study conducted during the mid-fifties, it was found that while in many countries of Asia and Africa about 2.5 to 10 work days were needed to produce one quintal of grain, the extent of labour time needed to produce the same quantity of grain was about 3 hours in parts of France and only 6 to 12 minutes in parts of the United States. The gap in the relative productivity of farm labour was therefore about 1 to 800 even over 20 years ago and this gap, which also represent the relative earning and purchasing power of farm labour, has been growing ever since.

In many of the poor nations, including India smaller farms have to be cultivated by the same or the even larger number of farmers. The percentage of work force employed in farming in India was 72.1 in 1971 and it is anticipated that this percentage will remain practically unaltered in 1981. The relative productivity of small farms, however, varies widely in the world. Japan could produce 6,720 kg of grain a hectare on very small farms in 1970, Africa 1, 270 kg, Asia 1,750 kg and Latin America 2,060 kg per hectare. Thus, the untapped production reservoir is very high in the tropics and sub-tropics.

Besides farm size and land and labour productivity, the other two major differences in the agriculture of the rich nation as compared to the poor ones, are in the pattern of agricultural growth and the nature of the food chain. The mechanised and low-labour consuming agriculture has achieved increased productivity largely on the basis of a high consumption of energy derived from the non-renewable resources of the earth. Such situation has now resulted in a widespread awareness of the simple truth that any finite resource, if exploited in an exponential manner on the assumption that the resource is infinite, will some day or the other get exhausted, thereby bringing the pattern of growth based on its consumption to ruin. It has also become clear that the tools of modernisation of agriculture, like pesticide, fertiliser, farm power and water, if indiscriminately used and excessively based on non-renewable resources, will end in crises, now referred to as "ecological crises", "energy crises" and so on. For example, 96 per cent of the energy input in the United States in 1970 came from oil, gas and coal, while in the same year non-commercial fuels like dung, firewood and wastes provided 52 per cent of our energy needs. The reserves of the fossil fuels are expected to decline rapidly in the next 30 years and even now, we have started witnessing some shortages of the most desirable fuels. Our agricultural production process is still predominantly based on the use of renewable resources but our current productivity is very low. Hence, there is urgent need for the development of technologies where the productivity of land can be continuously increased with diminishing dependence on non-renewable components of energy, by deploying recycling processes more and more effectively. A consequence of the agriculture of the high-energy consumption and low-labour-input pattern is the diversion of labour from agriculture to more industrial pursuits and a close linkage between farm and factory. Diversification of labour use, leading to a reduction in the number of people employed in the physical operations of farming, has historically been associated with a rise in the standard of living. Developing countries with a high population pressure on land will have to achieve diversification of labour use through the diversification of land and water use and by linking production and post-harvest technologies at the village level in the form of agro-industrial complexes. In countries where meat consumption is high, nearly 1 tonne of grain is needed per individual per year, while in India about five persons survive on one tonne.

To summarise, the major contrasting systems of agriculture we see today differ in the size of farm, the proportion of work force employed in agriculture, the types of linkages developed between farm and factory, the extent of consumption of non-renewable resources of energy, management efficiency, per capita productivity and income and the extent of use of animal products in daily diet. Our need is an agricultural system where benefits of a large human and animal population, robust soils, abundant sunlight, rich ecological diversity, availability of large quantities of organic wastes and a fairly extensive irrigation network are optimised in a manner that terrestrial and aquatic productivity is continuously increased without damage to the long term production potential of the soil and water, stability is imparted to the production as well as prices of foodgrains and labour and land use diversified, so as to increase real income and purchasing power.

Lessons of Past Experience in Planning and Developmental Administration

We have had the benefit of thirty years of education in the administration of a free country and, last year, our people reiterated their desire to combine bread and freedom for all. The time is hence opportune to look back and critically assess our successes and failures. The most striking success is in the field of infrastructure development, whether in education, industry, commerce or agriculture. We occupy an enviable place in the developing world in our educational and technological capabilities. In addition to a national grid of scientific laboratories, we have now more than 120 universities, 4,500 affiliated colleges, 40,000 secondary schools and 6,00,000 elementary schools. There are about 3.5 million teachers and 100 million students in this country. In industry, we are the tenth largest industrial nation. In agriculture, we have achieved a greater capacity to produce food in the last 30 years than in the preceding 10,000 years. The 10,000 year evolutionary history of agricultural systems in our country gave us the capacity to produce annually about 50 million tonnes of foodgrains in 1947. In 1977–78 the figure exceeded 125 million tonnes. Many more such figures can be given which indicate the commendable progress we have made in statistical terms.

However, when we measure progress in human terms, the deficiencies of the pathway of progress adopted so far become apparent. Our GNP and per capita income are among the lowest in the world. We have in absolute numbers probably more people going to bed hungry, more persons who are illiterate, more children who are drop-outs from the school system, more area denuded of forests and more numbers of unemployed than there were in 1947. There has been a drain of both brain and resources from the village to the town. On the other hand, the town and city experience a severe strain on their public utility services, particularly sanitary arrangements, due to the growing influx of the rural unemployed to urban areas. University campuses are in many instances the centres of origin of unrest and disillusionment. When adults cry for help, there is little time to attend to the needs of pre-school and primary school children, although this age group needs the greatest attention. Women, particularly in rural areas, have been mostly bypassed by extension agencies, although both by nature as well as due to economic compulsion, women are no more inclined to limit themselves to motherhood than men are inclined to limit themselves to fatherhood. The report of the Committee on the Status of Women drew attention to the fact that while according to the 1971 Census, there are over 31 million working women, 20 million of whom belong to the most needy sections of the society, yet day-care facilities for the children of those working mothers are scanty.

We can go on enumerating the positive and negative aspects of our socio-economic evolution since Independence. Statistical figures, however, hide the deep human dilemma we are faced with. I shall cite an example from one of the most crucial tests of human behaviour faced during the last 40 years, namely, the Bengal famine of World War II. Dr. Amartya Sen, in an article entitled "The Statistical Chickens" which appeared in CERES last year, makes the following remarks about this famine:

"I have a harrowing memory of an endless procession of emaciated men, women and children—more like skeletons than human beings—trekking in search of food. And of roads littered with corpses. One recalls families of labourers fishermen and craftsmen—all of whom had lost their means of livelihood. Today, when I look at the statistics of that period, I can see them in tables of destitution and mortality. Also in the charts on the epidemics that followed the famine. But I don't see them in the table on food availability per unit of population. The index of per capita food availability with 1941 as 100 had a value of 109 in 1943. While that figure stood high, people fell and perished, and that general problem is with us even today."

Today, we are fortunate in having in our country a large grain buffer. Yet, according to Prof. P.V. Sukhatma, about 25 per cent of the urban and 20 per cent of the rural population are severely malnourished.

This emphasises the need for social security measures which can insulate the economically handicapped sections of the society from want in the basic needs of man like food, clothing, energy and shelter. Management specialists can play a pivotal role in developing ideas for promoting a social security system, which will help to assure everyone born in this country certain basic needs, without, at the same time, generating an atmosphere of dole and patronage.

What can management specialists do to help in achieving the socio-economic goals of the current Plan? In my view, two important contributions can be made. First an interdisciplinary analysis of the attitudinal and organisational changes needed for promoting growth for social justice can be made in each area at the micro-level. Secondly, there could be direct participation in action plans designed to demonstrate how the goals can be achieved. I would like to avail the privilege of this opportunity in offering my own view on the major missing ingredients of Plan efforts so far and how management experts can make their own small contribution in providing these ingredients.

In my view, we have not benefited so far from two of the most potent instruments used by nature both in the origin and evolution of life and in the organisation of biological systems. The first is the principle of synergy. Synergy means behaviour of the whole systems unpredicted by the behaviour of the parts taken separately. It involves the generation of multiplier effects among the components of a system, so that the ultimate product is something more than the sum of parts. Buckminster Fuller, who has utilised very effectively this principle in engineering creations, has dealt with this phenomenon at length in his book *Synergetics—Exploration in the Geometry of Thinking*, published in 1973.

The compartmentalisation of institution and individuals who are to perform specific tasks in a developmental project denies us the benefit of synergetic interactions, which alone can help to give a larger end-result from limited inputs. Our project working model not only fails to derive benefit from potential multiplier effects, but does not often generate even additive effects. This explains our low growth rates. In fact, we have come to a stage in our agricultural advance where the absence of social synergy in terms of land use planning, water and pest management and post-harvest technology is becoming a serious handicap to further progress. This is why I stressed a few years ago in the Sardar Patel Memorial Lectures, that a prerequisite for achieving our national goals is the generation of social synergy.

What is social synergy? Ruth Benedict, one of the earliest anthropologists to apply the concept of synergy in social sciences, says and I quote, "Societies where non-aggression is conspicuous have social orders in which the individual by the same act and at the same time serves his own advantage and that of the group. Non-aggression occurs in these societies, not because people are unselfish and put social obligations above personal desires, but because social arrangements make these two identical."

"Cultures with low social synergy are those in which the social structure provides for acts which are mutually opposed and counteractive, and cultures of high synergy where it provides for acts which are mutually reinforcing. In cultures with high social synergy institutions ensure mutual advantage from their undertakings, while in societies with low social synergy the advantage of one individual becomes a victory over another, and the majority who are not victorious must shift as they can."

According to Abraham Maslow: "The high synergy society is the one in which virtue pays. High synergy societies all have techniques for working off humiliation, and the low synergy societies uniformly do not."

High synergy society seems to be another name for what Gandhiji described as the Sarvodaya society. It is also evident that our society as at present organised is a low synergy society. The joint family system, an experiment in social synergy, is vanishing. The exceptions are to be usually found in tribal communities. Strangely, much of the developmental planning for tribal areas stresses individual rather than group effort and thus will lead to these societies also becoming low synergy ones. What step can we take to ensure that we move from this to a better state of affairs?

The second important missing ingredient of the pathway of progress we have chosen so far is inadequate attention to the problem of self-replication of programmes. The secret of success of the chemical substance of heredity, the DNA molecule, lies in its ability to make an interminable number of copies of itself. If we wish to have a self-replicating movement, the project should promote self-help. The external input should have a catalytic role and not a self-perpetuating role. Unfortunately, we have very few projects, particularly in rural areas, which have grown on their own momentum when the external input is withdrawn. This is true of projects in the field of nutrition, health care, malaria control and soil conservation. This is why Government programmes do not usually trigger self-propelling growth, enabling small Government programmes to become mass movements. Yet, there are examples such as our wheat revolution which give us an insight into the making of developmental symphonies. The wheat revolution became a self-propelling movement, because of the synergy generated by machining a package economically viable technology with appropriate packages of services and public policies.

We often identify maladies but refrain from applying the appropriate remedies. Thus, the malady analysis itself becomes a sterile one and gives only psychological satisfaction to those who make it. While time passes by, we find that the emerging technology, whether, in agriculture or industry which is appropriate to our ecological and socio-cultural milieu, demands for its success a social infrastructure which can promote and sustain group action. Water harvesting in dry areas, crop planning to suit different weather models, pest-management and post-harvest technology, integrated sea farming involving a blend of captive and culture fisheries all demand for efficient adoption of community action on the part of a village or watershed community. If we continue to neglect this aspect of social engineering, the cost of production will rise to uneconomic levels, productivity will remain low and social disparities will widen.

Appropriate post-harvest technology at the village level is a potent method of increasing the wealth of the village through the production of value-added products from agricultural raw material. A rice or jowar based farming system can become the base for animal husbandry programmes for the rural poor, through the introduction of fortification procedures which make the straw or stem into a complete animal food. During 1976–77, about 5.8 million tonnes of cattle feed were exported. This included about 4.5 million tonnes of oilcakes. Our dairy experts calculate that in contrast to the earning of about Rs. 210 crores through the export of oilcakes, dairy products worth over Rs. 1,000 crores could be produced within the country utilising them in well planned dairy enterprises. Fostering mixed farming in ravine and degraded lands can also stimulate interest in sylvi-pastoral system and in planting leguminous shrubs and trees which can enrich soil fertility through biological nitrogen fixation, supply fodder and feed and provide fuel. We still have the opportunity for achieving self-sufficiency in energy requirements by by-passing the pathways which lead to an increasing consumption of non-renewable forms of energy. Under tropical condition, both growth and decay are accelerated. Hence, if the principle of recycling is used effectively, current liabilities like leaching of nutrients, mineralisation of organic matter and loss of run-off water can be converted into assets.

To help farmers with low risk-taking capacity, we need crop and cattle insurance based on an area approach, as recommended by Prof. V.M. Dandekar. If small and marginal farmers are insulated against risk, the diffusion of technological benefits will be more rapid.

There is vast untapped yield reservoir available even at current levels of technology in most production systems. The highest priority in the allocation of resources should go to deriving benefit from this reservoir. To do this however, we will need precise information on the constraints responsible for the gap between potential and actual yields. In inter-disciplinary constraint analysis of the kind undertaken jointly by biological and social scientists and students would help in developing programmes designed to elevate and stabilise yields.

To summarise, our experience during the last 30 years of agricultural growth has shown:

a) Our farmers are prepared to adopt economically viable new technology provided the technological package is supported by appropriate packages of services and public policies and is not characterised by high risk;

b) By and large improvement in productivity has been slow in spite of the large gap between potential and actual farm yields;

c) There has been differential rate of progress between regions, between crops and between different farming systems. Also, crop-livestock-fish production systems have not received the attention they deserve;

d) Unirrigated areas have by and large been neglected since the earlier strategies relied heavily on producing the food we need in irrigated areas;

e) Rural women as a class have generally been by-passed by most extension programmes though they play a key role both in the production and post-harvest phases of agriculture;

f) Though we have developed some capacity to grow more food, we are yet to develop for the entire population the capacity to purchase and eat food. This mis-match between the ability to grow and the ability to consume has resulted in severe problems of marketing, pricing and storage. Even a 5 per cent increase or drop in production hence tends to create all the difference between an uncomfortable glut and acute scarcity. Because of the relative high cost of production of most agricultural commodities due to the poor management of small holdings, the global cost-competitiveness of our agricultural products is poor. To promote agricultural trade, we cannot count on exceptional circumstances as was prevailing in sugar for a few years.

Our agriculture is now at the cross-roads. We cannot follow the same path hereafter. If we do so, we will stay where we are and we will find it very difficult to push up production except by a few million tonnes in good seasons. What we need now is a re-orientation with a view to using the infrastructure for growth already created for the following purposes:

a) Improved production through increased productivity of both terrestrial and aquatic farming systems and the development of crop-livestock-fish integrated production systems;

b) Making agricultural growth an important instrument of generating more income and employment by linking production and post-technologies in the form of an integrated chain;

c) Organisation of agro-industrial complexes in every district for the purpose of linking agriculture and rural industries. In such agro-industrial complexes, the landless labour should get the highest priority to become agents of production since it has been estimated that a majority of over 100 million severely malnourished people in our country belong to the households of landless labour. It is essential that some of the landless labour are withdrawn from the routine operations of farming;

d) Introducing a farmer-cum-area centred planning and intensification of location-specific research and extension.

The following are the three major components of agriculture advance:

a) technology development;
b) technology transfer;
c) technology sustenance.

In each of them there has to be an integrated approach to agriculture, animal husbandry, fisheries and forestry. Those responsible for each aspect should therefore have appropriate technical support in agriculture, animal husbandry, fisheries and forestry. They will also need to be co-ordinated in such a way that they work together in the same way as our own body functions with individual organs performing specific functions while at the same time the body itself functions as an organic whole.

Monitoring of agricultural progress will have to be done not only by the current yardsticks of production and expenditure but also by additional yardsticks such as the increased income which has accrued to those below the poverty line, the additional mandays of employment generated, the impact of new technology on the technological infrastructure necessary for sustained agricultural advance and the cost competitiveness of our products in the world market.

The most urgent tasks before management experts are, in my view, first the analysis of constraints which come in the way of realising the untapped yield reservoir existing in our major crop plants and farm animals, and secondly, delineation of the social and institutional factors essential for the successful spread of technology.

For the efficient management of small and marginal holdings, individual action by the farmer and his family, group action by a set of neighbouring farmers and finally collective action by a watershed community may have to be blended in an appropriate mixture. If the requisite degree of group and community endeavour is not generated, the introduction of low cost and ecologically beneficial technology like integrated pest management will be impossible under conditions of small holdings.

In countries like India, management experts will have to pay attention to the effective utilisation of not only the human, land, water and sunlight resources but also the vertical spaces both in water and air surfaces. Techniques like composite fish culture to get the maximum return from a cubic volume of water and multi-level cropping to get the maximum return from a cubic volume of air need to be introduced on a large scale. The need now is for effective land, water, air and sunlight management, based on integrated principles of ecology and economics. This would call for a new orientation to management training and education and the development of a cadre of managers well grounded in the principles of social scientific energy.

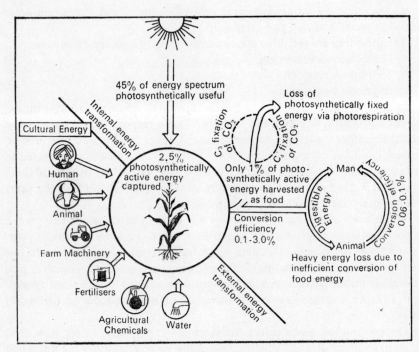

Figure 1

32. Food, Energy and the Environment— Modern Challenges in Agricultural Management

A.J. Vlitos

Prof. Vlitos is Director of Research and Chief Executive of Research and Development for the Tate & Lyle Group of Companies (U.K.). A specialist in the field of plant biochemistry, Prof. Vlitos is a member of the American Society of Plant Physiologists, the American Association for the Advancement of Science and the American Institute of Biological Sciences.

The three themes most likely to dominate the attention of governments, scientists and industrialists over the next 20 years are food, energy and the environment. These are universal topics—just as relevant in the highly developed societies as in the Third World. For the problems of growing, distributing and providing the food necessary to maintain increasing populations remain complex and are further complicated by the higher costs of energy and of the need to evaluate the toxicology of agricultural chemicals more critically prior to their use. How can the complexity of the problems facing agriculture, especially in the developing nations, be managed?

Agriculture is a multidisciplinary enterprise. The "farmer" in most nations represents not only a skilled labourer—he must also possess a variety of other skills ranging from economics and marketing to understanding some of the fundamentals of plant and animal physiology and soil science. Thus "management of agriculture" is likely to be sterile unless it is recognised that the farmer, especially in the Third World nations, represents the critical limiting factor in the chain of events which leads to a viable agriculture. Education is the key element and attention to rural elementary education aimed specifically at training the future peasant farmers could drastically alter the present, slow progress being made in achieving the minimum standards of agricultural management which required to keep pace with increases in population. Other factors likely to be of increasing importance in the near future are the demands to be made on agriculture not only for food but also for the chemical "feedstocks" which will be needed once the fossil fuels (coal and oil) run out or become more expensive. Examples will be given of the opportunities open to agriculture to meet *energy* demands as well as the demand for more food. The concept of agricultural management known as total crop utilisation will be examined and discussed in detail.

There are a host of problems which combine to frustrate agricultural development in the developing world. Some of these problems are technical others are social still others are economic and political. A simplified short list of the key problems is outlined as follows:

1) Economic constraints (increasing costs of seed, fertilisers, machinery);

2) Lack of markets and distribution facilities (not any lack of need but rather lack of ability to buy);

3) Social factors (which equate farming with the low end of the social scale);

4) Fewer people on farms to feed more people in cities;

5) Lack of agriculturally-based industries to utilise surpluses of perishable produce;

6) Education of farmer often neglected;

7) Increasing costs of energy both on the farm and in food processing;

8) Technical matters—lack of water or too much of it, salinity and aridity; etc., lack of adequate storage facilities for perishable foods, etc;

9) Insufficient use of agricultural wastes;

10) Long 'lead-time' from invention to application;

11) Other problems.

What can be done? There are international agencies which have spent years (FAO, World Bank, for example) attempting to attack each of the above problems systematically. There are no panaceas and no instant solutions. However within each nation and often within a given region in an individual country one can identify the single most important limiting factor or the two or three factors which are the most serious ones to limiting agricultural development. It might for example be a lack of irrigation during the dry season which prevents the farmer from growing dry season crops or, conversely, poor drainage which prevents him from growing vegetables during the rainy season. And if he did manage to grow two hectares of lettuce during the rainy season he might find it impossible to sell more than half the lettuce at a price which would pay for his labour, seed and fertiliser. He might not have anywhere to store the remainder of the crop until he finds new customer—so much of the crop might rot in the field. Many peasant farmers today learn what to grow each year through experiences of this sort. It is a costly inefficient way but often there is no other alternative. In some parts of the world the peasant farmer grows the crop that he is used to growing—a crop that his parents knew, one that he feels comfortable in growing. 1 know a farmer in Greece over 80 years of age who grew tobacco as a cash crop all of his life. When the oriental types of tobacco lost favour and were being replaced by so-called Virginia types he refused to switch—decided instead to grow watermelons.

When I saw him again recently and asked how the watermelon crop had done he replied "Fine, but I'm giving up farming. Its no fun growing watermelons—too easy! Tobacco was a much more difficult crop to grow but I knew how and I was proud of each crop. Watermelons! Anyone can grow those!" Resistance to change is almost universal in farming—especially so amongst peasant farmers. Switching, say, from growing rice to growing high-value perishable vegetable crops is not easy when the economic incentives are appealing.

This is why I feel that education in rural communities could be a key factor in alleviating some of the problems provided of course that rural education is designed to meet the specific needs of a rural people. Too often what is taught is not relevant to rural life—children seen in villages find it difficult to identify with the textbook characters. So a great deal of thought has to be given to designing an "appropriate technology" in rural education if I may apply that term in this context.

33. Managerial Implications of the "Nucleus Estate" Approach in Agriculture Development

Wagiono Ismangil

Dr. Ismangil is a Consultant at the Management Institute, University of Indonesia, Jakarta. He also teaches organisation theory in the Faculty of Economics of the University, and is a member of the Policy Research Team, Ministry of Manpower, Transmigration and Cooperatives and of the Supervisory Board, State Mining Corporation, Indonesia. Dr. Ismangil has several research projects in economics and management areas to his credit.

Introduction

The purpose of the paper is to examine some of the problems encountered in the nucleus-estate agriculture development scheme. The problems presented here are centred on the institutional and managerial aspects of nucleus estate agriculture development. The discussion is based on observations and interviews with participants of nucleus estate projects now being conducted in Indonesia. It is not intended to present a detailed study of the problems in the projects, rather the presentation will be limited to a general description of institutional aspects still faced in the operations of the projects. It is hoped that the exposure would suggest some steps where improvements can be initiated and developed.

The understanding of managerial and institutional implications of agriculture development is important in several respects. Firstly, it is imperative to study institutional implications in policy decisions. Secondly, such an understanding is also important now that agriculture development is considered urgent and that its interdependence to the rest of the economy is more apparent. The urgency of agriculture development is also seen in view of the ineffectiveness of industrial growth to prevent rising unemployment and continuing poverty of the great mass of people [1].

Furthermore, one cannot help the impression that agriculture development policies are still largely considered within a framework of agricultural techniques and seldom linked to a broader institutional considerations of development programmes.

Agriculture Development

The importance of agriculture in the development of many developing countries is widely recognised. For countries like Indonesia it is the leading sector of the economy. Figures for the year 1976 indicate that agriculture accounts for 31 per cent of Indonesia's GDP, 88 per cent of Indonesia's non-oil exports, and 58 per cent of the employment of the working population.

The strategic position of agriculture will be enhanced when the concept is broadened to include agribusiness. Agribusiness embraced industries that produces agricultural inputs and those marketing agricultural outputs. Exact figures on the role of agribusiness are absent from the official statistics, but this author would hypothesise that it will account for over 60 per cent of the nation's GDP.

Agriculture products in Indonesia has two pivots, namely food production and plantation. Food production, with very few exceptions is still performed by individual farmers or small-holders tending a limited area of arable land. Policies for agricultural development in food production are geared toward three general areas:

a) Development and rehabilitation of irrigation network;

b) Development and extension of advanced technology which uses high yielding seeds, insecticides and fertilisers; and

c) Expansion of farmlands through transmigration, etc.

In the export oriented plantations, development is usually done through the establishment of modern managed agricultural enclaves. This is done by assigning concessions to corporations for a certain areas of land and establish export agriculture utilising modern technology. Its impact on the neighbouring areas are generally very small except for the recruitment of manual labour.

The implication of such characteristics of agriculture is that there is an apparent dualism represented by the two extremes of agriculture described above. We have on the one hand food production performed in a traditional fashion by small farmers in a rural environment. By its very nature the traditional sector is usually characterised by a low rate of growth, narrow scope of operation and a personalised system of interaction.

In contrast, export agriculture is characterised by a modern system of management, within a framework of modern institutions tending hundreds of acres of land. The two extremes of agriculture production have little in common, and is not linked in a meaningful way. It is even supervised and developed by different governmental agencies in the Ministry of Agriculture.

Such a framework may develop to different growth poles, isolating one area to the other. In effect the dualistic nature of production is also seen in terms of the variables influencing their behaviour. The structure would make the nation dependent for its food supply upon traditional agriculture with a low rate of growth and a static rural environment. On the other hand, plantations producing for the world market are managed in a modern manner but are also highly vulnerable to fluctuations in the world agriculture market.

It can be generally stated that such a structure is a reflection of the dualistic nature of the society as a whole in less developed countries. Economies of these countries are generally characterised and contrasted in terms of a modern and a traditional sector, each influenced by a different set of factors in its growth. Differences in growth rates, technological dynamics, and managerial attitudes, will create disparities in income and productivity between the modern urban and the traditional rural. Different growth patterns for the two sectors may eventually create social tensions in the future.

Within this framework, it is often observed that policies of development are treated separately, using different sets of considerations, by different authorities in the ministry. Furthermore, in view of the scarcity climate surrounding developing countries, orientation, of development are geared toward producing more and hence the stress on growth. Growth is definitely important, but uneven rate of growth among sectors of the economy may be detrimental and works dysfunctionally toward the achievement of development goals.

It is within this framework that policies of agriculture modernisation should not be blinded by the goals of growth as such without consideration to the equalisation of this distribution and participation of the mass of the population. Increasingly, policy makers in less developed countries are realising that a one-sided growth should be compensated by a consideration of other social orientations of economic development. Therefore in the efforts to foster growth the following areas should also be considered :

a) A policy of growth that also includes a programme to enhance food production in the traditional sector, in order to keep up with the rate of increasing demand, and to prevent the import of food with hard earned foreign exchange;

b) A policy to prevent disparity of growth limited to that sector of the economy. The increasing gap between the modern and the traditional sector will create feelings of disharmony in the society and may induce social tensions.

Institutional Modernisation

Traditional efforts to institutional modernisation in rural areas are generally directed toward the development of cooperatives, or other farmer-grouping by any other name. These organisations are in the first place intended to protect their members from exploitation by traders and from usury. Such a protective function, and the development counter-balancing forces in the rural areas were an important gain for the farmers, but it was inadequate to pull the traditional sector up and linking it to the dynamics of the modern sector [2].

As a means of pooling of strength cooperatives did well in a closed and limited fashion. Many credit cooperatives in rural, and even urban areas, are successful. However these organisations are still closed systems, obtaining resources within the system itself, and developing it for internal use.

As a means of strengthening production capacity of rural production centres, food and otherwise, many cooperatives fail. They were faced by the reality of lack of modern management and promotional ability. In most cases observed by this writer in Indonesia, failure of cooperatives to develop can be traced back to their inability to link themselves to their environment, especially their inability to bridge their members to new marketing opportunities.

Linkages of traditional village producers to the outside world are performed by traders. Although these traders performed an important procurement and marketing function, their services are personal in nature. This characteristics of traders service coupled with their stronger bargaining position vis-a-vis the farmers resulted in (potential) exploitation by the traders. In any case the performance of these traders are very much dependent on their good will.

The above problems faced by rural organisations and the socio-economic "segregation" between the traditional and modern sector of the economy, necessitates the development of new approaches toward agriculture development. One of the experiments tried in Indonesia is the nucleus-estate approach.

The Nucleus Estate Approach to Agriculture Development

Briefly the nucleus estate approach involves the development of a processing and marketing centre linked to a number of satellite producers. Basically, the idea is to provide a linkage between the traditional producers, such as rice-growers, fishermen, sugar cane farmers, small-plantation holders, etc., to a modern processing and marketing enterprise. Such a linkage is expected to break the isolation of traditional farmers, producers in rural areas, and provide them with a means of communication and access to the growing modern sector, and to new opportunities beyond their traditional production and marketing scheme.

The idea is not new, linkages between large and small enterprises have been practised for a long time. In industrially developed countries where social and cultural barriers between rural and urban, between the weak and the strong, are at a minimum, such linkages are common. Unlike the less developed countries, in advanced countries a system of interaction among the various elements in the economy has been well established. There is little cultural barrier between the small farmer and his suppliers and traders in the cities. Social stratification has been less apparent. The dissemination of information relevant to business operation is fairly developed, thus minimising isolated areas in the economy, with the effect of an equalisation of bargaining positions among economic units.

The institutional link arranged between the "nucleus" and its satellites are various, ranging from a contractual voluntary arrangement, which can be classified as a vertical *cooperation* among economic units, to a more structured relationship, generally denoted as vertical *integration*. Consequently different nuances relationships are apparent in different arrangements.

The initiators of the nucleus system also differs from one project to another. The programme can be initiated by the participants themselves on the basis of mutual benefit. At the other extreme it can be introduced by a government decree coercing the participants to cooperate within a nucleus system framework.

The goals of the nucleus estate projects can be identified in the following terms:

1) To link the mass of the population, tied to traditional means of production, into modern commercial sector of the economy;

2) To enhance the development of the traditional agriculture by linking them to broader market and technological opportunities;

3) To bridge the gap between the development of the modern and the traditional sector of the economy;

4) To stimulate the development entrepreneurship. To develop independent, business-oriented agriculture undertakings, with potentials to growth.

The breakage from traditional means of production and exposure to modern ways of doing business is strategic in the effort of agricultural development in Indonesia, as well as in many less developed countries. It is rather presumptuous to assume that change toward modernisation can be achieved by means of financial and material assistance.

It is imperative to realise that most farmers in rural areas can only work and aspire toward what they can see, reach and understand. For centuries their horizon has been limited and conditioned by the cultural climate surrounding them. As has been pointed out earlier the cultural climate surrounding a rural way of life is characterised by its static and restrictive nature, and thus limiting farmers' scope of attention.

Thus a major key to agriculture development is the provision of a link to modern technology and markets. Such a link can provide the farmer-producer with the exposure and means of understanding the operations of other economic units. Institutional arrangements should be found where points of contact can be developed, so that the opportunities of a wide ranging economic inter-dependence can be realised through a corresponding network of social familiarity.

It is within this framework that an adequate institutional framework should be developed based on the nucleus estate approach. Theoretically, the arrangement is expected to overcome traditional approaches to rural institutional development, however observations in several projects now going on in Indonesia indicate that a careful preparation at the design and planning stage is in order to avoid unexpected consequence of the programme. The following discussions will be limited to some aspects of institutional and managerial implications of the nucleus estate approach to be considered by the participants of the programme.

A Systems Approach to Analysis

In order to analyse institutional arrangements and problems more systematically it is useful to conceptualise the nucleus estate approach within a framework of a systems approach. The concept of a system implies a framework of activities that are linked together in a systematic and meaningful way. There are interactions among the participants of the system, and inputs into a subsystem will be associated with outputs of another subsystem.

The conceptualisation is useful to the observer of managerial and institutional arrangements in agriculture development, since it provides him with a means of understanding how each of the activities is associated with the other in some way, how one subsystem, a participant to the programme, may affect activities of subsystems that have gone before or are likely to affect activities to follow afterwards.

Within the nucleus estate programme we can identify three subsystems of participants, namely the government agency responsible for the project, the nucleus corporation and the farmer-producer, usually organised in a group or cooperative. Although in its pure form nucleus estate arrangements can be developed on a voluntary basis involving a minimum of government intervention, such arrangements are not so common in developing countries, or when this happens it is less problematical and hence not relevant for the purposes of this paper. We will thus concentrate on government sponsored projects consciously designed within the framework of agriculture development.

Discussions on institutional arrangements will be centred on factors related to the government subsystem and the corporate subsystem for the following reasons:

a) The farmer-producer subsystem has been extensively discussed on many occasions related to agriculture development. I am especially referring to treatments of rural cooperatives or group farming;

b) The government subsystem is for our purposes, the designer and the coordinator of the system;

c) The government subsystem, the nucleus of the system, is the instrument in the implementation of the programme.

Conceptualising the nucleus estate programme as a system we can then classify the issues in terms of system attributes, namely systems goals, systems structure, systems input-output process, systems communication process and systems adaptation process.

Goals of the Nucleus Estate Project

In order for the system to succeed it is important that all the subsystems involved should be clear on the goals of the system as a whole. On the surface this seems to be a simple matter of announcing and communicating the goals designed by the initiator to be achieved by the system. A closer examination in the practice of nucleus estate programme indicates that the matter of goals clarification is not at all simple and should receive adequate attention at the initial stage of design.

In the first place nuclei estate project are usually burdened with a multiple of objectives. The goals enumerated are typical for a nucleus estate project. These goals do not always coincide with one another. Take the goal of agriculture development and relate it to entrepreneurial development. On the one hand the system is pressed for greater output. Efforts and resources are directed toward production increase. On the other the system is also required to develop entrepreneurial abilities of the farmer-producer. What is conflicting in such a situation is the orientation required of the managerial system. A production orientation requires a management system that is different from a development orientation of the nucleus estate project.

In practice the multiple goals situation would develop into a hierarchy of goals, ranked according to the urgency and felt pressures at the particular situation confronted by the coordinators of the system. Thus pressures in terms of increased production will gear the system orientation toward the combination of resources that may be detrimental to the efforts of entrepreneurial development.

Essentially an overall scrutiny of the goals to be achieved by the projected nucleus system is important to avoid any unintended consequence in the development of the project. In one case involving a fishery project, the input invested in the project did have an impact on the increase of fishery production, but failed completely in the development of artisan fishermen in the surrounding area. In fact the project seems to strengthen the already technologically advanced companies in this area rather than the small and the weak fishermen. In the process it is clear that only the well developed and strong fishermen can support the nucleus corporation in terms of productivity and the traditional fishermen are gradually pushed aside from the projects' scheme.

It is therefore important that all the participants involved have a clear understanding of each other's role within the framework of the system's goals. Government agencies controlling the system essentially have coordinative role. Such a role implies the functions of an arbiter, jury and conciliator at the same time. It should be realised that a project such as a nucleus estate would require constant monitoring and adjustment as it goes along. Conflicts and wrong perceptions of the participants' role are almost inevitable. The goals to be achieved should be seen in terms of a process that gradually evolves towards the ideal situation desired. As such government officials in charge of the system should be development-oriented and shy away from custodian type of supervisory attitude. This is easier said than done. Within the climate of government initiated development coupled with a stratification of the leader and the led, development orientation among government officials in the fields should be consciously developed.

The managers of the nucleus corporation should also be clear of its role in programme. If the stress is on development of the farmer-producer or the artisan fishermen in order for them to become independent entrepreneurs, then the role of the nucleus corporation should be that of a developer, trainer and provider of necessary inputs for the producer. Such a role should, again, be clearly laid down and specified to the managers of the corporations. Here, once more one should be clear on the type of orientation expected from a manager and develop them accordingly. Interestingly the understanding of roles for government officials and those for managers of the nucleus enterprise is interdependent to each other. Government's perception of roles determines the direction of coordination, and hence the orientation of nucleus' managers. This puts the responsibilities of government's coordination rather high on the list of prerequisites of success. The perspective will present itself that designers of nucleus estate projects should also include sufficient consideration on the mechanism of coordination and supervision of government officials on the project. This is important in view of the fact that often coordinative functions of government officials are considered lightly, and put as an "appendage" to a number of other functions already performed by the officials.

Structural Aspects of "Nucleus Estate"

In this section we are concerned with the variables influencing interrelationships among participants of the nucleus system. In the first place it must be realised that in view of the role performed by each participant it is clear that orientations of the three main participants differ from one another. Such a condition would result inevitably to a strain in relations among the participants.

Furthermore it is also important to realise that status and bargaining positions among the participants are unequal. This is especially evident with respect to status of the nucleus enterprise manager and the government officials on the one hand and the status of the farmer producer on the other. Within such a framework one must not expect that interaction will take place freely, since the participants are not on an equal plane.

The differences in status of participants is basic to the understanding of power structure within the system. The structure will in a sense influence system's effectiveness in terms of hierarchy of goals, direction of communication, process of equalisation basic to goals of participants and also commitment toward the system. Structural imbalances as a result of differences in status will steer the direction of goals achievement. There is a danger that the arrangement of hierarchy of goals tends to lean on the interests of the powerful rather than the weak. The farmer-producer groups, with the weaker bargaining position, will have a hard time voicing their interests and participating in the decision process of the system.

The structural imbalances among the participants are, in part, a reflection of the social stratification of the society as a whole. We can roughly observe the stratification of traditional societies in terms of rural, urban, leader and the led, those in power and the mass of the population. Within this framework the weaker bargaining position of the farmer-producer is apparently inherent to the structural set up of the society as a whole. As a consequence efforts to pull the farmer-producer into the mainstream of the economy and developing their understanding and access to modern technological and marketing opportunities should be considered within this broader structural framework of the society, so that policy decisions will not be based on unrealistic assumptions about the status of participants in the system.

The differences in status and positions in the system often is an underlying cause for tensions between the participants. It is not seldom that participants resent each other, blaming each other of misconduct and incapability of performance. In one instant at the Mitsugoro corn-project, a joint project between Mitsui & Co., Japan and Kosgoro (a retired servicemen cooperation), the nucleus corporation was blamed for importing a corn-disease with the import of high-yield Mexican strain, when the farmers experienced a crop-failure due to mildew. Word got around that such a disease only came with the imported Mexican seeds.

It so happened that the seeds imported were fully certified and cleared. But the incident illustrates the precious condition surrounding the interaction of the nucleus estate project. Cases of tensions among the participants are plenty, ranging from unsympathetic statements about the other participant to outright sabotage and pilferage of products. Such a climate, again, puts the coordinating government official on a strategic position to direct the system, provided they are rightly equipped with the needed development orientation.

The Systems Input-Output Process

Within a systems framework one can identify linkages between the various productive processes in the system. One significant classification—processing and marketing. The overall effectiveness of the system is highly dependent to the interaction between one process and the other.

In the nucleus estate system, the various stages of production are performed by different subsystems, specifically the extractive production process by the farmer or fishermen, the processing and marketing stage by the nucleus enterprise. The problem in such a system is to coordinate the activities of the various subsystems so that they are geared toward the overall systems' goal.

However, the different orientations among the participants with the responding different perceptions of their respective roles, make the coordination process a difficult one. Complaints of product quality and scheduling of incoming products from farmers are a common phenomenon in nucleus estate projects. On the other hand farmers' cooperatives are also heard to complain about the inconsistencies in standards required, and arbitrary decisions on the part of nucleus enterprise on rejections of delivered products.

Again here we see the need to evaluate the problem within a broader framework of cultural and social differences among the participating parties. In many cases it can be observed that farmers have a different perception of standards. Exact, scientific measures of quality requirements are unfamiliar to them. Time commitments are also strongly based on the cultural climate different from those used in the urban and modern sector of the economy.

The above variables should be used as a basis for consideration of policy decision-makers, so that targets and structural arrangements can be established on the basis of realistic forces operating in the society.

The Systems Communication Process

The problems of communication can be briefly described here, since most of the variables relevant to the problem have been discussed in the section about structure. One significant aspect to be stressed within this framework is that the socio-cultural gap existing between urban and rural subsystems would create barriers to effective communication.

This is especially important in the case of communication between the nucleus enterprise and the farmer. The relative lack of linkages between the rural and urban sector of the economy can be seen that in many cases they speak different languages, share very little in common by way of values and perceptions about society. The consequence of such a situation can be imagined if the participants are required to sit face to face in a conference room and discuss conditions of their relationship.

Within a development and learning context ideally communication should be open and frequent. Since the expected result of the project is mutual understanding of each other's way of thinking, and a transfer of modernisation to the rural farmers, it is clear that communication holds a central role in the process of nucleus estate system. However, environmental and cultural conditions surrounding the system make such a requirement difficult to achieve.

Here we see again the need for a development orientation both in the policies of government agencies and nucleus enterprise management. The willingness to adopt a "teacher's" position, understanding the circumstances surrounding the rural society.

The Systems Adaptive Process

By now it can be seen that the successful achievement of a nucleus estate project must be in a dynamic framework. Achievements of stated objectives is a process, gradually developing, and not always following a smooth path, toward success. Seen in this framework it can be concluded that institutional mechanisms to facilitate the growth process should be established.

The system should include a periodic review, if necessary redirections and reformulation of intermediate goals should be continuously done. The ideal forum for such a review is a tripartite meeting between government, nucleus enterprise managers and farmers. The adjustments should be seen from all three subsystems since each is faced with a different environment. Each subsystem is continually facing a problem of adjustments with respect to their environment, and also is faced with the adjustments toward each other.

The adaptive process of the nucleus estate project is in many cases complex. It may, in some respects, involve variables beyond the comprehension of any of the participants. It may therefore be pertinent to consider an outside adaptive system that has the capability to evaluate external as well asinternal environmental dynamics faced by the nucleus estate system. The outside adaptive system should ideally be not a permanently attached body to the nucleus estate system, but a complementary body to the tripartite forum suggested earlier.

Conclusions

Traditional patterns of institutional modernisation through development of cooperatives were successful in a limited way. However, with respect to agriculture production cooperatives an inadequacy was felt in terms of its inability to link themselves with a broader marketing environment. Another approach, the nucleus estate approach, was then considered to complement the shortcomings of traditional cooperatives. On paper the new approach seems ideal, however further scrutiny indicates that the requirements for success require a definite effort on the part of the subsystems, which on the surface seems hard to achieve.

Approaching the nucleus estate approach from a systems view, three subsystems were identified, namely government officials, management of the nucleus enterprise and farmer organisations. The performance of the system would be significantly influenced by the pattern of interaction among the three participants. Analysing the system in terms of goals, structure, input-output processes, communication and adaptive processes, several basic implications could be discerned. Most significantly is the need to clarify systems goals. Some of the goals aimed by the nucleus estate system are not comparable to each other. Consequently, a hierarchy of goals usually emerges on the basis of environmental and interest group pressures experienced at a particular time. Such a condition would confuse the real purpose of agricultural development, pulling the farmers into the mainstream of the economy.

In view of the fact that interaction among the participants of the system do not occur on the same plan, and status differences result in differences in bargaining positions, conscious efforts to coordinate the system should be an integral part of systems management. Furthermore a basic prerequisite of systems management in nucleus estate approaches is the developmental orientation and attitude as contrasted to custodian and production oriented attitudes of managers in general.

Achievements of the nucleus estate project should be seen in terms of a process, gradually adjusted toward a higher intermediate goal. Within this framework, an adaptive mechanism is an important instrument to scan the environment and a just activities toward systems goal. Such an instrument can be developed in the form of a tripartite forum consisting of the three participants complemented by an outside adaptive system periodically assessing systems achievements.

REFERENCES

1. World Bank. *Agriculture Sector, Working Paper*, June 1972.
2. United Nations Research Institute for Social Development (UNRISD). *Rural Cooperatives as Agents of Change: A Research Report and a Debate*, Geneva, 1975.

34. Management of Urban Communities

M.N. Buch

Mr. Buch is Vice-Chairman of Delhi Development Authority, India.

In the field of management of urban communities, I have tried to restrict my paper to policy issues. In fact, it is very easy to get involved in a discussion on the day-to-day management of urban communities and the difficulties faced by the municipalities in this behalf.

But, I find that in the context of muincipal government, both in India and in most countries—advanced and not so advanced—the real problems of municipal management stem from an almost total absence of any sort of a national policy and the management system which is ad hoc, is no system at all and therefore I will draw your attention to policy matters rather than to the details of the city management. It is the nature of man to be gregarious. I mean, people get together. Hermits are an exception.

The principal reason why they cluster together is economic. The organisation shifts from the tribal to the village, from the village to the towns mainly for economic reasons. As economic life becomes more complex and employment becomes more diversified human settlements tend to become larger and larger. The experience of Western Europe was that when a society moved away from the purely agricultural to the industrial, there was a spontaneous movement away from the village community into the cities. This is the main experience of the Industrial Revolution for example industrial production requires a certain minimum size before it becomes economical. Because of interdependence of the industrial production and the marketing of products, the towns continue to grow. Of course, the physical limitations of the States do create a diminishing curve of growth. This is the experience of Calcutta incidentally. In absolute terms, however, the larger the town is, the larger it becomes. In the developing world, the movement of towns have not always been as a result or a cause of growth. This is the major difference between the growth of urban communities in the West as a result of the Industrial Revolution and the growth of urban communities in the underdeveloped world. Population pressures on agricultural holdings which continuously reduce in

size because of sub-division and fragmentation together with the modernisation of agriculture has reduced the capacity of the village community to sustain employment. For example, if you extend electric power to a village, the man who irrigates his field by means of bullock power and therefore requires one man to attend the bullock and another man to attend the field, now can just switch on his motor and probably gets the same amount of lift in one hour which he would get in eight huors of working with the bullock and he himself can go and attend to the field and then he is free for the rest of the day. It replaces one and half labourers.

At the same time, the city with the diversified employment base offers an alternative to a person who can find no work in the village. A pickpocket cannot function in a village. He requires a crowd. So, even if you want to take to crowds you shift to the cities rather than to remain in the villages. Even though the standard of living in the cities and developing world is low, the wage is minimal because of an ever-enlarging labour force and even though opportunity for employment are really restricted, the cities offer some hope for a villager who would otherwise starve. A boot-black boy has the capacity to earn Rs. 20 a day. He may get less because there are ten bootblacks. Even then one may earn Rs. 2 a day. But, in a village he might not even earn that Rs. 2.

These two forces, the push factors in the villages and the gravitational pull of the cities have created a situation in the developing world where migration from the villages to the large cities is a continuing process. Surprisingly, the smaller towns because of relatively poor employment base tend to be bypassed in the process of rural-urban migration. So, the rural town, the smaller town with 30,000 or below tends to basically be uni-functional. It, still, is almost entirely dependent on agriculture and therefore multi-purpose employment opportunities are not available in the smaller towns. The people jump then to to go the larger towns or to the metropolitan areas. This prevents an orderly development of a hierarchy of settlements in which from village to the metropolis, every level of town or city has a part to play in the economic life of the country.

The cities do not act as a growth point for multiplying the economic base. Basically a metropolitan area does not have a finite hinterland. If you could cut Bombay out from the Indian mainland and float it into the sea, it could probably draw sustenance of labour and other materials from other countries and not depend on India. Take the case of Singapore, for example. So, a metropolitan centre by itself cannot act as a growth point for the hinterland. It can act as an independent growth centre. But it is not related to the hinterland.

In the case of the inexorable march to the cities, certain fundamental policy issues have to be decided before we can think of management of specific human settlement. Just as no industrial unit exists in isolation, similarly, no city is an island. In a state of anarchy, industrial management is an impos-

sibility as we are going through some of the industries now. In an environment of chaotic urban growth, no proper city management function can be performed because disorder breeds adhocism.

The poor wretched Municipal Commissioner busy dealing with the crisis of inadequate water supply in Colony A and sewage in Colony B, he just does not have time to plan a system; a framework of policy, therefore, has to be evolved before the management of a community becomes a feasible proposition.

The first concern of the planner, therefore, has to be the evolving of a national urban policy. The trend towards urbanisation cannot be arrested unless one is prepared to accept the radical options adopted by the Peoples' Republic of China.

You see, in China they recognise that the village, as such, is not an economically functional unit. Therefore, they reorganise village society into communes which are viable, which are large enough to be viable. The total reorganisation of the village community into a viable unit may not be possible in most countries in the developing world. The only alternative, therefore, available to the governments in these countries is to channelise the pattern of urban growth. Logically, the establishment of a proper urban rural continuum in which the next higher level of urban settlement is interlinked with its rural hinterland and the larger towns around it is the only sensible policy.

Such a continuum cannot be established directly between the metropolitan centre of the rural areas. The gravitational pull of the metropolis is overpowering. In a developing country, therefore, the decentralisation of industrial activity in a hierarchy of middle level towns, which continue to maintain links with finite rural hinterlands, is imperative if the regional balance of growth is to be maintained.

The metropolitan centre like Calcutta, for example, or Bombay, has a tendency to grow, and because it grows, it gives rise to problems and because it gives rise to problems, the fund generated by it, the capital generated by it just gets absorbed in itself instead of being available for development of the hinterland. There is no specific interconnection.

Therefore, any rational urban policy would take this fact into account and in a country like India, it would try to avoid what has happened in the United States. We cannot afford the megalopolitans of the growth which has taken place in the United States and its vast hinterland. I will come to that in a minute. Such a development has taken place spontaneously in some of the agricultural States in India. The Punjab is an example where interrelationship is established between market and service towns and the villages and the market towns and middle level cities. This development, however, is unplanned and has grown out of the increasing prosperity of the rural areas. The translation of this into a national policy which will ensure that even in areas where the villages are not prosperous has to be a principal objective of urban planners at the macro-level. The modernisation of agriculture with a view to

creating a marketable surplus and the building up of a hierarchy of urban settlement which will consume the marketable surplus and in turn provide industrial products both for the rural communities and the urban areas would be the keystones of such a policy.

In Western Europe I can think of France as an example in which there is this nexus between the village and market towns, and the market towns and the higher level cities. I do not think this is a result of deliberate planning. It just happens probably because the Frenchman still likes his land and does not want to be divorced from it, in fact he is practically Indian in that. When there is a national policy which channelises urban growth, the problem of city management becomes relatively simple. Unfortunately such ideal conditions exist nowhere.

We can take two extreme examples. The United States have passed from a metropolitan growth to a megalopolitan growth along the Eastern and Western sea coasts. Urban communities tend to merge into each other so that there is no well defined area to administer. The city governments as such fail under these circumstances. Services are not confined to a definite area, but because of overlapping political jurisdiction, a systemic approach becomes well nigh impossible. This is the very peculiarity of the United States that this is a vital society which abhors obsolescence. It is prepared to gear itself to meet a situation except in the field of government and social organisation. No community in the United States is prepared to give up its jurisdiction even though it means that the sewerage linkages with the communities adjacent to it cannot be set up, that the water supply system cannot be integrated. But they still are very reluctant to adopt any system which would permit them to have an overview of the entire metropolitan area.

, Given this model, a conflict is created between the needs to manage such an urban community and the need to provide a democratic option of local government in local area. This is the main conflict even in the States. Efficient management calls for centralised control. There can be no piece-meal infrastructure development of water supply system or a sewerage system in a metropolitan area requires overall planning and an implementation agency under a single control. This will be true of transportation systems, power systems, etc. At the same time, a management system which centralises an authority cuts into the very base of local government in which people living within a community decide their own priorities and take their own decisions. In the western world, a systematic attempt in resolving these conflicts seems to have been made in Toronto where a metropolitan government set-up has divided the functions into those which are city-wise and those which are of local implications. Metro government manages all city-wise functions. The purely local problems are dealt with by Burroughs which enjoy a great deal of autonomy within their own spheres. The Greater London Council also performs somewhat the same function. But from time to time there has been a reorganisation of the London Metropolitan area to suit changed circumstances. The effectiveness of the system, however, remains to be evaluated and the fact that Britain has had to set up commissions from time to time, to study the local government, means that no solution which is final seems to have been found for this problem.

The second model is of city management in India. I presume when I talk about India, I talk about many of the countries in the developing world. Here too the cities have tended to spill over beyond purely political limits. At the same time, the municipal government is restricted to municipal boundaries, extra municipal areas even within the main municipality without contributing anything towards municipal resources. For example, the settlements which have come up around Delhi like Ballabgarh, Ghaziabad and Faridabad etc., tend to draw upon the resources of Delhi, but contribute nothing to it. They have also increased the gravitational pull of Delhi because the volume of Delhi has increased. The boundaries have spilled over the Union Territory or Municipal Corporation limits and this has created certain problems. The problem of planning municipal services apart, even the financial burden of maintaining the existing services under these circumstances is enough to cause a breakdown in the city management. The picture of most Indian cities is that municipal bodies are so involved in the routine housekeeping jobs that there is hardly any element of future planning is visible. In other words, the general picture is one of a form of rudimentary administration, but with no modern city management concepts. At the macro-level, the city management involves in sweeping the streets, maintenance of water supply, provision of adequate sewerage and drainage, efficient management of city transport, provision of street lights, management of markets, maintenance of parks, etc. These are low level management functions. What I am trying to drive at is that planning for the future in which certain policy decisions have to be taken is a high level management function in the context of city management. Maintenance functions are a low level function because maintenance has to be done. It is an unfortunate fact that in most developing countries there does not exist an efficient management cadre even to fulfil these functions.

Service under the municipal government is considered less attractive than service under the State and therefore the recruits into the municipal service tends to be second grade. In cities in India, the Municipal Commissioner, who is the chief executive of the city government, is changed every two years. There is no continuity whatsoever. There is a certain amount of continuity in engineering services. But there also, as I said, we do not get the best people coming into municipal services. Training, both in-service and extra-service is minimal. The City Fathers are often engrossed in political matters rather than in the proper management of city functions. The leadership that they provide to paid cadres therefore is so ineffective, that the City Fathers are more bothered about their wards and one does not care whether what he plans for his ward has any relevance to what is being planned by the adjacent ward. In Indore, for example, one road passes through four wards. One City Father wanted the road to be widened in his area, the other man wanted a footpath and the third man wanted a drain and the fourth man wanted a market along this road. You can just imagine the chaos that existed; the road which is five and half miles has four different breadths. It has a pavement only in one section, footpath in one section, it has got a drain which does not lead from anywhere to anywhere. Well, this sort of narrow-minded outlook does create a totally ineffective city management. Under these circumstances, in many developing countries what a citizen could normally expect from a city government is just not provided. The inefficiency of managers is aggravated by the inadequacy of resources. The decisions are ad hoc and often contrary to what has been decided earlier. The case for at least developing a proper cadre of the city managers therefore cannot be over-stated.

Even in the absence of a national urban policy or a long-term perspective of city growth, many of the problems of cities can be tackled at lower levels if the city government is efficient and effective. Even the city of New York exemplifies poor city management, why quote Calcutta? If municipal government is our cake and unable to rise above inefficient housekeeping, is there a viable substitute or a parallel alternative? In India, we have created development authorities. These are sometimes authorities having a jurisdiction larger than that of a municipality. These authorities are expected to be divorced from day-to-day problems of city management. They are theoretically meant to develop a long-term perspective of city growth and to plan the type of activity which would optimise it. Unfortunately, no development authority has broken free from the narrow constraints of land use planning. All these authorities have ultimately come down to land use planning. Their perspective is restricted to land. They see a piece of land and decide what to do with it. That is all. They never have an overview of the city. The perspective has shrunk from the long-term overall view to the extremely limited one of which plot of land can be put to what use.

The authority I head is the main culprit in this. The blinkers are even more restricted than the ones worn by the municipalities because the municipalities are subject ultimately to a certain amount of popular pressure. The outlook largely is mercenary. The function is mostly regulatory. The exercise of police power may make an authority feared and the Delhi Development Authority is feared, I believe. But it cannot make it an effective instrument of city growth or city management. This is the major failure of the Delhi Development Authority, the Calcutta Metropolitan Development Authority and all other similar bodies. The development authorities should really convert themselves into planning commissions for urban agglomeration. Perspective planning with a very strong economic component should be the principal job of these authorities.

In fact, a city functions not because of its streets, but streets come in because there is a city. But the city functions because there is economic activity there. People produce things, people find jobs, people can earn a living. Now, if the authority which plans a city completely ignores these things and just thinks in terms of physical planning, well, that city cannot function. According to me, this is neither city planning nor city management. Various municipal bodies functioning within the planning area would be required to operate within the broad framework of the plan. But implementation and control should vest in the local bodies. Regulatory functions should be performed by the development authorities by exercise of budgetary control over municipalities. There need not be a sort of direct control by giving directives. It should be mainly by budgetary control. It is a very effective instrument. It could also have administrative control over those implementing agencies which are planning area-wise jurisdictions, may be, transportation system or water supply system. Those services which overspill municipal limits could be provided by specialised agencies which could work under the overall guidance of the development authority.

Under no circumstances should the development authority involve itself in the ordinary routine regulatory functions of a local body. To take an analogy from industry, the development authority should act as a board overseeing the company policy. The municipal body within the jurisdiction of the planning area could function as individual industrial units which together comprise the industrial undertaking. Just as the General Manager of a steel plant enjoys substantial autonomy within the general policy framework of the Hindustan Steel Limited, similarly the municipality would enjoy substantial local government powers within their own jurisdiction. At the same time, the entire urban agglomerate would function as a cohesive unit in which coordination policy and guidelines are provided by the development authority. This two-tier system of city management appears to be the only effective answer to the rapid metropolitan growth. The State, as I said initially, has been deliberately confined to major policy questions. We could get into a discussion as to where the funds come from and how resources should be raised. But I would suggest that those are matters of details. Actually, a community begins at the local level. Here, management functions devolve entirely upon the people living in that locality. The Area Councillor can provide a focal point for discussion. But how the people in the locality will live and interact must depend upon the local leadership. In this sphere, undoubtedly, the village community presents a much more closely knit picture than in the urban community. At the local level, therefore, the evolution of a pattern of community living akin to the village community could solve many local problems.

This calls for a view of the city as an interconnected cluster of village settlements rather than a homogeneous urban agglomeration. Basically, in a poor country if you think in terms of a city as a homogeneous unit, then you have to think in terms of expensive transportation system. Commuter distances are, really speaking, not a proper peg to hang city planning on. City planning in such a city must be confined to having residential and work areas adjacent to each other, really self-contained so that people can walk about or go by a bicycle to work, with certain central focal point which holds the entire city together. The average citizen need never cross-over from his community to any other community. But, whether the city planners can evolve such a pattern remains to be seen. Some of the new towns in some countries have designed interconnected village clusters as one. But to evolve such a design in an existing city would call for creation of city extension services within the municipal government. Delhi made an attempt at an urban community development service. But its effect has been marginal. The work has almost been given up. Community extension as a part of the city management needs to play a bigger role because it is out of this that an awareness of community needs and community responsibility would develop. If at the macro-level, a national urban policy could channelise urban growth and at the other end of the scale the realisation of the existence of a community at local level could create forces within a city which would awaken the municipal governments to their responsibilities and force them to work for community betterment rather than to function purely as a government.

tivity of man which means an organisation and other resources as well as specific management skills, be they conceptual, technical and leadership. What is therefore, called for here is the transfer of appropriate management technology in dealing with major problems of urban communities. These managers must adopt their ways and modes to the needs of communities which might adopt them. So we call for managers to be adept in the adoption and the adaptation of skills, technology and ways that should be called for in the management of communities.

Management must also be able to relate itself, with complimentary functions of planning and policy since the three are generally responsible for the development of communities. So, as I have earlier stated, the objectives of management in urban communities will be the main criteria of effectiveness and efficiency. To be effective, management must be able to achieve the results it has identified in a particular organisation in question. But to be efficient, it must be able to achieve these results at minimum cost. So, these are, what I consider the main parameters in setting goals and objectives in management of urban communities. Especially, in the light of focussing our goal to human welfare and efficiency.

The objective of business management is to minimise costs for maximising the profits. A recent development in the conduct of business enterprises, and this is also true of the Philippines, is the development of social consciousness among businessmen. Where even the goals in the hierarchy of the business world in the Philippines have come to associate the profitability in business with profitability of the human being, in the sense of social responsibility and social planning and social management, because, after all the goal should be human welfare.

Operating costs are usually fixed at a given budget so that the objective of management is to maximise the services that can be delivered out of the given budget. Non-business performance is not after all measured by the size of profit margin, but by the quality and quantity of the services rendered which are used to justify the budget.

Since the community goals are not attained by management alone, but in conjunction with the planning and policy functions, it is incumbent upon management to generate the necessary feedback information not only for its use but also for the improvement of the planning and policy functions, and thus what do we find? In the case of development of urban communities the immediate concern is goal formulation, so that appropriate goals are articulated and adopted and this has to do with the kind of participation that obtains in the community. In other words, we would like to see a good amount of public participation even in the policy formulation, even in the planning function and of course down the line to the implementation or in the management function. As a matter of need, therefore, management has come to be recognised as essential in the management of a community.

Let us now consider the primary factors that would be considered and understood in managing a metropolitan regional area such as Manila. In the concept of the metropolitan regions, it is good to stress this development model in terms of a National Human Settlement hierarchy, especially in the case of the Philippines, whose Government is central and whose expanse of territory involved is very very large. There is neen for establishing, first of all, a national policy framework for human settlements. And thus, we have created the Ministry of Human Settlements which will indeed take into account the development of settlements all over the country. Now Manila has recently been created as an agglomeration of four cities and fourteen munici-palities. The idea being that there will be economies rendered in the delivery of service because of scales and thus we have considered grouping, organisation of four municipalities and some thirteen or fourteen municipalitan posts in the Metro Manila area which is now being governed by the Metro Manila Com-mission.

Now, for the formulation of a metropolitan regional management model, we have thus far looked into certain basic considerations for such a model and this should include the concept of the metropolitan region and of its growth as well as the various aspects of integration.

Now to put management function in its proper perspective, a general systems framework of the development process will have to be presented. The process of national development is no less than the process of nation-building itself. If we have to build up a nation, then we have to consider national development first of all. The members of the society are therefore expected to contribute positively to national welfare through the proper uti-lisation of the Congress results including technology. Optimising the contri-butions of the different segments of the society is essentially the task of development plan, policy of planning and management. And it starts with the delineation of decision-making functions in the nation-building process. This process can be illuminated by a simplified systems model of the society where, human welfare, is achieved by the people through the consumption of goods produced by the system. In other words, this is making the society productive so that it can sustain some economic viability and in turn through the consumption of the goods produced by the community itself, it is hoped that welfare will be achieved.

This model shows the series of activities comprising the development pro-cess for the determination of the ends of development through the building up of a productive capacity or the means of development to the utilisation of that capacity to generate the things that people consume or the products of development in the milieu in which these activities take place. The model then delineates three functional levels in the process of the system depending on the kinds of decisions made, the nature of the actions involved, the speci-fications of the inputs required and the character of the output generated. These levels are subsystems of policy, planning and management which are responsible for generating the ends, the means and products of development,

clearly the duty of modern management and technology with respect to farmers' earnings.

International and national business are not interested in such a task, because they have insulated themselves from the results of their urban-oriented mercantilism. When prices go up, owners and managers increase their own pay—and even factory workers get 'Dearness Allowances', etc. But there are no Dearness Allowances for farmers.

In the case of India, at least, the structure of agribusiness is weighted against farmers by additional devices. For example, although many cotton-cloth mills in India are showing losses (and calling for tax-payers' money to make these losses good), there is a sizeable difference (up to 25 per cent) between what the farmers get for cotton and what the privately incorporated mills show as the price which they pay for raw material.

Moreover, as our farmers increase cotton production, imports are brought into the country and *subsidised*, in order to suppress the prices payable to our farmers. I wonder what would happen in an industrialised country if, say, motor cars from another country were imported and subsidised, in order to bring down the prices of locally made cars! That is what our Czars of Industry have done with imported cotton—although, thank heavens, our government is now more aware of the need to give our farmers control over their own produce.

The Roles of Other Institutions

Urban-oriented managers and administrators sometimes ask how such a system can work, when the farmers actually control the marketing and processing of their own produce. These urban-oriented people have in their minds an image of poor, illiterate rural producers—a lethargic mass with a fatalistic acceptance of poverty. Of course, this image is incorrect. Every community has its potential leadership and deep-rooted sources of adaptation and innovation, which are usually untapped. It follows that the rural manager must have faith in the rural community and its human resources.

When one views the urban orientation of our professional institutions, one is obliged to question whether they can be the source of the rural managers who are needed by rural communities.

By and large, perhaps, it is inevitable that Government and Governmental institutions, also, cannot fulfil our rural communities' management needs. Governments make policies; they set national goals; they provide guidelines for action, and, hopefully, they monitor progress and exercise a kind of "quality control" (for our milk cooperatives; for example, Government conducts the function of audit, which is very important). In other words, Government tends to work downwards from the top whereas rural management has to work upwards from the bottom.

Even voluntary agencies tend to suffer from the same weakness. They tend to be bureaucratised and urban-oriented. Often, with the best of intention, they have the idea of doing good for people, rather than enabling people to take over the show for themselves.

I hope I may be forgiven if I use this forum to point out that, by my observation, even multilateral and international agencies' efforts to do good frequently suffer from the same weaknesses and disabilities. Sometimes, their effect may be even worse than that, when the prestige and funds of an international agency are used to strengthen an urban-oriented bureaucracy which, once entrenched, may work against the rural people's own managers and professional staff.

Conclusion

In effect, rural management is not a discrete entity. It cannot consist of a group of individuals whose work is confined to, say, a factory (not even a dairy factory!). The rural management structure reaches right out into the rural producers' own communities. The secretary of the village milk cooperative is a manager in his own right, for example: he is the colleague of the Union's general manager and of the Union's staff. Thus, rural management includes the ability to recognise and respect the qualities of leadership and innovation that exist richly *within* the rural community. The rural managers have to be able to work with all their colleagues, including those in the villages. They have to be aware of the high present value of current income to the poor rural producer. They have to be able to perceive patterns of organisation which are capable of replication among thousands of rural families.

In India, for example, our 600,000 villages must each need 15–20 functionaries within the village, at least, say, one or two million trained functionaries. These functionaries can only be people *of* the villages: their work lies *in* the villages.... So, it is not enough to have read "Small is Beautiful" and then to sit in the city and say that one is a master of Appropriate Technology.

Of course, rural organisations need relevant technologies, whether they be big or small, just as they need relevant managers.

Rural organisations need built-in protection from vested interest. From where can they obtain such protection unless the control over their resources lies in their own hands? Ultimately, one sees that management *for* rural communities must become management *by* rural communities.

37. Management of Rural Communities

Washington A.J. Okumo

Mr. Okumo is Chief, Economic Cooperation Among Developing Countries, UNIDO, Austria.

Introduction

My own rather rudimentary technical acquaintance with the subject at hand counselled caution when I received the invitation from the organisers of this World Management Congress to come to New Delhi and address you on the subject of management of rural communities. However, I feel that such an invitation could come only from a recognition that rural development is an important factor in the economic and social upliftment of the poverty-stricken countries in the developing world. UNIDO considered it vital that its participation, through me, would highlight the industrial aspects of the management of rural communities within the context of technical cooperation among developing countries. The keen interest of Dr. Abd-El Rahman Khane, the Executive Director of UNIDO, in the subject cannot, therefore, be overemphasised. He wishes me to convey to this distinguished professional world gathering successful outcome of its deliberations and the adoption of concrete and forward-looking policies and recommendations for the benefit of the poor and underprivileged part of the human race.

In fact the scale and complexity of the issues which now confront us in the developing world is daunting. Old certainties are vanishing. Much conventional wisdom has had to be discarded. All is in a state of flux: the challenge of change is urgent and of great magnitude. The national state, while still in no danger of being subordinated to anything like world government, must adjust to pressures from both above and below, and the edges of sovereignty are being continuously trimmed. The concept of "national interest" is being redefined in a broader setting of mutual interests. The nature of the whole international system and its adequacy in relation to present and future needs, is being seriously questioned. Inevitably, the patterns of science and technology which sustain the existing international system are being critically scrutinised as never before. In this regard, I was greatly encouraged to see that this Congress has devoted a whole day to the discussion of the question of public policies on the management and transfer of technology to developing countries. The subject of appropriate technology is a very fashionable one these days, and it means many things to many people. Numerous papers and books have been written on it and many international seminars have been convened on the subject. Let us hope that this meeting will go beyond the purely academic and socio-political approach to this question and adopt concrete and scientific measures that will directly benefit the users of technology in the Third World.

It should be realised that the local development of appropriate technologies is normally both a high risk and an expensive activity in terms of time and finance. In practice, therefore, the choice of technology in rural areas is limited, largely determined by what is immediately or most readily available. The process of diffusion of new technologies is an uncertain one which seems to be difficult to influence or direct. For the shorter term it is likely that there would be a much greater return if priority were given to increasing awareness of the actual, as opposed to the theoretical, availability of proven appropriate technologies rather than to research and development in new technologies. Provision might then be made over the longer term for the import and adaptation of fresh technologies from other regions or countries as well as for the encouragement of innovation, particularly among smaller enterprises, for example, through the financing of pilot production facilities.

In all this, one thing is clear; *the inertial force of the status quo is the greater enemy of wisdom.* In an era of rapid change, the assumptions underlying existing policy over a wide front still resist that constant re-examination which they need. In few areas is this re-examination more critical to the human factor than in the orientation of world scientific effort. There has been no shortage of ideas and of exhortation on the subject; yet the pattern of science is so deeply embedded in existing political and economic structures that little has changed.

When we talk of rural development in the Third World, we must think and consider what progress in science and technology that has been achieved by the human race can contribute to the transformation and modernisation of the rural communities in these countries. The developing countries of Africa, Asia and Latin America have long recognised the crucial importance of rural development as an integral part of their national development effort. The fact that these countries share a common characteristic of having large proportions of their people in the rural areas has made cooperation among them to combat poverty in the rural areas a must. There is no doubt that in the past, many economic and social development programmes and projects from these countries have sought to develop and improve the rural population and the rural economy. The rural development strategies that have been used by many of these countries have been very diverse and much of the diversity has stemmed from the particular economic, social, political and physical environments of each country. So, attempts towards changes of rural areas have been going on for several years and under various names in developing countries of Africa, Asia and Latin America. The successes attained vary from country to country, but none of these countries claim to have achieved their desired objectives. It is in this context that I consider that technical cooperation among developing countries, which has as its objectives the fostering of self-reliance among them through the enhancement of their creative capacity to find solutions to their development problems in keeping with their own aspirations, values and special needs would make a significant contribution in the management of rural development.

The Definition of Rural Development

I know that many definitions have been proffered in this distinguished gathering of what is meant by the concept of rural development. I believe, however, that the commonly-held view of rural development is much too narrow, treating rural development as *a social category of programmes and projects with special characteristics*. Rural development programmes so far have concentrated largely on the agricultural sector and on the provision of certain social services, e.g., education and health. Although this had in most cases resulted in some improvements in the quality of life, the limited labour-absorptive capacity of agriculture in many developing countries constituted a serious constraint. In this speech, I consider rural development as a process of socio-economic change that involves the transformation of agrarian society in reaching a common set of development goals focussed on the capacities and needs of people. These goals include a nationally-determined growth process that gives priority to the reduction of poverty and unemployment and is aimed at the satisfaction of minimum basic human needs like shelter, food and clothing, and stresses self-reliance and the participation of all the people, particularly those with the lowest standards of living. In other words, the management of rural communities and/or development should have a multisectoral approach, whereby the "agents of change" should consider the promotion of a larger variety of productive activities in rural areas, if development was to be carried to the areas where people were, rather than to encourage further massive rural-urban migration with its concomitant social problems. The greatest opportunities for this multi-sectoral effort would seem to lie mostly in the non-farm group of activities consisting of manufacturing both traditional and modern—repair and maintenance, construction, and the tertiary sector.

I consider, therefore, that the aim of rural development is not only the development of rural situations in a narrow economic sense, but also the balanced social and economic development of particular areas or regions, with a special awareness for the optimum utilisation of local resources and a wide distribution of the benefits from the development. A re-ordering of priorities within the development process to achieve this aim must focus on the needs of the majority of the population who live outside the major cities, a significant proportion of them in conditions of absolute poverty.

In this regard, I can do better than quote a policy statement which the President of Kenya, His Excellency the Hon. D.T. arap Moi, made to the Kenya Institute of Administration on November 21, 1978. Mr. Moi said:

"I would now like to put one or two questions to you. When we talk of rural development what specially do we mean? Why do we talk about it every day and in every place? To answer these questions you must observe and understand your environment right there in the village:

— Look at that old man heading his cattle, camel, goats or sheep. Consider his social and economic needs.

— See that old woman weeding in that garden. See that other one carrying her gourd to fetch some water from a spring 10 miles away. Consider their immediate needs.

— Driving comfortably along a tarmac road, you look at the roadside and you see a boy with torn clothes playing with his equally unfortunate friends. Consider their immediate needs.

— What about that sick child on its mother's back? Why has it not had good nutritious food? Consider its wants.

"And after all this meditation, ask yourself, what can we do individually and collectively to help in the improvement of the social standards of these people? If you think that way and thus appreciate the problems facing our brothers and sisters everywhere in this Republic, you will not fail to see why the Government is fully committed to the idea of rural development.

"You are the vehicle the Government has chosen to deliver the social and economic goods to the *wananchi* and therefore you must face this difficult task boldly. You should not let the Government down in the eyes of *wananchi*. You will be given the necessary support and encouragement. I have already directed that from now on rural development funds will be channelled direct to the District Development Committees. This will facilitate faster implementation of district development plans...."

In other words, what Mr. Moi had in mind was that national development strategies need to emphasise and not merely recognise the agrarian core of most Third World countries. Rural development must be considered both as an integral part and the driving force of the entire development process. It cannot be pigeon-holed into a sectoral "box"; every sector of the economy must be considered to be part of rural development. When the anti-poverty, employment, distributive and participatory goals of development are added, rural development takes on a much wider significance, and demands far greater attention than it has received in the past in the majority of Third World countries, or in the allocations of external cooperation.

Although there is now a much wider recognition of the need for such re-orientation, particularly in international fora, there is a real danger that the urgency of national action will be lost with slogans such as "integrated rural development" that may give the illusion of global panaceas. Moreover, rural development threatens to become a casualty of the North-South debate on issues of international or domestic reform. It could be interpreted as an attempt on the part of rich countries, either to divert attention from questions of international resource and technology transfer, or to maintain Third World countries in their dependency status. At the same time, simple logic forces the countries themselves to give more weight to agrarian issues: the sheer mass of agriculture in most Third World economies; and the need to match growing populations with more food and more jobs. There is no denying that most Third World poverty and its associated problems are concentrated within rural society.

Further, rural development is not only a question of reversing urban bias and allocating more financial and technical resources to rural areas. The desired transformation of agrarian society, in most cases, requires a change of the structure of society as well as a change of the structure of political and economic power, both local and national. It is understandably difficult for an international organisation to confront the implications of the fact that rural development depends less on finding and applying the right technical solutions or filling a gap in capital resources, than on the occurrence of the appropriate social, institutional and political changes. On the face of it, this places an upper limit on the role of external cooperation. The justification for nonetheless strengthening efforts to promote rural development rest on the assumption that this limit still allows worthwhile contributions by the international system in this area. Given the numbers of people involved, even a modest improvement in the effectiveness of these contributions could have a tremendous impact.

Strategy and Policy Issues for the Manager

I have read with great interest the article in the Congress Papers by the distinguished and world-renowned management author and specialist, Professor Peter F. Drucker of the U.S.A. In his keynote address Prof. Drucker talked about the "issues facing management to-day and tomorrow". He talks about the role of the manager in the rural development process as an entrepreneur in the "Schumpeteranian mould". I entirely agree with him, especially on the role the managers can play in providing the necessary training and provision of capital for the development of rural communities. However, I should like to point out that the utilisation of the conventional approach without modification where necessary and supplemented by a grassroots process to rural development will not do the trick in many developing countries. In other words, there must be room within any rural development strategy for both top-down and bottom-up approaches, and that these should be complementary. I believe that this was the basic thrust of the Prime Minister's address to us.

For example, the distinctly "village" type of rural industrial production which is closely related to local resources and initiatives and serving highly localised markets, and which are undertaken mostly by small enterprises in craft, service-type and pre-industrial activities, could be influenced mainly by bottom-up policies and strategies; whereas the more organised and specialised forms of production, often undertaken by larger enterprises of the factory type, serving wider markets and perhaps requiring aggregate resources beyond the limits of what may be available in the local community could be influenced by top-down management strategies which Professor Drucker has amply talked about. In my view, however, I believe that both components are necessary ingredients in the management of the development of rural communities, since smaller enterprises and handicrafts alone would rarely be sufficient to catalyse rural development.

It is also extremely important that, in the management of any rural industrial development programme, there must be, at the policy-making level, clearly defined views as to the kind of products that are to be given priority so that public resources for long-term investment and assistance can be channelled accordingly. These priorities need to be established on the basis of resource endowment, availability of raw materials, energy supplies and skills, and the identification of market opportunities. Such priorities can only be properly established in the context of considerable depth of understanding of the local market and the nature of existing and anticipated demand. Both forward and backward linkages within the economy will help to identify the main areas for specialisation. Once national priorities have been established they will form a framework for the organisation of specialised institutional assistance and serve as the basis for integration between policies directed towards different sectors.

The range of product priorities and/or possibilities in any rural industrial development programme should consist of the following: the production of agricultural inputs, i.e., industrial enterprises with forward linkages with agricultu e; the production of consumer goods and basic needs items as well as the provision of services for rural communities; the processing of agricultural produce both for local and regional markets; the production of building materials, minerals processing, artistic crafts and non-rural resource-based industries which tend to be governed by competitive conditions in regional, national and international markets, provision of repair and maintenance facilities, including the production of spare parts; and finally, the provision of inputs and services for other local industries (subcontracting and perhaps ancillary units).

It goes without saying, therefore, that the establishment of growth of industrial enterprises in rural areas are conditioned primarily by the availability of entrepreneurial skills, the availability of credit and the removal of infrastructural constraints. The nature of rural enterprises, in terms of scale of production activity and the production technology employed, is largely influenced by these primary factors, which are closely interlinked. Government assistance to rural enterprises therefore has to be tailored to take these relationships into account as well as the form of social organisation of production. In many rural areas standard packages of assistance are likely to fail because they are inappropriate to local needs. Most forms of industrial activity require managerial qualities of flexibility and sensitivity to changes in demand, which have to be developed through experience and training. In rural areas such qualities of entrepreneurship can often be identified in emergent commercial and service-type activities.

The Management of Rural Communities in the Context of Technical Cooperation Among Developing Countries

I have said at the beginning of my talk that since the politico-cultural traditions of countries and regions vary enormously the choices between public or private enterprise and entrepreneurial or more cooperative forms of production units within a rural setting are more apparent than real. It is in this context that countries of the Third World could cooperate with each other in the identification and analysis together of the main issues of their development and to formulate the requisite strategies in the conduct of their international economic relations, through pooling of knowledge available in those countries and joint studies by their existing institutions. Here international management can play a vital role to increase and improve communications among countries, leading to a greater awareness of common problems and wider access to available knowledge and experience as well as the creation of new knowledge for tackling problems of development, especially of rural development.

I know that the subject of *appropriate technology* has been dealt with by another group, I would like, however, to bring to your attention that the Government of India, in cooperation with UNIDO, has just ended the deliberations of an International Forum on Appropriate Industrial Technology which was held in New Delhi from 20–25 November 1978 at the technical level and later at the ministerial level in Anand from 28–30 November, 1978. These meetings adopted recommendations calling for appropriate international cooperation to strengthen existing technological capacities in the Third World, including the rural sector, and to improve the effectiveness with which such capacities are used and to create new capacities and capabilities and in this context to promote the transfer of technology and skills appropriate to their resource endowments and the development potential of the developing countries so as to strengthen their individual and collective self-reliance.

In fact, the ministers endorsed the Buenos Aires Plan of Action on Technical Cooperation among Developing Countries which called, in general terms, for the improvement of the capacity of developing countries for the absorption and adaptation of technology and skill to meet their specific developmental needs. Specifically, it called for the promotion of greater technological self-reliance in the following terms:

"Developing countries should make every effort to strengthen their scientific and technological capabilities to suit their special needs, values and resource endowments by formulating, where necessary, technology plans as an integral part of their national development plans; establishing scientific and technological data banks; encouraging indigenous research and development activities for the attainment of their development objectives; combining research efforts and sharing their results with one another by means of agreements on scientific and technical cooperation; strengthening national design, national laboratories, research centres and scientific and other institutions; and linking their national research and development institutions, where appropriate, to those in other developing countries inclu ding linkage through the regional centres on transfer and development of technology. Developing countries should undertake special efforts to strengthen their national potentials in engineering and consultancy services by improving the professional standards, organising training and research. Broad exchange of experiences in this field among developing countries is an indispensable component of national and collective self-reliance."

It also called for the formulation, orientation and sharing of policy experiences with respect to science and technology in the following terms:

"In view of the important role of science and technology in the development of developing countries, and bearing in mind the successful experience of several developing countries in applying science and technology in their development process, developing countries should, wherever possible, exchange among themselves their experiences in the formulation and implementation of their plans and policies for the orientation of science and the transfer and development of technology to their own development objectives, needs and capabilities.

In conclusion, I would like to point out that I was deeply struck by the simple, wise and down-to-earth address which the Prime Minister of India, Mr. Morarji Desai, gave to us at the beginning of our deliberations. It should be clear to us all that the aim of a poverty-focussed approach to rural development is the raising of incomes and the satisfaction of basic needs for a minimum acceptable standard of living. The industrial component of the basic needs basket is substantial. These have been identified as processed food, clothing, footwear, housing and construction materials, basic drugs and medicine, bicycles, matches, soaps and detergents, textbooks and stationery, domestic utensils and household items, low-cost furniture, and energy supplies for heat and light. Although the production of many of these items does not require sophisticated technologies or a high degree of organisational skill, each may require that the existing production and distribution systems should be radically reformed to make them more appropriate to the requirements of the rural poor. This would be the appropriate task of management in the developing countries.

majority of the organisation gets busy with the tasks.

I am not suggesting that the structure is rigid or airtight. Two-way communication and upward mobility are encouraged if not built into the structure. But the fact remains that the job at the top, middle and the bottom is perceived to be qualitatively different. Equally important, the persons engaged at different levels, other than at the very top, are responsible for and therefore tend to have only a partial view of the organisational objectives. This is not to say that many sophisticated corporations do not encourage everyone within the corporation to understand overall objectives as a desirable attribute. But that understanding is not perceived to be critical. There is generally sufficient clarity about what is to be done at different levels of organisation, in what time-frame and with what resources to permit exclusive focus on the segment without serious consequences for the aggregate.

This pyramidical organisational arrangement has worked well in market situations in most countries even with different political and economic systems when the purpose of the organisation is to produce economic means in the form of either as goods or services. Here the enterprise is engaged in satisfying specific consumer needs. Once the basic management decisions on the objectives of such an organisation are made, much of their implementation can be sufficiently routinised into tasks to be performed by staff. The objectives here lend themselves for sequential distribution into tasks because the end results are in sharper focus and somewhat predictable.

In social services, such is not the case. Social services deal with ends or the total recipient in meeting his needs. The contrast here is between specific needs of a consumer versus the total consumer. Let us examine these social services and determine whether a different kind of management practice is necessary for them.

The broad range of social services are grouped into six major systems [4]: (1) education; (2) income transfer; (3) health; (4) housing; (5) employment training; and (6) general or personal social services. The last category includes child welfare, family services and counselling services for the aged, community centres, information and referral programmes, nutrition, services to the handicapped and disadvantaged groups, services to mentally retarded, counselling programmes for all age groups, family planning, and others. The term "social services" is internationally recognised as covering essential forms of communal provision. In the socialist economies, these are described as major forms of collective consumption. Social services are more specifically defined as the organised system of services under public or private auspices that directly support and enhance individual and social well-being, and that promote conditions essential to the harmonious interactions of persons and their social environment, as well as those services directed toward alleviating or contributing to the solution of social problems [5].

In capitalist or mixed-economy societies, all of these services become part of the non-market sector because they define and maintain the society's self-

protective and control mechanisms and its way of dealing with those who need help. Society meets some or all of the need because the market does not respond, or responds inadequately, and/or the societal stake in provision is too great for it to be left to chance, and/or because there is recognised economy of scale and need to escape from producer monopolies in order to protect standards and assure access. The socialist thinking which guarantees certain items of collective consumption is quite similar despite differences in vocabulary. There are several important relatively centralised or decentralised national models of social services and their local delivery [4]. For example, the U.K. has developed a comprehensive freestanding centralised social services system with local delivery points. Poland assigns social work as an adjunctive service, often a residual one, to institutions regarded as having fundamental life-cycle roles. France also organises social services as adjunctions to all major institutions. The Federal Republic of Germany stresses cash benefits as an overall social policy perspective, where people need services, e.g., home nursing care, there is a tendency to cash them out, to provide a grant which permits the individual to make a private arrangement, even with a relative or neighbour. Yugoslavia offers a unique approach to planning and programming of social services in which formal structure of self-management permits considerable initiative from the consumer. In 1974, Yugoslavia added "communities of interest", a third category to the other two fundamental units—neighbourhood and work units—which may join together to create programmes. In any given field of activity there is a council of providers and a council of beneficiaries who join in an assembly which is the policy body for the field of activity. The social work centre in Yugoslavia, like the local authority social service office in the U.K., is conceived as a place of leadership and responsibility by social workers [4].

In the U.S., social service history is one of creating categorical voluntary programmes of a quite specialised sort to meet specific needs, differentiating favoured "problem" groups out of the public assistance social service "mass", and leaving the most complex, multi-problem "unattractive" cases to what is in many States an overextended and poorly staffed public welfare system. Recently, a significant concern with service integration has led to numerous experiments with multi-service centres that cover several social services such as employment, housing, health, public assistance and other services [4].

The Canadian model is similar to that in the U.S. with a series of interesting and somewhat contradictory initiatives and an unclear direction for country as a whole. In Israel, all basic social services have local outlets [4].

Despite these national models and differences stemming from cultural and historical variations, there is clear evidence that social services are here to stay. However, much is yet to be settled that has management implications: the scope and scale of the services, their degree of universalism and selectivity, and their delivery systems. Most countries are going through change, reorganisation, growth and experimentation with these services. There, however,

appear to be some areas of agreement. Let us examine these to determine what they might portend for management [4].

1) Demographic, cultural and political variations within a country lead increasingly to recognition of the need for a delivery outlet based on and responsive to local needs through local participation and control. There is further recognition that these outlets should provide multiple social services. Across nations, fragmentation of services is of growing concern and there appears to be commitment to case integration and programme coordination [4].

2) There also seems to be an agreement on the need for a "generalist", practitioner or team at the core of the local service system. His new role includes [4]:

a) giving information and advice and making referrals about all social services;

b) giving access to these services;

c) providing front-line counselling;

d) coping with emergencies;

e) carrying out appropriate ongoing social treatment;

f) providing case integration and programme coordination;

g) being accountable for services; and

h) making decisions.

In some countries this role is performed by a local team such as in the U.K. While in others, it is either the responsibility of an individual, such as in France, or a combination of the two.

The major point to be made here is that the practitioner has qualitatively the same responsibility of access, integration and accountability as does the head(s) of the department(s) of social services. His role includes all the three tiers of the organisational pyramid that Anthony talks about. The only difference between him and the chief is difference in the magnitude or quantity of elements under his purview. In reality, he cannot reflect a part of the purpose of social services and be effective. He must know just as much, understand just as much, and represent just as much of the mission of the services as would be expected of the head of the organisation.

Let me illustrate this point by citing the example of higher education, an important social service, with which I am closely associated. Having worked with more than 100 colleges and universities, I have found that unless the purpose of the institution means the same both to the President of the university as well as to a professor of English, the institutional management becomes full of conflict and adversary relationships. I have also discovered that the professor of English, for him to have the same interpretation of the purpose, needs to know as much about where the institution stands and where it is headed in its totality as does the President of the university, unless the institution has the kind of management information system that permits both of them to look at the institution together, they cannot come to an agreement as to

what each must do to move the institution closer to its purpose than where it is, and the management of the institution remains less than satisfactory; unless they begin to share each other's concerns such as the President with quality of English and the Professor with the quality of English and balancing the budget, the student will not be adequately served. Finally, unless what either one does is understood by both to be interdependent, it either does not get done or gets done reluctantly in response to pressure. I suspect that similar is the case with doctors in health services, and service workers in housing, employment training and general services.

I can of course continue with examples but instead let me attempt to generalise what I perceive to be the principles essential to the practice of management in social service.

1) The management of social services equals a common understanding of the purpose(s) of those services by everyone engaged in the organisation responsible for those services.

2) Common understanding of the purpose equals perception by the organisation, an assessment of their present state and a considered judgement about where they should be in terms of the purpose.

3) Total perception of the services equals what needs to be done by everyone and how that will be interrelated to bridge the gap between where the services are versus where they ought to be.

4) What needs to be done equals rethinking of the content of routine by all so that it uniformly reflects the purpose.

How can these principles be implemented? Because of the time constraint it is not possible to elaborate on several reasonable options. But let me at least show you a process [6] that has been attempted with measurable success by a number of institutions in higher education in the U.S. The first stage in implementing the principle is to give the organisational mission a programmatic interpretation through participation of all organisation levels. No matter how well stated the purpose is, it remains meaningless unless it is given an interpretation that is commonly understood in programmatic terms. This attempt in itself is often a unifying force for the organisation. The search for valid answers to the question—what does the purpose of health services, for instance, mean in terms of access, integration and accountability—brings a focus to the deliberations of the top, middle and bottom levels of the organisation and energises them in a stimulating way.

The second stage is to detail the programmatic interpretations of the purpose jointly arrived at through participation by the practitioners into specific goals. These encompass areas through which programme ideals become realities, for example, hospitals, community health centres, special, general and other services. The goals taken together provide a level of detail in terms of which the purpose can be concretely achieved.

The third stage in the process is to integrate organisation with the goals. It is important that organisational subdivisions derive their responsibilities

from the overall service goals rather than traditional functional definitions. Such responsibilities might or might not be very different from the previous ones. But their execution would tend to be purpose rather than procedures oriented. Eventually, the concept of the job itself will change to mirror the purpose.

The fourth stage is organisational coordination of the major tasks. Much frustration in social services stems from an inability to foresee and plan activities that are interdepartmental in nature. Responsibilities, therefore, must be translated into a plan of activities within the resource framework.

The fifth stage is the alignment of budget, both resource acquisition and utilisation, so that the budget allocations reflect achievement of service delivery goals.

The sixth stage is evaluation. In the context of this process, evaluation is concurrent with formulation and implementation of the service purpose. Evaluation of this kind is both corrective and predictive. Corrective evaluation means that the mission, goals, responsibilities, activities, and budget are internally consistent and externally viable and that results correspond to the purpose. Predictive evaluation means that the actual results are evaluated in terms of their future implications. Thus, evaluation provides the process with continuity and momentum.

These stages are documented into multi-purpose matrices so that everyone within the organisation can perceive them in their entirety and act to actualise them. They are outlined here in sequential order only for clarity and convenience. In reality they represent points on a continuum rather than steps of a chain reaction.

The practice of management, that emerges out of this process, does not depend for its effectiveness on the disappearance of the pyramidical construction of the social service organisations. Such dependence would be tantamount to expecting a miracle since bureaucracies never die. The process depends instead on a premise that if the content of the organisation is strengthened, the form of the organisation, even if it is not ideally suited, will become less significant.

The function of management in social services is not limited to any part of the organisation but is a responsibility of the entire organisation. Here there is not the orderly sequential progression of purpose into products through organisation hierarchy like in market activities where products themselves are means. In market activities there can be those at the top who can assume the responsibility and develop expertise to scan the external stimuli such as changing market conditions, competition, and health of the organisation to provide renewed direction to the segment when needed. For management as we now know it, provides organisations with powerful tools for exploiting external opportunities through pragmatic distribution of assignments that are qualitatively different at different levels of organisation.

Greater the success in exploiting external opportunity, greater are the

rewards for everyone concerned. For regardless of the economic system, management of economic activities is designed to generate goods and services that are used as *means* by the consumers to achieve their own ends. A purpose of the market organisation is to create means for the consumer. The purpose of social services, on the other hand is to create ends for the outside to detect opportunities, for the other, the focus is on the inside to achieve its mission. If I were to transpose Maslow's hierarchy of needs to demonstrate the difference, market oriented institution's primary need is survival, for social service organisations, this primary need is self-actualisation. In my judgement, these two types of activities are at different poles sharing between them the heritage of management tools and techniques. But they do not share the same approach.

In social services, purpose is the product. Purpose is end. Purpose is the organisation at the top, middle and bottom. Purpose is the recipient. Many of the conflicts that are common for these services stem from the practice that follows the pattern established by the management thought as applied to commercial activities. It is not uncommon that institutions engaged in health care, education and other social services find central administration to be more of a hindrance than help in obtaining results. This is so mainly because the purpose of the organisation delivering those services has different interpretations to those who are in management and who are in operations. And no two individuals in the same organisations are able to perceive together the institution as a whole.

The management of social services does not require segmentation of the institution into its parts and assigning them as responsibilities at different levels of organisation but systematically helping all of the functions however small or large they may be to reflect the totality of the organisation and its purpose, much the same as a drop of the ocean reflects the properties of all of the ocean.

REFERENCES

1. Koontz, Harold. *Toward a Unified Theory of Management*, McGraw-Hill Book Company, New York, 1964.
2. Shay, Philip. "The Emerging Discipline of Management," A Chapter in *Handbook of Business Administration*, McGraw-Hill Book Company, New York, 1967.
3. Anthony, Robert N. *Planning and Control Systems, Harvard University: A Framework for Analysis*, Harvard University Press, Boston, 1965.
4. Kahn and Kamerman, *Social Services in International Perspective*, U.S. Department of Health, Education and Welfare, Washington, D.C., 1977. [The author is indebted to this study for the comparative social service material included in this paper.]

5. U.S. Department of Health, Education and Welfare, *Social Work Education, Planning and Assessment System*, Washington, D.C., 1976.

6. Parekh, Satish B., *Long-Range Planning. An Institution Wide Approach to Increasing Academic Vitality*, Change Magazine Press, New York, 1977.

39. Management of Social Services

Mario E. Albornoz Galdamez

Dr. Galdamez is associated with the Catholic University of Chile since 1960. Dr. Galdamez has been in charge of its various programmes in Economics and Business Administration. He is currently vice-rector of Economic and Administrative Affairs of the Catholic University. Prof. Galdamez is also a visiting professor and consultant with several leading institutions.

Introduction

The private business firm constitutes a basic cell of the western society. There are many reasons to justify this statement, and it would not be worth to explain such an obvious matter. Nevertheless, permit me just to mention that, business firm is, and has been, the vehicle through which human beings of the western world have had access to a better standard of living.

At present, there are two outstanding aspects of business firm, which should be noted:

a) The interests of different groups affecting the business firm: employees, executives, stockholders, government, town councils (municipalities), consumers, etc.

Each of these groups observes business firm from its own point of view creating real and potential conflicts that influences the development and the policy of management. Business firm responds internally trying to do the best it can do.

b) The quantitative and the qualitative changes that countries of the western society experiment, regardless of these countries being post-industrialised, industrialised or developing countries.

These changes, political, social, economical, technological, etc., varying permanently, characterised a day by day more turbulent environment [1] and with consequences for business firm difficult to predict.

These two aspects make that business firm depend more and more, on the environment it operates given that the turbulent changes and the individual

331

interests pressure business firm equally.

Facing this, a business firm has two alternatives: to be prepared in advance for the changes or to stay static and wait for their impacts. To be prepared means to look forward in order to foresee the problem and then develop feasible strategies, in order to continue its progress and to offer welfare to society in an efficient way.

If the social environment is observed, it can be noted that many changes happen in areas such as: social security, justice, participation, pollution, consumer movements, education, health, etc. Most of these changes have taken many companies by surprise.

A group of these problems is called social services, concerning aspects which can be considered on-business tasks of society or services for which business firm has not been interested in getting profits out of them. The social services can be included in the concept of the social responsibility of business, and for this responsibility goals must be established and results assured [2].

Thus, this paper pretends to relate the strategic decisions business firm adopts, with the social impact they have in a definite set of problems, called social services.

However, we must not forget that a business firm has to produce profits both to the stockholders and to maintain itself in competition in the long-run; to provide jobs for the labour force; to demand products and services from other economic activities; to satisfy the demands of the society.

Social aspects cannot be considered as something outside the firm; on the contrary it is something that it is part of the firm; up to now social needs have not been included, neither within the areas of the business firm, nor within the areas of social influence. The strategic approach helps us to consider these aspects as a part of the business firm.

The Evolution of the Social Responsibility of the Business Firm

In recent years many words have been said about the social responsibility of the business firm.

Some authors, as Richard M. Hodgetts [3], define the social responsibility as "the moral obligation that the business firm must assume in relation with the welfare of the society where the firm operates. Obviously this responsibility differs among different firms."

Even though not all the authors on this topic agree that the concept of moral or ethic obligation is taken by business top executives as an important problem to be considered, many of these authors emphasise that the firm, whether she likes it or not, has to develop explicitly this responsibility and it is forced to two situations:

a) To adapt the firm to the social expectations and to the pressures coming from the community.

b) To cooperate in the efficiency of the social services.

The traditional approach of the social responsibility and its evolution

Traditionally, the business firm has understood that its social responsibility is related only with its nearest environment (Table 1):

—The owners or stockholders of the company;
—The consumers;
—The government;
—The suppliers;
—The employees and workers;
—The community more directly in relation with the firm.

Table 1

**THE SOCIAL
RESPONSIBILITY OF THE
BUSINESS FIRM**

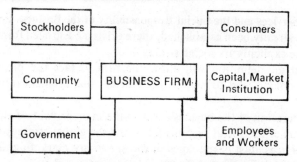

Richard M. Hodgetts, *Introduction to Business.*

However, in recent years this traditional way of visualising the social responsibility has been overcome, mainly because of two reasons:

a) Social changes, more frequent and variables day after day;
b) The change of the public opinion about the business firm.

As the very well-known Prof. Bernard Taylor [4] states, the body of the laws affecting business firm in most of the western countries is growing and growing; the number of lawsuits presented against business firms has increased in great proportion; for example, only in the U.S.A. the claim for goods raised from 50,000 in 1960 to 1,000,000 in 1975; if we add to this the antipathy movements against business firms, we have a picture that can be considered a real challenge to the firm.

Trying to find a solution, the most advanced western business firms are replanning and redefining their social responsibilities once again.

The alternatives of the business firm

To face these problems business firms can follow different approaches and alternatives. Among the alternatives that can be mentioned, we have:

a) To sensibilise the executives towards social and political aspects;
b) To combine the production, finance, personnel development, marketing,

investment projects, strategic and operative plans, with certain social aspects in order to foresee future social contingencies, which may affect the plans of the business firm.

c) To develop a social strategy of the business firm, from its global policy and strategy. This would allow to minimise the risk: of the social environment changes, and to be prepared to meet what we can call the strategic surprises.

In this way it is possible to encounter the social changes, neither affecting the business firm, nor wasting resources [5].

In other words what we consider important is that the business firm takes the initiative in order to look for the social problems (and for sure it will find them), that the business firm takes the responsibility of solving efficiently these social problems, assuring in this way for a better future for itself.

The Social Services and the Social Responsibility of the Business Firm

As it has already been established, there exists a basic need for the business firm to define explicitly its social strategy.

This strategic definition will allow the firm to face the problem of the social environment, and to help in the efficient management of many social services.

The cooperation of the business firm in the management of these services must be a part of the social responsibility and the global strategy of the firm.

Social services must be managed in the same way marketing; finance, personnel and production are managed.

The business firm must be creative, must take the initiative, and should meet its social responsibility goals.

Classification of the social services according to the contributions of the business firm

When the term social services was mentioned at the beginning of this paper, it was associated with the non-business tasks of the society.

When the social services are included within the context of the social responsibility of the firm, the area of their action increases; and this is so because the firm must satisfy its basic objectives of survival, real and potential profits, growth, and human and social responsibility.

Table 2, first column, shows the principal kinds of social services. This list includes social services relevant for different world environments and communities and, even though it does not pretend to be complete, tries to cover the main types of social services.

Types of problems from the management point of view

Each social service mentioned in Table 2 presents different kind of problems. The second column of Table 2 shows the corresponding ones for some types of social services, as an illustration.

These problems may vary from one society to another; the illustrations given pretend to show those problems that can be considered more frequent.

Table 2

Social Services	*Problems*
1. Economic Development	Investments, Technology, Proper development of technology
2. Education	Financing, Quality
3. Employment and Training	Financing assistance to handicapped and disabled groups, Permanent education
4. City Planning	Shopping centres, Transport,
5. Ecology	Pollution Unpleasant noise, Forest and animal preservation
6. Culture and Art	Diffusion Support orientation at Financing
7. Health	Hospital administration, Financing, Improvement of health services, Public medicine
8. Government and Legislation	Assistance to government to properly legislate on the business firm-society problem, To improve public administration, Assistance to improve social services
9. Consumer's Movements	
10. Equality of Sex	
11. Race and Colour	
12. Extreme Poverty	
13. Drug Addiction	
14. Labour Unions	Strong unions, Collective bargaining, Infant programmes management
15. Nutrition	
16. Demography	
17. Ethics, Morals, Religion	
18. Sports, Recreation	
19. Unemployment	

How can the Business Firm Help to Efficiently Manage Social Services?
A Methodology

When the business firm is aware of social responsibility, and wants to help in an efficient way to manage social services, she must develop a method to comply with it.

A methodology is described, and its five steps are closely related among them (Table 3).

    a) To define objectives and social priorities.
    b) To develop feasible strategies.
    c) To determine the strategic zones of social influence.
    d) Summary table: application.
    e) The institutional approach.

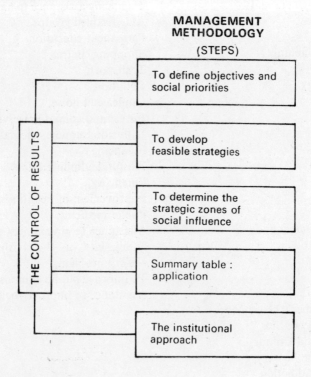

To define objectives and social priorities

At this stage the business firm has to wonder about the future social environment it will face:

—Which are the potential social problems?
—How will they affect it?
—In what direction?
—With what degree of intensity?

This must also be analysed from the external point of view:

—How does the social environment see us?
—Which pressure social groups exist and may exist?
—Other questions alike.

The firm, then, has to decide what priorities will assign to the different types of social services of the environment and it has to identify the kinds of problems she will help to solve.

The firm must set explicitly its social objectives, both qualitatively and quantitatively (the specific results the firm pretends to achieve).

These objectives has to be in accordance with the firm's long-run objectives and with the different types of business the firm operates or will operate in the future.

It must also be taken into account that the social objectives are influenced by:
— The value system of the owners or stockholders of the company.
— The value system of the executives.
— The influence of the firm employees, workers and labour unions.
— The value system of the society itself (culture, religion, etc.).

To develop feasible strategies

The definition of the social objectives and priorities permit to visualise the final results which may be reached.

The problems that must be solved when designing the strategy are:
— How to obtain the final results?
— Which human and material resources are needed?

The social strategy has to be feasible, that is to say, its application; should be possible for this reason it must consider the strong and weak characteristics of the firm and also the different types of business the firm is interested in.

To determine the strategic zones of social influence

The firm must understand that she can neither solve all the problems of its environment, nor attend the interests and needs of all groups.

For this reason, it is essential that business firm determines within its environment the zones it will assist.

The selected social areas constitute for the firm strategic zones, because in each one of them the firm must apply a different strategy.

The firm can choose one or several zones, depending on the influence it wants to achieve.

Anyway, the non-selected areas may act over the firm, either pressing it or giving negative opinions about it; but what really matters to the firm is to be effective in the area chosen, because this one matches in a better way with its social objectives and priorities, with its strategy and its business.

At the same time, the company must design a communication programme to and from the strategic area chosen to apply its influence. This programme must include the adequate research in order to find the interests and needs of the people of that zone in order to provide adequate solutions.

When the social services are applied to each strategic zone they really mean something to the business firm. If the firm helps to administrate efficiently these services it will assist its area, and will obtain a more outstanding social influence.

Summary table

The above methodology can be summarised as follows:

    a) The strategic zones of social influence must be defined;

    b) The business firm has to determine for each zone selected:

— The types of social services the firm wants to administrate or to attend;

— The types of problems the firm will help to solve inside each social service selected;

— The priorities given to each social service and problem selected;

— The assumptions about the future trends.

An extension of Table 2 can be useful at this point.

Institutional approach

The firm must decide whether if, for solving these problems, it will act individually or through industrial associations, by means of pressure groups, or a combination within these alternatives. Given that each alternative offers advantages and disadvantages, the firm must consider its objectives and priorities, its strategies, and the results it wants to reach.

An Alternative: to Combine the Creation of New Business Areas for the Firm with a Probe Solution for Essential Social Problems

A proper way to apply most of the mentioned ideas is to put into practice an Administration Plan of Social Services, with the chance of looking for new areas of business.

As an example: an American company has made good business, solving important social services at the same time. This is the Control Data Corp., company of Minneapolis, which, among other things, has worked the following social services, in an efficient and lucrative way [6]:

— It reduced considerably the health problem of the Indians, in the Rosebud Sioux reservation in the State of South Dakota, U.S.A., applying a computered health programme, tried out in a reservation.

    Result: Possibility of applying it in developing countries.

— A plant was built, in the North of Minneapolis, in a zone characterised by unemployment, the personnel had no experience in the job. The people had judicial problems and a high alcoholism rate.

    Result: Though it meant much money and time, new sources of work were created getting a high standard of efficiency at the same time (110 per cent of normal standard), with a very low rate of defective production.

— It applied a complete educational problem of reformation, and penal assistantship, through a computer, allowing prisoners to study their lessons, while the computer supervised their answers.

Result: At present, the programme is being applied in youth centres and other prisons.

"People do not want philanthropy, and they are willing to pay for the solution of their problems" states William Norris, President of the Board of Control Data Corp.

The idea developed herein is the following: if a social programme is applied, as it has been stated, it is not known in advance, if it is going to generate, or not, new products or services, which may be considered business to the firm.

However, it sounds logical to capitalise this type of experiences and open, through this channel, new business horizons.

In this way, an excellent combination is obtained: the solution of social services with the firm participation and a lucrative way of business.

Conclusions

From the preceding pages we can conclude the following present trends in Business Administration:

a) The business firm, each day, depends more and more on its environment.

b) The business firm should foresee and solve the problems of its environment in advance, in order to minimise the impacts upon itself.

c) The social responsibility (and the social services) is part of the new conception of business administration: creativity and anticipation, more than reaction facing a given pressure.

d) The business firm can actively cooperate in the management of social services, designing a social-strategic action plan. These areas of social needs become normal areas of business.

e) If, in addition, it is possible to create new areas of lucrative business, the firm can efficiently solve its own problems and those ones of the community.

f) With all this, we can conceive an efficiency concept, in three dimensions:

— Through productivity, measured in physical quantities, per unit of time (traditional approach);

— Through maximising profits: economic efficiency;

— Through social efficiency: the firm covers its social responsibility.

REFERENCES

1. Ideas expressed by Prof. H. Igor Ansoff, in the EIDEP Program (ESADE International Development Executive Program). Barcelona, Espana,

April, 1977.
2. Humble John. *Social Responsibility? Myth or Reality?* Revista Empresa Icare No. 6, May, 1970.
3. Hodgetts, Richard M. *Introduction to Business,* Chapter 25, Issued by Addison-Wesley Publishing Co., U.S.A., 1977.
4. Taylor, Bernard. *Strategic Planification for Social and Political Changes,* Long Range Planning Magazine.
5. Ibarra, José Ricardo. La Gerencia Estratégica "Las Empresas ante un entorno Turbulento" Revista Empresa, edita-do por ICARE No. 1. Santiago, enero, 1978.
6. *International Management.* McGraw-Hill, July-August 1977, Volume 32, Number 7/8, p. 32.

BIBLIOGRAPHY

Ansoff, H. Igor. *Corporate Strategy,* McGraw-Hill, 1965.
Ansoff, H. Igor. *Management of Strategic Surprise and Discontinuity Problem of Managerial Decisiveness,* European Institute of Advanced Studies in Management, Working Paper No. 75–29, July 1975.
Ansoff, H. Igor, R. Hayes, and R. Declerck. *From Strategic Planning to Strategic Management,* London, John Wiley & Sons, 1976.
Humble, John. *Social Responsibility.*
Hodgetts, Richard, M. *Introduction to Business,* Addison-Wesley Publishing Co., U.S.A., 1977.
Taylor, Bernard, *Strategic Planning for Social and Political Changes,* Long Range Planning.
Drucker, Peter F. *Technology, Management and Society,* Pan Books Ltd., London 1972.
Drucker, Peter F. *Reflexiones para un Director,* Association para el Progreso de la Direction—APD, Madrid, 1973.
Romani, J.M. *Empresa empresarios..para que?* Revista Jano Management Enero 1975, Barcelona. *International Management,* McGraw-Hill, July-August 1977, Volume 32, Number 7/8.
Truitt, N., D. Blake, E. Valenzuela, J. Elias, C. Olavarria and R. John Pate. *Opinion Leaders and Private Investment: An Attitude Survey in Chile and Venezuela,* Fund for Multinational Management Education. December 1976, New York.

Managers' Concern in the Next Decade

40. Managers' Concern in the Next Decade

Sir Adrian Cadbury

Sir George Adrian Hayhurst Cadbury is Chairman of Cadbury Schweppes Ltd. He is also a director of the Bank of England and IBM (UK) Ltd. Sir Adrian is involved in a number of social activities and is particularly interested in management education, being a member of the Council of Industry for Management Education, the Council of the University of Aston, the Council of the Careers Research and Advisory Centre, and a trustee of the International Students Trust. He also has a special interest in regional affairs, and was Chairman of the West Midlands Economic Planning Council during 1967–70. Sir Adrian is an active sportsman.

At the outset, I accept that my point of view is influenced by my background as a manager. Nevertheless, I believe that the concerns which I have will be shared by the managers all around the world at least in some degree and I find it of particular importance and interest that this Congress should be held in India where different points of view can be reconciled, because India is a bridge between the world of advanced technology and that of rural industries, between the less advanced and the developed countries of the world.

My first concern is simply our ability to manage effectively under conditions of economic turbulence and rapid social change. Our task is to meet the changing needs of the consumer by making and marketing the goods people want at prices they can afford. In doing that our first responsibility to society is to manage scarce resources efficiently because an inefficient or unprofitable business is no asset to society. In the decade of the 1960's we had uninterrupted growth and growth was the accepted goal; the rate of inflation was predictable; raw materials were steady in price and readily available and so our budgets were based on annual increase in output and companies like ours were looking to widen their product range by diversification and by geographical expansion and we thought we could not go wrong by using other people's money.

The oil shock, the depression which accompanied it and the rising demand for protection has changed the picture completely. We face inflation rates which are high and fluctuating, wide movements in exchange rates, a challenge to growth in a world of finite resources and the reality that we have had to manage without growth any way.

If you take my own trade, the food in the United Kingdom, we are still in volume terms doing less business than we were doing in 1973. So, it is not just a question of no growth, we have had negative growth. We are now managing not for the growth of our companies, but for their survival. This means concentrating on our basic businesses, doing better with what we have, learning to react more quickly in our planning and systems of organisation and measuring our results in terms of cash flow because cash flow is real, while our balance sheet and profit and loss accounts have been distorted by inflation. There are countries where the rate of inflation has been very much higher than it has been in India and perhaps we can account for your better record over inflation in India by the calibre of the people who manage the financial affairs of this country.

So, our first concern must be to do a better job as managers against a more unpredictable economic background without being able to rely on growth to bail us out.

Of course, how we do that job is also a matter of great concern. So, let us look at the external and internal implications of our work. Looking outwards focusses attention on how our work as managers relates to society as a whole. Our obvious point of contact with society is through the government. Government intervention is here to stay in all our countries; if not through mutual admiration, through mutual need—a need which has grown as the economic climate has deteriorated. I am down in my published paper, by a happy slip of the pen, as suggesting that a goal government can only achieve through industry's help is *expert* growth. I meant *export* growth, of course. Not that I am against expert growth as well, but the Prime Minister implied that we should be chary of offering advice to experts. Governments through their policies of intervention have had to share some of their powers with managers and with trade unions; but government intervention is not going to go away. However, there is a change in the way in which governments and businesses are being perceived, at least in many western countries. There is widespread disillusion about the ability of governments to cope with major economic and social problems and by contrast business is being turned to as having resources of efficient administration and the capacity to find solutions to problems. So, the trend in a number of developed countries is to demand lower taxes and lower public expenditure, a greater degree of individual choice and a greater reliance on individual initiative in improving levels of housing, education and other services which were referred to by Mr. Fernandes this morning.

There is also a move away from the centre to the local level (again in line with the provision of district industry centres in India), away from thinking that governments have the answer to everything and towards saying that partnership with business which has scarce management skills might be more fruitful. As a practical example of this, two of our managers in the United Kingdom are taking part in a local government project team which is looking at ways of reviving employment in city centres.

So, I see our relationship with society as being a form of contract. In earlier days, the contract was that provided we delivered economic benefits without inflicting any obvious damage on the community, then we were licensed to manage. Now we are rightly expected to produce social as well as economic benefits, and to make use of our resources of skill and experience to help the community. That is admirable, but we do need to watch that this changed view of our role does not go so far that social performance becomes the test by which business is judged, which is about as sensible as judging social institutions by their profitability. I remember on an earlier occasion hearing Peter Drucker say that he did not want the hospitals to be run like businesses, he just wanted them to be run like hospitals.

I hope to see better contracts between government and management at the grass roots. I think we should take to heart and accept that agreement between businessmen, politicians and administrators at our levels is useful and important but that what matters is how it is implemented on the ground—that is where the action is. Let us encourage contacts at local level and be prepared to release managers for joint ventures with government and encourage them to run for public office. So much for my second area of concern which is the relationship of managers to society.

My third area for concern is within our own business and relates to how we manage. How do we manage when authority has to be earned, when the people we manage are not only better educated, but have been educated in a more questioning way and have higher expectations? I have no doubt this means that we must adopt an open style of management to achieve results in the next decade.

I am convinced that a greater degree of involvement and participation for everyone in our businesses makes sense for the individual and makes sense for the company. We not only get better decisions as a result, but we win commitment to those decisions. For my part give me a second best decision at any time provided it has the full backing of all those involved.

We have to do a far better job of making people feel that they belong to the enterprise where they work. It is our job to create a sense of identity and a feeling of common purpose in the businesses we manage. We have to explain what we are aiming to do, why it is important and how the individual employee fits in. Just as essential we have to listen and take into account the views of the people affected by a decision before taking it. We cannot improve the efficiency with which we use resources without change, but change is uncomfortable. As I was leaving England, the *London Times* had just suspended production because they could not get agreement to the acceptance of technological changes which they believed were essential for the future of the newspaper. As managers, we have the responsibility to initiate change and win acceptance to change by putting all our cards on the table and by showing that we have trust and confidence in the people with whom we work.

If we go along this path, then we have a massive training task ahead of us. Training for managers so that the first line of management—who are the company to the employees—can put across what needs to be done and why and answer questions about the company's plans and figures. In effect participation starts at home. We must make sure in the first place that we have taken our own managers fully into our confidence all down the line. Then the training effort needs to be extended to all those employees who want to play an active and informed part in the participative structure.

The second area of training for managers is concerned with answering such questions as "how do you manage in an open way"? Does it work? Does it mean all talk and no action? The answer is, yes it does work, but it is more demanding. The manager remains responsible for the final decision (we must never confuse participative management with permissive management.) He remains responsible because that is the job he is trained to do and because he must take account of all the relevant factors in coming to a decision; the views of those for whom he is responsible is one such factor and an important one, but it is not the only consideration.

I would like to finish by pulling together some common threads running through the three areas of concern I have outlined—managing the business for survival, managers in society and involving people in the business through open management. They relate to the way I see the managers as essentially the man or the woman in the middle. Managers make things happen and they are continually resolving the problems set them by consumers, customers, governments, their bosses and the workforce. Each of these groups exerts a force on the manager and out of the sum of these pressures he has to produce constructive and acceptable results.

What changes of emphasis will there be in this role in the decade ahead? First the frame of reference of managers will continue to broaden. We have to be more alert to the signals from society concerning what is expected of us and we have to act on them more quickly and efficiently. A wider range of managers will be involved in the company's external relations, so the influence of managers will become more diffused within society, leading to a better understanding of the managerial role.

Secondly, we will have to spend more time in resolving conflicting demands. Managers are asked on the one hand to produce goods and services and on the other to conserve natural resources; on the one hand to raise productivity and on the other create more jobs; on the one hand to be more innovative and on the other to conform with the increasing weight of regulations and legislation. Well, finding the right balance between conflicting demands has always been a part of the manager's job. It is going to be a bigger part and we are going to be more exposed in carrying it out.

In the West pressure groups have been growing in power. The problem is they are rarely representative and usually against something. As managers we have to be positive and so we have to make the best sense we can out of these negative pressures and still come up with constructive answers because that is what the community looks to us for.

The third strand follows on from this issue of pressure groups and it concerns what the collective role of managers in society should be. How do managers ensure that their point of view is heard and that their professional standards and systems of value are maintained? I think it is vital that managers should be able to exert a collective influence, not down the trade union road, but through the strengthening of their own professional organisations. This in turn requires a much clearer lead by those organisations on codes of managerial conduct and business ethics. An issue I know in which the World Management Congress has been actively engaged. As managers we cannot influence by force of numbers, we have to do so by the logic of our arguments and by ensuring that we have the trust of government and the community and that trust will depend on establishing a clearer and more visible set of standards which as managers we agree to abide by.

Fourthly, we have to find ways of simplifying and decentralising the organisations in which we work. Businesses will not survive in an unpredictable world, unless they can speed up their reaction time and that means cutting the number of levels of authority. Apart from anything else if involvement and participation are to be made effective, we must make them effective at the place of work, because that is where the majority of decisions are taken which affect people most directly.

Managers at that level must have the authority to take the necessary decisions, otherwise all our talk of involving people more effectively is humbug. One way of simplifying our organisations and reducing the size of the units in them is what I have called in my paper disaggregation, we must unburden ourselves of the great range of services which most large enterprises gather within the company and instead we should consider buying these services in from small independent businesses outside.

The last point I would like to see in the next decade is a greater emphasis on continuity in relationships. Arguably, the best way to get ahead for a manager in the sixties was to keep on the move and this has two major disadvantages. Too often managers were not in the job long enough for their mistakes to catch up with them and the people who worked for them felt they were being used to provide a career path for their managers. I believe that we should rely more on team work and on involvement in the areas ahead and that these depend on personal relationships which must be allowed to grow. Of course, movement of managers is necessary to bring in new ideas and to reward performance, but let us weigh more carefully the costs of movement against the benefits.

I may seem pessimistic about the next decade, but I hope not. I have no doubt that the job will be more difficult and that more will be expected from us. But that is a challenge we should welcome. We have chosen to be managers, the initiators of change and not caretakers preserving the past. Let us build from the bottom up—on our side is a movement of power away from the centre towards the local level in all our countries and there are signs of a fresh evaluation of the contribution business can make in economic and social terms. I have no doubt that managers have an essential role to play in meeting society's needs over the next decade—my hope is that we have the confidence to meet that challenge to the full.

41. Managers' Concern in the Next Decade

L.K. Jha

Governor, Jammu and Kashmir, India.

Despite our very different backgrounds, I find myself in agreement with most of what Sir Adrian has said. In particular I should like to underscore what he had said about the widening of the role and responsibilities of managers in the years to come. "How the work of managers relates to society as a whole"—as he has aptly put it—is indeed going to be a crucial test of the managers' performance.

I also agree with him when he says "government intervention in industry is not a passing phase." Authorities on management have recognised three tiers of management: the top management dealing with corporate strategy, the middle management focussing on functional responsibilities for production, finance, marketing, etc., and operational management at the foreman or supervisory level. I would add that the top management itself operates in an environment which is, to a greater or lesser extent, subject to management by the government and up to a point by international force as well.

At this point I must proceed to develop and dwell on some differences between his viewpoint and mine. He has referred to a swing in government-business relationship in the direction of government placing greater reliance on private managers to fulfil some of the economic and social goals to which governments attach importance. This may well be true of developed countries. I believe in developing countries the pendulum is still swinging in the opposite direction because of the feeling that private management pursues its own objectives with scant regard to the wider goals of economic and social policy. In developing countries "distrust of the motives of companies particularly large international ones" does not belong to a "past period", but is a continuing factor. If managers can succeed in eradicating it we should have a far healthier climate, beneficial alike to managers and the community as a whole.

The other major point on which I should like to present a different alternative scenario from that of Sir Adrian is in regard to the international setting. I agree with him that the economic framework within which the goal of growth was being pursued in conditions of stability and predictability has broken down. It could well be as he has argued, that in the next decade "conditions of much greater uncertainty" will prevail. But it is also possible that just as the trials and tribulations of the thirties led the nations of the world to open a new chapter in economic policy after World War II, so the struggle and sufferings of the seventies may be the stepping stones of a new international economic order which would provide stability and certainties which would be wider and deeper than what we have ever known in the past.

In the rest of what I have to say I shall attempt to speculate on this possibility, particularly from the viewpoint of developing countries thoughti will be my endeavour to argue that such an order will be beneficial to developed countries as well and indeed to mankind as a whole. I should also add that the success of such an order will depend upon the managerial skills of a high order being deployed not only at the level of enterprise but also at the national and international levels.

The main features of the economic system to correct the malfunctioning of their economies which they had experienced in the thirties which was brought into being by developed western countries after World War II were the following:

a) The adoption of techniques of macro management of the national economy through fiscal and monetary measures evolved by Keynes in order to prevent recession and unemployment;

b) The introduction for the first time of an instrument of international management in the shape of the International Monetary Fund headed by a Managing Director whose approval was necessary to changes in exchange rates and restrictions on current payments;

c) The setting up of the GATT which sought to minimise governmental interference in international trade, to eliminate non-tariff barriers and through negotiations to bring about a reduction in tariffs.

This system—I shall refer to it as the Bretton Woods system—was not universal. The socialist countries of East Europe were out of it *ab initio*, partly by political choice and partly because their external economic relations were conducted by the State itself while the system was aimed at minimising the role of the State. Japan and West Germany as defeated countries were not brought into the system to start with though they joined it later. Similarly the developing countries many of whom had not even emerged as sovereign States, had little voice in the evolution of the system though most of them joined it.

For managers this system meant a great deal of freedom in their operations. Some of the risks affecting their international operations, such as those arising from changes in exchange rates or tariffs were minimised or eliminated. Even in their domestic operations the macro-level management by developed country governments was based on the concept of maximising growth by leaving micro-level decisions to enterprising managers. In developing countries managerial decisions were, no doubt, subject to a much greater degree of control. But it was essentially a benign control intended to speed up industrial development. The virtual absence of effective competition, both internal and external, gave managers in developing countries much greater effective freedom than would appear from a superficial reading of the various restrictions to which they were seemingly subject.

For at least a couple of decades the Bretton Woods system seemed to work well. Both developed and developing countries achieved much higher rates of growth than they had in the past. Impediments to international trade were being steadily reduced. Although there were occasions when individual countries had to revise their exchange rates to correct a disequilibrium in their balance of payments, by and large stability of exchange rates characterised the whole period.

Then suddenly in the seventies things have begun to go wrong. The whole system of stable exchange rates which was the bedrock of the Bretton Woods system had been abandoned. The problems of unemployment, inflation and recession can no longer be tackled on Keynesian lines. Protectionism has been revived. If the world is not to re-enact the tragedy of the thirties, all of us —particularly those with managerial talents—must consider what the alternative to the Bretton Woods system should be.

The breakdown of a system is not a reason for having no system. We have only to contrast the chaotic conditions prevailing after World War I with the stability and high growth rates achieved after World War II to recognise that despite its many shortcomings, of which I shall be speaking presently, the system did serve the world community well. With the growing economic interdependence of nation-states the need for an international economic order has, I feel, to be accepted. But it must be free from the weakness of the Bretton Woods system.

From the standpoint of developing countries, its most disquieting feature has been that under it the gap between rich nations and poor nations has been widening and the share of the latter in world trade, production and consumption has been dwindling. This growing disparity is not an accident but a byproduct of the system which from its inception ignored some of the special problems of developing countries, particularly the following:

1) The export earnings of developing countries are heavily dependent on the prices of primary commodities in international markets. As their buyers are few and have considerable bargaining strength while their sellers are many with little staying power, commodity prices are generally low and often drop perilously. When the decline in exports causes a balance of payments crisis in any developing country, the IMF usually joins a devaluation of its currency which leads to a further deterioration of its terms of trade and worsens its plight. The GATT has stood in the way of producer countries getting together to improve their bargaining strength. In regard to export of manufactures, whenever developing countries succeed in establishing a foothold in

developed country markets discriminatory non-tariff restrictions are imposed on them, the GATT notwithstanding, by forcing them to accept restrictions "voluntarily".

2) Developing countries are in dire need of capital for their development. Though some international financial institutions had been set up to help meet this need as a part of the Bretton Woods system, with the weighted voting system the commercial interests of developed countries have tended to dominate the lending operations of these institutions, particularly as they are also at the mercy of developed countries for the resources they need for their work. Commercial lending to developing countries has usually been short-term and at high rates of interest. They face considerable difficulties in re-paying these credits—not because the projects which they financed did not generate the neccessary resources but because of the balance of payments constraints to which the developing countries are subject for the reasons I have just explained.

The price which developing countries have to pay for the technology which they import from developed countries is usually dictated from a mono-polistic position—through the patents and secrecy which protect technology and know-how. And even when the high price has been paid, the technology does not effectively pass into the hands of the importing country.

Developing countries, as more and more of them acquired sovereign status and joined the U.N., began to voice these concerns in different internation-al fora fairly forcefully from the mid-sixties. Their dissatisfaction with the Bretton Woods system was mainly because:

1) It minimised their operational options to deal with their emerging problems individually without bringing into being instruments of collective corrective action, the whole emphasis being on what governments shall not do and not on what grovernments shall do.

2) It covered only a limited area of international economic relations, mainly trade in products, but not the international movement of the factors of production: technology, capital, labour and primary produce.

The emergence of multinational corporations as the principal actors on the world economic stage heightened these anxieties. The fact that the global production of the multinationals surpassed the total volume of international trade was symbolic of the change which had come about in the international economic scene, namely, that the movement across national borders of in-puts had outstripped the significance of international trade in outputs. The view that multinationals brought benefits to developing countries by providing them with the technology, the capital and the skills they were most short of ceased to impress developing countries once they began to calculate the costs at which these benefits were derived. Their attitude and policies towards multinationals further hardened with the discovery that through national legislation alone they could not be subjected to the discipline which governed national enterprises and that in certain situations their economic power could well pose a threat to political power—to the very sovereignty which most newly independent countries cherished most.

From the point of view of developed countries the Bretton Woods system worked well for a couple of decades. Then problems began to appear on the international monetary scene. Some of these were met by imaginative innovations, such as the replacement of gold by SDRs. But when some major industrial nations, particularly the United States, began to face a chronic disequilibrium in their external payments and when speculative capital movements began to cause an intolerable strain on the stability of exchange rates, a fundamental rethinking on the whole concept of stable exchange rates began.

The possibility of placing restrictions on speculative capital outflows which the Articles of the IMF permitted was ruled out as such interference was considered to be both undesirable and difficult to enforce. A strong body of opinion developed in the U.S. that the very fact of having officially determined exchange rates was responsible for encouraging speculative movements and if market forces were allowed free play new steady rates of exchange would come into being at levels which would restore equilibrium.

This hope has however been belied. Speculative capital movements have continued. The dollar has continued its downward plunge. Although no one is yet talking of restoration of stable exchange rates attempts to revive the dollar are being made from time to time.

In the process a re-examination is one of the deeper causes of the malfunctioning of developed country economies of which the disequilibrium in external payments is the most obvious symptom. The real problem which developed countries are facing is that they can no longer deal with problems of unemployment and recession by a stimulus to domestic demand on Keynesian lines, without running into problems of two-digit inflation and a drain on their balance of payments. In this situation while some lobbies advocate protectionism as a method of safeguarding domestic unemployment deeper thinkers are taking a different view. At the Bonn Summit the U.S. pressed Germany and Japan to step up their growth rates in order that the pressure on the dollar may be reduced. The U.S. for its part was urged to raise domestic oil prices in order to reduce the yawning gap in its balance of trade. Side by side there was recognition of the importance of steps to help developing countries raise their standard of living.

As things are today, the Bretton Woods system, although in form it is still there, in substance has ceased to be an effective instrument for managing the world economy. The nature of managers' concern in the next decade will depend very much on whether a new order takes its place and what its main features will be. I believe and I hope that slowly we are inching forward towards a more comprehensive and a more equitable economic order which should come into being in the early eighties. I have already outlined the directions in which developing countries would like to move. Among the developed countries too a respectable body of opinion is gathering strength which urges that there is sufficient mutuality of interest between developed and developing countries for a new international economic order to be brought into being, even though there are sectors where, particularly in the short term, a conflict of interests is in evidence.

Furthermore, those who look upon the world economy not in terms of the sectoral interests of developed and developing countries but from the viewpoint of the human race as a whole are convinced that the problems that lie ahead can only be solved within a framework of global cooperation. Among these problems are those of pollution, energy, soil erosion and exhaustion of natural resources on the one hand and the formidable task of finding a thousand million additional jobs by the end of the century on the other.

Already in response to these new thought trends, the concept of stabilisation of commodity prices has been accepted in principle and discussion is proceeding on the machinery to bring it about. Ways in which the technological needs of developing countries can be most appropriately answered are being discussed with increasing seriousness. While at one time developing countries alone were speaking of a code of conduct for multinationals, today developed countries also are giving the most serious attention to this issue. The question of reform of international financial institutions to enable them better to serve the needs of developing countries is on the anvil. Developed countries have endorsed a reasonably high target for the transfer of resources to developing countries though most of them are well below it.

From these straws in the wind I am encouraged to believe that a new international economic order will evolve perhaps not dramatically but gradually. What is lacking at the moment is the kind of public awareness of the advantages of North-South cooperation which would generate the necessary political will for this purpose. The setting up of an independent Commission of International Development Issues under the chairmanship of Willy Brandt is a significant and important step towards such an awakening.

From the point of view of developing countries one of the prime objectives of the new order must be to reduce income disparities between countries and of course within countries. Almost all developed countries subscribe to this aim in their domestic policies. What stands in the way of its wholehearted acceptance internationally is the assumption of a zero-sum game—the belief that the poor countries can only get richer by impoverishing the richer ones. However once the importance of external demand in stimulating domestic employment and correcting balance of payments disequilibria is recognised, as it was at Bonn, it is but another small step from this premise to see the contribution which rising income levels in developing countries can make to the economies of developed countries. The trouble is that this potential has not yet been recognised. Not many people know for example that U.S. exports to what are known as developing countries—leaving out of account the oil producing and exporting countries—are higher than total U.S.

exports to the European Economic Community, the socialist countries of East Europe and China put together.

The basic problem which faces developing countries today in my view is that thanks to technological advance their per capita productivity is rising faster than their per capita consumption of goods. Despite all the efforts made, through advertising and high pressure salesmanship, to create new needs, there is a point of satiety beyond which physical consumption cannot be pushed. In developed countries even the unemployed are assured of reasonable incomes and standards of consumption, which was not the case when Keynes outlined his approach. A stimulus to domestic demand by fiscal and monetary measures does not lead to a quantitative increase in consumption which would create new jobs, but has the effect of bringing about qualitative changes in consumption patterns which raise prices and increase imports. A rise in income in poorer countries where people are far from being able to satisfy their basic needs can result in an increase in the volume of demand for the sophisticated products of industry which developed countries can produce most efficiently and in the process create more jobs and more exports for them.

Side by side some of the other concerns which growth has given rise to in developed countries can also be mitigated by a global approach. Pollution is one such problem. Essentially it is the result of over-concentration of certain types of industries in particular areas so that the harmful wastes which they generate are higher in volume than nature can cope with. In contrast there are vast stretches of land where industrialisation is totally absent or at a very low level. A wider dispersal of industry can cater to human needs without the undesirable concomitants.

I have now to relate the kind of scenario I have presented of a new world economic order with the theme of managers' concerns in the next decade. The concept of concern is capable of conflicting connotations. It may signify an area of interest and attraction; or it may indicate an area of anxiety and aversion. There are things which you are concerned with and things which you are concerned over. Whether the managers will be involved in the kind of goals at national and international levels that are slowly beginning to get acceptance, or whether they will try to get around and circumvent these objectives will determine the concerns of managers in the next decade.

For my part I shall seek to sum up and draw some conclusions relevant to managers at the enterprise level from what I have said today in the following terms: Sir Adrian has emphasised how the work of managers has begun to relate to society as a whole. He was referring primarily to society at the national level. I believe in the next decade the relationship between managers and the human society as a whole will begin to influence governmental attitudes towards management. The open style of management which he has advocated will have to be observed not only at home but in all the countries in which a company operates.

Sir Adrian has emphasised and managers have long recognised the importance of catering to the changing needs of the consumers of their output. They will in future have to pay increasing attention to the need of the suppliers of their inputs. Just as they have got used to respecting trade union opinion in dealing with labour, they will have to pay attention to the legitimate inerests of those who supply them with primary commodities for further processing. Their objective must be to imbue them with a sense of common endeavour in their operations.

Despite the concern which managers show for consumers it is clear that even in developed countries consumers have been compelled to set up organisations to watch their interests. The State too has been playing an increasing role in this area, particularly in providing protection to the consumer in the field of drugs and foodstuffs and electrical appliances so as to minimise hazards. I see an attempt in the coming decade for steps being taken to protect the interests of the consumer over a wider field, not only of the domestic consumer but also of the consumer overseas, not only of the consumer of products but also of the consumers of factors of production such as technology and capital.

Sir Adrian expects the next decade to be fraught with uncertainties. He may well be right. On the other hand it has been my endeavour to show that a search is on for restoring conditions of stability. The success of this effort will depend upon the ability of governments to cooperate with each other. At least those managers who dislike a climate of uncertainty and instability will I hope encourage rather than discourage attempts to ensure a better management of the world economy.

In fact I would like to conclude on the note that the next session of the World Management Congress will be not just a get-together of managers from all over the world but a session devoted to the problems of world management which will have begun to take a new, concrete shape in the coming decade.

42. Managerial Realities of Global Interdependence

Bohdan Hawrylyshyn

Dr. Hawrylyshyn is Director of the Centre for Education in International Management (ECI), Geneva. A leading consultant, speaker and teacher in management, Dr. Hawrylyshyn is Vice-President of the European Foundation for Management Development, and a member of the Club of Rome. He is currently Senior Fellow at East-West Environment and Policy Institute, Honolulu.

It has been said that we are dealing with a very complex subject. I will try to simplify it somewhat, and will structure my presentation in the following fashion:
— First, I will make some comments about the reality of global interdependence as seen through an historical perspective;
— Secondly, I will talk about the present and prospective nature of interdependence;
— Thirdly, I will try to deal with some of the effects of interdependence at the levels of the nation-state, the firm, and the individual manager and ways of coping with them;
— Finally, I will describe some of the characteristics of both nations and individuals which will be required to do well in a truly interdependent world.

History shows that there has not been a straight-line progression toward greater interdependence. It has been a cyclical type of evolution. There have been periods of opening up and increasing interaction between various political entities, and periods of drawing apart and isolation. Also, we have to distinguish periods of enforced "interdependence" achieved by military conquests and periods of more voluntary interaction.

Imperialist conquests resulting in unilateral type of dependence, while normally economically beneficial to the conquering nations, tended to be destructive of indigenous cultures, value systems, and economic structures. There have been exceptions, but such periods can be classified as periods of digression in the general evolution of mankind. The examples of the destructive effects mentioned above are many, be it the eradication of Inca and other Indian civilisations in Peru or the near extinction of Hawaiians within a generation of "discovery" of the Hawaiian Islands by the Anglo-Saxons.

Periods of increasing voluntary interdependence through commerce and cultural exchanges can be associated with an acceleration of cultural, technical, and economic progress.

The current reality is the inevitability of interdependence. We are simply condemned to it. The long term prospect is that even continental-sized countries will have to co-exist and interact with each other. Full economic independence, thus self-sufficiency, is beyond the reach of even the biggest and the best endowed countries. China is the most recent example of a continental-sized country which is confronting this particular new reality. The risks of an increasing technological gap and the opportunity cost of ignoring the laws of comparative advantage are simply too high. I have just visited China and by luck could observe it during the effervescent period of opening up to the world, a consequence of what the Chinese call the "second liberation of China".

If we accept the proposition that we are condemned to co-existence and interdependence, we need to have some working assumptions about the forms of such co-existence. We can readily exclude the feasibility of a single world order imposed by a single nation. A world hegemony is beyond the reach of even the most numerous or the most powerful. Given the destructive power of atomic weapons, the risk of undertaking the "conquest of the world" is sure to discourage any such initiative. This is why it is legitimate to talk about interdependence when we talk about the future. The interactions between nations will be essentially voluntary, determined by various countries' perceived needs and their complementarity. They will take place within a political world order influenced by a multitude of nations and groups of nations, hopefully with some sense of responsibility toward the world system which they will help fashion. The experience of a little country like Switzerland is significant; the more possibility people have to influence a system, the more responsibly they behave toward it.

Given the above assumptions about the shape of the world to come, how do we cope with the effects of interdependence?

1) At the country or macro-management level, there has to be good scanning and proper understanding of geo-political, world economic, monetary, and technological trends. By way of example, it is important for most countries now to assess properly the likely long-term consequences of the current flirtation between China and Japan. The consequences are likely to be very significant. The balance of political power at the world level will change, so will the pattern of trade and a number of other things will have to be reordered. Given the accelerated dissemination of technical know-how, new countries emerge quickly and develop real competitive advantage, particularly in older sectors of industry. Greater interdependence, therefore, implies also faster restructuring of economies. Some countries have demonstrated the

ability to do it well. Sweden, for instance, has been successful for over forty years in upgrading its economic output, by phasing out some activities and by expanding the more capital and skill intensive ones. Labour was being retrained and upgraded, and was shifting to higher productivity occupations.

In the recent period, a number of countries, particularly in the Western world, have been rather inept in coping with the industrial restructuring. The desire of parties to remain in power or to accede to power make them readily yield to expedient measures of preserving existing jobs, subsidising dying industries at the expense of the vigorous sectors which could be expanding more rapidly, creating new jobs and maintaining a country's competitiveness in international markets.

2) Firms which operate at the international level also need good scanning systems to detect trends and forecastable events, but they also need good filtering systems to select only those changes in the world environment which can have an impact on companies' corporate strategies. Such firms have to frequently evaluate the shifting opportunities in order to match their internal capabilities or to develop in time the requisite capabilities. They also need to carry out a periodic review of their organisation structures. Structures must reflect the external world with which the firms are interacting and also the changes in strategic postures. Thus a company producing and marketing a homogeneous line of products in a limited number of countries can manage quite well with a functional structure. As it goes for product diversification, it has to anticipate a change to a product division structure. As it goes for significant geographical spread, it may have to opt for an area type of structure, etc. One cannot design a structure which can remain effective when external realities or the nature of company's operations change. The common consequence of greater interdependence for all sizeable firms is the need to internationalise their managers. It is they who have to build world-wide organisations, to provide couplings between the firm and the heterogeneous external world.

3) The effects of growing interdependence on managers vary primarily as a function of the degree of involvement of managers in things international. Let us analyse them in a descending order:

a) The greatest impact both in terms of need for understanding and nature of work, is on managers who have some world-wide, or at least cross-boundary responsibilities. Such managers have to be equipped with multiple "adapters" to be able to "plug in" to various national "currents". This implies the *capacity* to understand different political and economic systems, different priorities, objectives, modes of behaviour, willingness to accept their legitimacy, and *ability* to think in other people's terms and decide using somewhat different sets of criteria. This is particularly technologically and economically advanced and big countries, since home country standards weigh very heavily in such cases.

b) At a somewhat lower level, we find expatriate managers, who work in a country and a culture other than their own. The need for personal adapt-

43. Managerial Realities of Global Interdependence

Frederick G. Harmon

Mr. Harmon is President of American Management Association-International since 1975, responsible for AMA's activities outside the U.S., including centres in Europe, Canada, Mexico and Brazil. Prior to joining AMA, he was editor-in-chief of the journal "International Management". He also contributes special columns to several leading periodicals.

The world today is in a constant state of flux. Deeply ingrained attitudes and long-held concepts are being questioned more frequently and with greater vigour than ever before. Traditional ideals and personal values, once presumed to be in conformation throughout the world, are rapidly being altered with each successive generation.

Caught in the middle of all this change are the established institution which strive to keep the wheels of the world's various countries oiled and running smoothly. Yet even these foundations of society are feeling, and in some cases reeling, from the effects.

Business, the backbone of almost any economy, has been wracked by crises within the last decade. Three major ones—identity, authority and integrity—are, I believe, reflective of the overall state of the world today. The identity crisis is, perhaps, foremost in intensity. What exactly is business' role in today's society? What should it be?

The next crisis facing the corporate sector is that of authority—how much power and authority should business wield and where should this power come from? The third crisis it that of integrity. While business as an institution has never enjoyed total respect, the recent scandals in England, Asia and the United States have merely confirmed the general public's feeling that business is suspect. At present, as we all know, codes of conduct are being developed to guide and restrict business behaviour.

Today, I'd like to examine the crises and the ways in which they relate to society and the corporation. I also want to share with you my thoughts on what we as management education specialists can do to help alleviate the pro-

To provide for consumer participation in bodies controlling the quality and performance of certain types of products (e.g., control of services rendered by nationalised industries, etc.);

To provide for participation of consumer in bodies concerned with questions of general economic and social policy having an impact on consumer interests (anti-inflation policies, anti-pollution programmes, policies against restrictive trade practices, price and wage controls, trade agreements, etc.).

Programmes
For (voluntary) collaboration of consumers with non-governmental bodies concerned with consumer protection issues (e.g., standardisation institutes, research and testing facilities, etc.);

For collaboration with "allied movements" such as trade unions and consumer cooperative, political parties, opinion groups, etc., to obtain the right of consumer representation and participation ("lobbying" information campaigns, contacts, etc.).

4. Economic self-help of consumers

Legal measures
To permit the establishment and functioning of consumer self-help organisations (on co-operative lines);
To assist in the establishment of consumer self-help organisations.

Standards
Defining criteria of consumer self-help organisations (on the basis of which they are recognised as cooperatives and can be affiliated to central cooperative bodies, etc.).

Programmes
For promotion and development of consumer self-help organisations at national and international levels;
For representation of consumer self-help organisations in national and international consumer movements and in government bodies concerned with consumer protection.

APPENDIX II

International Activities for Consumer Protection
(Source: Consumer Protection: A Survey of Institutional Arrangements and

Legal Measures—Report of the Secretary-General of the United Nations (E/1978/81). These conclusions are based as responses from 19 countries).

a) There is an increasing awareness of consumer protection problems, particularly in certain areas, as evidenced by existing and planned national measures and institutions;

b) The type of institution used to deal with the various problems, and the nature and scope of measures taken to deal with different problems in specific products or services vary from country to country;

c) In a number of countries the formulation and implementation of activities concerned with different aspects of consumer protection is in a state of evolution, with varying degree of comprehensiveness;

d) In developing countries, priorities for action in consumer protection often differ and problems are particularly acute because of limited infrastructure and resources;

e) Problems relating to basic needs, especially in the areas of food and health, are of special relevance, particularly in developing countries;

f) Issues such as price, safety and quality standards, and consumer information—including labelling and advertising—are of growing importance, particularly in relation to the activities at transnational corporations;

g) There is no systematic exchange of information on consumer protection measures and institutions among countries, although considerable progress has been achieved in this respect in certain industrialised regions;

h) Although some international standards exist or are being developed by United Nations bodies for certain products and services, i.e., food and drugs, or certain commercial and industrial practices which also serve the interests of consumers, there are no generally agreed international standards in other areas of consumer protection.

Many United Nations Organisations and other bodies are dealing with specific aspects of consumer protection, but their efforts need to be strengthened, broadened and in some cases, better coordinated.

There are a number of areas in which cooperation and assistance can be of use to developing countries, for example:

a) Advice and assistance to Governments on policies, institutions and measures for consumer protection;

b) The establishment and enforcement of safety and quality standards for food and drug products, and their pricing;

c) The establishment and implementation of standards covering quality, safety, weights and measures, packaging, testing, etc., for industrial goods destined for consumers;

d) The establishment of general, internationally agreed, norms for the responsibilities of transnational corporations for consumer protection;

e) Consumer information and education, including labelling for goods and services, in addition to foods and drugs, which may cause injury or harm to consumers;

f) Training of personnel concerned with various aspects of consumer protection;

g) The effect of advertising, particularly as it affects consumption patterns and consumer choice;

h) Means of redress, particularly with respect to product liability and collective action by consumer organisations.

Expert examination of the whole scope of issues and measures relating to consumer protection, particularly modalities of exchange of information and technical cooperation could be useful.

In conclusion, I would also like to share with you the seven deadly sins against the consumer:

The Seven Deadly Sins against the Consumer

The First Deadly Sin is to deny the consumer adequate basic goods and services; food, clothing, shelter, medical care and education. The consumer should have access to a variety of products and services at competitive prices. In the case of government or private monopolies he should have an assurance of the satisfactory quality and service and fair prices.

The Second Deadly Sin is to sell the consumer dangerous, unsafe goods. The consumer has a right to be protected against the marketing of goods which are dangerous to health.

The Third Deadly Sin is to deny the consumer correct and adequate information. The consumer should be protected against dishonest, deceitful or grossly misleading information, advertising, labelling or other practices. He must be given the facts needed to make an informed choice.

The Fourth Deadly Sin is to deny the consumer representation wherever consumer interests are involved. The consumer must be assured that the consumer interest will receive full and sympathetic consideration in the making and execution of government policies. There must be effective representation and consultation.

The Fifth Deadly Sin is to deny the consumer compensation against damage. Whenever there is misrepresentation or shoddy goods or services, he must be adequately compensated. Free legal aid, when needed, should be available or an accepted form of arbitration for small claims must be established.

The Sixth Deadly Sin is not to prepare the consumer, not to give him consumer education, not to provide in our educational system the mechanism by which the consumers can prepare themselves for the realities of life.

The Seventh Deadly Sin is to degrade the environment in the name of progress in such a way that the whole basis of the source of our life is destroyed.